The Burning Forest

Praise for the book

'A very important and interesting book which should be widely read… A deeply disturbing analysis of the sacrifice of tribal lives and communities caught between the camouflaged barbarity of the security forces and the violent arrogance of a deflected rebellion. The appeal for reasoned humanity cannot be any stronger – or more eloquent – than this.' **Amartya Sen**

'Thoroughly researched, devoid of any sensationalism, and therefore all the more harrowing is this narrative of what has been happening in Bastar since 2005 when State violence was unleashed on the tribals there, trapping them between the Salwa Judum goons and the Maoists "intent on securing their rights". Nandini Sundar lays bare how, now that the inaccessibility that protected their centuries-old culture has been ripped off to reveal a vulnerable community sitting on immense mineral resources attractive to capitalist investment, a deliberate strategy of murder, destruction and devastation has been shaping the contours of "Development" in the region. Un-putdownable. Indispensable to students of Indian democracy.' **Girish Karnad**

'Nandini Sundar is one of India's most distinguished anthropologists, and the leading academic authority on Bastar. But she is also one of Indian democracy's most passionate voices, throwing a spotlight on the deep relationship between violence, development, state formation and social movements. This unique combination of talents is on full display in this book on contemporary Bastar. This is a textured, deeply researched, committed and evocative portrait of lives and communities caught in the crossfire of violence in Bastar. It is a searing critique of the state, but one that Indian democracy needs to hear.' **Pratap Bhanu Mehta**

'Nandini Sundar, an extraordinary anthropologist-activist, has mined twenty-five years of experience in the region to write an account of Bastar's civil war that is both gripping and harrowing. She pulls no punches in describing the greed and cynical violence of state agencies, mining companies, politicians and immigrants. Her account of life in the Maoist rebel zones is graphic, full of empathy but by no means uncritical. This is a story that everyone who cares about India must read.' **Partha Chatterjee**

'This disturbing book, written with deep knowledge and passion, shakes us out of our complacency as it exposes the brutal realities of the war in Bastar.' **Sharmila Tagore**

'Here is a politically important chronicle of the struggles of the adivasis of Bastar in Chhattisgarh, which challenges the Indian state's dominant narrative that overemphasizes Maoist violence alone, ignoring the state's culpability in alienating these adivasis by evicting them from their lands and unleashing terror on them. Combining rigorous theoretical analysis with intensive fieldwork, Nandini Sundar has come out with an excellently critical narrative which reiterates the basic principle that no state can ever be exonerated from crimes against humanity, and provides a compelling case for the withdrawal of security forces from Bastar, and initiation of dialogue with the Maoists there. It is a must-read for both academics and social activists.' **Sumanta Banerjee**

'Every thinking Indian, every citizen who is concerned about the present and future of the Republic, should read *The Burning Forest*. It is an impeccably researched and finely written work of scholarship, redolent with insight, and displaying enormous courage as well.' **Ramachandra Guha**

'How does democracy affect the prosecution of civil war? Nandini Sundar explores this question with untold courage and fierce determination in her remarkable extended ethnography of counter-insurgency in Chhattisgarh (India) – a desperate struggle to clear the land for mineral exploitation… A rare and brilliant treatment of a topic few social scientists would dare to touch, let alone examine at such close quarters and for over two decades.' **Michael Burawoy**

'This meticulous and powerful book not only documents a brutal regime of internal colonialism in the world's largest democracy. It reveals the insidious ways in which consent to state oppression is manufactured and amplified. Everyone interested in the commingled fate of democracy and capitalism in the post-colonial world should read this book.' **Pankaj Mishra**

'Among the most important works on the conflict in southern Chhattisgarh' *India Today*

'There are enough questions that have been answered in *The Burning Forest* to keep you sleepless over several nights, thinking about what we have done to our own people. It is a book that all of us need to read.' *Indian Express*

'One of the most rounded accounts of the strife [in Bastar]' *The Telegraph*

'[A]sks for no glossing over of any kind… a thorough, diligent and finally credible effort' *The Caravan*

'[A] razor sharp critique of the institutions that make India feel good about itself – its parliamentary democracy, its judiciary, its free press, its vibrant civil society' **The Wire**

'[E]ven if you disagree with her views... there is no way you can read it and not feel harrowed by the war India has unleashed against its own people in Bastar.' ***Business Standard***

'[T]he work needs to be celebrated for its scholarship, for its independence and for its courage.' ***The Tribune***

'[A] balanced and incisive narrative of the ground reality in Chhattisgarh' ***Force***

'Sundar's book is a must-read for those interested in the genesis and the nature of conflict in Bastar and for those willing to think beyond "development" achieved through the dispossession of land from the Adivasis to whom it belongs and for whom it is a source of livelihood.' ***The Hindu***

'[A] timely and pro-Adivasi book written with utmost honesty and a deep sense of empathy' ***Open***

'A compelling account of the real-politik of "democratic nation building"' ***Seminar***

'Sundar's book is an exceptional expose of the scandal of rural governance in India, a chronicle of State excesses, an anthropologist's view about how conflicts perpetuate themselves and an account of how India's democracy is degraded when few are watching. Policymakers ought to take away the key lesson from it that there really are no military solutions to social conflicts.' ***Hindustan Times***

'If many places are like Bastar, few books are like *The Burning Forest*... it resonates with classics on frontiers and dispossession.' ***Journal of Agrarian Change***

'The message of this monumental social science inquiry is loud and clear – citizens have to assert their rights to get justice from the Indian state.' ***Contributions to Indian Sociology***

The Burning Forest

India's War in Bastar

Nandini Sundar

juggernaut

JUGGERNAUT BOOKS
C-I-128, First Floor, Sangam Vihar, Near Holi Chowk,
New Delhi 110080, India

First published in hardback by Juggernaut Books 2016
Published in paperback by Juggernaut Books 2022

10 9 8 7 6 5 4 3 2 1

P-ISBN: 9789393986153
E-ISBN: 9789393986160

Typeset in Adobe Caslon Pro by R. Ajith Kumar, New Delhi

Printed at Thomson Press India Ltd

To Manish Kunjam – who has fought for his people with honour and retained a sense of humour through terrible times

To Ashok Desai and Nitya Ramakrishnan for striving to make the Constitution of India meaningful

Contents

List of Maps xi
Preface xiii

Prologue: Dandakaranya, the Forest of Exile 1

I. The Landscape of Resistance

1. Burnt Rice 7
2. Iron in the Soul 27
3. 'Because I Want Peace' 48
4. The Maoist State 68

II. Civil War

5. A 'Peaceful People's Movement' 89
6. Between Fear and Courage 112
7. The Sorrow of the Sabari 129
8. Border Crossings 148
9. Notes on an 'Operation' 162
10. The Renegade and the Rifleman 186

III. Institutions on Trial

11. Security or Development? 219

12. The Amnesias of Democracy 238
13. The Rights and Wrongs of Human Rights 257
14. To Talk or Not to Talk? 279
15. The Propaganda Wars 291
16. Praying for Justice 310
17. The Legal Death and Reincarnation of the Salwa Judum 332

Epilogue: A New Compact 351

Notes 353
Appendices 377
Appendix 1: Official Data on Deaths in the State–Maoist Conflict in Chhattisgarh, 2005–16 378
Appendix 2: Timeline 380
Acronyms and Abbreviations 384
Glossary 388
Acknowledgements 393
Index 399
A Note on the Author 416

List of Maps

1. Bastar Division in Chhattisgarh xvi
2. Mineral Map of Bastar 30
3. The Dandakaranya Guerrilla Zone, c. 1999 70
4. Bijapur: Origins of the Salwa Judum, 2005–6 98
5. Konta: Spread of the Salwa Judum, 2006–7 106
6. Tadmetla, Neighbouring Villages and CRPF Camps 172
7. Health Centres in Undivided Dantewada District 231

Preface

A colleague at the Delhi School of Economics, Rabindra Ray, once told me a story which had circulated in the 1970s, in the days when he was a 'Naxalite' or an armed revolutionary, drawing inspiration from communist struggles around the world. A policeman taunted a youth he had arrested: 'You Naxalites talk so much about Vietnam,' he said. 'Show me where it is on the map.' The youth – who was illiterate – put his hand on his chest and replied, 'It is in my heart.'

Today, in the former undivided district of Bastar stretching over 39,114 square kilometres in the south of Chhattisgarh, the landscape of the heart is like a torn map, fluttering between resistance and anguish. The region is at the core of the Indian government's war with Maoist guerrillas. The Government of India is represented by barbed wire camps, helicopters, roads and mines that cut deep gashes through the forest. The *janathana sarkar* or 'people's government' of the Communist Party of India (Maoist), on the other hand, has unmarked boundaries and mysterious circuits of information. Its citizens face an uncertain, perilous journey, on which they have embarked with determination but no clear destination. They are not always sure who their fellow travellers are. When I asked a man whom he preferred, the government or the Maoists, he replied, 'I know what is in my own heart, I cannot speak for the hearts of others.'

Starting in the early 1980s, the Maoists established a strong base in Bastar, helping the villagers resist the petty tyrannies of the bureaucracy. Years of sporadic battle followed. In 2005 the Indian government began concerted operations to bring the area back under its control. The fabulous mineral resources of Bastar and practical sovereignty were both at stake. The first step was to prop up a so-called people's movement named the Salwa Judum, which in Gondi, translates literally as 'purification hunt'. Vigilantes accompanied by security forces went through villages, burning, looting and killing, forcibly removing villagers to government-controlled camps. By 2009, the Judum had been converted into a full-fledged police and paramilitary operation, named Operation Green Hunt. In the years since, the number of deaths, rapes and arrests of civilians has only grown, quite apart from the deaths of security forces and Maoist cadres. A standard feature of such wars is the impossibility of fixing numbers and even identities.

In Part I of this book, I attempt to locate the war in the social fabric of exploitation and describe the beginnings of resistance. In Part II, I explore the varied forms that counter-insurgency has taken and what it means to be an adivasi citizen of India caught in armed conflict. In Part III, I ask what difference it makes, if any, when a counter-insurgency campaign is conducted in a democracy rather than a military regime or colonial government. How have different institutions and actors reacted, ranging from the welfare bureaucracy to political parties, human rights organizations, the media and the judiciary? The tragedy of India is not that there are only a few fringe elements or brave dissenters who oppose its wars, but that, despite a well-developed institutional structure, even the most basic of checks within the state fail in the face of corporate and political greed and official indifference.

This book is written against both the government's militaristic understanding of the Maoist movement as a law and order problem that must be crushed and the revolutionary certainties of the Maoists and their sympathizers. It is written for all those who hate the impunity and arrogance of the Indian state, who admire the Maoists for their sacrifices but disagree with the wisdom of their path, and who recognize that violence, even against injustice, can degenerate into brutality and corruption.

This book is written for all the ordinary adivasis I know, who make difficult moral choices within complex constraints, and many of whom are heroic beyond bounds I can scarcely imagine. In today's conditions, it requires superhuman effort for them to merely survive.

This book is written because, in the absence of justice, at least the truth must be on record.

This book is written for myself – as catharsis, as helpless witnessing, as rage about the annihilation of a people and their way of life.

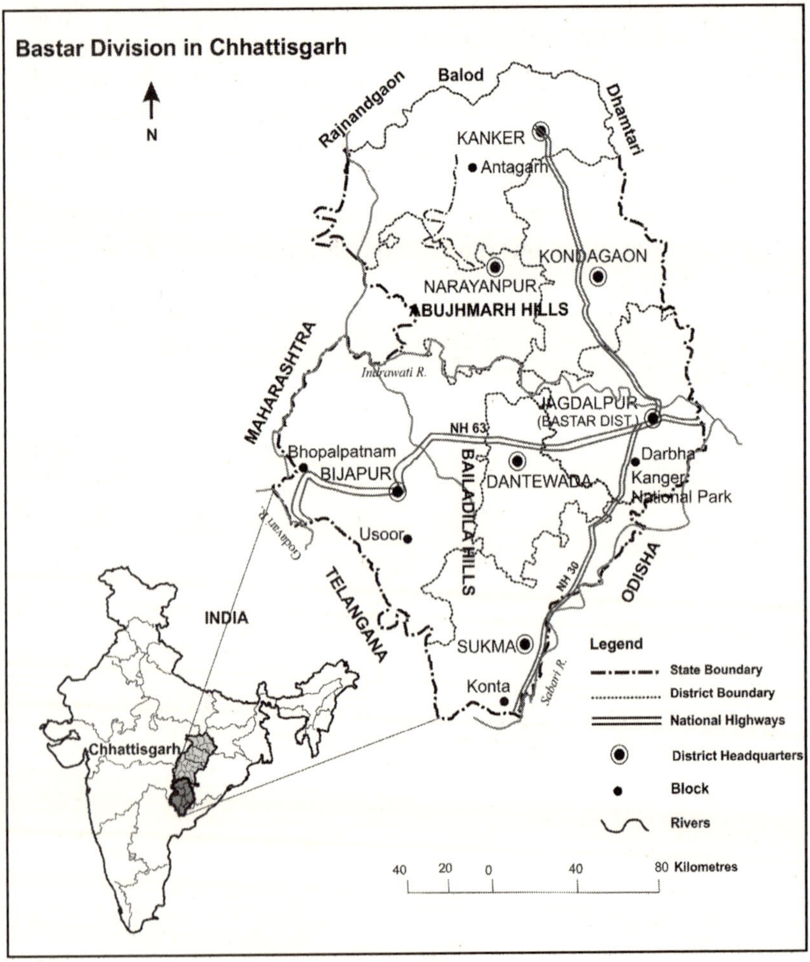
Bastar Division in Chhattisgarh
N
Balod
Rajnandgaon
Dhamtari
KANKER
Antagarh
KONDAGAON
NARAYANPUR
ABUJHMARH HILLS
MAHARASHTRA
Indrawati R.
JAGDALPUR
(BASTAR DIST.)
NH 63
Bhopalpatnam
BIJAPUR
BAILADILA HILLS
DANTEWADA
Darbha
Kanger
National Park
Godavari R.
Usoor
TELANGANA
NH 30
ODISHA
INDIA
SUKMA
Konta
Sabari R.
Chhattisgarh
Legend
State Boundary
District Boundary
National Highways
District Headquarters
Block
Rivers
40 20 0 40 80 Kilometres

Prologue: Dandakaranya, the Forest of Exile

> do not forgive truly it is not in your power
> to forgive in the name of those betrayed at dawn
>
> Zbigniew Herbert, *The Envoy of Mr Cogito*

February 2006

Hungi lay counting the stars as they slowly faded into half-light, putting off the moment when she would have to start her morning chores. The goat kid had kept her up half the night by running up and down below her bed, rubbing its back against the ropes that made up the cot and nibbling at her toes. Pandri, the white rooster her father was training for a prizefight, had just started crowing but was not yet insistent. Her mother, Deve, had got up earlier to defecate while it was still dark – a time when only the dim shapes of people would be visible. But Hungi was being lazy that morning. Suddenly, 16-year-old-Masa, one of the village sentries, came running through the village, shouting loudly, 'The Judum is coming.' Nearing Hungi's house, he said breathlessly, 'They have come to Itapalli…and it's our turn next.' On her feet instantly, Hungi grabbed her baby brother and ran in the direction she had seen her mother going. Her father, Rama, who had been up for a while warming his hands around a small fire, went inside the house and gathered as much grain as he could in a small cloth bag, quickly untied the cattle and followed her. In half an hour, the entire village was deserted, except for the squawking chickens and some pigs.

They came from the east, some 400 men dressed in camouflage fatigues, some with black scarves around their heads, carrying Kalashnikovs. They reached the village just as dawn was breaking. In front was the former Maoist Kiche Handa, now working with the police as a 'Special Police Officer'. His task was to point out houses. 'That's the house of the headman,' he said, 'where the Maoist leaders always stay when they visit the village. And that's the house of Hadma, an active sympathizer.' The force went inside the houses and took whatever they found – rice, money, jewellery. In Hungi's house, they kicked at the sack of beans she had so carefully collected, spilling them around the house before setting fire to it. The fire took time to catch since the houses were at a little distance from each other. But by 11 a.m., all seventy mud and thatch huts in the hamlet were burning. The forces were tired and the local commander called a halt. They moved a little way off and began to cook, feasting on the frightened chickens they had captured and the rice they had looted. By the time lunch was over, it was two in the afternoon, and time for the next village.

Jogi's house on the western edge of the neighbouring hamlet was shielded by a grove of mango and tamarind trees. She had been out since 4.30 a.m., gathering the mahua flowers used to make the local liquor, and had just come home. Jogi's father, Hunga, had a bad leg after he had fallen off a tree some years ago. As he did most afternoons, he was sitting outside the house making a bamboo basket. When the forces came, neither Jogi nor her father was prepared. Two of the men hit Hunga with rifle butts, and when Jogi ran to save him, she was caught and pushed inside the house. After they had finished raping her, the soldiers shot Jogi. That evening, back in camp, the force commander called a press conference. He proudly displayed a woman's corpse dressed in an olive-green uniform. A guerrilla squad commander, he said, captured after a heavy encounter in which both sides fired several rounds.

The villagers of Koruthguda did not come back that night or even the next. From the forest, they watched the flames devour their houses. Luckily Hungi had found her mother and some others from the village in the forest. They cooked what little rice they had brought, hushing the babies in case the forces were still out there. Hungi's father, Rama, went back to the village briefly to try to retrieve some grain, but the houses were still smouldering. When people came out of hiding on the third day, they found only the charred remains of their homes, an occasional mud wall still standing, and in some places the twisted metal mouth of a blackened vessel visible through the ashes. Even the sounds of the village were missing – the chickens gone, the pigs no longer grunting.

After two weeks of trying to live in the forest, the entire village left. Most went across the border to Khammam in Andhra Pradesh, a day's walk away, where they had contacts among the Telugu farmers who employed them seasonally to harvest chillies. A few took shelter with relatives in villages which had not yet been burnt. Some tried to take a few head of cattle with them and some just let them go, defeated by the enormity of what had happened. The cattle became feral, appearing together in wild groups at the edge of the forest, and fleeing again. Grass began to grow out of the houses, and the tracks disappeared as the forest took over. The village died.

April 2009

Rama was the first one to return to the village. He went up to the herd of cows grazing nearby, and found his favourite brown cow, Moti. He gently touched her face and called her by her name, and Moti quietly followed him home. For both man and cow, there was real joy in this reunion. Others began to come back in ones and twos, reclaiming their cattle, cleaning the debris of burnt grain and broken pots from their homes. The men went into the forest and cut down fresh logs. Slowly, slowly, the village began to grow again.

In the neighbouring village, Itapalli, some families had been captured by the forces, and had been living in the Salwa Judum 'relief' camp at Dornapal, along with people from other villages. They were ostensibly refugees from the Maoists and under police protection. When they heard that the villagers of Koruthguda and Itapalli had started trickling home, Hidma and Mahesh, who had been living in camp, sent a letter asking whether they too could come back: 'Our lives have been miserable, without forests and fields, without the sunrise on the river, and the sound of the birds. Forgive us for staying on the other side.'

February 2016

The villages were tense again. The fields had yielded little this year because of the drought. A paramilitary camp had come up 2 kilometres from Itapalli, and the forces went out patrolling every day, raiding villages at dawn, arresting men and taking them to the camp. The women spent the days pleading with the police to release their men. Two boys had been picked up while cutting wood from the forest between Itapalli and Koruthguda. A week later, the Koruthguda villagers found out they had been killed as Maoists.

Hungi had got married the previous year and was living in a neighbouring village, but had come home to check on her parents. The family talked late into the night. Hungi's mother, Deve, said, 'When we came back seven years ago, we vowed we would never leave again.' 'But who knows,' said her father Rama, 'what the future will bring?'

Part I

The Landscape of Resistance

1

Burnt Rice

From before the time of human life, in the heart of Gondwana, as the earth pushed and pulled itself into shape under heat and pressure, Archaean granite metamorphosed into gneiss. The plateaus thrust upwards, while water flowed from the rocks to form the landscape familiar to us today as Bastar, clasped between the rivered boundaries of the Sabari and the Godavari, which separate the states of Odisha, Chhattisgarh, Maharashtra and Telangana–Andhra Pradesh.

The Indrawati cuts across the district, flowing south-west from its origins in Kalahandi in Odisha, past Jagdalpur, the former capital of Bastar state, before joining the Godavari near the Chhattisgarh–Telangana border. To the north of the Indrawati ascend the unmapped hills, the Marh, and to its south lie the districts of Bijapur and Dantewada.[1] Each night the moon rises on the sandy banks of the river, reflecting in the water, before disappearing as the mist settles over silent, forested tracts. But the Indrawati is dying, its waters flowing backward into a former tributary, the Jaura nala, a symptom of all that has turned upside down in this part of the world.

For those whose bearings depend on roads rather than rivers, two old trading routes, now national highways, run south and west through Jagdalpur, taking in wooded hill passes, before descending into the hotter, less shaded, plains. These roads connecting

Chhattisgarh to Maharashtra and Telangana form the arteries of both commerce and state control.

The plateaus are ancient, but the first geological phenomena in the region, older even than the gneiss, are the Dharwar rocks formed over 500 million years ago. These form three distinct ferrous hill ranges each running north to south: the Chargaon–Kondapakha–Hahladdi hills and Raoghat in the north and the Bailadilla hills in the south. It is from here that iron entered the soul of the nation, hardening it to all human emotion, from here that the origins of time return to haunt the present.

In these hills, there once lived a civilization. Over the centuries, people here named the gods on the mountains and the mountains for the gods: Raoghat for the horse-riding Rao who guards the entrance to the Marh, Omalwar for the Kunjam clan god, Urru Morka Dado. They etched the landscape with stark and simple names: Biere Metta or Big Mountain, renamed by outsiders as Bailadilla for its bull hump shape, Inda referring to the wide water of both river and sea, now Sanskritized as the Indrawati. The Savada became the Sabari, and the entire region came to be known as Dandakaranya, or the forest where Rama was exiled, in an attempt to fit the region into a national epic imagination, where the locals were fierce and savage, and fair-skinned Aryans brought civilization.

For the adivasis, the forest was an intimate, if also dangerous, home. They battled the tigers and the wild boars to collect colourless gum from the white *dhaora* tree, pressed the yellow *tora* fruit for oil and learnt to peel away the round red skin of the *tendu* fruit to eat the sweet, pulpy flesh beneath. They found that the *bija* tree bleeds red like a human being when hacked. Where they had to clear the forests, they left mahua and toddy trees to mark the bunds, and planted tamarind trees to shade the village. In empty forest fields, the clap of a wooden trap blowing in the wind reminded humans and animals of each other's presence. 'If you peer into the deep caves,' said Dulsai, in a village north of the Indrawati, 'you can see the marks of tigers.'

In the cities, however, these forms of life find no favour. The gods that live in the mountains are signed away to mining companies, whose infra-vision does not see the splendour of the forest, the flower tucked behind the ear, the feather in the dancing headgear, but only the minerals beneath.

The colonial-era principle of eminent domain, which gives the state the right to acquire all land, has no room for local notions of property. In Bastar, the Earth, known as Bhum, Jaga or Mati, was sovereign, giving permission to certain lineages to settle; if the Earth was unhappy, people fell sick and had to leave. The first founders gave land to others, interceding on their behalf with the Earth. Every village knew where its forest began and that of their neighbours ended; they made sure that each forest spirit got its own due. The Mother Goddesses – every village has at least one – love, fight and visit each other, just like their followers.

The central Indian forest tract out of which Bastar is hived is peopled by several Gondi-speaking groups, who refer to themselves as simply *koi*, *koya* or *koitor*, meaning human. The major scheduled tribe (ST) or adivasi communities of Bastar include the Halbas, agriculturists who worked as soldiers guarding small forts like Chote Dongar or Hamirgarh; Bhatras in north-east Bastar whose language is a mixture of Halbi and Oriya; Dhurwas (formerly known as Parjas) who occupy the areas surrounding the Kanger forest; and the Dorlas of the southern plains bordering Telangana/Andhra. The best known are the southern Madia, whose distinctive bison horn headgear embellished with tassels of cowrie shells has been appropriated by the government to showcase tribal diversity, and the northern Muria famous for their *ghotuls* where youth were initiated into work and life. Among the other communities who make up the special character of Bastar are several classified as other backward classes (OBCs), such as the Dhakads, Marars (gardeners), Rauts (cowherds), Gadhwas (bell metal specialists), Kumhars (potters) Kallars and Sundis (distillers). The scheduled castes (SCs) – Maharas, Pankas and Mrigans – were the traditional weavers and musicians. There are several other OBC and SC communities who have come in from neighbouring states like the Telgas and Mahars from Andhra Pradesh and Maharashtra respectively, now settled in Bijapur district.

But political and economic power is concentrated in the hands of immigrants who have come in the last century, especially in the last five decades: traders and businessmen from Rajasthan, Uttar Pradesh, Bihar and Punjab; those working in the Bailadilla mines and the lower state bureaucracy; and Bengali refugees from the 1971 war, officially called East Pakistan Displaced Persons, settled by the government in what it saw as the empty forests of Koraput and Bastar.

~

When I first visited Bastar in 1990 as a PhD student researching colonialism and resistance, the newspapers occasionally reported 'Naxalite incidents' such as police–guerrilla encounters, along with accounts of murders and human sacrifices. But all these were 'far away', in places like Bijapur or Golapalli or Kistaram at the western and southern extremities of the state. In the Dhurwa belt where I lived, the Maoists were still exotic. There was little in the newspapers then about who the Naxalites were or what villagers thought about them. This kind of reporting that obliterates, even as it names, has remained constant over the decades.

From the bureaucratic redoubts of Delhi and Bhopal (Bastar was still part of undivided Madhya Pradesh), the government ruled over a vast tract in principle if not in practice, replacing the ritualism of the old kingdoms of Bastar and Kanker with an indifferent administration. The main problem I saw was exploitation by immigrant traders, mostly Thakurs from Uttar Pradesh, who ran the trade in minor forest produce and illegal tin mining. Together, the traders and local officials devised ways in which they could profit from government schemes meant for adivasi welfare. But thanks to the parliamentary Communist Party of India (CPI) which had been active in this area for a few years, the days when the forest guard or the patwari (revenue agent) would demand chickens and free labour from the villagers had gone, and land was still mostly in the hands of adivasis. Across the region, children went to village schools, regularly if the teacher came, and irregularly when the teacher absconded; government health services were few and far between, and people's only hope – both then and now – was the *wadde* or local healer. On soundless summer evenings, the wadde's long, low incantations can be heard from afar, rising suddenly to a crescendo and then falling again to an intimate mutter, as he implores the Mata, the Mother Goddess, to spare the patient she has infected.

I was young then, and divided my time between other young people and village elders, learning to speak Dhurwa and discovering the intricacies of village politics. I remember it as a time when I laughed a lot. My days were spent carrying out a household census and collecting genealogies, attending rituals, chatting to women as they husked grain or cracked tamarind pods, and watching the Panka weaver at his loom. Returning home on full moon nights, I would pause by the fields to see how brightly each stalk of grain was lit. Friday, the weekly market day, was like a mini festival when nobody did any work, coming home happy and exhausted after a morning negotiating with traders and meeting friends.

I made occasional trips further afield, for instance to a small village haat at Bade Karkeli near Kutru in Bijapur where we drank *landa* or rice beer and my friend Kala bought baskets of small dried fish. Near the dilapidated mansion of the former zamindar of Kutru lay the grave of a Parsi shikari, Peston Naoroji Kharas, gored by a wild buffalo in 1948. The Elwin Cooper Company of Nagpur used to organize hunting expeditions in the area. By 1998, the grave was in disrepair and the wild buffalo were no longer so plentiful in the Indrawati National Park. My field notes spoke of barricaded police stations: 'Fortified police camp at Kutru with barbed wire all around. Police shining wary torches at night at all passing vehicles and calling out to find out who is there.'

The war had already begun, though I did not know it. What I remember more vividly is the everyday humiliation and loss, of friends dying suddenly for want of a doctor, the tense silence of village elders before a visiting policeman. It was hard not to feel angered by the casual racism of outsiders: bus conductors kicking elderly adivasi men and shoving women off the seat to make way for some minor official, a constant litany of complaints about how adivasis did nothing but drink and did not want education or modern medicine.

I recall occasional delirious nights of dancing during fairs and weddings, and tense moments at the cockfights, but voices were rarely raised. Village disputes involved extremely complicated negotiations, such as one in which the priest made off with an entire pig rather than just the head, which was his customary due. But arguments usually ended with the male elders drinking together and laughing.

In 2005, all this suddenly changed for the villagers living in the Maoist strongholds of Dantewada or South Bastar district, when the government began its devastating counter-insurgency operations. My life, which had taken me on to new research interests elsewhere, changed too, as news of violence began to trickle in from Bastar. My first encounters with the Salwa Judum were through human rights investigations or 'fact-findings' in November 2005 (with a PUCL/All India Fact-finding team, henceforth All India Fact-finding team) and May 2006 (with the Independent Citizens' Initiative, henceforth ICI). After that, over the past decade, I have made repeated visits alone or with different friends. In 2007 three of us from the ICI, Ramachandra Guha, E.A.S. Sarma and I, filed a petition on human rights violations and state-sponsored vigilantism before the Supreme Court. Litigation reduced the licence I had as a sociologist to travel freely and talk to every side. But in the beginning, when I saw what I saw, I could not sleep, and a permanent ache entered my heart.

Chronicles of Counter-insurgency

In telling the story of counter-insurgency, where do I begin – with the flame or the candle snuffer, with the dream or the death, with the living forest or the hardened iron?

I learnt from my lawyer friends that the first page of any petition must contain a 'timeline', a narrative of dates and events relevant to the issue, to help the judges understand and contextualize the matter. But what are the relevant dates here that the reader should know about? Should one start with 1910, with the Bhumkal, when the adivasis of Bastar rebelled against the colonial administration, asking for their lands and forests to be left alone, whose memory is invoked in the songs and tracts produced by the Maoists? Or 1947, when independent India promised a new democracy but sold the adivasis short by keeping several old colonial laws? Some might want to start with 1967, when a small village in West Bengal, Naxalbari, became synonymous with hope, and young men and women took to armed struggle against oppression; or the 1980s, when the first Communist Party of India (Marxist-Leninist) (CPI [ML]) People's War squads left Telangana for Bastar; or 2004, when the CPI (Maoist) was formed by the merger of the People's War and the Maoist Communist Centre of India (MCC), signalling a higher level of strength. One could also reel one's historical timeline close and start with 2005, when the mineral-rich hills of Bastar suddenly became the most valuable piece of real estate in the country, and those who stood in the way of their exploitation – like the Maoists – became, in former prime minister Manmohan Singh's words, the 'Biggest Internal Security Threat to the Indian State'.

The Biggest Security Threat contains many smaller stories from across the country, of both individual lives and community sorrows. In writing a history of the Indian Maoists in the late twentieth and early twenty-first century, appropriate space must be given to the desperate struggle of the dalits or SCs of Bihar against upper-caste landlords for wages and dignity; the corruption introduced by the faction-ridden, extortionist gangs of Jharkhand which call themselves Maoist but are propped up with police support, like the 'Tritiya Prastuti' or the People's Liberation Front of India; the police-atrocity-induced Lalgarh movement in Bengal which flared briefly and ran its own health centres and schools before it was appropriated and betrayed by Mamata Banerjee's Trinamool Congress (TMC); the tragic story of the Kuis of Odisha, whose entirely constitutional agitation for land rights was labelled Maoist by the state and repressed; and the virtual overground disappearance of the Maoists in Andhra Pradesh, following aborted peace talks in 2004, repression, and new economic and political opportunities.

My account is focused on Bastar or the southern part of Chhattisgarh, where, over three decades, the Maoists established what is almost a parallel state, distributing land, settling disputes, taxing contractors and entering into the minutiae of intimate relations. But my story is not about the Maoists, though they inevitably figure in it. My narrative is really about Indian democracy, when it reduces what are essentially political contests over rights, distributive justice and alternative visions of the good to law and order problems, and when it would rather fight against its poorest citizens than talk to them.

Unlike insurgency, which has many local characteristics, counter-insurgency draws on a global repertoire. The political histories of places like Malaysia, Vietnam, Guatemala, El Salvador and Colombia, or even Sri Lanka, Algeria and Kenya, the kinds of movements (nationalist, Marxist, Islamist), and the kinds of regimes in power (colonial government, authoritarian regime or democracy) may be quite different, but the software of counter-insurgency that circulates through manuals and military training colleges across the world is common.[2] The basic aim is to exhaust and coerce civilians into abandoning support for insurgents. The similarities are especially stark when it comes to indigenous people dreaming of a Marxist revolution.

To borrow a term from the historian Ranajit Guha who wrote on the elementary forms of peasant insurgency in colonial India,[3] one might discern certain 'elementary aspects' of counter-insurgency. The counter-insurgency may be conducted directly by the police or army; cloak itself in the guise of popular anger against rebels; or employ vigilantes, including death squads, with the state claiming it is helpless to identify and act against criminals. Most counter-insurgencies, however, officially deploy a combination of state and state-supported non-state actors against insurgents. Former insurgents turned pro-government mercenaries are organized as 'home guards', 'special police officers' or paramilitaries who work as informers and also serve as the first line of attack. Often, villagers are also armed and conscripted into 'civil patrols' or 'village defence units' to fight against insurgents.

In addition, counter-insurgencies have similar consequences for civilians. Looting and/or burning of villages is standard as are murders, rapes and widespread arrests of the civilian population. Forcing villagers into camps, often called 'model villages', under police, paramilitary or army surveillance in order to isolate the insurgents and break the support of the civilians is part of a widespread strategy variously called 'grouping', strategic hamletting or forced population removal. Both grouping and conflict more generally lead to widespread displacement. Starvation and denial of basic services are often used as weapons of control and are not merely by-products of unsettled conditions.

Finally, counter-insurgencies also rely on control over the media, and the use of special laws which give the government emergency powers to arrest, detain without bail and so on.

In Bastar, as I show below, almost all of these elements have been present; only the combination has varied over the years. This book concentrates on the early years, since they set the pattern for what came after, but also shows how violence mutated over the decade.

A Very Statist People's Movement

When it started in 2005, the Salwa Judum was presented in the media as a popular uprising against the Maoists, and even a decade later the government continued to insist it was a 'spontaneous, self-initiated people's movement against the Naxalites'. In practice, it was the police and politicians who mobilized the 'people'. The ruling

Bharatiya Janata Party (BJP) ministers and Opposition politicians like Congress leader Mahendra Karma held public meetings and rallies (Jan Jagran Abhiyans or Public Awakening Campaigns) against the Maoists; villagers who attended these official summons were conscripted into marching on other villages.

In earlier, but similar, counter-insurgencies in India, as in Telangana and Mizoram, the police and army carried out the operations. However, at least initially, using the army against the Maoists would not have been seen as legitimate, since fighting for social and economic rights is treated differently from secession. Moreover, the popularity of 'people's movements' made this a desirable label to appropriate. The experience of both Delhi 1984 and Gujarat 2002 proved useful, when the pogroms of Sikhs and Muslims were blamed on 'mob anger', even as they were clearly organized by members of the ruling Congress and BJP respectively. In a model public–private partnership, the governments ensured police inactivity and complicity.

From 2009 onwards, the government gave up the pretence of using non-state actors, launching 'Operation Green Hunt' or a nationwide action against the Maoists, using the Central Armed Police Forces (CAPF) comprising different agencies such as the Central Reserve Police Force (CRPF), the Border Security Force (BSF) and the Indo-Tibetan Border Police (ITBP), along with the Chhattisgarh police. Recruiting locals into the paramilitary forces and police to 'wean' them off the Maoists was a critical part of this strategy.[4]

Despite having a large force at its command, the government is loath to let go of vigilantism. Indeed, with the coming of the Modi-led government in 2014 and the growing incidence of vigilantism against minorities and liberals, the Salwa Judum has gone mainstream across the country. For every protest against the violence of right-wing non-state actors, there is a counter protest supported by the police. Emboldened by this national atmosphere, in 2015–16 the police encouraged their urban acolytes to form groups like the Samajik Ekta Manch (Social Unity Platform), Naxal Peedith

Sangharsh Samiti (Naxal-affected Struggle Committee) and Bastar Sangharsh Samiti (Bastar Struggle Committee) to hold anti-Maoist rallies, threaten human rights activists and display public affection for the police.

The Mass Burning and Grouping of Villages

Between June 2005 and 2007, entire villages in (then undivided) Dantewada were forcibly taken to live in roadside settlements. To avoid violence, many villages came to camp on their own. The camps were officially described as 'relief camps', but the Judum leaders referred to them as Salwa Judum 'base camps', from where attacks could be launched. Villages that resisted joining the anti-Maoist rallies were burnt. Men, women and even children were killed, and many women were viciously gang-raped. The Maoists retaliated by killing Judum leaders, including headmen who had convinced their villages that it was safer to side with the government; their frightened relatives then took refuge in the government camps.

British-controlled Malaya (1948–60) is famous as the classic prototype of grouping. Some 5,70,000 Chinese were uprooted and moved into internment camps glorified as 'New Villages' to 'wean them away' from the Communist Party of Malaya. The strategy was borrowed by the Americans who created 'strategic hamlets' in Vietnam to isolate the peasants from the Viet Cong, and deprive the latter of supplies and information on troop movements. The process is euphemistically described as 'protecting' the civilian population from being 'preyed on' by insurgents, and has been deployed with devastating effect on civilian populations across the world.[5]

What colonial- and emergency-era Malaya did, however, democratic India did in parallel time. Between 1949 and 1951, some 1000 Koya villages in Khammam in Hyderabad state were burnt, cattle impounded and the people forced into large military camps euphemistically called Ashokanagar, Gandhinagar, Jawaharnagar and so on, after the national leaders of those days. This was just one of the tactics used, apart from raids, arrests, torture and sexual violence, to repress the Telangana armed struggle (1946–51), when guerrilla squads of the CPI (then undivided) assisted by village defence units fought both the *razakars*—the private armed militia under the Nizam of Hyderabad—and, subsequently, the forces of the Indian Union.[6]

However, the Indian army counts Mizoram as its most successful use of grouping when 82 per cent of the population was moved from several small, scattered villages into larger villages called grouping centres, in order to defeat the Mizo National Front, which had declared independence in 1966. Even then, participation was portrayed as 'voluntary':

> Darzo (Mizoram) was one of the richest villages I have ever seen in this part of the world… My orders were to get the villagers to collect whatever moveable property they could, and to set their own village on fire at seven in the evening. I also had orders to burn all the paddy and other grain that could not be carried away by the villagers to the new centre so as to keep food out of reach of the insurgents… I called the Darzo Village Council President and his village elders and ordered them to sign a document saying that they had voluntarily asked to be resettled in Hnahthial PPV (Protected and Progressive Village) under the protection of the Security Forces as they were being harassed by the insurgents, and because their own village did not have communications, educational, medical and other facilities. Another document stated that they had burnt down their own village, and that no force or coercion was used by the Security Forces. They refused to sign. So I sent them out and after an hour called them in again, this time one man at a time. On my table was a loaded revolver, and in the corner stood two NCOs with loaded sten-guns. This frightened them, and one by one they signed both the documents.[7]

In India, grouping has only been applied to 'tribal' populations. Apart from Telangana and Mizoram, grouping was used to subdue the Srikakulam Naxalite uprising (1957–70s) and the Naga armed struggle for sovereignty in the 1950s. In Telangana, while the entire population was resisting, it was only the adivasis who were confined to camps. But this is not surprising, since adivasi ways of life are seen as lacking value. Even before grouping became a popular counter-insurgency tactic, indigenous people were being 'settled' by colonial governments who saw shifting cultivation, hunting gathering and nomadic herding as a wasteful use of resources. Modern governments also justify grouping in the name of a more efficient delivery of services, which traditionally scattered habitations make difficult. This rationale fits neatly into the 'winning hearts and minds' approach made famous by General Gerald Templer in Malaya. The new villages where the Chinese were settled, it was argued, would be models of benevolent and efficient administration in contrast to what they were leaving behind. The Salwa Judum camps too were initially promoted as model settlements, before the endemic corruption of both the state and the Salwa Judum leaders ensured there was nothing exemplary about them.

From Displacement to Starvation

Scorched earth policies are so common in war that international conventions have explicitly outlawed them:

> Starvation of civilians as a method of combat is prohibited. It is therefore prohibited to attack, destroy, remove or render useless, for that purpose, objects indispensable to the survival of the civilian population, such as food-stuffs, agricultural areas for the production of food-stuffs, crops, livestock, drinking water installations and supplies and irrigation works.[8]

When the Judum attacked, they burnt not just the houses with everything inside, but also any stocks of stored grain they found in the forest. They even destroyed hand-pumps. Those who were not forced into camps fled into the forests, taking shelter with the Maoists; some 1,00,000 fled into neighbouring states, particularly Andhra Pradesh.[9] They survived on the water used to boil rice or on grain recovered from their burnt houses. In normal times, the smell and taste of burnt grain is hard to stomach, but humans will eat anything to survive. In the camps, corruption in food supplies meant that people were always hungry. As in Malaya and Mizoram, the government also imposed restrictions on the transport of rice to markets in the interior.

The battle raged across roads, trees, schools, transformers and hand-pumps, fought each bitter inch of the way. The government clears the forest and expands the highways, and the Maoists mobilize villagers to cut the roads at night, deep incisions that slow vehicles down to a crawl. The most visible signs of the infrastructural war are the abandoned schools, their ceilings half fallen, creepers growing out of the sides of blasted walls. In the early years, the schools were occupied by troops during their combing operations, and destroyed by night on Maoist orders, to prevent permanent police bases in the villages. But even before this, as soon as the Judum started, the government ordered the schools to shut down and the teachers to move to camp. For several years, interior weekly markets also closed, and those left in the villages – even when ill and desperate for medical help – were too scared to come out for fear of being captured and killed.

In 2015–16, after a spell of relative calm, terror resurfaced, with reports of cash, jewellery and poultry being looted from homes, bans on traders transporting rice to the interior, and villagers, especially men, scared to come to the market for fear of being arrested.

Recruiting Local Youth as Auxiliaries

The government initially proposed to create 'village defence committees', which would be armed as in Kashmir or Nagaland,[10] much like the civil patrols of Guatemala where there was mass conscription of civilians into the 'dirty war'.[11] However, this didn't work out and, instead, it created a force of special police officers (SPO) out of civilians. Many of these SPOs were former Maoists or their village-level workers, called *sangham* members, who had been forced to 'surrender' at Judum rallies and join the police to identify and track their former comrades.

Here too the government borrowed from well-tested counter-insurgency models, using renegades like the Ikhwanis in Kashmir, SULFA (surrendered United Liberation Front of Asom) members in Assam, or the 'Cats' of Punjab.[12] These men form a shadowy force, unaccountable because they are not officially on police rolls. Even if formally absorbed into the local police, they often continue as an indisciplined presence inside the force. Hated as a class by the local population for being collaborators and traitors, some among them become particularly infamous among civilian victims even as the state celebrates them as counter-insurgent warriors. The Kashmiri Ikhwani Ghulam Mohammad Mir aka Muma Kana, who by his own claims had assisted in the arrest of some 5000 militants, was given one of the nation's highest honours, the Padma Shri, in 2010.[13] In Bastar, the SPO Kartam Surya, notorious among locals for his role in arson, rape and murders, was given a gun salute by the police when he was killed by the Maoists in 2012.

In 2011, the Supreme Court declared the use of local youth as SPOs in counter-insurgency operations unconstitutional. Not only were the state's economic policies neo-liberal, it said, but when faced with the inevitable consequences of these disastrous policies in the form of increased social unrest, its response was equally misguided – such as the reliance on revenge-filled renegades or jobless youth to fight the insurgency rather than on well-trained forces.

The state government immediately responded to this order by renaming the SPOs an 'auxiliary armed police force', continuing to use them in much the same fashion as before, as undisciplined storm troopers and guides. In 2013, the state police changed their name yet again, creating a 1700-strong 'District Reserve Guard' (DRG) of 'former Naxalites of lower cadres, Maoist sympathisers, and villagers displaced during the Salwa Judum'.[14] In 2016, the police also resuscitated the idea of village defence committees.

The Tyranny of the Law

The law has always been more efficient as a companion and aide to counter-insurgency rather than as a check on its excesses. In September 2005, the government announced a ban on the CPI (Maoist) and all its front organizations, and in December 2005, the Chhattisgarh state assembly passed the Chhattisgarh Special Public Security Act (CSPSA) (based on an earlier ordinance). Among other things, this made it illegal for any person to 'assist or participate in any manner in the unlawful activities of such organizations or through any medium or means'. Any villager attending a Maoist meeting or contributing to a village pond whose construction was organized by a guerrilla squad might technically be violating the law. However, the police do not need the CSPSA when it comes to ordinary adivasis, liberally invoking charges of murder and attempt to murder. The clauses related to the Arms Act, dacoity and waging war against the state (Sections 120–121 of the Code of Criminal Procedure, CrPC) are also used, even when people are found with nothing more than axes or bows and arrows.

Policing strategies to deal with adivasis and Naxalites appear to have changed little over four decades. As Amrita Rangasamy wrote in the 1970s:

> The Central Reserve Police were brought to Srikakulam to hunt down a small band of Naxalites and their followers. They now hold the entire tribal community suspect. Police bewilderment is evident in the transporting of scores of tribals to prisons all over Andhra Pradesh and 'sieving operations' are perhaps carried out in jail in the hope that the 'Naxalites' would surface... By tradition, the Indian tribal has never received justice. But in Srikakulam denial of justice has been made a canon of official policy.[15]

Prison statistics in Chhattisgarh are shocking, and have only got worse over the years. In 2013, the Chhattisgarh jails were running at a capacity of 261 per cent, or 15,840 prisoners as against a capacity of 6070 prisoners, the highest levels of overcrowding in the country. Of this, Kanker had an occupancy rate of 428 per cent, Dantewada of 371 per cent and Jagdalpur jail of 260 per cent.[16] Most of the prisoners are undertrials, who are eventually acquitted because there is and can be no evidence against them. But in the meantime, they have spent several years in jail. Rather than rethinking its policy of mass arrests, the Chhattisgarh government sanctioned Rs 21.66 crore in its 2016 budget for additional barracks to address the problem of overcrowding.[17]

Shackling the Messenger

In times of counter-insurgency or war, the media's tendency to follow the state's narrative is well known – whether through the visual and aural imaging of war and casualties, or the front-page coverage given to the administration's view versus the space given to dissenters.[18]

In Chhattisgarh, the local media has been intimidated when it has not been actively co-opted by the state. At the height of the Judum, few in villages or towns barely 50 or 100 kilometres away knew what was happening since all they read in the press was a litany of violent Maoist attacks.

The national media has been largely indifferent, with coverage of the armed conflict in the last 10 years ranging from silence on state atrocities to uncritical praise for the state in its battle against the Naxalites. From 2005 to 2007 there was a virtual media blackout. Between 2008 and 2011 there was some exposure of human rights abuses, followed by comparative silence till 2015–16, when the revival of vigilantism and attacks on human rights activists, lawyers, journalists and others made it impossible to ignore. Much of the coverage has focused on middle-class interlocutors, but a decade of war in Bastar means there is much more reporting even on ordinary adivasis now than there was at the start of the Salwa Judum. The major difference is that villagers are now willing to talk about what they have suffered compared to the terrified silence with which they endured the Salwa Judum.

In general, the national media is sanguine about the effects on civilians when it comes to national security. In the 1960s, when almost the entire population of the north-eastern state of Mizoram was being forcibly displaced into army-controlled camps, the *Indian Express* accepted, with apparent approval, that 'Operation Security will involve a measure of force'.[19] In Kashmir, despite the discovery of unmarked mass graves, thousands of disappearances and some estimated 70,000 to 90,000 deaths since 1989 when the Kashmir movement began, these are scarcely issues for national debate.

The Ebbs and Flows of Counter-insurgency

As the seasons have passed, the war has both receded and redoubled in intensity, naming and renaming itself – Salwa Judum, Operation Green Hunt, localized operations like Operation Maad, Kilam and Podku, or Mission 2016. The conflict has expanded to new areas, spreading north and east into the Dhurwa and Koya villages of the Kanger National Park, and to Kanker, Antagarh and Bhanupratappur in the far north. Encounters, ambushes, mass arrests and civilian killings are reported from across the district. Combing operations now go on even during the monsoons, with no thought to the deep vulnerability of people during this season when food stocks are traditionally low.

Uniformed guerrillas march through the night, crossing pebbled streams by foot, wary of snakebites and brambles, trying to keep themselves and their janathana sarkar alive. Uniformed paramilitaries march through the heat of the day, many praying for a transfer out of the place. Occasionally, the Maoists launch a devastating attack, like the 76 CRPF men ambushed in Tadmetla in April 2010; and sometimes the security forces notch up deaths, as in the 17 villagers shot in Sarkeguda one night in 2012. The silent forest has learnt to listen for the sound of death.

The security forces have come to stay. Like an occupation army, they have spread their tentacles, setting up camps every 5 to 8 kilometres, tearing down the forest, ringing large areas with concertina wire, their lumbering green armoured vehicles flattening the forest roads as helicopters and unmanned drones fly overhead. Villagers say the camps come up overnight, sometimes on land they have been cultivating for decades. Six-lane highways are being built through forest villages. Right now there are perhaps five or six vehicles that might pass in an entire day – some couples on a scooter, interstate trucks, the very occasional car belonging to some official, and on market days crowded jeep-taxis and buses carrying people and produce. On village roads one might go for miles without seeing a single person, leave alone a motor vehicle. The population density in Dantewada, according to the 2011 census, is 59 persons per square kilometre, while in Bijapur it is 39. But the planning is clearly for a future where ore-laden trucks will make their way out in a continuous stream.

While most villagers have returned from the Judum camps or Andhra Pradesh where they fled between 2005 and 2007, some who left then will never return, because even desperate flight produces new roots. Some have settled in the Salwa Judum camps where their children have become part of the police, and some have struck roots, albeit tenuous, in Telangana/Andhra Pradesh – their children study in Telugu, and they have new identity cards and, in some cases, new religions.

Even for those who have returned, staying in their villages is contingent: frequent combing operations by security forces, torture and mass arrests as well as the lack of work drive youth to leave, at least for a season, and often for much longer. Under the pressure of paramilitary camps and police payments to informers, the Maoists are also turning on villagers, killing 'informers' and beating people for collaborating with the police. In conversations, people report 'calm' or 'disturbed' as if they were reporting the weather on a weekly or monthly basis. And whenever there is a major 'encounter' between the security forces and Maoists, a silence descends on all the villages around, as villagers collectively hold their breath, waiting for state retaliation.

In the areas which have not been directly affected by the Judum or subsequent operations, other kinds of divisions have surfaced. Each tribe has its own association, like the Halba Samaj or Koya Samaj, which lays down rules regarding marriage and food. There are fights between Christian converts who refuse to pay their share of contributions for village fairs, saying they no longer follow the gods in whose name these fairs are held, and those following the traditional path who argue that these are collective village events and not just religious festivals. The Hindu chauvinist Vishwa Hindu Parishad is now in on the act, infusing a wider Hindu–Christian antagonism into a very local conflict.

Future historians will note the passing of a civilization that understood the forest, and the rise of a society of middlemen, contractors, paramilitary forces, and of divisions induced by religion and political parties.

2

Iron in the Soul

In April 2015, I was sitting in a tea shop in Nagarnar, 16 kilometres to the east of Jagdalpur (the headquarters of Bastar district), where the state-owned National Minerals Development Corporation (NMDC) was building a steel plant. As in Kirandul and Bacheli in the Bailadilla hills, the first public sector mining townships in the region, the roads within the Nagarnar steel plant were wide and well paved. However, the road to the village outside was earthen and bumpy; it ended in a chowk, with the usual shops selling tea, soft drinks and cold samosas, a bus stand and a panchayat bhawan. The conversation in the tea shop was about the ongoing land acquisition. The shop owner said, pushing stalks of sugarcane through a press, that the government was now acquiring land for Rs 28–30 lakh an acre, when in 2001, they had forced people to sign away their land for Rs 11,000 an acre. Most land had been acquired then. The villagers had been lathi-charged and arrested when they protested. A balding man, Shankar, chimed in, saying he had got Rs 73,000 for his 5 acres. This was too little to buy alternative land; the family now survives on the class IV or manual job one son had obtained in NMDC. Since then, politicians and traders from Jagdalpur had bought up the land, in their own names if purchasing from non-adivasis like the Sundis, or in the name of a trusted adivasi servant (*benami*), since the law prohibits adivasi land from being sold to non-adivasis. A tall, thin man with a sharp moustache, who worked at the Punjab National Bank, insisted that it was the market at work; the locals kept silent, and almost tangentially, as if it was part of someone else's story, or in separate conversations with me, described what they had lost.

On the other side of Jagdalpur, in Lohandiguda, where a Tata steel plant was to have come up following an agreement in 2005, the villagers had been living in uncertainty and tension for eleven years. In 2007, the state carried out rapes and arrests to cow the villagers, organized by the CPI, into parting with their land to the Tatas.[1] The company was silent on this, but ran sports programmes in schools, and operated a clinic as part of its corporate social responsibility (CSR). Villagers continued to cultivate their own land, but officials refused to give them loans or fertilizers since the land had been officially 'acquired'. The only people who were really happy were the *dalals* who have a finger in the manipulation of land acquisition and sales. In August 2016, the company formally wound up its project, ostensibly because of delays in land acquisition, and the consequent loss of a captive iron ore mine, but also because of the glut in steel production worldwide.

The Wealth Beneath the Earth

In May 2015, Prime Minister Narendra Modi visited Dantewada and announced investments of Rs 24,000 crore, for an 'ultra mega' steel plant at Dilmilli to the south of Jagdalpur, a 10 million metric tonne processing plant at Bacheli-Kirandul near the existing NMDC iron ore mines in Bailadilla, a railway line to bring iron ore from the planned Raoghat mines in the north to Jagdalpur, and a slurry pipe and pellet plant in Nagarnar.[2]

If the government had its way, Jagdalpur would be surrounded by steel plants and the entire region criss-crossed by pipelines, roads and railway lines carrying iron ore and other minerals. Where there are no mines, there will be dams and reservoirs to supply power to industry: the Polavaram dam in Andhra Pradesh, if it comes through, will submerge much of Konta block, while the Bodhghat hydroelectric project – once shelved but now revived – will flood villages in Dantewada. Between the mines, the dams and the defence establishments like the defence base at Mardum and the Jungle Warfare College in Kanker, the dense biodiversity of the region will be a thing of the past.

If the late nineteenth century belonged to the forest department, where forests were reserved to meet the shipbuilding and railway needs of the British, and the twentieth century belonged to the public engineers who built dams, the twenty-first century is undoubtedly – at least so far – the century for public–private partnerships in mining. The 2000–8 global commodity boom or, in the longer term, commodity supercycle, driven by demand from the BRICS countries (Brazil, Russia, India, China and South Africa), led to a major rise in prices for primary commodities and a greater financialization of these commodities, as well as the development of new mining technologies. In the first decade of the twenty-first century, iron production worldwide went up by 10 per cent. New areas were opened up for mining, with state intervention in these areas taking on the form of a roll-out of rural infrastructure – roads, power, telecom towers, etc.[3]

This global phenomenon is visible in Chhattisgarh. During 1982–90, 96 per cent of the acquisition was for projects involving water resources, dropping to 49.9 per cent between 1991 and 2007. In contrast, acquisition for industry, mines, defence and roads (34.72 per cent of all acquisition) went up dramatically in the latter period, while acquisition for health and education stayed at zero. Between 1991 and 2007, 3703.75 acres of land were acquired for defence in Bastar alone.[4]

Bastar's mineral wealth includes 10 per cent of the country's iron ore reserves, apart from bauxite, platinum, corundum, dolomite, limestone, etc.; minerals contribute greatly to the state's revenues.[5] Much of this is headed into private hands.[6] From Kalinganagar and

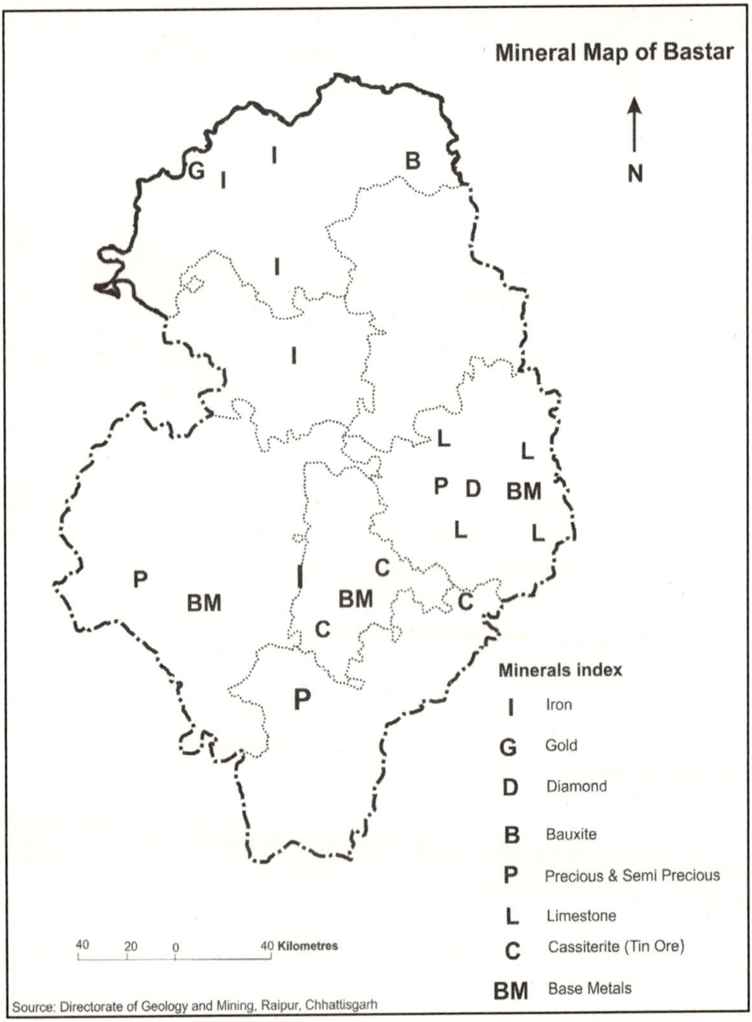
Mineral Map of Bastar
N
G
I
I
B
I
I
L
L
P
D
BM
L
L
C
P
BM
I
BM
C
C
P
Minerals index
I Iron
G Gold
D Diamond
B Bauxite
P Precious & Semi Precious
L Limestone
C Cassiterite (Tin Ore)
BM Base Metals
40 20 0 40 Kilometres
Source: Directorate of Geology and Mining, Raipur, Chhattisgarh

Kashipur in Odisha to Noamundi in Jharkhand and Raigarh in north Chhattisgarh, landscapes are being transformed where sponge iron plants belch dense black smoke, coal mines destroy swathes of green forest, and mining for iron ore or bauxite displaces small helpless villages, turns their waters red with sludge and sucks up the springs.

Formal mining coexists with informal private extraction. I have passed rivers in Antagarh in the north where gold panning occurs, and in Tongpal in the south I have seen traders take out illegally smelted tin in bags strapped to the sides of their motorbikes, headed over the border to Odisha and Andhra Pradesh. All the police stations en route, said the traders, take a cut, giving me exact figures of how much they paid. Every night, according to a Dantewada journalist, 14–15 trucks with 16–40 tonnes of iron ore, illegally pilfered from the NMDC mines, are sent off from Bacheli and Kirandul to sponge iron plants in the state.

The emptying of villages by the Judum meant a great deal of unchecked smaller-scale prospecting and felling. In 2008, in a government guest house in Chintur on the Andhra Pradesh side of the border, waiting to cross over to Chhattisgarh, I met a Telugu businessman who had just acquired 3 hectares of land for a granite quarry in a village, all of whose inhabitants had been moved to camp. Three hectares, he figured, would get him a profit of Rs 10–20 crore. Under the Panchayats (Extension to Scheduled Areas) Act (PESA), 1996, the villagers must be consulted before any lease for the mining of minor minerals is given in their village. But since there was no one left to ask, the administration simply usurped this right. The businessman said he sniffed opportunity at times of conflict when competition was low: his company had acquired some 100 hectares in different villages in small lots and under different names to circumvent the laws requiring federal clearance for diversion of forest land.

From Mining to Militarism

Mining and militarism have a deeply intimate history. In 2003, when India liberalized its mining policy, the de facto Maoist control over the region was seen as constituting a major obstacle to rapid industrialization and land acquisition. Industry associations like the Federation of Indian Chambers of Commerce and Industry (FICCI) explicitly supported the government's offensive against the Maoists and called for the involvement of the private sector in this effort:

> The growing Maoist insurgency over large swathes of the mineral-rich countryside could soon hurt some industrial investment plans. Just when India needs to ramp up its industrial machine to lock in growth and when foreign companies are joining the party – Naxalites are clashing with mining and steel companies essential to India's long-term success.[7]

Human rights activists argue that it is not a coincidence that Salwa Judum began just when the state government had signed a memorandum of understanding for a steel plant with the Tatas in June 2005. Around the same time, Essar was acquiring land for another steel plant in Dhurli and Bhansi villages, and both the Tatas and Essar were given captive iron ore mines on the Bailadilla hills. 'Public hearings' were held in Lohandiguda, Dhurli and Bhansi, in order to fulfil the official requirement under PESA of eliciting villagers' 'consent':

> The villagers under the leadership of Dantewada Adivasi Mahasabha and Sangharsh Samiti Dhurli, said that on 9th September the police forced them to sign No objection letters. Two constables were posted in each house. No outsider was allowed at the meeting place. People were not allowed to leave their homes or to talk to each other. According to villagers, at 9 a.m. they were forced into vehicles, and taken to the meeting location. Supporters of the opposition

leader (Mahendra Karma) also helped the police in this process. The villagers related that they were taken into a room in twos, and pistols were placed at their temples to make them sign where told. They were told to not step out of the village afterwards.[8]

Those villagers who refused to sign were arrested, and Section 144 (prohibitory orders on assembly) was imposed on the area.

In North Bastar, 22 paramilitary camps fortify the prospective Raoghat mines. Villagers near the mine told us that some 10 years ago, when the project was being proposed, the police took away all their bows and arrows, leaving them vulnerable to attacks by wild animals. Since then they have arrested several village leaders protesting against the mines and railway line. Even the prosaic words of the Rapid Environmental Impact Assessment report on the Raoghat mines reveal how incalculable the loss to both people and nature would be if the mines and the railway line linking Dalli Rajhara to Jagdalpur came up. The country would lose:

> 26 plant species that are included in the red list of rare and endangered species of vascular plants of India; high average growing stock and ultimately, the presence of 22 mammalian species of which 15 are in either Endangered or Vulnerable list of IUCN appendices or WPA schedules; large number of insects including a few rare ones (identification in progress), 28 species of Butterflies and 102 species of bird from 38 families.[9]

The site proposed for the mining waste dumps, the report warned, would destroy the drainage of the entire valley; and indeed the entire culture of the people would likely become extinct.

A Concert of Interests

Important as mining and resource extraction are, they are not the whole story. Land acquisition has been taking place across the country, and while the police often work as corporate agents, firing on villagers protesting against land acquisition,[10] they have not resorted to Salwa Judum–style grouping elsewhere. Instead, what we see is the coming together of several interests – the security establishment in Delhi, local politicians, the police, the mining industry, the Hindu chauvinist Rashtriya Swayamsevak Sangh (RSS) and unemployed youth. The Indian state may have let its sovereignty slide in the abandoned adivasi homelands of India, untouched for years by basic services like education or health. Elsewhere in Uttar Pradesh or Bihar, the police coexist with and are often subservient to the armed power of local big men. However, Maoist control over vast areas is untenable for the state. A casual glance at the topography through which the Salwa Judum moved and the burned villages it left in its wake will show that there is no one-to-one correlation between the villages attacked and the mining areas. Instead, major Maoist strongholds were targeted for the first attacks, and others that fell en route were burnt almost randomly.

The RSS has always seen the left as its primary enemy. A report by an RSS think tank talks of the history of conflict between the Maoists and Sangh organizations such as the Vanvasi Kalyan Ashram, Vidya Bharati and ideologically similar groups like the Gayatri Parivar, and proudly confirms the RSS hand in Salwa Judum:

> The participation of Gayatri Parivar, Sangha Parivar and the Divya Seva Sangh [sic] situated in Gumargunda village of Dantewada is incredible... This movement [Salwa Judum] started fifteen years ago through the peaceful People Awakening Programme. The overall objective of the movement is to form a village security committee. This movement stays completely away from any publicity or propaganda. This is their main strength.[11]

~

For Congress politician Mahendra Karma, the alleged leader of the Judum, the campaign was a chance to make a name and money for himself and his followers. In 2005, several people also told me that Karma got involved in the Judum so as to save himself from CBI prosecution in the *malik makbuja* scam, in which timber had been illegally felled on a large scale. For at least a century before mining became the main attraction, Bastar's forest wealth has been a source of huge profit for both the state and private traders.

Before 1947, felling teak or fruit-bearing trees on private land was prohibited except when shade or falling leaves upset standing crops. After Independence, peasants were given the right (malik makbuja) to cut trees on their own land, after taking government permission. Contractors used this to persuade peasants with little understanding of market prices to sell them teak trees – which cost lakhs – at ridiculously low rates. The contractors also removed timber from government forests, which was then passed off as coming from private lands. Several hundred truckloads of timber were thus taken away. In response, the government enacted the MP Protection of Scheduled Tribes (Interest in Trees) Act, 1956, under which the sale of trees from adivasi lands has to be sanctioned and supervised by the Collector, to ensure the adivasis are not cheated.

However, the administration proved an unreliable protector, colluding with timber merchants to subvert the law. Agents, usually immigrants, contacted villagers, tempted them to sell trees and offered to pursue the complex paperwork involved in return for a commission. But their profits went beyond any reasonable commission, helped by the widespread illiteracy in the area. In 1997, while researching the malik makbuja scam, I interviewed a man called Mundru in Kukanar. The agent kept Mundru's bank passbook and merrily withdrew whatever he wanted from the account. Of the Rs 2,72,000 deposited in his account for sale of trees, Mundru got merely Rs 16,000. Timber merchants bought not just trees but, where they could, the land itself, in order to fell trees. Rich adivasi politicians from both the Congress and BJP, like Mahendra Karma and Rajaram

Todem, were legally able to buy land from other adivasis. Again, land records and timber transport permits were fudged with the help of forest and revenue staff, to enable theft from government forests.

Manish Kunjam, who was then a CPI MLA, raised questions about the scam in the legislative assembly and the Bastar Collector complained against his own superior, the Commissioner, for collusion in the malik makbuja scam. However, between 1993 and 1996, the Madhya Pradesh government did nothing. An environmentalist in Karnataka, S.R. Hiremath of the Samaj Parivartana Samudaya, and Ratneswar Nath of Ekta Parishad, an NGO in Kanker, then took the matter to the Supreme Court. In 1997, the court banned all felling in Bastar. It also set up an independent enquiry by the Lokayukt, a government watchdog body. Charges were filed against several people, but nothing came of it.

The Lokayukt report specifically names Mahendra Karma, who was then MP for Bastar, for defrauding five residents of Kasoli village whose land he bought. In the registered sale deed, while the land itself cost merely Rs 22,050, the 25 teak trees, two bija trees and seven mahua trees standing on it were valued at Rs 1,61,000. The total was thus Rs 1.83 lakh. Karma claimed to the Lokayukt that he had paid the full amount, but the sellers said they got only Rs 1.5 lakh. Karma then resold the trees – and it turned out that there were actually 79 trees on that piece of land and not merely 34 trees as mentioned in the sale deed – and got Rs 17.5 lakh for it. In short, Karma made a profit of Rs 16.5 lakh within six months, while the actual landowners got practically nothing. As the Lokayukt report dispassionately notes, all this was possible because of collusion at all levels of officialdom:

> These officers (forest and revenue officials responsible for supervising sales) granted permission freely in favour of other influential persons also like Mahendra Karma (the then Member of Parliament), Rajaram Todem (presently Dy. Leader of Opposition in M.P. Legislative Assembly) and other influential merchant families like

> Suranas, Awasthis, Brij Mohan Gupta and many others who have entered in this trade of purchasing land with standing trees and selling the timber. It is observed on the basis of scrutiny of records that their cases were decided with utmost promptness whereas cases of other ordinary persons were decided in a routine manner.[12]

Once the Judum started, however, all this was quickly forgotten.

The Police Stake in a Continuing War

The presence of the Naxalites has been hugely beneficial for the police, as Shivraj Patil, who was Union home minister at the time, admitted to the ICI in 2006. Police stations compete to be declared 'Naxal affected' since this brings with it the promise of 'security-related expenditure', free central government (taxpayer) money without any metric of accountability. The police also want the promotions, which come with a high kill rate of insurgents, never mind if these are 'genuine encounters' or extrajudicial killings.

On the other hand, every time there is a major encounter or ambush in which the police or CRPF get killed, it becomes an occasion for the security forces to demand more money. The press dutifully reports violations of standard operating procedure, the need for better equipment and better coordination between states and the Centre.

In the police narrative, they never have enough personnel to fight the Maoists. They claim that the administration initially relied on Salwa Judum vigilantes because decades of neglect had resulted in low people–police ratios in Chhattisgarh, and this was a prelude to establishing full control by the police. However, the police–population figures in Chhattisgarh have for long been higher than in many other states with a Maoist presence.[13] It is true that the police–area ratio in Chhattisgarh is among the lowest in India – 31.8 police personnel per square kilometre (2009) up from 17.59 (2005–6) – but again, this is higher than in some neighbouring states.[14] What the security establishment ignores is that Scheduled Areas were meant to be sparsely policed and lightly administered as a matter of policy.

The lack of police has been overcompensated by the presence of armed personnel sent by the Centre. In 2016, 116 battalions of CAPF were posted to 10 states across central India, with more forces in the pipeline. Of the 93 battalions deployed the previous year, over half (48 battalions) were in Bastar alone, with four battalions earmarked just for the Raoghat mines.[15] This meant an estimated 0.1 million 'boots on the ground' in Bastar for a population of about 3.09 million (2011 census).[16] Coupled with unmanned aerial vehicles to spot Maoist movements, helicopters to drop security forces, bulletproof mine vehicles and a whole host of other equipment, in the 11 years between 2004 and 2015, central India has become a bristling war theatre. The air force has started practising strafing, though their official position is that this is only for self-defence. But nothing is ever enough for the security establishment.

Middle-class Dreams

Life in this region is marked by a duality. Larger-than-life statues of dancing Gond women – their naked black bodies adorned with bronze-paint jewellery – mark the roundabouts of Jagdalpur, gratifying settler fantasies, even as the presence of real adivasis diminishes in the city. Wide roads with yellow dividers now cut through small towns like Sukma and Bijapur, formerly just a huddle of small shops, petrol pumps and an occasional roadside eatery. Bijapur now boasts a district library, a swimming pool and glass-fronted government buildings. The country is full of youth looking for jobs; if adivasis must be sacrificed to make way for industry, so be it.

Most of the middle class actively supports the idea of mining (even if it comes with severe police repression), claiming that this is the route by which adivasis will be 'civilized' and 'mainstreamed'. In 1938, Wilfred Grigson, the administrator of Bastar state and author of the authoritative *The Maria Gonds of Bastar*, wrote:

> As the Maratha Amil sixty-seven years before, so now the Victorian Englishman: develop trade and civilisation would follow. The isolation of centuries was to end, Bastar was to be opened to the world by land and water, and its 'savages' to exchange their freedom for the 'allurements and comforts of civilisation', trade and traders, clothes, tobacco, a better system of criminal and judicial procedure, vaccination and copper coin… A land free from rules and regulations and a race that had no use for copper coin did not square with that passion for uniformity that characterised the Victorian rulers of India and still marks the framers of constitutions for the India of today.[17]

How little has changed in ideas of progress from then to 2010, when home minister P. Chidambaram declared that 'while implementation of laws such as PESA and FRA [Forest Rights Act, 2006] might give rights to forest dwellers, the long-term solution lay in the basic development which would bring them out of the forests. "They must know that the government is friendly to their way of life, but wants to help them change their way of life," he added.'[18]

The major change, though, from Grigson's time to Chidambaram's or Narendra Modi's is the development of a local constituency of immigrants. In the last few decades, many of the adivasi areas in the country have seen significant demographic change, leading to a rapid increase in the percentage of non-tribal settlers. They occupy the bureaucracy and control trade. Inevitably, they have also slowly taken over adivasi land, helped by the weak implementation of laws meant to protect adivasi holdings, and have come to dominate electoral politics. In Bastar, the non-adivasi population has expanded so rapidly in the last few decades that Jagdalpur, formerly 'reserved' for an adivasi in the legislative assembly, can now be electorally represented even by a non-adivasi, and inevitably the seat has been won by a moneyed Marwari. The non-adivasis have settled in small urban clusters along the roadside, dominating the highways. Over the years, their children have grown to consider themselves even more indigenous than the adivasis, whom they despise as backward and incapable of fully utilizing the advantages of the area. The desperate poverty of the adivasis is turned against them, to justify displacing them for more productive uses of land. From 1947 till the turn of the century, approximately one in every four adivasis nationally had been displaced for dams, industries, mines and similar projects.

It is this immigrant constituency that is especially vocal in demanding a railway line, mining and industrialization, which they think will get them jobs. In 2009, when the CPI organized a public hearing in Lohandiguda on the proposed steel plant to counter the fraudulent public hearing organized by the government, these non-adivasi youth barricaded the road to try to prevent them, with tacit support from the administration. Compared to these assertive 'insiders', everyone who comes in the way of their exploitation of resources – Maoists, human rights activists, metropolitan journalists – is an outsider.

The immigrants retain close connections to other parts of India, speak the same languages and share the same aspirations as the metropolitan urban middle classes – who, since liberalization began in 1991, have been fed on a story of accumulation with growth and learnt to love private capital as the saviour of their times. Even when the weight of 'scams' or instances of collusion in utilizing natural resources between corporates and government became apparent in the last days of the Congress-led United Progressive Alliance (UPA) regime, public anger was directed not at the model of growth predicated on the use of adivasi resources but at the money being made by politicians. This is the constituency that broadly supports the government's counter-insurgency efforts, even if the way the Salwa Judum initially played out, with the unchecked power it gave adivasi SPOs, was not to their liking.

The crew-cut, fatigues-wearing Brigadier B.K. Ponwar who has run the Jungle Warfare College in Kanker since its inception – and who fancies himself as both Rambo and boy scout – once described his vision of paradise versus the deficits of the area he found himself in. Bastar has some of the most biodiverse forests in the country, populated by Gonds (and not Bhils), but, said Brigadier Ponwar sadly: 'There are no malls here, only Bhils and Bustars. In Gurgaon [the suburban sprawl known for its malls], you can live in India, but shop like foreign [sic].'[19] At his college, overweight policemen are transformed into hardy guerrilla fighters, and as one newspaper helpfully mentioned, his training has great benefits for the sex lives of the troopers. They train to the aggressive chorus of 'Let the Bodies Hit the Floor', Drowning Pool's hit song. I have no idea if the brigadier borrowed it from the Guantanamo Bay camps where it was played as an instrument of torture in 2003.

In comparison to immigrant youth, local adivasi and 'Bastariya' youth are much more conflicted about the effects of mining and industrialization. They know that projects like the Bailadilla mines have brought them nothing but displacement and ruined their environment, but at the same time, they see no alternative model of employment. While education and literacy have been hugely neglected in adivasi areas, there is a growing population of youth who have been schooled up to class 12 or college, and who, in part because of the alienating nature of their education, do not wish to return to farming. Lacking the kind of family contacts that non-adivasi youth have, their main hope lies in the formal government sector in which a certain number of jobs are reserved by law for the SCs and STs. But given the downsizing and contractualization of government employment, these jobs are almost impossible to get. In 2015, 75,000 persons applied for 30 peon positions in Chhattisgarh's Directorate of Economics and Statistics.[20]

In 2005, when the government started the Salwa Judum, adivasi youth had few choices. Many were attracted by the Maoists, who had been a familiar presence since childhood, and their argument that people should support them in order to defend their lands had a deep resonance. This was strengthened by the brutal Salwa Judum attacks on their villages, which forced many to join the Maoists in pure self-defence. But many – especially the SCs and OBCs who saw the Maoists as a predominantly adivasi party – were attracted by the prospect of government jobs as SPOs.

Dehumanizing Adivasis

Decades of upper-caste racism have so naturalized the association between adivasis and animals that they are often described as subhuman, as in the Bastar tourism website which ran for a few years from 2005, before middle-class adivasis finally succeeded in having it scrapped. Describing Maria drinking habits, the government proclaimed: 'when drinking water from a stream they do not take up water in their hands but put their mouth down to it like cattle.' It added pruriently, 'The tribals of this area is famous for their "ghotul" where the prospective couples do the "dating" and have free sex also [sic].'[21]

The Maoists have become the national vermin, competing with the national animal and the national song, and 'infesting' a whole red corridor of their very own. While the Maoists and the villagers they represent occupy the lower end of the animal scale, the sort that humans like to crush and exterminate, the security forces are exhorted to bring out the animal in themselves, the fiercer the better. The police and paramilitary units specially trained in anti-Naxalite operations are called Greyhounds in Andhra Pradesh, Jaguars in Jharkhand and Cobras (Commando Battalion for Resolution Action, a unit of the CRPF) in Chhattisgarh. The forces also employ dogs to discover explosives and sense ambushes, importing Belgian Mallinois for the task.[22] On one trip, the police unleashed a dog to check our car. This one happened to be a particularly enthusiastic puppy which licked our faces, but doubtless, this was not the effect they intended. The use of dogs also has a symbolic value in reducing the enemy to hunted prey.

Even when talking of welfare and not war, the prose of dehumanization is evident: if food rations or other services are denied to villages, it does not matter, because it is only Naxalites who 'infest' these areas. Conversely, if villagers are to be given services, it is only because they are 'Naxal-hit' and need to be 'weaned away' from the Naxalites, not because they have entitlements as citizens. At a meeting in June 2015 organized by the Surya Foundation, a pro-BJP think tank, a 'security expert' from a reputed government security think tank, waved a list of solutions. One of them included stopping all rice-carrying trucks from entering Abujhmarh, considered the headquarters of the Maoists, so that the Maoists could not stop the trucks and offload supplies for themselves. When I pointed out there were villagers living in the Marh, he declared, 'There are ways to get rice to them, such as going house to house and distributing rice.' 'But then the Maoists can simply ask each household to set aside some rice for them,' I said. He replied, 'The villagers will then refuse and this demand will help to alienate them from the Maoists.' I gave up at this point. How does one begin to explain the complicated overlap between adivasis and Maoists to those blinded by hubris?

To summarize, the repertoire of counter-insurgency may be common to different parts of the world, but in Chhattisgarh it is inflected with a particular character that draws on the nature of Indian democracy: the location of adivasis as the poorest and most 'backward' section of the Indian population requiring to be weaned away from their forest-dependent lifestyles into urban mainstream society; the constellation of classes, especially the growing middle classes, which want economic growth at all costs; and the attractions of government employment in the police or paramilitary forces, especially given the lack of other jobs. Counter-insurgency, especially in order to clear the way for mining and industrialization, is justified as a massive employment exercise, and displacement of the poor is sanitized and celebrated as growth and development.

Retelling This Story

Inevitably, the commentary on the conflict, like the conflict itself, is polarized on distinct lines. Police officers and security experts have generated a large amount of what one might call 'Naxology'. This is similar to colonial Indology, which came about as a form of knowledge that would help the British to control the population better. There are some relatively more sympathetic semi-official analyses focusing on the 'root causes', such as a Planning Commission report written in 2008, which highlight the discrimination and poverty in so-called Naxalite areas. But thanks to nearly two decades of concerted counter-insurgency propaganda, such narratives are disappearing from public discourse. Police officials frequently claim that military action rather than dialogue is justified because the Maoists have lost any ideological basis they may once have had. However, their own tactics are based on the premise that civilians will obey whoever exercises greater force, that is, that control is simply a function of power, and ideology has no purchase.

In hard-nosed quantitative social science, there is equally little room for ideology. Some analysts like to plot the overlap between forest cover, mining, adivasi populations and insurgency as if one automatically leads to the other. While there are indeed strong correspondences, they are not explanatory in and of themselves. Jhabua and Dantewada districts have very similar percentages of forest cover, poverty and adivasi populations, but where Dantewada has been the epicentre of Maoist insurgency, in large part because of its proximity to Andhra Pradesh, Jhabua has been the site of experimentation for a number of Gandhian 'people's movements'. To understand the Maoists in Bastar, or indeed anywhere, one must look at Maoist ideology and organizational structures, individual lives of sacrifice, and historically learnt repertoires of resistance and solidarity among the local population. Even within Dantewada, there is a wide variation in villages, with some considered Maoist strongholds and others relatively neutral.

In the currency of journalism and human rights, analysis depends on your political position. For the right-wing commentator, gullible adivasis are brainwashed by manipulative Naxalites. For liberals, adivasis are 'caught' (sandwiched) between the Maoists and the state.

For a radical, whose battle is often as much with the liberals as with the state, the liberals are 'sandwich theorists', naive at best and state apologists at worst, who commit the ultimate sin of 'equating state violence and Maoist violence'.

These would-be revolutionaries see only resistance wherever they look, assimilating the figure of the adivasi Maoist into the glorious fight against corporate displacement, regardless of the multiple reasons why people join the Maoists. Of course, resistance and courage exist, in remarkable measure, especially for a people as exploited and under siege as the adivasis of central India. However, the urban radicals are unable to cope with the moral complexity of multiple affiliations and desires, the differences across regions and over time as people's allegiances change, and the desperate yearning for peace. People want both the Maoists and the state, but for different reasons: the former provide freedom from a hated bureaucracy and the latter holds out the promise of welfare on a scale that no one else can provide. Even as villagers hate the government for what it is doing to them, they want justice from this very government. And even as the Maoists curse the Constitution, they invoke its principles when criticizing the extrajudicial killings or the arrest of their leaders. India's constitutional democracy, because of and in spite of all its failures, is a predicament and promise that no citizen can escape from.

Counter-insurgency and Democracy Today

A small cottage industry of quantitative political science literature is devoted to assessing whether democracy makes any difference to the conduct of counter-insurgency. Some argue that democracies are less likely to produce internal insurgencies; that public reaction to the deaths of soldiers as well as to human rights violations increase the costs to the state; and that democratic states are more likely to take a 'balanced' or 'moderate' approach, avoiding indiscriminate killing and combining counter-insurgency with welfarism and co-optation of elites. Other scholars contest this claim, arguing that there is no empirical evidence, when comparing regime types, that democracies handle counter-insurgencies any differently from colonial or authoritarian regimes.[23]

That India has an electoral democracy, a free press, statutory institutions like the National Human Rights Commission (NHRC), an independent judiciary and a flourishing human rights movement should surely mean something. But what they mean may not be what we expect. In fact, I argue, it is these that provide the cracks through which Indian democracy falls – both through their institutional weakness and the official legitimation they provide.

Electoral democracy seems to be of limited use in stemming massive human rights violations due to counter-insurgency. Evidence includes: the collusion of the two main political parties in conducting the Salwa Judum and the acquiescence of all the major political parties to similar operations in their own states; the use of electoral victories to justify pogroms or avoid culpability; and the role of mining companies in funding elections. If the media contributes to a freely functioning democracy, its very freedom undermines that democracy when it fails to report on certain things or slants the story. The courts or statutory institutions like the NHRC may choose to check the government, but when they don't, their power to conceal human rights abuses is far greater in a democracy than in a military regime.

What has changed is that counter-insurgency now has to compete with international cyber-activism, though of course, both the traditional and new media can also be an effective extension of state propaganda. There are other institutional features that introduce some checks. India's federalism is often seen by the police as a problem for cross-border operations, but it also means that the victims of Salwa Judum had the option to flee to Andhra Pradesh, where for all the hardships they faced, life was a little more secure. And because popular followings cannot be totally suppressed, events like funerals or memorial meetings can become spaces for the enactment of alternative allegiances. When Mallojula Koteswara Rao, popularly known as Kishenji, was killed by the security forces in West Bengal in November 2011, thousands of people gathered at his funeral, including members of the legislative assembly: 'Since morning people started pouring in from places as far as Nizamabad, Adilabad and Visakapatnam. A serpentine queue could be seen at Kishenji's house at Brahmana Veedhi (street), where his body was kept.'[24]

If the Maoists are the spectre haunting the state today, they have also influenced its imagination in more positive ways – at least enough to enable other groups like the Campaign for Survival and Dignity or the National Alliance of People's Movements (NAPM) to press for legislation like the Scheduled Tribes and Other Traditional Forest Dwellers (Recognition of Forest Rights) Act, 2006, popularly called the Forest Rights Act (FRA), giving security of tenure to forest dwellers, or the Land Acquisition Act, 2013, which introduced clauses on social impact assessment and consent. That these acts passed by the UPA regime are being undermined by the Modi government, which came to power in 2014, is another matter.

Above all, democracy gives those who dissent a basic advantage: the ideals of the very Constitution and rule of law in whose name they are declared illegal. Ultimately, then, the story of Bastar will go down in history not just as a moment when democracy failed and fell by the wayside, trampling the lives of its citizens, but also a moment when it was rescued by its people – men like Podiyam Panda who managed to keep their sanity and humour in the most difficult conditions, or women who bravely testified to rape by the security forces, despite unbearable intimidation. When the state falters, it is citizens who intervene to prop up the state idea, demanding accountability and the rule of law, if only as a sign of hope that flourishes despite the anomie and despair. These are signs that stand for wonders in the parched landscape of civil war, the signposts to a democracy that is always in process, never achieved, but never abandoned.

3

'Because I Want Peace'

Because I want peace
And not war
Because I don't want to see
Hungry children
Or emaciated women
Or men with silenced
Tongues
I must keep on fighting...

Because there are territories
Now liberated
Where those who don't know how to
Are learning to read
And the sick are treated
And the produce of the land
Belongs to everybody
I must keep on fighting
Because I want peace
And not war

Claríbel Alegria, 'Because I Want Peace'

The Hindi-speaking Chhattisgarh government constantly describes Maoists as Telugu-speaking outsiders, even though by now over 90 per cent of the Maoist cadre and even high-level commanders in Bastar are local adivasis, and all meetings are conducted in Gondi. But Bastar has always been a zone of north–south crossings, and the two movements that have changed the course of Bastar's history have both been from south to north. In the fourteenth century, the Kakatiya king Annam Deo fled from Warangal (now in Telangana) and established the kingdom of Bastar, which lasted till its accession to the Indian state in 1947. The second fateful journey north was of Naxalite squads in 1980.

The Early Years

> Q: When and how did you join the People's War?
>
> A: In the 1980s, KS [Kondapalli Sitaramaiah] told us to go into the forest. We asked why we should go to the forest when there were so many problems in the plains, and the forests appeared to have no problems. KS told us, 'Wherever there are people, they will have problems. Find out what their problems are.'
>
> Interview with A. Reddy, 2010

The mostly young Telugu men (and later women) who came to Bastar in 1980 were steeped in Maoist ideology and long family traditions of sacrifice and resistance. I interviewed several in 2009–10 in Warangal. Some came from families and villages that had participated in the Telangana armed struggle (1946–51). Some villages were known for their contribution of cadres. One woman activist, Manju, came from a village where 11 people had been 'martyred', including her brother who ran the local youth club and was killed when a grenade left by a squad leader in their house exploded. There were a few older and married men like Sivanna, who came from a caste of toddy distillers and had directly experienced feudalism in their villages. When he went underground, his wife supported the family by rolling beedis. Yet others had spent time in jails during the Emergency. Many were swept up by revolutionary student politics, including a 1978 campaign exhorting them to go to villages and learn from the people. Some joined barely out of school, like Lachanna whose elder brother was killed in an encounter and who went underground at the age of 15. Another leader, Prashant, was 17 when he joined the party in 1985 and left it only 28 years later. Jannu Chinnalu, a local organizer, played an important role in recruiting youth in Warangal.

Few parents were happy with their children's decision to abandon career and comfort for the hard and dangerous life of a 'professional revolutionary', but equally, few of them came in the way, since they too were in general sympathy with the party. Even today, in less selfless times, parents writing to their children in the forest tell them that while home is always open for them, they are free to continue living their ideals. The mothers simply ask the questions that all mothers ask: 'Are you well, are you eating?' Through the 1980s and up to the 1990s, despite the severe repression, entire localities in Warangal were with the movement. If there were police on board a bus, the driver would sound a special horn so that any guerrillas in the area would be alerted and run away.

These recruits belonged to the CPI(ML) People's War, founded by Kondapalli Seetharamiah, and traced their genealogy to the CPI (ML) of Charu Majumdar.[1] Armed struggle remained the ultimate line, but the People's War also advocated mass organizations, and indeed the party was well entrenched in the popular imagination through the Revolutionary Writers' Association or Virasam (founded in 1970), the Jan Natya Mandali (1971), and mass fronts like the Radical Students Union, the Radical Youth League and the Ryotu Coolie Sangham which took up, among other things, the issue of agricultural wages and unpaid labour for landlords. As the movement spread, police repression intensified.

The government helped reinforce the notion that peaceful

resistance was impossible through incidents like the one at Indravelli in Adilabad in 1981. A meeting of the Girijan Ryotu Coolie Sangham, which had been scheduled to coincide with market day, was refused permission at the last minute. But people did not know this and congregated in large numbers. The police opened fire without warning. Officially, 13 Gonds and one police constable were killed; the unofficial figure is about a hundred deaths. For the anthropologist Christoph von Fürer Haimendorf, hardly a proponent of armed struggle, the Indravelli massacre merely confirmed his bleak prognosis for adivasi futures. In a postscript to *Tribes of India*, he wrote that the 'sentiments of protest and revulsion' in a few Indian publications comparing Indravelli to Jallianwala Bagh were 'the only ray of hope in an atmosphere of otherwise unrelieved gloom'.[2]

In 1979, the party decided to take military matters seriously. As the party history, *30 Years of Naxalbari*, notes:

> The movement in AP by 1979 had reached such a critical stage. To advance now meant making necessary preparations to take on not only the landlord classes, but also the police and para-military forces. Preparation for such an eventuality meant not only adoption of new forms of struggle, not only new methods of organisation, but also the military preparation of the party.

The party drew up a 'Perspective for a Guerrilla Zone', in which the Dandakaranya forest was to be used as a rear area to escape to when repression intensified on the Andhra side of the Godavari. Organizing local adivasis was a secondary task. From there begins the story of Bastar.

Crossing the Godavari

The attempt by Andhra communists to mobilize people in Bastar has a long history. P. Sundarayya, the chronicler of the Telangana armed struggle, writes that in 1951 the then undivided CPI made the first attempt to cross the Godavari into Bastar. But they found no welcoming chord among the people whose language they could not understand. Instead, they found a distinctly unwelcoming police. When three members were shot in Bhopalpatnam, the communists retreated.[3] For the next 30 years, there would be only minor attempts to enter Bastar, including a cycle rally with red flags demanding better wages for tendu leaf pluckers in 1963. In 1968, the police, ever on the lookout for real and suspected 'extremists', arrested one Y.S. Murthy when he was putting up posters and doing 'wall writing' in Jagdalpur town. When Shankar Guha Niyogi, who later became one of India's most revered trade union leaders, came to intercede for him, the police promptly arrested him too. In 1974, Sharuni Vijay Kumar, with an MBBS from Warangal, set up as Dr Srinivas Rao in Bhopalpatnam, accompanied by his compounder, Tushar Kanti Bhattacharya aka Mohan Singh. Bhattacharya later started an independent clinic in Tarlaguda. They lasted only a year before the police raided their houses.[4] Thereafter, the trail runs cold, till the first People's War squads came in 1980.

The first seven squads, or *dalams* as they are locally called, sent in June 1980, comprised five to seven members each. 'Initially,' the party history tells us, 'they faced immense problems in getting roots amongst the tribals, specifically in the light of the police repression and combing operations, that started immediately. Yet, before the enemy's first suppression campaign began in 1985, the movement spread like wildfire, even beyond the Party's expectations.' By 1985, all the squads were linked, even if irregularly, in south Bastar. In 1987 a Dandakaranya state conference was held, including Gadchiroli, Adilabad, Bastar and the Andhra–Odisha border region; locals began to be involved, and the party began to take up new issues. This Maoist history is corroborated by police sources.[5]

Taking Up People's Issues

> It took me three months to learn Gondi. It was initially very difficult to form sanghams. People debated with us and said even before you came, we were managing fine. Then we fought to raise the price of brooms, in the Marh we taught people to boil the water they collected by digging holes in the sand, we started medical aid.
>
> Interview with Lachanna, 2009

When the squads first came, they wondered what to do since Bastar's apparently egalitarian adivasi communities did not fit into the model of class struggle they had learnt in feudal Andhra Pradesh. Initially, the dalams focused on making state institutions work, rather than on establishing a parallel state. They held meetings in the villages at night, carried out surveys and identified local problems. Subordinate government staff would occasionally get a visit from a Maoist in disguise, to enquire about the status of government schemes and the official wage rates. They threatened foresters and contractors who paid less than the minimum wage, teachers and health workers who drew their salaries without teaching a single letter or curing a single ailment, land revenue officials and police who demanded bribes for routine practices like land mutation or registering cases, and shopkeepers who cheated the villagers. They protested against the physical abuse and sexual exploitation of women and forced labour. In those days, government staff would demand to be carried around from village to village on a cot in order to carry out land mutation and other such work. They also demanded ghee, chickens, goats and liquor from the villagers. V.P. Patel who did a few 'extended case studies' of Maoist 'incidents' notes that all cases of beating and – much more rarely in those days, killing – had previous histories in which the individual concerned had been warned.[6]

Not all encounters were confrontational. Many lower-level government staff – peons, electricians and others – have described to me their cordial meetings with the Maoists. In the interior villages, primary school teachers too would attend their meetings, and as time went by the Maoists also established extensive networks among traders who acted as couriers for them. Maoist leaders would visit the weekly markets in civilian clothes and, for a long time, were as open as an underground movement could be.

These early Maoists appeared to the villagers as Robin Hoods. They wore khaki uniforms and had rudimentary weapons. One guerrilla recalled, 'The only training we were given was to wear a gun and go into the forest. Our only weapon was Marxism Leninism.' Initially, he said, their weapons manufacture was extremely basic: they used iron and discarded rifles to make guns and worried about how they would function in the monsoons. Their other equipment was also primitive. Sivanna remembered their footwear coming apart in a week on the stony tracks of the Karegutta mountain. Eventually, they went barefoot to save the Rs 100–150 they spent on shoes every week.

In several Konta villages in the south, residents said that their first memories of the party were of squads, armed only with axes, and dancing to drums. In north Bastar too, villagers would joke with the guerrillas, threatening not to feed them till they sang for their supper. Initially, the revolutionaries asked only for leftovers, but later people themselves decided they deserved fresh cooked food. Now, when the dalam comes visiting, they give them grain because the numbers are much larger. In several villages, some of the land redistributed within the village is kept aside for collective cultivation to feed visiting squads and to provide seeds for poorer farmers.

After a few years, forest and revenue staff stopped demanding bribes and moved to the smaller block centres. Since the exploitative state had receded, if not completely disappeared, the Maoists were again at a loss. Their struggles became seasonal, concentrated on raising tendu leaf rates.

But once people saw that the Maoists had the power to fight against the rangers and local police, they began to come to them with all sorts of problems, including marital disputes. Initially, according to Lachanna, the party told them to sort it out locally. Between 1983 and 1987, there was an intense debate within the party on the agrarian structure: as to whether internal class differences among adivasis mattered, or whether the major contradiction was with the state. The year 1987 was an important one: the then Maoist leader Shivaji who favoured focusing on the state as the main enemy was expelled from the party; a forest committee was formed for the Dandakaranya region; and the party decided it would be necessary to form sanghams in the villages on a class basis. These sanghams are village-level committees, mostly composed of youth, who implement the everyday programme of the party.

The Indrawati National Park dalam found that, when they tried to organize villagers to protest against displacement from the park, their work was being subverted by local headmen, who warned the villagers not to attend for fear they would be harassed by the police as Maoist sympathizers. No one would show up for rallies. In the south too, the local commander Ramanna (who later went on to carry out some major attacks against the CRPF) found that the priests and headmen were sabotaging the newly formed sanghams from within.

One particular incident in 1987 changed this. Kalma Deva, a Madia originally from Pentapad in Sukma, had colonized some 100 acres near Konta. The local Dorlas asked the party to redistribute some of this land to them. The dalam, of which Rajanna was the commander and Ramanna the deputy, held two or three meetings in the village to persuade Kalma Deva to give up some of his land. There happened to be a wedding in the village, and the dalam was dancing too. Kalma Deva informed the police, and in the ensuing raid, while the rest of the dalam escaped, Rajanna fell into a ditch and was arrested. The following week, Ramanna killed Kalma Deva for betraying them. The villagers, however, saw this as a signal that the party was ready to take up land issues seriously and began coming to them in large numbers.

The 'Bastar Aryans'

> It took us a long time to realize there were class struggles among adivasis.
>
> Interview with Sivanna, 2010

Land has been the driving force of all migration and politics in adivasi India. From my own field research in the 1990s, I found that the Dhurwas and the Dorlas tend to stay in their own villages. But the Gonds in the surrounding hamlets, which stretch into the hills, are always in search of land. Lachanna described these southern Gonds as the 'Aryans of Bastar', ever ready to colonize new tracts. In the 1980s, a group of Gond men from Jangampal and other villages near Kukanar, assisted by the CPI, settled old village sites in the Kanger National Park, such as Bhadri Mahu and Chandameta. These villages had been deserted by their original inhabitants due to illness or during harsh droughts such as in 1935 and 1965. The settlers resisted repeated evictions and arrests by the forest department. Sometimes, the father would leave the land in the care of his sons and find new land and occasionally a new wife as well, but more often it was the sons who went in search of land. Others, especially from the areas around Gadiras, Sukma and Kuakonda, migrated further south to the forests of the Golapalli and Kistaram range, where they cut down forests or settled abandoned Dorla villages. Traditionally, soon after the harvest, some 60–70 men from different villages would go on hunts that lasted two or three months, across long distances. It was during these hunts, called *judum*, as compared to the shorter hunts around the seed sowing time, called *vetta*, that they would identify suitable lands. From Konta, the search for land continued, across the Andhra Pradesh border.

The Maoists gained many recruits by helping Gonds occupy forest land and settle villages in south Bastar in the 1980s. Mankuram, of Palpocha village along the Andhra Pradesh border with Konta, described to me how he arrived there in the early 1980s. A Congress worker who spoke fluent Hindi, he was the first person that the newly arrived People's War squad met. At the time, this was all forest land. Mankuram identified the land he wanted to settle on. The squad kept a lookout for the right moment, and when the forest department carried out felling, they burnt the stacked logs. The ranger called Mankuram and asked him to help get the remaining timber out in a bullock cart. In exchange, the ranger gave 25 families a Preliminary Offence Report (POR) for 'encroachment' without fining them. This POR, though a marker of criminality, also serves as proof of the villagers' presence in the area, and in subsequent years, with the government regularizing 'encroachments', the POR becomes the first step to a legal title.

Once the first few families were settled, there were fights between people from different villages, but the squads drew boundaries between them; in Kistaram the boundaries are still marked by white flags hung from a rope across the road. They appointed headmen for each village, and warned the forest department not to harass the villagers. From then on, whenever the forest department wanted any work done, such as felling trees in a coupe or creating fire lines, they would enlist the Maoists' help. This practice continues. Individual foresters – because of the nature of their work – often have an understanding with the Maoists. One surrendered Maoist showed me photos of himself in a ranger's uniform given to him by a sympathetic forester, along with the relevant fabricated ID. Six feet tall, he towered over everyone else in the meeting, just as a ranger might.

In March 2012, I rode through the Kistaram forest on a friend's motorcycle. We were surrounded for miles by fallen red leaves and leafless teak. Intermittently, we came across a mahua tree with small burning rings of fire and ash underneath. The administrator W.G. Grigson aptly described the difference between north Bastar 'with its evergreen moist forests, cool climate, abundant water-supply and often thick population' and the 'hot dry regions of deciduous forests, deficient water and sparse populations' of Konta and southern Bijapur.[7] Whether or not there was any other evidence of the Maoist state, almost every village among the dozens I visited between 2005 and 2015, across Bhairamgarh, Bijapur, Dantewada, Sukma and Konta blocks, had experienced some land distribution. For instance, a family with 1 acre might be given an additional field taken from someone better off; the land of someone who died childless would be distributed to others.

Under the directions of the sangham, the villagers cooperated to build embankments, or level the lands and carry out improvements on the fields of the poorest. Even in January 2016, at the height of a wave of renewed repression when people were finding it difficult to sleep at home because of police raids, I saw gangs of villagers doing such collective work. Villagers said they would leave for coolie work in Andhra Pradesh only after they had fulfilled this obligation. The party gave the poor bullocks, set up grain banks and lent money without interest. Sometimes, forest produce was collectively sold and the money used to help people with loans, wedding expenses and the like. In its core areas, since official *pattas* or land titles no longer reflected actual ownership, the party told people to burn them and issued their own pattas instead, in the name of both husband and wife.

The party got villagers to collectively build ponds, a critical need, since even by 2011 (according to the decennial census), only 1.49 per cent of cultivable land in Bijapur district and 1.63 per cent in Dantewada district was irrigated. They also set up agricultural cooperatives, which have exhibited varying success. In the traditional system, groups worked on each other's land in exchange for meat and landa. But this favoured the rich who could afford more days. In the Maoist system, everyone puts in and receives an equal amount of labour, and the poor get wages over and above that for any extra work done. The best groups seem to work with a small number of households who own roughly the same amount of land. In 2013, the wages were around Rs 100 a day. In some of the villages with longer Maoist presence, people told me the work groups and the janathana sarkar were on autopilot, while in other villages, especially the newer ones, they were still struggling to institutionalize them.

The Leaf That Can Make or Break Governments

If land is the most important source of livelihood, forests are the next. The fall and new flush of leaves regulate the cycle of life, subsistence and celebration, and it is the careful harvesting work that adivasis carry out in the forest that brings tamarind and tendu, *char*, *baheda*, sal seeds, *aonla*, resins and a variety of other products to the urban market. For the villagers, the sale of forest produce, especially tendu leaves, is their main source of cash income.

Non-timber forest products (NTFPs) in Chhattisgarh are classified into two categories: nationalized NTFPs (currently tendu or *Diospyros melanoxylon* leaves, and different types of gums) and non-nationalized NTFPs (all the rest). Officially, only the Chhattisgarh State Minor Forest Produce Co-operative Federation can trade in nationalized produce, either directly or through agents who must then pay royalty. Traders can freely buy the other forest produce directly from villagers at local weekly markets, and sell them onwards at the agricultural exchange.

The traders and contractors in Bastar are almost without exception non-adivasi immigrants. Many of them came in relatively poor and have made their fortunes from the forests or from trade in illegal mineral smuggling. One indication of this wealth are the over 6000 trucks registered in the Bastar Parivahan Sangh, the transporters' union, all of which are owned by these traders. At the top of the merchant hierarchy are the Marwari wholesalers, whose trading links stretch across India. The Marwaris purchase forest produce and grain in bulk, through a network of smaller merchants, and also import goods from other parts of India, which are then retailed downwards. At the bottom are the small agents known as *kochiyas*, who actually weigh the produce on market day. Under-weighing the produce and cheating the villagers is routine.

The government and the Maoists have long battled over who would purchase tendu leaves from the villagers. Tendu leaves are used for rolling tobacco into beedis. The tendu bushes are pruned in February–March and the leaves plucked in May. Villagers get wages for pruning the bushes, and are paid for the number of bundles of leaves they collect. In 1988–89, the Madhya Pradesh government set up a state forest produce marketing federation, with primary cooperatives at the village level. The forest department appointed an agent in each village to purchase, dry and bag the tendu leaves. This was to replace the earlier system of having contractors bid to purchase leaves from demarcated areas, on payment of royalties to the government. The idea was to raise the returns to the villagers and, also since much of the tendu plucked was from government land, to increase revenue for the government.

However, the government has been stymied by a bureaucratic approach and lack of funds to buy all the tendu available. In practice, moreover, in Maoist-controlled areas, where the forest department has little say, the agents are paid by the contractors. Over the decades, the Maoists have been more successful than the government in ensuring benefits to the villagers, organizing them to strike and refuse to pluck leaves if the contractors do not increase their rates. In several villages, I was told that the rates were fixed in public meetings covering a cluster of villages, with both the dalam and contractor present. The rates offered by contractors are now much higher than those set by the government. For the contractors, it is worth paying this higher rate to the primary collectors and a tax to the Maoists, in order to be allowed to collect tendu from any given area. According to a tendu leaf contractor I interviewed in 2005–6, they paid 80 paise for a bundle of 100 leaves. For 1 kilo or roughly 14 bundles, the cost of purchase was Rs 15.70 (Rs 11.20 for purchasing the leaves, Rs 3 for transport, Rs 1–1.50 for royalty at the rate of Rs 500 per sack). Income on 1 kilo, on the other hand, was Rs 20–25, leaving a profit of at least Rs 5–10 per kilo. In 2013, in North Bastar,

I found that where the party was strong, the contractors were even willing to pay the villagers Rs 40 extra per 100 bundles over and above the government rate of Rs 110. The rates vary depending on what the party can enforce in any one region. On average, a villager can collect 100 bundles a day. A small percentage of the villagers' earnings is set aside as contribution to the local janathana sarkar.

Displacing the Old Power Structure

> For three years we did not interfere with internal village politics, only taking up issues against the state like tendu leaves. Then we realized we had to enter into people's lives or else we would not belong anywhere.
>
> Interview with Lachanna, 2010

As it began to take up land and forest issues, the party also found itself grappling with the local power structure. Traditionally, the offices of both priest (pujari, *perma*) and headman (patel) were hereditary within the lineage that had founded the village. In addition, there were *pargana majhis* who headed a cluster of villages or pargana, an old administrative unit. Some pargana majhis, like those in the egalitarian Marh, were clan heads, while many of those in south Bastar were descendants of the small chiefs who ruled over the *garhs* (like Bhairamgarh). In some areas like Bijapur or Kutru, there were no pargana majhis at all, and it was the village headmen who were powerful.[8]

Starting from the 1930s, in areas like Bastar, Chotanagpur and the Santhal Parganas, the government codified and standardized the local political structure, creating headmen where they did not exist. In the process, they became the link between their own communities and the government. The Maoists saw them as representatives of the state in the village, and elements of a feudal order that had to be demolished if they were to create their own sanghams and janathana sarkar.

When the Maoists started setting up their parallel sanghams, some of the headmen and priests accepted the growing power of the sanghams and their own displacement quietly, while others who had been abusing their powers in petty ways resented it. In Abujhmarh, there was little distinction between the patels and others, but in parts of Dantewada, there were 'big men' who controlled vast acres and dominated their areas. In the words of 'P. Shankar', the pseudonym adopted by the author of *Yeh Jungle Hamara Hai*,[9] a chronicle of the early years of Maoist presence in Bastar, men like Burka Samayya, Dubba Kannayya, Borja Sayanna and Kursam Ramayya were 'feudal obstacles' and 'cruel landlords', some of whom 'died a dog's death at the hands of people'.[10]

Lachanna told me the story of Bandi, the patel of Bedre whose killing enabled the 1990 Jan Jagran Abhiyan, or the first police-supported vigilante movement against the Naxalites. Bandi controlled some 25–30 villages: his henchmen would comb villages and force people to pay huge fines in chickens and rice for minor misdemeanours. In 1988, emboldened by the guerrillas, but in their absence and without their knowledge, one of the village sangham leaders kidnapped Bandi. The police retaliated by kidnapping members of the sangham leader's family. After Bandi was killed, police repression became very intense and villagers fled their homes. Bandi's younger brother Masa then started the Jan Jagran Abhiyan in September 1990, with police backing.

In general, though, Maoist policy has been quite pragmatic, and the degree to which sanghams have overthrown the traditional leadership varies from village to village, depending in part on how stratified the village is. Moreover, when they come to a new area, the Maoists, like everyone else, contact and work through the local leaders. If there are big men who are bitterly opposed to the Maoists, there are also others that exercise great influence in their areas who work closely with the Maoists. As one villager described it, 'Such men are neither armed Naxals nor are they mere sympathizers. They are trusted men who know how to deal with all sides.'

Because of their greater visibility to the administration, the local leaders are in a particularly difficult position: on the one hand, they are asked to perform errands for the Maoists, which may range from getting fish stock for collectively built village ponds, books, radio equipment, uniforms and other supplies, to interceding with the police when villagers are arrested. Some demands are harder to meet than others – for instance, when the Maoists ask for things like the cleaner for a gun nozzle. On the other hand, these big men are kept on a tight leash and not allowed to stand for elections or contract for government works for fear they will then be corrupted and co-opted by the administration. One of these leaders, though clearly unhappy about the situation, conceded: 'We are only 10 per cent, and the remaining 90 per cent of the people are happy with the Maoists because their main ambition is to keep the forest, revenue and police departments out.'

Financing the Movement

> Q: Why not aim for Tata and Essar, why beat up only the small *karamcharis*?
>
> A: But people haven't seen Tata and Essar, these are their local representatives.
>
> Interview with Lachanna, 2010

As with local leaders, the Maoist stand on traders has been largely driven by practical concerns. The traders on their part have played both Maoists and police, sometimes willingly and sometimes under coercion. The relationship between contractors and the Maoists is unhealthy, based on mutual and simultaneous mistrust and dependence, enabling the rise of networks of corruption, patronage and protection. The Maoists need the contractors for funds and in turn they require Maoist permission to work in their areas or get contracts, or else they risk boycott and the burning of their vehicles, including dumpers and trucks. RJ, a contractor from Sukma, told me that Maoists had a rate card to allow vehicles to operate in interior markets like Chintalnar. For each jeep, the owners had to pay Rs 3000; for a tractor, Rs 5000. Like everyone else, RJ's family was friendly with both sides, but after the Judum started, the Maoists told them to choose.

It is ironic that the tendu contractors, many of whom bankroll the BJP, were the only ones to travel to interior villages when the Judum had stopped every other form of public service. Had it not been for them, rice and other supplies inside would have been impossible. Police attempts to stop them led to the shopkeepers and traders holding a big rally in Geedam in protest. When the government shut down existing weekly markets after the Salwa Judum, the Maoists and traders jointly identified alternative sites from where the weekly market could function.

There was also a less materialist relation. Youth from Uttar Pradesh, Bihar and elsewhere, bored of their rural or small-town life, were attracted by the glamour of the Maoists, the glamour that attaches to men with guns, and were therefore willing to act as couriers and messengers. However, the Salwa Judum gave many of them a chance to become instant leaders and acquire guns and contracts from the government instead.

The Maoists repeatedly claim that their deals with companies and contractors do not come at the expense of their own constituency. For example, even when they have a deal with a contractor, they insist on minimum wages or appropriate rates for tendu leaves. However, this scarcely enables transparent alternatives to the system of industrial capitalism. And when it comes to which companies they will allow to work and which are prohibited, the line seems a bit arbitrary. One Maoist leader said that they take money from companies other than 20 big ones, which they have listed as Comprador Big Bourgeoise.

Another denied this, and said that road construction and mining are never allowed, but certain other kinds of companies are. At one point, under pressure from the villagers, the party toyed with letting villagers form cooperatives to engage in illegal mining and sell to smugglers, but as people and cattle began to fall into the mining pits, they abandoned this idea.

Industrialists often try to work out private deals with the Maoists. A US embassy cable on Wikileaks quotes 'a senior representative from Essar, a major industrial company with large mining and steel-related facilities in Chhattisgarh', who 'told Congenoff that the company pays the Maoists "a significant amount" not to harm or interfere with their operations; when the Maoists occasionally break this agreement and damage Essar property or threaten personnel, Essar sets different Maoist groups against each other to suppress the situation'.[11]

Jaganna, who used to lead the Andhra Pradesh–Odisha border committee but has since surrendered, told me that a senior official of the Essar Group appealed to him to allow a pipeline to pass through his territory. This pipeline was meant to pump iron ore from mines at Bailadilla in Chhattisgarh to Visakhapatnam port. He said the Essar official told him: 'Since you are the local government here we will pay you the same rate of royalty we pay the government.' Given that this rate was Rs 27 per tonne, less than US $1, and that the market rate for iron ore was Rs 5600 or US $120 per tonne in 2010,[12] this did not constitute much hardship for the Essar Group. The Maoists decided to divide the Rs 2.8 crore they got annually between party funds and local development, but in the first year they spent it all on roof tiles for 60 villages. The following year, however, the Chhattisgarh state unit of the Maoists objected to the mining by Essar on the grounds that it devastated the local environment and provided no benefit to the people of Chhattisgarh. Consequently, the Maoist Central Committee called off the deal with Essar, and ordered the Odisha committee to break the pipeline. A Chhattisgarh Maoist, however, claimed that Jaganna had made his own private deal and there had been no sanction from the Central Committee in the first place. He also claimed that Jaganna's surrender was engineered by Essar. By the time the party established its Darba division, Essar had already built the pipeline. In 2008, when I travelled to Chitrakonda, I saw the black remnants of the Essar powerhouse; the Maoists also burnt 76 trucks belonging to Essar, and in 2009 blasted the pipeline.

Attacks on the pipeline and repairs to it keep alternating. In 2011, the police arrested the general manager of Essar, along with a contractor, B.K. Lala, and an adivasi schoolteacher, Soni Sori, along with her nephew Lingaram Kodopi, for allegedly passing on money from Essar to the Maoists. According to one security expert who says he got his information from the police, the arrest occurred because Essar refused to pay the local police the same rates it paid the Maoists. Usually, the government is easily managed. An affidavit filed by the Centre for Public Interest Litigation in May 2015, based on 'internal emails and documents from Essar Group of Companies', describes how 'corporates use their money power to change public policies, plant questions in Parliament, get access to internal government documents/cabinet papers, grant favours to politicians and bureaucrats for receiving benefits in return, and plant stories in news media'. It describes how Essar arranged cars and accommodation for the personal visits of senior officials in the Chhattisgarh government, as well as Congress leaders like Mahendra Karma in Delhi.[13]

In a world of contractors, Maoists, politicians and middlemen, money flows are often difficult to track. In one case I tried to follow, an Andhra Pradesh–based company under contract from the Tatas, which carries out sample prospecting to check the ferrous content of iron ore, used a local journalist to route money to the Maoists in order to be allowed to work in Bailadilla. The journalist's version is that he had been initially approached by the company through a police officer, and given Rs 10 lakh. In turn he gave a contractor Rs 3.5 lakh to pass on to the Maoists. He then informed the company they could start work. The company started by paying their workers Rs 100 a day. After a couple of weeks, a Bijapur squad came and asked for Rs 120 a day for the workers and burnt the vehicles. The Maoist version is that they never received the money. They only came to know that the journalist had taken money to arrange the deal when they got a complaint routed by the company through their Central Committee. Whatever the truth, the whole episode shows close links between the police, the Maoists and those who travel in-between. In 2014, the police arrested contractor Dharmendra Chopra, who revealed that he provided supplies to the Maoists, in exchange for fixing deals for BJP and Congress politicians and mining companies like Jayaswal Neco and Godavari Ispat.[14]

4

The Maoist State

> In reading the military literature on guerrilla warfare now so fashionable at the Pentagon, one feels that these writers are like men watching a dance from outside through heavy plate-glass windows. They see the motions but they can't hear the music. They put the mechanical gestures down on paper with pedantic fidelity. But what rarely comes through to them are the injured racial feelings, the misery, the rankling slights, the hatred, the devotion, the inspiration and the desperation. So they do not really understand what leads men to abandon wife, children, home, career, friends; to take to the bush and live gun in hand like a hunted animal; to challenge overwhelming military odds rather than acquiesce any longer in humiliation, injustice or poverty.
>
> I.F. Stone, *In a Time of Torment, 1961–1967*

The Maoist state in Bastar has taken shape over three decades, and its boundaries have expanded and contracted with the power of insurgency and counter-insurgency. At one level, the Maoist state is a virtual phenomenon, an idea, an emotional identification that has little to do with physical frontiers. At another level, the contours of the Maoist state can also be mapped by the absence of any visible welfare markers provided by the Indian state, such as roads, schools or health services.

While Indian states are identified with the dominant linguistic community, the borders of Maoist state committees follow the spread of exploited communities, languages and topographies suited for guerrilla fighting. The 'Dandakaranya guerrilla zone' once included parts of Chhattisgarh, Andhra Pradesh, Maharashtra and Odisha, though it is much smaller now. The region that outsiders derogatorily called Abujhmarh (unknown hills) – because it has never been surveyed – is considered the ultimate Maoist stronghold.

As the party grew, it established its own structures, from the politburo and central committee downwards to various state committees or special zonal committees. These state/zonal committees straddle existing state boundaries. For instance, the Dandakaranya Special Zonal Committee (DKSZC) covering undivided Bastar in Chhattisgarh and Gadchiroli in Maharashtra has eight divisions under it. Below the divisional committees are area committees, which oversee the (secret) party cells and the mass organizations: the Chetna Natya Manch (CNM), locally called Cinem batch, the Dandakaranya Adivasi Kisan Mazdoor Sangathan (DAKMS) and the women's wing, the Krantikari Adivasi Mahila Sangathan (KAMS).

For the villagers, however, the main distinction is between the dalam, the 'professional revolutionaries' or armed squads, and the sangham or village-level workers of the mass organizations. By dalams they usually mean the local organization squads (LOS) and local guerrilla squads (LGS), which are armed, but fighting is not their main task; instead their work is ideological and organizational, the LOS especially.

By contrast, the People's Liberation Guerrilla Army (PLGA) is designed to fight. It has a main force, a secondary force and a base force. The main force consists of platoons of about 21 people, who come together as a company of 70–80 people and a battalion of 250–300 people when required. Their primary work is fighting.

The Dandakaranya Guerrilla Zone, c. 1999

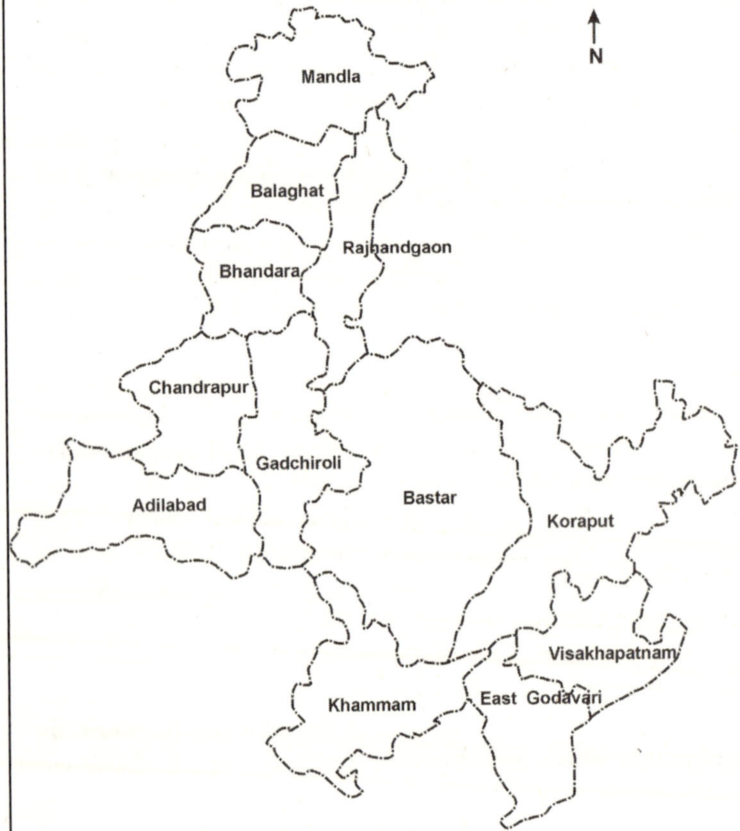

Source: P. Shankar. 1999. *Yeh Jungle Hamara Hai*, p. 20. New Vistas Publications.

* The Dandakaranya Guerrilla Zone presently (c. 2016) excludes East Godavari, Khammam, Visakhapatnam, Koraput and Mandla districts.

The secondary force consists of the local armed squads (especially the LGS), which also do other work. The base force consists of *jan* militias, made up of *gram rakshak dals* or village defence committees. The militias are mobilized for specific actions. In 2009, in a village north of the Indrawati, I met the commander of the jan militia, wearing a lungi with an incongruous military belt. He lived out in his field *kothar* (open shelters with thatch roofs put up in the fields to watch over the ripening crop) along with his unit of approximately 25 boys and girls, armed with 12-bore guns, and a wireless set which alerted him to the movement of the security forces. Others reported, however, that their militias only had bows and arrows or knives.

In 2004–5, the Ministry of Home Affairs reported that Naxalites had 'an assessed strength of around 9300 hard-core underground cadres and a holding of around 6500 regular weapons besides a large number of unlicensed country made arms'.[1] Most of the Maoist weaponry is looted from police armouries or captured from police personnel killed in encounters, though there is also some indigenous weapons manufacture. In 2006, defence analyst Rahul Bedi estimated that the Maoists had acquired AK-47s for all their leaders, as well as 'carbines, 7.62 [millimetre] self-loading rifles, grenade launchers, mines, improvised explosive devices and mortars'.[2] But even up to 2015, police accounts of encounters suggest that the rank and file have outdated weaponry: 'Bastar Police recovers 4 dead bodies of Maoists in uniform with a 303 service rifle and two 12 bore rifles. Dead Maoists are all women Naxals.'[3] It is debatable, of course, whether those killed were actually Maoists or ordinary villagers.

Maoist military prowess relies less on weapons and more on guerrilla tactics, and above all, as Amitav Ghosh writes, albeit in a different context, in *Flood of Fire*, 'the look that appears on men's faces when they fight for their land, their homes, their families, their customs, everything they hold dear'.[4] But much as the Maoists may claim that guns are subordinate to their politics, the militarism on display in their writings – and in the video images of encounters and ambushes they create and circulate – goes far beyond what is needed for self-defence. The Maoists are proud of their military actions, such as breaking open the Jehanabad jail and the Koraput armoury; looting ammunition depots and explosives from the NMDC warehouses in Dantewada; blasting transformers; and attempting assassinations of prominent politicians. In 2008, they ambushed and killed 38 members of the elite Greyhound forces on the Balimela reservoir in Odisha, while in April 2010, they killed 76 personnel of the CRPF in Chhattisgarh. On 1 December 2014, the Maoists killed 14 CRPF men at Kasalpad in Sukma. The list could go on. A Gondi song that became popular after the Kasalpad incident talks of how Delhi sent the CRPF to attack villages, and, instead, they were wiped out.

Why Women Fight

One evening, while visiting a village, I was summoned by a woman wearing a red sari and a spangled black shawl, and carrying a small handbag. She had clearly just changed out of her uniform. She gave me and other women a lecture on the origins of Women's Day in New York. 'Women join us,' she said, 'not because of domestic oppression but because they too want to fight the forces which kill and rape, and they believe equally in the cause.' To my cynical ears, this initially sounded like a memorized speech, but what else, I thought to myself later, could explain the fortitude of these adivasi women, in the face of brutal rapes by the security forces? Women constitute about 40 per cent of the cadre now.

A booklet published by the Maoists, *Women Martyrs of the Indian Revolution*, describes the attraction the party exercised in areas where they were well entrenched. Comrade Oyam Yenki

> came close to the party since she was a child. Since her whole family was participating in the activities of various sangams she never used to miss even one programme. She was very much interested in songs, dances and meetings. She had good attachment with the party. As a child she worked in the *Bal Sangam* at first and then worked in

> the KAMS. She wanted to join the squad but party did not agree as she was too young. But she insisted and got recruited in January 2003 at the age of 16. (p. 66)

My own interviews reinforced the importance of idealism in motivating youth. Soni said she and her school friends in the Marh spent hours discussing the party literature which squads brought them. They joined as soon as they turned 16. Many women joined for personal reasons, such as parental pressure to marry, domestic disputes or simply to wander. Lakke, a Dorla woman, entered the party to avoid being married off by her parents. She married a Telugu comrade and they had a daughter. But since the party discouraged children, they had to leave the girl behind with a childless couple in one of the villages. 'She doesn't recognize me any more,' she told me sadly.

After 2005, many young men and women were propelled into the party because of the Salwa Judum. Neela, a cheerful young woman with a beautiful smile, who I met by chance in 2012, was studying in the Basaguda *ashramshala* (school hostel) when the Judum started attacking villages in that area. Her parents asked her to come home because it was so unsafe. Neela sounded regretful about leaving school, but said, 'Anyway, what kind of job would I have got after studying?' She then smiled and added: 'Now I study in the party school.' Neela said she had been attracted to the Maoists from childhood onwards, because the *dada log* or elder brothers as they are popularly called, talked to her seriously and gave her things to read. Her companion in the squad, a tousle-haired youth called Sanna, was also studiously inclined and was lugging around a thick class 11 history textbook. He said he was particularly interested in British history. He too had been studying in the hostel when some of the boys in his school joined the Salwa Judum and accused him and a couple of others of helping the Maoists. So he went home and, after the Judum burnt his village for the second time, decided to join the Maoists. One of the first duties that Neela carried out as a squad member was to recover the body of a young woman, Gantal Sridevi, from the forests around Lingagiri, where she had been gang-raped and killed. She recalled with a kind of compressed sadness: 'Her body was swarming with flies, and she had her periods when she was raped… She loved clothes and they stole all her clothes before killing her.'

Life is hard for women Maoists, walking long hours, even if menstruating, struggling with recurrent bouts of malaria, sometimes wearing the same clothes for days. And there is always the threat of rape if the security forces capture them. A typical dalam day, as described by Lakke, starts at 4 a.m. After ablutions, they get ready to walk to the day's target village. When they reach, there is a roll call and duties are assigned. After spending the day in the village, the dalam leaves again at about 4 p.m., walking a couple of hours to their next village halt. Again, there is a roll call, followed by meetings which last till 10–11 p.m., and then another walk into the forest to sleep. Depending on how safe the area is and the situation, dalams may even sleep in villages. This is a life where there are no holidays. The local cadres get to meet their families once a year, if even that; and since they get no salaries, the party gives them a small gift to take home, bed sheets for instance. The villagers are appreciative of the cadres' sacrifices. As one told me: 'Once gone, these children belong to the party. It is as if they had died for us.'

Many women are active fighters. *Women Martyrs of the Indian Revolution* describes Comrade Karuna:

> Comrade Karuna participated in many military actions during her revolutionary life of 9 years from 1997 to 2005. She was a steeled woman fighter and once again she proved that a woman is no lesser than a man in any way in military field. The ambush near Torrem village near Basagudem was her first military action. In that action, 16 police personnel were killed and 17 were injured. Karuna felt very proud of her participation in this successful ambush. Later she

> participated in Kongupalli, Wakulwai ambushes etc. as a member of support team. She showed her fighting spirit through participating in the ambushes conducted in Bajrangbali of North Bastar division and Tigeta, Motukupalli, Usikapatanam, Saalpalli etc. of West Bastar. She also took part in Tallagudem, Motu, Vedire, Geedam etc. police station raids. She was Deputy Commander of ambush batch in Geedam raid. With her martyrdom, PLGA lost a capable and efficient soldier especially an aspiring woman fighter. (pp. 49–50)

Learning to read and write, in Hindi and Telugu, is also a critical part of the training. For villagers, this is the most memorable feature of their encounters with the dalams. Several people told me: 'The dalam members keep reading at meetings.' 'Whoever joins them learns to speak Telugu and read.' 'All their posters are handwritten – how much must they write!'

Children are also assigned a role, as members of the *bal* sangham. Their main task is usually to carry messages. The children take immense pride in their work. One small sentry, who stood at a river crossing between two villages, helped us to wade through after asking us our names. He then smiled broadly, evidently pleased with himself, and said: '*Main dost lagta hoon na?*' (Don't I look like a friend)?

In this atmosphere, the Maoists do not need to use force to recruit, contrary to the police allegation. In certain periods, Lakke told me, the party got many more recruits than it could handle, and had to turn people back. This was so especially after the Judum. The size of a village makes a real difference to its local influence. In the bigger villages with more people to spare, households are more likely to allow their children to leave and join the Maoists. Proximity to the thana is also a factor determining how much people can support the Maoists.

Establishing a New Administrative Structure

> The JS (janathana sarkar) shall be the newly formed People's Democratic State and the power of a government. This power shall attain a complete character and a form with the formation of countrywide People's Democratic Republic federation. Depending on the common minimum program prepared by the Party the janathana sarkars forming in the process of development of revolutionary struggle in DK [Dandakaranya] shall make efforts to implement the people's government power as the new state power.
>
> Policy programme of the janathana sarkar,
> CPI (Maoist) document 2004

> When there are two governments, whom should we follow?
>
> A woman in Basaguda camp, 2008

Having displaced or co-opted the traditional power structure, the Maoists set up a parallel administrative structure by the mid-1990s: the revolutionary people's committees (RPCs) or the janathana sarkar (JS). In theory, anyone could be elected to these committees, not just members of the sanghams or mass organizations. In practice, of course, the sangham members also double up in the JS. The dalams liaise with the forest department and tendu contractors, and visit the villages once a month or so; day-to-day supervision of the work is done by the sangham.

An average JS comprises four or five villages with a population of 500–3000 and is run by a committee of 7–11 members, along with a president and vice-president. My surveys in Bhairamgarh and Konta blocks revealed significant variations in the number of hamlets or villages under any one JS. The JS has eight departments: financial, defence, agriculture, judicial, education–culture, health, forest protection, public relations. Each department has its own workers. As the villagers described it, the agriculture department encourages the formation of cooperatives to cultivate and share plough bullocks, and the construction of ponds for irrigation and fish rearing. The forest department has two people in every village who check out the forests once a month to see what was cut and whether it was authorized. They also ensure that houses are built collectively. In many ways this builds on traditional forest protection measures in the area where people would either hire a guard based on contributions from every household or collectively pay a small amount, called *devsari* or *maan*, every year to a neighbouring village if they used its forests. Every month or so, a general body meeting is held by rotation in the different constituent villages, where all issues are discussed. Everyone attends, including women and children, unlike traditional meetings which only men attended.

The sangham exercises close supervision over every household in the village, maintaining a record of arrivals and departures. This surveillance has tightened after the Salwa Judum began (and increases whenever repression intensifies, such as in 2015–16) with people having to ask for permission to leave the village. They have to specify how long they will be away and where they are going, to prevent them becoming informers. Gangu from Tatapadu, who had been forced to stay outside his village to recover some money he was owed, was panic-stricken, convinced that the sangham would take action on his absence. People wishing to return from the Salwa Judum camps had to write to the sangham asking for permission. However, I was also given more benign explanations for the controls. The reason why anyone leaving the village for more than a month had to inform the party was so that it could look after any family member who fell sick, or prevent the trafficking of women, which is rapidly becoming a big problem in these areas. There is no doubt, however, that the sangham members can also become petty tyrants. In many Judum camps, I heard that while the dalam members were good, the sangham members enacted their own prejudices while taking decisions and misinformed the dalam. At the peak of the Judum, the sangham members were captured, killed or fled the village. But it did not take long for them to be re-established, albeit even more secretively than ever before.

Normally, the sangham or the judicial wing of the JS settles disputes, and unlike the traditional system where the offender has to pay fines, under the Maoists, conflicts are settled by agreement alone. People told me that both parties to the dispute have to shake hands. If a fight cannot be settled within the village, it is referred to the dalam, who might also decide to hold a *jan adalat* if it is really serious. Everyone gets two warnings before they are finally exiled or killed. The militia then implements the decision taken at the dalam meeting. It is hard to know the degree of popular participation in the jan adalats, but certainly, there is deep fear of contravening any decision. Villagers describe Maoist beatings as brutal, saying that sometimes spouses and even the children of the accused person are forced to participate in the beating, or at least look on. Even if people feel that someone branded an informer is actually innocent, they are powerless to protest. I was told that after the Maoists killed an SPO, Dasru, of Bangasai, the villagers were reluctant to allow his mother to bury the body in the village, for fear of being seen as soft on the family. Dasru was finally buried in Maraiguda where he was living as an SPO. In another case from 2015, when a man had been killed, the squad banned the entire village from cultivating, especially the patel, perma and sarpanch, till they found the murderers. Soon enough, the villagers identified the killers, who turned out to be lumpen youth who had been hired because of some personal enmity.

Changes in Social Relations and Rituals

> Mahendra Karma says adivasis are not museum pieces when it comes to the changes brought by Tata and Essar. Then why does he have a problem if the Maoists are also changing adivasi culture?
>
> Interview with Raju, 2011

The Maoists claim that when they reached the area, it was an 'ocean of darkness'; 'women were no more than chattels slaving away from morning to night'; they were forced to dance before the adivasi raja [sic] at festivals, and children led 'wasted lives'.[5] While this bleak picture of adivasi female serfdom is exaggerated, and women here are often better off than those in other more feudal parts of India, they do have a number of problems, including very little access to health and nutrition.

Lakke told me that she, along with another woman from the KAMS, the Maoist women's wing, had been tasked with covering some 25 villages, in which they would hold fortnightly meetings and recruit women to the KAMS, reading out their manifesto line by patient line. They talked of local problems like forced marriages, wife beating, bigamy, bride price, the fact that women are not allowed to sow or to attend collective rituals where animals are slaughtered. Hidme of Medulpenta, a village woman I met in Andhra Pradesh, recalled the messages she took away from the KAMS meetings: 'They used to say that men with two wives should have their noses rubbed in the ground. A man who leaves his wife has to pay Rs 8000, and if a woman leaves, she has to pay or her new husband pays.' When I asked how this differed from existing custom, she said: 'They tell us to follow our own customs, not government customs.' In fact, punishments like making men grovel are likely to have been the innovation of the local dalam rather than the high command. Hidme went on to say, 'Since the dada log came, there has been no forcible abduction of girls, and marriage is only by mutual consent. The amount of bride price has decreased. Earlier people took cattle in bride price, now they are content with goats and pigs. People are still drinking, but not as much.'

Many of the changes that the Maoists propose require time. Rava of Dulatong, a strong Maoist supporter whom I first met in 2011, was deeply upset because his son had married the neighbour's daughter, a girl from a fraternal clan, who should have been considered a sister. The girl was four years older than his son, and had had two abortions previously, but that wouldn't matter, said Rava, if only she had been from a *saga* (affinal) clan. The Maoists and his other progressive friends kept trying to convince him it wasn't important, but as a *siraha* and a respected man in the village, Rava was vulnerable to criticism from relatives who blamed him for allowing his son to violate social norms. As a middle path, Rava stopped talking to his son and daughter-in-law, but did not sever them from all family rituals. In pre-Maoist times, they would have been outcast. In 2015, I learnt that Rava had left the village and was living in Andhra Pradesh, out of sheer embarrassment.

The party has a vision for every aspect of village life, and is entrenched to a degree the government never can be. In Matpalli village in Konta, I was told how the squads were training people to tether their cattle in the fields to fertilize them, and not near their houses where they brought in flies; they were also persuading people to cultivate and eat green vegetables to improve the local diet. While the Maoists have not banned cockfights, they regulate how they will be conducted: there will be no drinking and nobody can spend amounts over Rs 10 while gambling. Most people don't mind this: I saw men returning from such a fight chatting cheerfully to the local squad leader, a woman, about whose cock had won. However, some of the youth, especially those who have studied outside, resent the bans on film shows and the insistence that only the traditional dhol be used at weddings, as well as the fact that rich villagers are not allowed to buy tractors without permission, while there is no such ban on traders.

The local festivals are closely tied to the agricultural cycle: *beeja pandum* occurs in the summer when the seeds are sown, *karum* or *kurmi pandum* during the monsoons when the first stalks of millet appear, and *korta pandum* when the first stalks of rice emerge. 'P. Shankar', the Maoist chronicler, describes these festivals as needless superstition, while the fines imposed for violating rules (such as the prohibition on eating new mangoes before the *marka pandum*) are seen merely as a way for the village priest and headman to make money on the side. But as the ethno-botanist Madhu Ramnad writes, these practices allowed the trees to regenerate sufficiently and follow a sustainable rhythm.[6] Indeed, some of the Maoists themselves came to realize that these rules enabled a degree of egalitarianism. Lachanna pointed out that richer families wanted to abandon these rules and turn to faiths like the Gayatri Parivar so that they could begin to sow early.

In areas controlled by the Maoists, for all their official dismissiveness, the traditional festivals continue to take place – more so than in areas exposed to the market and outsiders where Holi and Diwali are now taking over, along with gambling. The Maoists have introduced some changes, such as persuading villagers to coalesce kurmi pandum and korta pandum into one event rather than celebrate them a week apart so as to minimize drinking and wastage of time. Moreover, under the conditions of the Salwa Judum and Operation Green Hunt, the timings of these festivals have to be decided in consultation with the local militia. Security is required since any village assembly could be considered a Maoist meeting. Moreover, the seed-sowing festival is a time when land and seed distribution is decided, so dalams may be involved.

The Maoists have been much more successful at establishing a presence among Gonds than among other castes, in part because all the meetings are conducted in Gondi and the songs are in Gondi. The other castes are usually in a minority and more integrated with the state. As ironsmiths (Lohars), weavers (Maharas, Pankas), distillers (Kallars, Sundis), cowherds (Rauts), they are not as dependent on land. Dorlas in the south are more dependent on public works than Gonds, and hence are somewhat more resentful of the curbs on taking up government wage labour. The Gonds are also more centralized in their decision-making than the Dorlas or Dhurwas, where consensus takes longer to arrive at.

It would be rash to generalize, however, that the other castes do not support the Maoists. The Maoists also get support from across formal political affiliations. For instance, Prem Raut was running the RSS front Seva Bharati in Matkapal, engaged in Hinduizing adivasis. However, he also attended sangham meetings because everyone in the village was with the Maoists; he thought they were doing good work, redistributing land, cattle and grains to the poor. He said regretfully that he couldn't be active in the sangham as he had to look after his old parents.

The Ritual Trappings of a State

> The People's Democratic Government shall guarantee all kinds of freedom and rights of the broad toiling masses... It guarantees the following fundamental rights to the people: right to express (speech, write, publication); right to meet; to form organization; to conduct strikes and demonstrations; to live according to one's wish; to have primary education; to have primary medical treatment; to gain minimum employment. In addition to these rights the people will have to fulfill the following duties: to protect the country; to respect the constitution and law, to protect the government properties, to provide military services, to pay taxes.
>
> Policy programme of the janathana sarkar

A state requires not just an army and an administrative structure, but also the visible symbols of rule, like a constitution, a flag and commemorative days. The Maoist calendar of Martyrs' Week (commemorating Charu Majumdar's death), from 28 July to 3 August, and Women's Day on 8 March has also been integrated into the annual cycle of agricultural festivals. During Martyrs' Week, the dead are remembered; local vehicles usually stay off the road knowing there will be Maoist roadblocks. Whereas earlier, the villagers' calendar was tied to agriculture and forest produce collection, now it is also tied to fighting. March–May is the period for attacks (tactical counter-offensive campaigns), but with the police stepping up operations year-round, this calendar no longer works.

Maoist architecture consists primarily of memorials. Across the Maoist state huge red cement structures topped by a sickle dominate the landscape, with no concession to the beautiful artwork seen on traditional stone menhirs or wooden pillars which portray the life of the person. The only allowance for local custom is that these memorials are inaugurated around January–February, at the time of *gaddi pandum*, the festival when the spirits of the dead are worshipped. It is the party that decides where a memorial will be built and brings in outside masons if necessary. A prominent Maoist leader like Azad might have several memorials strategically placed on crossroads. The memorial to Patel Sudhakar Reddy in Malkangiri in Odisha is located on a spectacular site, overlooking the river launch at Jambai, which leads to the 'cut-off area' – villages which have been isolated by the Balimela reservoir. It is starkly visible against a wide expanse of hill, forest and plain. The memorial, on which someone had ironically inscribed 'Last bus stop for martyrs', cost Rs 3,15,000 and took 30 days to build. People of four panchayats participated and on any one day 400–500 people worked on it. The police could hardly have missed the construction, but evidently thought discretion was the better part of valour. There are also local memorials to popular leaders who may have died of illness for which the villagers bear the costs. In 2015–16, the security forces began demolishing Maoist memorials, establishing a gloating victory not just over the living but also the dead.

The Maoist state necessarily has its own flag, which the policy programme of the JS describes: 'Name: Janathana Sarkar; Flag: Hammer and Sickle with red flag with the length and breadth of the ratio 2:3. Song: Must sing Communist International in front of the flag.' The Indian state's celebration of Independence Day and Republic Day, accompanied by the unfurling of the Indian tricolour, is countered by black flags in Maoist areas.

The Pros and Cons of Keeping the Indian State Out

> Q: What are the Maoists fighting for?
>
> A: Complete equality and an adivasi Raj where if one person has a motorcycle, so will everyone else and we can run things in our own way... But [he laughs] when that will happen, I don't know. I'll grow old and die and still we'll be fighting for it.
>
> Conversation with a villager in Matpalli, 2012

Maoist literature claims that they have engaged in considerable development work since 1980. For instance, they write that in south Bastar and Gadchiroli, by 2000, they had established 135 people's clinics, started six primary schools and 10 night schools, built 25 huts for government teachers, set up 10 village libraries and so on. The maximum work had been in the field of agricultural and livelihood improvement: 81 tanks in Dantewada district, 4 lakh fish seedlings distributed in the Konta squad area, 16,200 saplings distributed (of which, like any government department, they complained that only 30 per cent survived because of people's neglect), bullock carts built in 10 villages, diesel pump sets introduced in nine, 268 cattle detention yards built, five rice mills introduced, and people trained in forest protection, cooperative paddy banks set up and agricultural cooperatives created in 220 villages. All of this, they say, had been done through the janathana sarkars.[7]

Apart from land distribution and ponds, however, given the sweep of the area under their control and the fact that this comes with the state being kept out, the effects are inevitably thin. Dealing with the soft arm of the state is the Maoists' weakest spot, in terms of both internal debate and how the villagers see it. The Maoist argument is that the entry of government funds into the village leads to corruption and encourages class differentiation, and that it is far better to have villagers build their own assets through collective labour.

Even the most committed Maoist supporters, however, are

unhappy about the Maoist policy of not allowing government funds. As one of them said to me wistfully, 'If we could take money from government, we could develop our village. But instead we have to go to Andhra for labour which only benefits the Telugu farmers.' Mass migration to Andhra Pradesh has intensified – in part to escape the arbitrary arrests of young people, but also because people desperately need some money, and there is no work available in Chhattisgarh.

In some areas, the overwhelming presence of the CRPF makes little difference to people's support for the Maoists. 'Only a few of us will be able to go to meetings,' one villager from Tatapadu told me, 'but they will relay the information.' In other areas, however, attitudes have changed due to repression and propaganda by the police, and an angry implosion by the Maoists. One winter night in 2013, in a village deep in the Kanger forest, over a fire and glasses of mahua, a group of men and women evaluated the advantages and disadvantages of having the Maoists around. This area was not a traditional Maoist stronghold and had become a site for their activities only in the last six or seven years. The advantages included: first, agricultural cooperatives had been set up and there had been an increase in the wage rates; second, there were far fewer fights in the village, and those disputes that occurred were settled without money; third, the forest department no longer bothered them. The disadvantages included: first, the Maoists only allowed public works as they saw fit – they allowed road building inside the villages, but disapproved of connecting roads between villages for strategic reasons, making it difficult to take sick people to the hospital; second, there was intensive police combing because of the Maoists and youth were arrested; third, the Maoists beat up people who did not obey them. In 2013, the majority of the villagers felt they were better off with the Maoists, but by 2015–16, a drought year, their views had changed somewhat. The demand to attend meetings or surrender a share of their earnings from tendu and mahua, and the restrictions on engaging in government-funded wage labour had begun to seem onerous. They were also upset at some of the surrendered Maoists getting jobs with the police, while they themselves were struggling for employment.

In an ideal world, the government would not be repressive and thieving, and there would be no need for Maoists. But given the choices the villagers have, their best option is for the government and Maoists to coexist peacefully, or at least to train their guns solely on each other, leaving the villagers alone. For most of them, having no Maoists at all is not a good option, since there is thus no countervailing power to confront exploitation. The Maoists argue that they should be judged not by what they have done, but by what they have kept out – pointing to the devastated mining belts of north Chhattisgarh and the rapid reduction of the adivasi population in Jharkhand following an influx of non-adivasis.

If there is one major change the Maoists have introduced, it is to give people a new confidence. Citizens of the Maoist state now look one in the eye and shake hands, compared to the evasive glance with which adivasis traditionally greeted strangers. And it is thanks to the Maoists that the rest of India now knows of the existence and incredible bravery of the people of Bastar.

Part II

Civil War

5

A 'Peaceful People's Movement'

> A holy battle, launched by Chhattisgarh's forested people against leftist extremism…
>
> A peaceful Gandhian movement created by a spontaneous reaction of the tribals to counter Maoist atrocities…
>
> Raman Singh, BJP chief minister of Chhattisgarh, 2007, 2010[1]

June and July are peak sowing months in Bastar. After the tendu leaf season is over, the new mangoes have been eaten, and the village priest has sown the first seeds at the shrine of the Earth, the cattle horns begin to call out to each other. Young and old – boys and men – set out on hunts, sometimes for a few hours, sometimes for a few days, before the serious work of ploughing begins. People rise early to work before the heat settles. In the half-light of early dawn, women sweep the floors and plaster the courtyard with dung. The men go round and round the fields, prodding the cattle, dropping seeds in the wake of the plough. After the work is done in the fields and the afternoon fades, with an occasional cock crow breaking the silence, women sit in their yards pounding the grain, their poles flying in and out, stretching forward to pile up the husks with one hand while using the other hand to strike. The buffaloes come home after wallowing all day in tree-shaded, clear streams. On the stonier, forested slopes of the hills, trails of fire sometimes snake across in the evening, as the undergrowth is burnt for broadcasting seeds in the ash.

This is a time when traditionally everyone attends to their own business. The villagers cultivate their fields, the Maoist leaders retreat to military camps, and the security forces stay in their barracks. Through all the recorded history of the last 200 years of peasant rebellion in India, it is difficult to find a single one which has started in the summer. The time for rebellion in an agricultural calendar is after the harvest. And yet, when news started filtering through towards the end of June 2005 of a major 'people's uprising' against the Maoists, no one thought fit to ask a simple question: why would 'the people' do this now, when the loss of a sowing season would mean the loss of an entire year's food?

Planning for Spontaneity

Far from hinting at any public dissatisfaction with the Maoists, all through the first half of 2005, the police and district administration wrote fortnightly reports complaining to their superiors that the Maoists had people's support. These were included by the NHRC as annexures in their 2008 report to the Supreme Court, and made available to us by the court's permission.[2] Even a botched Maoist attempt at raising the price of tendu leaves from the government rate of 45 paise to 85 paise for each bundle of 50 leaves – which resulted in the contractors refusing to purchase leaves in the Konta area in 2005 – finds no mention in these reports. (It was subsequently invoked as a central reason for the 'spontaneous' uprising.)

There were the usual 'encounters' between the Maoists and the police, in which villagers were killed, either in the crossfire or as 'Maoists'. A typical police entry dated 8 January 2005 describes an encounter in Peddakorma village near Bijapur: 'One villager was wounded in the cross firing. Three women with him were sobbing with fright. On searching their house found one country made gun and explosives in a small plate.'The Maoists attacked official outposts like the Jagargunda police station in the south in January 2005, and a forest department office in Kanker in April. On 24 May there was an ambush in Karremarka in the west of the district in which five policemen were killed, and on 29 May, a blast between Bheji and Konta in the south.

But clearly, everything was not business as usual. In the early twenty-first century, several factors came together: the formation of Chhattisgarh in 2001, the liberalization of the mining policy in 2003, and the formation of the CPI (Maoist) in 2004 through the merger of the People's War and the MCC. There was a renewed urgency for the government to do something about the Maoists. In 2004–5, the Chhattisgarh government contacted the National Remote Sensing Agency in Hyderabad to map Maoist camps in Abujhmarh. It set up a Jungle Warfare College in Kanker, and it requisitioned additional forces from outside the state, including India Reserve Battalions (IRB) from Gujarat and Nagaland.[3]

The central government, for its part, promoted a policy of creating 'local resistance groups'. Lango village in East Singhbhum in Jharkhand had shown the way when villagers poisoned 11 members of a People's War squad who had come to settle a local land dispute. Lango's police-supported Nagrik Suraksha Samiti (Citizens' Protection Committee) was rewarded with Rs 2 lakh and promoted by the home ministry as a popular uprising against the Naxalites:

> Recent developments in Jharkhand, where CPIML-PW encountered strong resistance from villagers in Lango village, P.S. Dumaria, Distt. East Singhbhum show a strong anti-naxal feeling among sections of villagers. This feeling needs to be harnessed and channelised in making peoples' resistance groups to counter the atrocities committed by the naxalite outfits. There is a need to encourage and promote these local resistance groups. The States have been requested to explore the feasibility of appointing Special Police Officers (SPOs),

> Nagrik Suraksha Samitis (NSSs) and Village Defence Committees (VDCs) in the villages affected by naxalism. These local groups are required to be encouraged to come out against Jan Adalats and also to expose other misdeeds of the naxal outfits and their leaders. This will help reduce the over ground support to the naxalites.[4]

Chhattisgarh is one state that appears to have taken the home ministry's instructions seriously, though it did not need to look as far afield as Jharkhand for a model of a 'local resistance group'. It had its own Jan Jagran Abhiyan (JJA) of 1990–1. A police note on the JJA claims they heard that villagers were upset about forcible recruitment to sanghams, whereupon 'fanning the flames of discontent, [the police] made a plan for a Jan Jagran Abhiyan (JJA). On 3 September 1990 at Gram Ermnar, thana Bijapur, among 800 villagers from 13 villages, the Jan Jagran Abhiyan was started.' JJA meetings were subsequently held at different places in Bhairamgarh, Bijapur, Usoor and Konta blocks, mapping a geography similar to the one that the Salwa Judum would follow in 2005.[5] When I met Mahendra Karma in 1991 – he was even then the official face of the campaign – he told me that 3000 sangham members had surrendered at the JJA meetings held across Bijapur. The CPI had also initially joined the JJA, but withdrew after the Maoists killed their leader Gopal from Basaguda in 1992. The CPI later admitted it had been a mistake to join the JJA, but that was the turning point: their mass base started going over to the Maoists.

The Maoist explanation for the origins of the first JJA locates it much more in local factors and the resistance of village elites like Bandi Patel than in police planning. Lachanna recounted how the JJA people would visit villages and greet people with 'Lal Salaam', the traditional communist greeting. If anyone responded in kind, they were beaten. People were made to swear oaths – on rice mixed with the blood of goats ostensibly sacrificed to Danteshwari, the goddess worshipped by the former princely rulers – that they would not feed the Maoists. Women were raped; some people committed suicide out of fear. Unlike the Salwa Judum reign when entire villages were burnt, during the JJA only some houses in each village were targeted. Initially, the shaken Maoists blamed themselves, but then decided to fight back by killing some of the JJA's leaders. Some of the headmen who had participated in JJA processions fled to Bijapur.

A 1991 news clipping from *Navbharat* gives a glimpse of the Maoist resistance to the JJA:

> The bandh call by the Naxals was successful. It is said that two days prior to the bandh, explosives were prepared in Chintalnar, and the Kanker–Jagargunda buses also stopped. Pits were dug and logs placed across the Jagargunda–Basaguda road and banners against the BJP hung at various spots. Police vehicles were told to return and were told that a Jan Jagran *shivir* [camp] was not wanted.[6]

It took a year before the JJA was defeated, and after this, said Lachanna, the party decided the sanghams should operate more secretly. In 1998, there was another smaller JJA but it was limited to a few villages around Bhairamgarh.

The 1990 JJA was supported by the Sivananda Ashram at Gumargunda and the followers of Baba Bihari Das, a 1970s Hindu revivalist leader who advocated vegetarianism and temperance.[7] His followers refused to eat or intermarry with those who refused to convert. In the course of countering the JJA, the non-converts took revenge by making Bihari Das's followers (Bhagats) eat beef. They also forcibly cut off the tufts of hair the Bhagats wore at the back of their heads in imitation of Brahmin priests. The media dutifully ascribed this to the Maoists' contempt for religion, even though this had little to do with the Maoists and was aimed at restoring disrupted village solidarities. By 2005, the Gumargunda ashram was active again in anti-Maoist activity. The ashram's pujari Nandlal formed village defence committees under the banner of the Dantewada Samanvay Samiti (DSS), helped by men like Sudru Ichami, the sarpanch of Satwas (who was subsequently killed by the village sangham for corruption), and Chaitram Atami, who later became the leader of the Kasoli camp, a model Judum camp run by the government.[8] Many Salwa Judum leaders prominently displayed DSS badges.

In 2005, the Chhattisgarh police decided to dust off the JJA model. Fortnightly police reports as well as a police-commissioned video speak of launching 'overt and covert operations, increased patrols, information based operations and propaganda' in the form of posters and leaflets in Bijapur and Bhairamgarh from January 2005 onwards.[9] Two 'NGOs', Bastar Bandhu and Janwadi Mukti Morcha, were also mobilized. No one seems to have heard of them before or after, just as no one had heard of the mysterious Sodi Deva in whose name invitations were sent to attend Jan Jagran meetings.

The Maoists do not seem to have been fully aware of the planning under way. There were stray incidents of action taken against one or two of these operators – for example, official diaries from April 2005 mention a 'Jan Jagran Sainik' called Lakshmayya being knifed by the (Indrawati) National Park Squad of the Maoists on his way home and earlier, in September 2004, the Maoists beat up Kummaram Karma of Takilod village for going to Pharaspal and complaining about them to Mahendra Karma. But there seems to have been no concerted effort to address this new threat.

The Spark That Lit the Judum Fire

> The Salwa Judum consists of all those who come to a meeting and say they will fight against Naxalites.
>
> Madhukar, Judum leader, May 2006

Despite the planning, the JJA needed a spark to set it off again. This is locally attributed to an ambush on 13 May 2005 when sangham members of Karkeli village looted a truck ferrying rice to a CRPF paramilitary camp. The FIR filed by the police on this occasion

(Crime No. 4/2005, Nelasnar thana, 17 May 2005) records that truck drivers Jagtar Singh and Sheikh Riyazuddin were taking 570 sacks of rice valued at Rs 1.71 lakh from Jagdalpur to Bijapur when, between 7.30 a.m. and 11.30 a.m. on 13 May 2005, some 25 men and women stopped the truck, blindfolded the drivers and looted the rice. As the Karkeli villagers later told us, the police responded by arresting and beating up all the adult males of Karkeli. On 15 May, a crowd of some 1000 villagers surrounded Nelasnar thana to get the men released. The police agreed on condition that they hand over the Maoist leaders.

In a round of interviews I conducted in 2009 with local leaders of what became the Salwa Judum movement, I got slightly contradictory accounts of the exact sequence of events in 2005. Of the 20–25 men from Ambeli, Karkeli and Bandipara who started the campaign, only a few are alive now. But all agree that Todsa Ganpat of Ambeli, or Gannu Patel as he was called, played a major role. Gannu Patel was a strong leader. Initially, he was the main point man and supplier for the Maoists in the locality; however, he always tried to ensure that the Maoists did nothing to invite reprisals for the villagers. (In July 2005, soon after the Judum started, the Maoists killed Gannu Patel, his son Budhram and Enka Kishore, the sarpanch of Ambeli. Gannu Patel's other son Mangal became an SPO.)

Purushottam of Gudma, one of the early organizers, told me that village leaders met on 26 or 28 May 2005 at Ambeli. They decided to stop working with the Maoists or give them rice, and also to beat up the hard-core sangham members. People complained of not being allowed to participate in elections and access government funds. Other organizers, however, like Micha Tugge of Bandipara and Lachman Poyam of Ambeli, as well as some women in Ambeli claimed the first meeting took place at Mandimarka village on 4 June, following which two other meetings were organized in the forests between Ambeli and Uskapatnam villages. This was the time for the annual hunt and people were congregating in Ambeli anyway for beeja pandum or the seed-sowing ceremony on the 5th.

On 5 June 2005, which is now ritualized as the beginning of the Salwa Judum, the leaders asked Raju, a sangham member from Gattapalli who had led the rice-looting operation, to come unarmed to Ambeli. He was beaten up and handed over to the police in exchange for the Karkeli villagers. The next meeting was held at Gudma village on 14 June. The organizers then decided to split into two groups: villagers around Gudma would go to Kotrapal village about 15 kilometres away, and the Ambeli/Uskapatnam villagers would go to Tadmendri village. Both these villages were considered Maoist strongholds. By this time, the police were openly involved.

The Tadmendri and Kotrapal meetings, on 18 and 19 June, appear to have been the point at which the operation escalated. Villagers who participated in the Tadmendri meeting told me 5000–6000 people from about 50 villages were present there. Police documents record the numbers as 3500 people from 35–45 villages. Locals reported that there were orders to the villages that all sangham members had to surrender before the Tadmendri meeting, go to their local thana and join as SPOs.

At the Tadmendri meeting, the JJA beat up the patel for refusing to reveal the names of the sangham members in his village. The sangham members retaliated and a fight ensued. Some sangham members managed to escape. They reported the fight to the Maoists who were camping nearby. The JJA procession, meanwhile, shifted to an open field. The Maoists, led by a woman commander, entered Tadmendri and started firing in the air and let cattle loose on the crowd. Everyone ran, leaving behind their cycles. The police record concurs with this description, but adds that 27 people were injured in the stampede, and when people did not return home that evening there was panic. Within five days, however, everyone was home and the cycles had been returned. Eventually, all the Tadmendri sangham members too were forced to become SPOs, and some of them died in a Maoist attack on an SPO camp in Rani Bodli in 2007.

On 18 June, the same day as the Tadmendri meeting, a meeting was held at Matwada on the national highway on the day of the weekly haat. According to the Collector's monthly report, 5000–8000 people from 32–50 villages attended the meeting, which was addressed by Congress MLAs Mahendra Karma and Rajendra Pambhoi. The crowd surrounded 15–20 sangham members who tried to escape by shooting arrows at the mob. In the stampede that followed, Sarve Mohan aka Mohan Singh was left injured in the forest; he later died. Although a decision had already been made to attack Kotrapal, the Collector writes that since no one from Kotrapal came to this meeting, villagers decided to go to Kotrapal the next day and 'make them understand'. On the 19th, 15,000 people went in procession to Kotrapal, but before they reached the village the sangham members fired on them, and kidnapped 12 persons. Bhuvaneshwar, a Thakur, was killed; the rest were released. The security forces accompanying this procession first looked to their own safety by hiding behind a culvert. Eleven days later, on 1 July, Mahendra Karma led another procession to Kotrapal. The Collector records: 'During this period, not a single resident of Kotrapal was to be seen. Everyone had locked their houses and left.'

What the Collector did not report was the killing of two old men, Uike Sannu and Vanjam Mangu, and the wholesale burning of Kotrapal. The news spread quickly. From across the mountain, the Karremarka villagers could hear the crackle of falling wood and see the flames leaping into the sky. Kotrapal was attacked at least twice more that year, before the sangham members surrendered and all the villagers were forced into camp. Eighteen people from the village were killed between 2005 and 2008. The police recorded none of these deaths, even as 'encounters'.

The Maoists provided the Raipur press with a wireless intercept of the Bijapur Superintendent of Police (SP) D.L. Manhar, speaking to his subordinates sometime around the first attacks on Kotrapal. Apart from telling his subordinates to kill any journalist who tried to cover the Naxalites, to tell villages which joined the JJA that they

Bijapur: Origins of the Salwa Judum, 2005-6

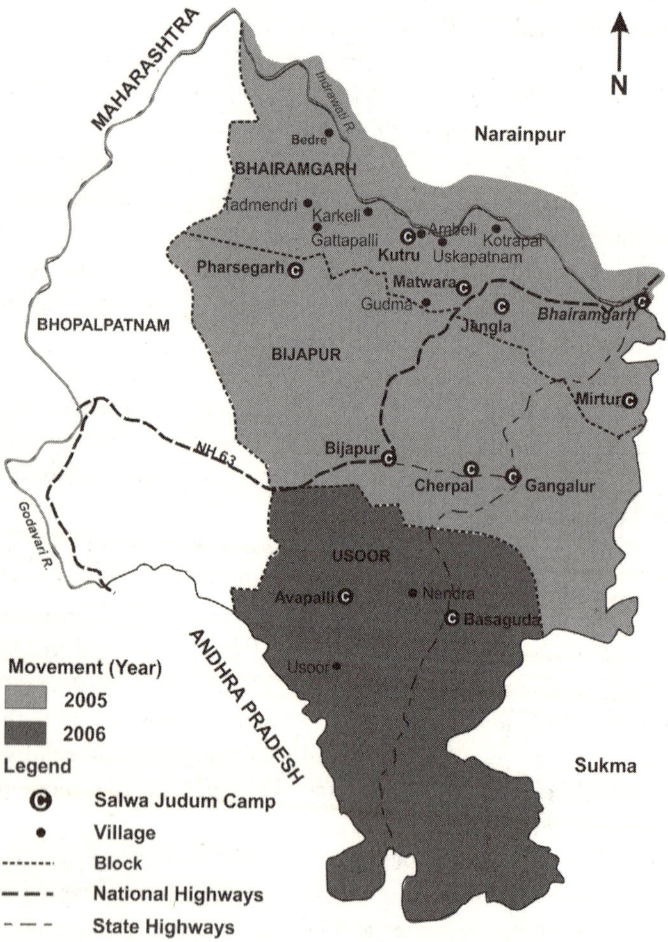

would get 2 lakh rupees (as in Lango, Jharkhand), to spread the word on rewards for turning in weapons, and to make a list of all the sangham members in the area, the SP says:

> 8.43 The Jan Jagran people are clearly telling villagers that if they don't join them, the third time around they will burn their villages
>
> 9.01 The Kotrapal sangham members will surrender today. Once they have surrendered, we will include them in a team and send them to your area
>
> 9.09 The Jan Jagran people are telling us (police) 'you don't need to do anything. We will go with our bows and arrows, and bring them back on our shoulders after killing them, as we do in hunts.'

In November 2005, when the All India Fact-finding team met the Collector, K.R. Pisda, he claimed that the first he heard of the JJA was after the Karremarka ambush of 24 May, when he started getting letters from villagers asking for protection. In the record room of the Supreme Court, I later saw these 12 identical letters dated 14 June (the date was overwritten) written in the same handwriting, ostensibly from villages around Kutru, complaining that the Naxalites were forcibly recruiting 'mothers, sisters, young men and women'. 'Save us from the Naxalites,' the letters said, 'or leave us to kill or be killed on our own.' They looked very much like an official alibi.

The Long and Deadly Marches

Sometime between June and August 2005, the movement changed its name from Jan Jagran Abhiyan to Salwa Judum, which the government translated as Peace March. 'Purification hunt' is, however, a more accurate translation. In Gondi, 'salwa' is the process of pacifying or purifying (like coming into the shade from the hot sun or sprinkling water on an ill person to cleanse them from disease), while 'judum' is the term used for the long summer hunts.

From 18 June onwards, rallies were held almost daily in different villages in the Bhairamgarh–Bijapur area, addressed by ministers and accompanied by a heavy deployment of security forces. For instance, the Collector's 'Fortnightly Returns' note that on 24 July 2005 Kedar Kashyap, *prabhari mantri* (minister in charge of the area), Lachu Ram Kashyap, Chitrakoot, MLA, Rajaram Todem, BJP member of the Chhattisgarh Scheduled Tribe Commission, and Vijay Tiwari, Army Welfare Board Member, attended the JJA rally at Bhairamgarh. The politicians were ostensibly there only to provide moral support to the 'people', while the police were needed for security given the risk of Maoist retaliation. As described by the media:

> From a handful number to thousands. This is how the anti-Naxal movement is gaining grounds in the main heartland of Naxalites in Bastar… After keeping their mouths shut for decades, the tribal people are getting united to battle against the People's War… It is a decisive moment for the government as the tribal people are eagerly waiting for support from police and administration. If the government backtracks and withdraws its support, the people who stood against the Naxalites may turn against the government. The Chief Minister Dr. Raman Singh calls it a historic moment. Addressing people at Dhamtari, he said that this is for the first time in the history that a major tribal movement is taking place.[10]

In reality, it was the public which was being forcibly conscripted into the police's war on Maoists. Police and Judum leaders sent out letters and verbal messages to village headmen. They were asked to join Judum meetings and to bring the sangham members from their villages. Many of these sangham members were then forced to become SPOs. The headmen were in a difficult position: they were damned by the Maoists if they took people to the Judum, and damned by the police if they did not. The villagers were equally unhappy about having to spend two or three days out continuously on these processions. They had to carry their food with them, and lose out on work during the critical sowing season. Inevitably, some participated in the looting of the villages they went through. People recounted that they were threatened they would be fined Rs 700, their houses and animals would be looted, and they would be declared Naxalites, if they did not come. They were taken in trucks to rallies. One woman who could not go told me she had to sell a field to pay the fine. When I asked Purushottam, the Salwa Judum organizer, if force had been necessary to get people to come to these meetings, he denied it at first, and then said: 'Perhaps a little, to create the right atmosphere. It was a revolutionary situation.'

Videos of the meetings, made by both the police and independent sources, show the police marshalling large crowds dutifully waving bows and arrows and shouting slogans of 'Salwa Judum Zindabad, Naxalwad Murdabad' (Long live Salwa Judum, death to Naxalism). As the police, or leaders like Mahendra Karma, read out the names of sangham members from lists, cowering young men and women were brought to the front. Vermilion was smeared on the foreheads of those present, symbolic of religious incorporation into the campaign.

The Judum meetings usually ended with all the houses in targeted villages being looted and then torched by the Salwa Judum activists or by the security forces (this part of course was not shown on government videos or reported in any newspaper). The objective was generally villages considered Maoist strongholds, but often those which fell en route a procession might get attacked as well.

The Salwa Judum leaders, and sometimes the police and paramilitaries acting on their own, hunted down those who did not capitulate, hiding in the forests and raiding villages repeatedly till they found sangham members. In Sagkeli, for instance, where five people were killed between September and October 2005, all except one were sangham members. Two of them were identified while ploughing, with the help of a young boy who had been picked up and taken away in an earlier attack.

The Government's 'Humanitarian' Response

According to the government's propaganda, the Maoists were furious with the villagers for deserting them, and as revenge, were burning the houses of people who attended the Salwa Judum meetings. People were forced to seek refuge in the sheltering arms of the government, which responded by setting up roadside relief camps, and providing food and medicine. The media reflected this faithfully with headlines like: 'Maoists have made us refugees in our own land', even as a paragraph way down revealed: 'At another relief camp, Channu of Palnar village or Mangu of Irauli knew nothing about how they came to camp... Many of them were brought from remote areas.'[11]

In November 2005, the chief minister sanctioned nearly Rs 86 crore for the Salwa Judum. But camp infrastructure, sanitation and food for the inmates appear to have been the least of the 'movement's' concerns. Far more money was spent on banners, hoardings and leaflets praising the Salwa Judum and condemning the Maoists; these were visible everywhere, pinned to trees by the highway and at the entrance to camps. One such leaflet read:

> Who is a Naxali?
>
> - anti-national, terrorist, someone who puts an obstacle in the nation's progress
> - they have relations with ISI [Pakistan's Inter-Services Agency] and the Nepali Maoists
> - they kill villagers; have killed thousands of innocent villagers
> - Naxalis loot – they have looted money, the respect of women, the houses of the poor
> - The Chinese have left Maoism and turned to democracy; the Maoists are destroying democracy and turning to Maoism
> - The Naxalis are bringing the ghost of Mao to Bastar and making the people sad
> - Naxalis are enemies of society and enemies of the nation

The media reported that the villagers 'strongly felt the need for setting up village-level groups. And were also demanding weapons from the State Government to counter the Maoist menace.'[12] It was this popular demand that forced an ostensibly reluctant government to act. The state's highest-ranking police officer, the Director General of Police (DGP), O.P. Rathore, said, 'Desperate situations call for desperate remedies. A stage had now come when there was no alternative to training local tribals to defend themselves – with firearms if necessary.'[13] The priorities for this 'people's movement', we are led to believe, comprising some of the poorest citizens of the country, also included paying for the expenses of all the ministers and politicians who attended the rallies.

The Salwa Judum Manifesto

The Collector of Dantewada in 2005, K.R. Pisda, was an adivasi himself but from another part of Chhattisgarh – a 'promotee', as those who graduate up the ranks are contemptuously called by their peers who come in through direct recruitment. With henna-dyed hair and a soft voice, Pisda was an unlikely planner of such bloodshed. When the All India Fact-finding team met him in November 2005, Pisda was scornful about Mahendra Karma, who was widely considered the leader of the Judum. Pisda said Karma was doing it only for political mileage. Proudly fishing out a blueprint he claimed to have prepared for the Salwa Judum,[14] 'Work Proposal for the Jan Jagran Abhiyan' (written in Hindi), Pisda showed how systematically everything had been planned, starting with the appointment of SPOs, the distribution of 'traditional weapons like bows and arrows, axes, hoes, sticks, etc. to villagers', to the evacuation of villages. This document betrays deep envy for Maoist organizational forms:

> If we want to destroy the Naxalites totally, we will have to adopt their strategies, or else we will not be successful. However many police forces we get, we will find they are inadequate… For this we too

> will have to form village defence squads like the Naxalites. For this SPOs and trustworthy people from the village defence committees will have to be given licences and guns. Such a squad of 15–20 armed villagers and 50–60 villagers with bows and arrows should patrol the villages in their areas for three to four months continuously. (Chapter 4, paragraph 18, all translations mine)

As for targeting sangham members, the government's justification was that they were the local backbone of the Maoist movement, even though they were clearly unarmed:

> A Naxalite is one who wears a uniform, carries weapons, moves with a squad, but their role is at one level that of a director. Their real strength lies in the sangham members in each village and in the villagers themselves... To finish off the Naxalite problem, it is not enough to kill Naxalites – the system they have created in every village must be smashed and destroyed... From one perspective, the sangham member is just an ordinary villager who, like others, does daily labour to feed himself and his family. They have neither a uniform like the Naxalites nor any arms. (Chapter 4, paragraph 13)

The document was surprisingly candid:

> Police must now become aggressive. Sometimes, for unknown reasons, some excesses take place during the course of such operations and some innocent persons become victims of this action. The support of higher-ups is necessary through keeping silent on such matters during big operations... When they see Naxalites being killed or running, they will at once come over to the side of the police. Therefore it is essential to link this activity to the others. For this Superintendents of Police must be given targets. (For action, Home Department, SP Bijapur and all Thana Prabharis). (Chapter 4, paragraph 10)
>
> It is essential to curb the enthusiasm of the media. This is not

> a proposal for a ban on the media, simply for restrictions on it. At the state level, a meeting should be called of all editors and news channels and they must be reminded of their responsibility to the people. (Chapter 4, paragraph 28)

The Collector's 'Work Proposal' was a far more accurate description of what actually happened than the 'self-initiated' people's movement reported in the media.

The Judum Invades New Areas

In early 2006, the movement spread from Bijapur and Bhairamgarh in the west to Usoor and Konta in the south. In Usoor, inmates of the Hirapur camp told me in 2008 they had been brought there directly from a Salwa Judum meeting held in the local market centre, Awapalli, on the afternoon of 3 February 2006. At this meeting, led by Mahendra Karma, sangham members of Basaguda, Lingagiri, Dharmapur and Hirapur surrendered, but no one came from Korsaguda; later, the Judum went to Korsaguda, and other villages, and burnt them. People fled to the forest or to Andhra Pradesh.

In the Konta area further south at the border with Andhra Pradesh, everybody had been dreading the arrival of the Salwa Judum. The words they used described it as a pestilence which swept over people and homes, and over which nobody had any control. In February 2006, Mahendra Karma's men first persuaded some villagers from a roadside village, Dubbatota, to join them. These Dubbatota people in turn caught villagers from neighbouring Misma who had come to the Dornapal Monday market on 20 February and took them to the thana. They were told that unless everyone from Misma came to camp, they would not be released.

Other visitors to the Dornapal haat had similar experiences – of being captured and taken to Konta in trucks, and kept for three days till they agreed to bring others. Six or seven trucks of people were brought from Bijapur and there was a big meeting at Konta over 24

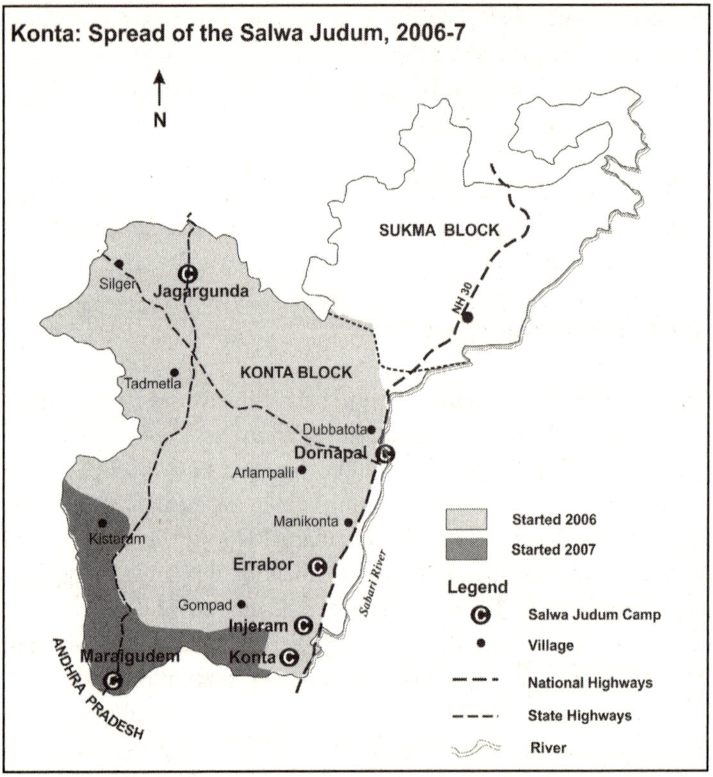

and 25 February, attended by Mahendra Karma, the Collector K.R. Pisda and others. The Judum burnt Birla village during that time. On the following Monday, market day in Dornapal (27 February), another Judum meeting was held, followed by attacks on several villages. A day after this, the Maoists blasted a truck full of Judum processionists returning to Konta, killing 28 people. People were furious not just with the Maoists but also with the Judum for putting them in this situation. One distraught survivor told me in May 2006, '*Judum hame chutiya bana kar le aye*' (The Judum fooled us and brought us).

Throughout 2006, the Judum burnt hundreds of villages around Konta and forced people into camps in Konta, Errabor, Dornapal and Injeram. In some cases they lured people by promising rations if they attended the Judum meetings, and then took them into camp. In early 2007, the Judum moved to fresh areas like the Kistaram range on the Andhra Pradesh border. The numbers of refugees on the Andhra Pradesh side ebbed and flowed, depending on the intensity of the attacks in Chhattisgarh. The Andhra Greyhounds and Chhattisgarh paramilitaries and SPOs also conducted combing operations on the Andhra Pradesh side of the border, and repatriated villagers to the Judum camps in Chhattisgarh. The Maoists on their part killed SPOs when they could, including in weekly markets on the Andhra Pradesh side.

On the Bijapur side too, the Judum and police raids continued between 2005 and 2008. The same villages were attacked repeatedly in an effort to smoke out the remaining villagers to camp. Different gangs of SPOs might visit the same village. In 2008, I visited Pulam in Bijapur. Huge trees had been felled to block the road. However, given how often the police had been coming, this hardly seemed to have been very effective. When we reached Pulam, the villagers ran away when they saw us, and then sent one small boy to scout. Slowly they came, carrying bows and arrows (it was June so they could have legitimately been hunting), and one man had a belt to carry cartridges. We met a youth, evidently a sangham member, who maintained a diary on the basis of which information was passed on to the dalam:

> **September 2005**: 2 men killed in the village; **13 July 2006**: 4 people killed while working in their fields, including two women, one of whom was pregnant; **2, 9 and 26 December 2006**: Police and SJ came to Pulam and looted on their way to other villages; **June and 8, 23, 25 July 2007**: Police from different thanas visited repeatedly; on two occasions they looted goats and hens; **20 August 2007**: SJ came and took away people, they kept one of them, Hemla Santu, and released the rest; **27 August 2007**: Police came and took 4 more people; they were beaten and freed. They burnt 70 houses; **24**

> **September 2007**: The Bhairamgarh Salwa Judum came and took 15 goats, 1 hen; **December 2007**: 9 people were killed in the village. Hearing firing at Tokadi, 3 km away, all the villagers gathered in one place; but the force came from an unexpected direction and shot at them. The police version is that the villagers gathered for a meeting with the Maoists. A couple of days later, the police came and fired again, but everyone ran away.

As of January 2007, a government memo notes, 644 out of 1153 villages had 'joined Judum' in 6 out of the 11 blocks of Dantewada district. Forty-seven meetings and 139 *padyatras* had been held; 2008 sangham members had surrendered; there were 47,238 people in 20 camps; 4048 SPOs had been appointed. Rs 11.17 crore had been spent on the relief camps from 2005 to 2007.[15]

The maximum damage took place between 2005 and 2007: the police claimed that the Maoists killed 412 people, including police personnel, during this period. However, these numbers are suspect, and include many killed by the security forces. For litigation, we compiled a list of some 3000 homes burnt, and 537 civilian victims of the Judum and security forces, which is itself an underestimate.

Resisting the Salwa Judum

> It is amply clear that the government has opened up this 'new front' – the tribal genocide operation under the name of Salwa Judum – to crush the economic and political aspirations of the people of Bastar Chhattisgarh, and to perpetuate their kingdom of loot.
>
> 'Salwa Judum: A New Front of Hidden War', CPI (Maoist), 2006

The Maoists and the sangham members resisted the Salwa Judum as best as they could – firing on processions before or after they entered a village (so that the villagers would not be held responsible for having Maoists in their midst, and also because it was difficult to manually operate the improvised explosive devices [IEDs] when the Judum was swarming over the village). They warned local headmen not to take the villagers to Judum meetings and tried to convince people to join them in the forests instead. Complaints registered by the police, for instance this one at Mirtur thana, give us a glimpse of these efforts:

> Hapka Lachman s/o Aitu Ram r/o Halur complained that on 15.10.05 at Halur at 10 pm, LGS leader Santosh r/o Timenar, Joga, Ursa Aitu and 100 other sangham members came to the house of the complainant and accused him of informing on sangham members in Salwa Judum rallies and looted his house.

The only news that came out of Dantewada during the first year of the Judum was Maoist attacks on sarpanches favouring the Judum, who then left their villages and became the backbone of the Judum in camps. The Maoists claimed that the bulk of the villagers were with them, and it was only a few villagers close to the headmen or sarpanches who were keen to participate in the movement. But inevitably, once people were forced to choose sides in a situation of terrible uncertainty and the constant threat of attacks, the situation became more complicated. In Teknar, in Bhairamgarh block, when the Judum started, the Halbi-speaking Kallars – a 'backward caste' whose traditional occupation is brewing liquor – thought it safer to come into camp in 2005, after their village was attacked, but the Gondi-speaking Murias stayed behind.

A similar divide developed between the Maharas, who are SC, and the Muria adivasis. For instance, the day after the Judum held a meeting in Gangalur on 24 August 2005, a prominent market village in Bijapur, the Maoists held a meeting in Patnad village and noted the names of 10 people who were accused of taking people to the Salwa Judum. Their protestations that they were doing it to save the village did not cut much ice. On 4 September 2005, the Maoists told the Patnad villagers to camp in the mountains with them, a sensible precaution because when the Judum attacked on 21 September, they found the village empty. However, the Maoists also killed the patel and sarpanch, along with two Mahara boys who had joined the Judum. Soon after, some 50 non-adivasi households left for Bijapur, while the remaining 250–300 Muria households remained with the Maoists in the forests.

But the adivasi–local-non-adivasi Bastariya divide was not absolute. The government and media initially made much of a Dorla–Gond divide in Konta, claiming that the Dorlas were with the Judum and the Gonds with the Maoists. But the Judum also attacked Dorla and Telga villages, and there were both Dorlas and Gonds in the ranks of the Maoists.

From early 2006, the Maoists began full-scale retaliation for the Judum, beating it back but also escalating it to an even more intense civil war. The first major incident was the attack on the truck carrying Judum processionists on 28 February 2006. In July 2006, as part of a strategy of 'liberating' people from camps, the Maoists struck Errabor camp. Thirty-two people died in the fire that ensued, including a small child.

The Maoists also held jan adalats where they punished people who were active in the Salwa Judum rallies. In one such jan adalat in Manikonta in April 2006, 13 men were killed. The police had forcibly brought the Manikonta villagers to Konta camp a couple of months previously. On 25 April, when they returned to the village to retrieve their grain and household goods, the Maoists kidnapped some 50 of them. A boy from Gapapalli, who had escaped to Andhra Pradesh, described to me a year later what happened in vivid eyewitness terms, all the while claiming he had only heard of it from others:

> The Maoist leaders asked the men they had captured how many villages they had burnt and how many pigs, etc. they had looted while accompanying the Judum on procession. They forced the men to talk. People in the crowd also identified these 13 men as the worst. They were beaten to death by the dalam and some 50–60 people.

> The meeting lasted about an hour. People from all the neighbouring villages had come. These men had been warned three or four times before but they didn't listen, so the public said, 'Kill them.'

In May 2006, we had met a few of the widows of these 13 Manikonta men in Dornapal camp. They were resentful of both the Maoists who had killed their husbands and the Judum which had brought them to camp. The government had given them compensation of Rs 2 lakh each, but they had no idea what their bank passbooks contained.

The Judum was beneficial for the Maoists in many ways: it increased their strength and helped them spread to new areas, and it gave people the experience of defending themselves and cultivating in the forest even during conflict.

In 2006, following Maoist retaliation, the government officially declared its intention to 'gear up the Salwa Judum movement in two blocks before extending it to new areas', an admission of how government-controlled this 'people's movement' really was.[16] But in at least two blocks, Bhopalpatnam and Sukma, it was the residents who stalled the Judum. The villages in Sukma block were saved from the Judum because of the resistance of Manish Kunjam and other CPI cadre.

In Bhopalpatnam too, the Judum never took off because of opposition by local leaders. In Bhopalpatnam 19.67 per cent of the land is irrigated compared to the average of 1.49 per cent for Bijapur as a whole (2011 census). From Usoor, those who could not flee to Andhra Pradesh went to Bhopalpatnam instead, looking for work. After hearing about the Judum from their farmhands, the Bhopalpatnam farmers were determined not to let the force into their area. In the summer of 2006, panchayat members from Bhopalpatnam who attempted to go to Raipur to complain to the higher authorities were stopped en route by Judum leaders and beaten; they tried again in November, through different routes, taking 12 days to get there. Somehow, they managed to resist the Judum.[17]

6

Between Fear and Courage

> Fear binds people together. And fear disperses them. Courage inspires communities: the courage of an example – for courage is as contagious as fear. But courage, certain kinds of courage, can also isolate the brave.
>
> Susan Sontag, *On Courage and Resistance*

Till mid-2007, it was difficult to get anyone to testify freely about their experiences. Access to the villages – indeed any movement off the highway – was blocked off by the security forces, claiming it was for the visitors' own security. The Salwa Judum camps dominated the highways, barricaded with sandbags and preceded by checkpoints manned by SPOs. The SPOs, in plain clothes, searched vehicles and took whatever they pleased. Sometimes, the same vehicle was repeatedly searched every hundred yards by different groups of SPOs. When we protested that their leader had already allowed us to pass, one said, 'There are no leaders here, everyone is a leader.' At night, gangs of SPOs and Judum leaders patrolled the camps with sticks, ensuring that no one went in or out. I remember travelling on a bus in 2007 past the camps on the Konta road, my face covered with a scarf, terrified that some SPOs might pull me out and declare me a Maoist.

The camps were effectively open-air prisons, unlike relief camps organized after communal riots, which are places of safety run by co-religionists or human rights organizations. Here, the Salwa Judum leaders and SPOs carefully monitored conversations with reporters or human rights groups. In November 2005 when the All India Fact-finding team was trying to have a conversation with villagers in Gangalur camp, the SPOs quickly turned aggressive, asking, 'Where were you when the Maoists were killing people?' Even had they wanted to intervene, the local administration was helpless before the Judum leaders and SPOs who, in front of us, freely gave them orders to stop us travelling further.

In May 2006, when the ICI visited, the situation was scarcely better. Even though we had a letter of permission from the Chief Secretary, the CRPF stopped us. One team, consisting of Ramachandra Guha, Farah Naqvi and me, tried to cross the Indrawati at Nelasnar to visit affected villages on the other side, but the villagers said no boats were available. So we went on to Kutru where the CRPF commandant gleefully told us that if we did not return soon we would be blown into little bits by a Naxal bomb and our flesh would hang on trees. On our way back, at dusk, we were stopped by a mob at Bhairamgarh thana. By now, rumours were circulating that we had offered the Nelasnar villagers Rs 1 lakh if they helped us cross, which fevered imaginations further translated as an attempt by Maoists to flee at any cost. The driver had some green pants in a bag in the boot, which the SPOs fished out with great triumph calling it a Maoist uniform. Ram was taken into the thana, and Farah and I followed behind, worried that something might happen to him. The Judum leaders and SPOs inside were drunk, and refused to read the Chief Secretary's letter. Luckily, we managed to get through to Himanshu Kumar, the head of a local NGO who was on good terms with the Salwa Judum leaders – and his word counted more with them than the Chief Secretary's. A Judum leader took away my camera; I got it back some months later, from the Collector, without any apology.

People did not feel safe even in Andhra Pradesh. When J.P. Rao and I started touring the Khammam villages in 2007 in search of Judum refugees, they insisted that they had come there several years earlier in search of land. They did not want to be identified with villages that had been burnt, because that would have suggested they were Maoist supporters. While not implausible, their claims were belied by the testimonies of their Andhra neighbours and the fragility of their homes.

The Cherla Testimonies

Though several human rights reports based on information from villagers appeared between 2005 and 2007, direct testimonies by villagers themselves came only in June 2007, when the CPI held a rally at Cherla, just over the border in Andhra Pradesh. This was the first mass public demonstration against the Judum. Thousands of villagers came for this, and handed over petitions to the CPI leaders. While returning, senior activist Sukal Prasad Nag was severely beaten by SPOs at Errabor camp; the others escaped only because they were forewarned and took a different route.

Written in broken Hindi and Gondi, on scraps of paper or ruled pages torn from school notebooks, the testimonies gave a vivid and first-hand glimpse of the Judum's operations.[1] The villagers wrote of houses and entire villages being burnt, poultry and cattle eaten on the spot or taken away to the Salwa Judum camps; of people being beaten and killed, burnt alive, or drowned in the river if they happened to be found there fishing or bathing. Several accounts mention women being raped, sometimes with names, but more often as 'x's wife or daughter'. Sometimes they just wrote: '10 women were raped in our village'. Quite often, the names of those arrested or forcibly taken to camp find mention even before those killed, prioritizing the living dead; they were all taken as equally lost to the village. Naga and Mizo villagers can recall the precise dates on which their villages were burnt in the 1950s and 1960s, perhaps because of a history of Church-taught literacy. By contrast, the adivasis of Chhattisgarh have much less sense of chronological time, so all dates are approximations.

Many testimonies carried lists of household losses. *Khapra* or baked-brick roof tiles are often the only item of construction that is purchased while building and therefore priced; the rest of the house is usually built of local wood and mud. However, people also specifically noted doors being looted. There is no furniture beyond one or two wood-and-rope cots. There may be an occasional transistor or a cycle, a few steel pots and plates, a few clothes, a couple of blankets and some agricultural implements. The main wealth – if one can call it that – is in the form of poultry and goats, and the sacks of rice, millets, mahua, tamarind and other forest produce that the villagers store. The Judum took all this, as well as any gold jewellery and cash they could find. Few households had more than Rs 10,000–20,000 in cash and, certainly, no one had bank accounts. Occasionally, in the testimonies one comes across something unusual that was looted, like fishing nets or a musical instrument.

Because people have so little, they are able to detail every single loss. The tragedy is that it adds up to so little. In Pochampalli, one entry notes:

> Apart from raping Bhima's wife and setting their house on fire, the Judum looted everything in the house: Paddy: 10 sacks; Salt: 1 kg; Millets: 5 sacks; sulphi or fermented palm juice worth Rs 1500; 10 items of clothing; 10 utensils; 10 chickens; Rs 2000 in cash; 3 goats and 5 kg oil.

Many of the complaints mentioned SPOs and security forces finding the bags of paddy that had been hidden in the forest and burning them. Others complained that if they refused to give chickens to the SPOs, they were beaten with rifle butts. Sometimes the losses were estimated village-wise: in Bhendaras, the village as a whole, which had some 100 houses, lost Rs 50 lakh. In Gapapalli, villagers estimated they had lost Rs 3–4 crore of property, as the Judum had attacked soon after the harvest when everyone had stocks of grain in their houses.

The Sawapalli villagers were graphic: 'The Salwa Judum also throws the small children in the fire besides beating and killing pregnant women… If the Salwa Judum catches people it kills them, tears apart their body, slits their tongue and heart etc… We are very frightened these days.' The villagers of Kottapalli were much more matter-of-fact. Attaching a detailed list of losses household-wise, they wrote:

> We are writing a short letter to you. The whole village has fled. We eat once a day, if even that. We have left our villages and wherever we go there is no land. All our poultry, cattle, pigs and utensils have been forcibly taken from us by the Salwa Judum people. They have raped and killed girls in our village and beaten many of us. Having written this, we wish to bring to you that this has been happening for the last three years. The Kottapalli people have been beaten a lot. How can any villager live in such circumstances? With this we end our letter. Please do what you have to. Thank you.

Some of the letters betray a touching faith in the government and in mainstream political processes, addressing their letters to the 'Mantri Mahoday' (minister) and asking for an immediate investigation. Many of the letters were addressed to Manish Kunjam as president of the Adivasi Mahasabha. The Korpadar villagers wrote:

> Going to the police does not help as the officers do not listen to the villagers. The frightened villagers of Gangaloor, Cherpal and Bijapur, seeing the Salwa Judum, have fled into forests... Why is this happening in our country, why is this happening in Chhattisgarh? Why has the Chhattisgarh administration been running this? Has our chief minister been elected only for this?

Eighty-three Maraipalli villagers signed off on a tragic letter that ended: 'We want to say and write much more but our pen fails us here. We end this report with an urge to please understand our problems.'

Indiscriminate Targeting

Initially the Judum targeted sangham members, especially those who refused to come to camp and surrender. Rapidly, however, as the orgies of looting and burning took over, the killings became completely arbitrary. Those who could not run away in time – especially the old and the sick – were killed, sometimes burnt alive in their huts or on their threshing fields. Charred bodies were found later – 'looking like broiled fish', one man told me. Old people also sometimes got abandoned in the confusion that followed after a village was attacked. Even when villagers fled well in advance of an impending attack, those who were old, very poor and landless did not have anyone to go to. A testimony from Pakapad in Konta notes:

> All the villagers have left their homes. Some are wandering in towns and some are wandering in the dense forests. One of the residents, Bainda Lakmayya, and his father, Bainda Buchayya, died after being bitten by a snake while they were in the forests. One old woman, after getting no food or water, died in thirst. And one resident, Korsa Bukka, died after the village was evacuated, while wandering in search of food and water.

In Vengaipadu, villagers told me that almost all of the seven people killed in their village were old men. Around Diwali 2005, Joga did not go to camp because his *sulphi* tree was giving sap. Outsiders can rarely conceive how important these palm trees are to the locals; fermented palm juice is a seasonal and much-loved drink, and these trees are individually bought and sold, separately from the land on which they stand. When the Judum came to find Joga because he wasn't in camp, he ran towards the forest. But because he was drunk and couldn't run fast, he was caught and axed to death by the SPOs. Madda, another old man, had stayed back in the village. In July 2006, the Judum came and tied all the fowl of the village on a stick and made him carry it to the river. There the SPOs knifed him, leaving his body by the river but taking away the poultry. A third man was killed by the Naxalites for being an informer and taking people to camp, while a fourth was killed by the Judum. He was tied to a post outside his father's kothar and axed in the neck and back. His corpse was left there, still tied up.

Children were also vulnerable. In Hiranad village, the testimonies tell us of Oyam Sannu's daughter who was 'killed and thrown into the pond by the Judum. She was six years old. The SPOs who did this are Punem Shankar, Bindu, Modiyam Hunga.' In Rigarnad, 'one three-year-old girl child, Korsa Mangli, was beaten unconscious and her hand was broken by the Salwa Judum.' In early March 2007, I was told by an Andhra medic of how the Judum burnt 24 houses in Durapalli. Apart from an old woman who was forcibly pushed into the fire, a three-year-old girl and a three-month-old child died when they could not be extricated in time from their burning home. The children's mother then went into deep depression. In her case, the Médicins Sans Frontières (MSF) was able to provide some counselling, but there were many other parents whose children died and who then died of grief themselves, like Madvi Mase of Nendumango who left her baby in a hammock and went to get water. By the time she came back, the Judum had attacked the village and burnt the house with the baby inside.

Despite government claims that no air power was used and that helicopters were only used to evacuate injured jawans, villagers talked of helicopters being used as combat vehicles. A Rigarnad testimony from 2007 talks of an 'eliapte' landing and killing them. The police claimed it was a Maoist meeting, but the villagers later told me that they came in the midst of a village festival; those who were sober ran away, the drunk ones got killed or picked up. It is not clear how many were killed in that one incident, but some seven people from

Rigarnad were killed between 2005 and 2007. Surpangada villagers told Human Rights Watch that in 2006, 'police came in three helicopters, landed there and set huts on fire'.[2]

Often, villagers were picked up on combing operations and passed off as Naxalites. Civilians being killed in 'crossfire' was another convenient alibi for the police. A villager from Padpalli in Cherpal camp testified to the NHRC that in November 2006 the Salwa Judum, CRPF and SPOs came to his village and burnt and looted the houses. The CRPF took four men to the Cherpal camp that day. After two days, CRPF men told the villagers that there was a Naxal attack on the camp, and when they counter-fired, these four men were killed in the crossfiring. The Bijapur district SP and Sub Divisional Magistrate (SDM) came and praised the CRPF, while the chief minister visited Gangalur and gave Rs 1000 as reward to each SPO of Cherpal camp.

Beating was a common complaint in the testimonies: 'The Salwa Judum broke the hands and legs of Madkami Joga's daughter.' In Patel Kankapal, 'the Salwa Judum beat five people unconscious. The injured were admitted to Bhadrachalam hospital. They had to sell their cattle and goats to arrange for treatment. Around Rs 20,000 was spent on their treatment.' But getting treatment was rare; most people found it too dangerous to venture out and risk arrest. Those injured by bullet wounds when the Salwa Judum attacked their village relied on forest herbs instead.

Some days appear to have been absolute carnivals of looting, arson, rape and killing as the Judum swept through several villages. The villagers' testimonies name the people killed, and the SPOs who did the killing. Mahendra Karma and Salwa Judum leader Ram Bhuwan Kuswaha, several wrote, were present when their village was burnt.

The villagers never abandon the dead. People told me that after every attack, some people went back and recovered the bodies of those killed, and either cremated or buried them with whatever rituals they could muster in those troubled times.

When Stones Are More Truthful Than Official Records

Apart from the Salwa Judum processions, which resulted in killings in the villages, there were reports of regular 'encounters' during this period. On 6 September 2005 the *Hitavad* reported a press release issued by the DGP Chhattisgarh saying that 10 armed Maoists were killed in the Bijapur forests in an encounter during Operation Green Hunt. This was the first use of a term that later became synonymous with the war on the Maoists. But the Maoists claimed in the January 2006 issue of *People's March* that the dead were unarmed villagers killed in cold blood. Later that summer, the Cherli villagers then captive in Mirtur camp told the ICI that the 10 people were killed in crossfire between the police and Maoists. Not surprisingly, no policemen died in this 'encounter'.

In 2009, when we visited Hariyal Cherli, there were 10 rough-hewn stone memorials at the entrance to the village. Seven of them had 'comrade' scrawled on the stone: '*Lutere Sarkar Salwa Judum ka naam liye Gram Cherli Comrade Kadti Chinna umra 25 saal san 2005 shaheed huye. Comrade ko lal salaam*' (The looting government under the cover of Salwa Judum killed comrade Kadti Chinna aged 25 years. He was martyred in the year 2005. Red salute to the comrade). The seven were probably sangham members, aged between 18 and 40. One of the the 'comrades' killed, Kadti Kumma, was a 12-year-old boy, perhaps a bal sangham member.

We met the wives and sons of some of those killed, who said that they had all fled to the forest when the Judum and Naga forces attacked the village in 2005. Five houses had been burnt in that incident. 'The Naga police caught all 10 in the forest, gathered them together and shot them dead.' The women said they found the bodies lying in a straight line in the evening, and by the time they put them on cots and brought them back to the village, it was late at night. They reported the deaths to the police the next day.

The police records of the time, which I found in the NHRC annexures,[3] contradict each other, as if the police had not quite made up their mind what story to tell about these 10 corpses. One FIR says that the villagers recovered five bodies on the 2nd, while another says the police found three bodies on the 3rd. One deceased person is common to both accounts.

A third FIR (13/05), based on information provided by Naval Kashyap, platoon commander, gives a graphic description of the alleged 'encounter'. The police received intelligence from an informer that the Naxalites were having a big meeting with sangham members about a plan to attack the Salwa Judum and police. Accompanied by Salwa Judum guides Raghu Ram, Chandu, Phaninath and Devi, the police set off to corner them:

> We surrounded the mountain around 5 p.m. The firing last 1.5 hours. The Naxals fired about 200 rounds. 3 Naxals were grievously injured, we saw them falling. The Naxals were loudly shouting to each other [they always make it convenient for the police to identify them], Santosh, Jaggu, Lakhu, Joga, Manglu, Meshram, Kamlu, and firing. Then taking advantage of the darkness and the dense forest, they ran away. There was a possibility of more people being wounded, but because of the dark, we could not search the area.

The fact that compensation was given to anyone killed by the Naxalites, but was not available to anyone killed by the Judum or security forces, skewed the records enormously. In 2008, when the NHRC investigated the incident, they concluded that seven of them had been killed by the Naxalites, since the police had recorded their families as having taken compensation. However, at least three of the allegedly compensated families told me in 2009 they had refused the money, but that the sarpanch kept their passbooks with him in Mirtur camp and took the money out as he pleased. The relatives of two other families who refused to accept compensation were declared Naxalites. People who start off their recorded history as Naxalites in the police version become victims of the Naxalites once the NHRC is done with them. Their own existence as ordinary villagers or sangham members drops out of the story altogether.

The Lying Women of Our Country

> Girls are put up by the underground to say they have been raped.
>
> Brigadier Ponwar of the Kanker Jungle Warfare College, personal comment, 2008

Rapes were brutal and widespread. To prevent young men being picked up, it was often women who went to the market to either sell wood or buy rice, but this made them even more vulnerable to assault and rape. Villagers wrote of 12-year-old girls being raped, of women being 'penetrated with sticks and killed', of the Judum members pulling off women's clothes, their saris, blouses, lungis, etc., and stealing the money pouches tied to their waists. Old women, pregnant women, young girls – no one was spared.

In 2008, a villager from Vengaipadu told me two young girls had been picked up from the village. They were both at home when the Judum attacked, because one was ill and the other one was looking after her. Both were raped and then arrested. Their hair was cut off and they were made to wear uniforms so that they would look like Naxalites. Another young girl was taken to Mirtur thana and made to pose for a photo with a gun. The girl's father had paid a senior lawyer Rs 10,000 to have her freed, but she was still in jail.

In villages across the Indrawati, I was told of young girls who had been arrested from the local *mandai* or fair. The police insisted they were taking part in a Naxalite meeting. The girls were kept in camp, raped and then married off to much older men, under the supervision of a renegade dalam member, who had made this his own particular occupation. One girl testified to the NHRC on the commonality of rapes in camp:

> Two days after we reached the camp, the SPOs of the camp asked me and some other girls to come with them, because they wanted to interrogate us. It was about 7 or 8 in the night. They took 7 of us in a vehicle out of the camp to the nearby forest. There they raped all of us again and again.

In 2008, I collected testimonies from two young girls in villages around Chintalnar, accompanied by CPI activist Podiyam Panda. Had it not been for him, they would never have talked; their eyes were already dead with pain. They described how they had been held in the Judum camp as sexual slaves. Somehow, they managed to escape, and their testimonies bear witness to a complex web of negotiations – with the local police, the tendu thekedar and camp leaders:

> I was three or four months' pregnant and was visiting my parents' house when last year in June 2007, Salwa Judum leaders and SPOs attacked my village. It was about 9–10 p.m. and I was sleeping when they surrounded my house. They beat up my parents and dragged me to the main road. From there, along with another girl and a young boy I was taken to Jagargunda camp. There I was kept for a week and raped every night by different SPOs. I do not recognize the others, but I recognized Bhima aka Ramesh of Jonaguda village and Somdu of Kunder village. We [Maite and I] were kept locked up in one house and Unga was kept separately. We were given only a little food and not allowed out at all, except to relieve ourselves. My clothes were in tatters and my jewellery was taken away. After a week, I was given a small cloth to cover myself. When we were being taken to Jagargunda, my parents tried to stop them, but they were chased away with guns and knives. On our way to Jagargunda, we were told that we would also be killed and our bodies thrown near the nala but one saab [policeman] from Jagargunda saved us.

> After a week, our parents and other villagers came to rescue us and the SPOs finally let us go. But even then they threatened us and we would have been killed/beaten on the way back if we had not got a lift back in the tendu thekedar's jeep. Unga was badly beaten and was ill for a long time. Maite and I were also ill and could not work for two months. After all this, the Chintalnar police took Rs 1500 from each of our families, for having 'saved' us. The Chintalnar police told our parents they had wirelessed to Jagargunda camp and we were safe.

In another instance, in Narsetti village, three girls were raped inside their houses when the Judum attacked their village. Sreedevi Panikkar recorded their statements for a fact-finding report:

> In July 2007 when the Salwa Judum and security forces came to our village I had just come back from the fields and was going to fetch water. Four men who had their faces covered stopped and forced me to take them to my house. One of them forcibly took my father and mother out. The other three men forced me inside the house. One of them stood guard at the door while the other two men raped me. They kept saying, 'You are a Naxalite and we have taught you a lesson today.' They raped me and then forced me to go outside where a crowd had gathered. They left.

A mother testified in another case:

> We could hear her screaming. My husband ran to the door, banged on it and asked them to leave our daughter alone. At this point, the man standing at the door started to beat my husband with the rifle butt. The two men who had taken my daughter inside the house also came out and beat my husband. My husband was unconscious. My daughter was crying. Her clothes were torn.

Fortunately, adivasi society, unlike the rest of 'civilized' India, does not stigmatize women who have been raped, and many have subsequently got married.

The New Legal Category of 'Naxali Offence'

The police invented the category of 'Naxali offence' to arrest whoever they liked. Sometimes sangham members were identified by former Maoists turned SPOs when they went to the market or were found during combing operations, and kept in handcuffs close to the police station in the camps. But far more often, the arrests were completely arbitrary. When some of us visited Jagdalpur prison in May 2006, at least two prisoners described how they had been conscripted as guides by the CRPF and Border Roads Organisation (BRO), and then arrested. In one case, it was because he refused to join the Judum. They had not seen their families for several months.

Women who were arrested were often brutally gang-raped before reaching jail – like one woman we met in mid-2006 who had been travelling on the back of her brother's cycle to visit their sister in another village. The CRPF shot her brother before raping her right there on the road where they caught her, and again, in the police station. The other women around her confirmed that when she reached the jail she was so swollen she could hardly walk. She was arrested under the dacoity and arms act. In 2015, the Jagdalpur Legal Aid Group (JAGLAG), a collective of lawyers, got a young woman who had spent seven years in jail, Kawasi Hidme, released. Newspapers reported her reunion with the village: she was so changed by the torture and suffering she had undergone in jail that her family did not recognize her when she was released. She had suffered a uterine prolapse because of the torture she had undergone.

The charges against prisoners often had no relationship to anything they might have done. The International Association of People's Lawyers (IAPL) described the case of Dodi Nanda, who was 'lying drunk on the roadside near Jagargonda when a mine blast took place at Tarrem. He was transported by army helicopter and when he came to, he found himself in Dantewada jail!' The IAPL found from the records that he had been charged under five separate and serious criminal cases, such as attacking police stations and killing policemen. Though these cases had been assigned to various lawyers in the Legal Aid Panel, meant to provide free legal aid to those who could not afford lawyers of their own, and two matters were at advanced stages, no lawyer had ever met Dodi Nanda.[4]

In later years, it became common for the police to arrest all the youth in a village en masse, causing entire villages to empty out. All the youth would escape to Andhra Pradesh for the mirchi harvest and only old people would be left behind. Several people were charged under cases they had never heard of, or that they had no idea they had been implicated in. Whenever there is a bomb blast or an attack on a government building, the police enter the accused as 'xyz and unknown others'. These unknown others are then fleshed out whenever the police need to charge someone with a crime. They get stock witnesses to say they heard the Maoists calling out certain names as they were firing or retreating.

Finding out what has happened to someone taken away is tortuous – with villagers running around between the local police and the jail, contacting their local MLA and any influential person they know to help. Women often land up in large groups at the police station to try to recover people who have been taken away. For Manish Kunjam, CPI leader in Konta, getting distress calls about villagers arrested and taken away has been a frequent occurrence over the last 10 years. Once found, the relatives sell their goats, their lands and whatever else they have to pay the lawyers who charge the maximum fees they can extract, starting from a minimum of Rs 20,000–30,000. Almost all the lawyers in Bastar are non-adivasi.

Even in ordinary cases, the legal system does not cater to adivasis, who are unfamiliar with Hindi or the kind of documentary evidence that courts require. In Chhattisgarh in 2007, there were 2.5 lakh cases pending, penalizing adivasis for minor forest offences. Across

India, many thousands languish in jail on minor charges because they cannot find the money required for bail or get any legal help. They very rarely meet their families, who live in distant villages and do not have the money or the resources to visit. Cut off from their homes, their fields and the blue sky, many of these prisoners fall into deep depression.

But so-called Naxalite prisoners face even more serious problems: they are not produced in court on security grounds, or hearings are endlessly delayed till an adequate security guard is made available or the witnesses – policemen or members of the paramilitary forces who had arrested them and who are subsequently posted elsewhere – turn up. They are routinely denied bail. Even if they are finally acquitted, most of them have already spent years inside. Sukal Prasad Nag, who was with the CPI when arrested, described how, on these court visits, all the prisoners would be lined up and repeatedly counted under heavy police presence. Often the police were so spiteful as to prevent them from meeting family members who had come to court.

In December 2007, there was a spectacular jailbreak in Dantewada, when some 370 prisoners escaped. I later met one of them in a village across the Indrawati, happy to be free after two years in jail on false charges. He said the jailbreak had been planned by two dalam members in jail: Suresh, who had been captured after an encounter in Konta, and Somru alias Verghese of Gettepatta village, who had been betrayed when planning an attack on the NMDC in Bacheli. It was Sunday around 5 p.m. when food was being dished out, and they went into the guardroom on the pretext of needing medicines. There was only a single guard there who they pushed into the sentry room, after which they broke open the cupboard and took out guns. He said the jailor was a good man, and even if he had been present, they would not have harmed him. The jailor was subsequently arrested.

Sukal Prasad Nag described his daily routine: tea between 5 and 6 a.m., which had no sugar and was sometimes so awful that prisoners threw it away; rice and dal at 9 a.m. The so-called dal was usually just water, and as for vegetables you had to be lucky to get even one radish leaf. The rice would smell so bad they couldn't eat it. Once a week they got some chickpeas and jaggery, but all the nutritious stuff the prisoners were supposed to get was sold off in the black market outside the jail. They got tea at noon and dinner at 4 p.m., were allowed out for 10 minutes after that and were then back in the lock-up. Another former prisoner talked of the white worms floating in the food, and the lack of medicines: whatever the illness, there was only one medicine available. Kopa Kunjam, an NGO worker who was framed and spent time in jail, described the awful overcrowding: they had to measure out sleeping space between the elbow and the hand. 'It was impossible to even turn over in one's sleep,' he said. 'You had to get up and lie down in the new position.'

After the CPI prisoners led a strike, Sukal Prasad Nag said, they got a fan and a television, but were not allowed to watch news, only songs. They were given no newspapers, and not allowed letters from home – only one postcard once a month was permitted. They were allowed meetings once a week for five minutes, but any food that the families brought was taken away by the jail authorities.

Little appears to have changed by 2016. The overcrowding has only got worse over the years and in 2015–16, the police have renewed their drives to arrest large numbers of youth.

7

The Sorrow of the Sabari

We have no roof over our heads
No goat to beat
No cock to crow
No vessels to cook in
No rice to eat
What sin have we done
That we should live like this
Who can save us from this
And let us go home?

Song sung by Usoor villagers living in the forest, 2007

The Judum was a time of massive dispersal and displacement. After Judum attacks, people either fled to the forests or were forcibly taken to camp. Some came on their own to forestall arson; others came only after repeated assaults. Sometimes half the village came, especially non-adivasi villagers, or sarpanches and their relatives who had been attacked by the Maoists; others stayed back. Suspicion grew like a thick wall between those in camps and the others. When people left, mothers were parted from sons who became SPOs, and husbands from wives, not realizing how deep the divide would become.

Many people lived in the forest for a few months or a year before finding life was too hard, and migrating to Andhra Pradesh after that, especially from villages around Basaguda and Konta, which were close to the border. A much smaller number went to Maharashtra or Odisha, where there was less employment available, while people in the villages across the Indrawati migrated further into the forest of the Marh. Some took refuge with relatives or contacts in the parts of Bastar that were not affected, such as Bhopalpatnam. Entire villages lay desolate, their inhabitants were scattered, the fields grew hard and the cows went missing. Sometimes, gangs of thieves rounded up the cattle and sold them in Andhra Pradesh.

No Relief from 'Relief Camps'

Images taken by a local photographer in Konta in February 2006 show long lines of villagers, including children, in a Salwa Judum procession which turned into a forced evacuation. Most of the men are armed with sticks; a few are carrying small bags. Judum leaders bring up the rear, the last one smiling for the camera. People came with just the bare essentials because they thought this was only temporary; in any case they could carry no more.

The geography and timing of the camps can only be explained by the course of the Judum attacks on villages, rather than any desire of the villagers to find relief from the Maoists. The first camps were set up by the government along the Bijapur highway in 2005, next to police stations – in Jangla, Matwada, Bhairamgarh, Gangalur. In 2006, as the Judum spread to Konta, camps came up along the Sukma–Konta highway – at Dornapal, Errabor, Injeram and Konta. Sometimes, people would be brought to one camp and then moved to another if the first one was too full. Following a third wave of Judum attacks on villages along the Konta border, a new makeshift camp came up at Maraigudem in early 2007.

Initially in 2005, the camps were mere rows of tarpaulin, occasionally covered with a blue plastic sheet, allowing in both the sun and the rain. The floor was bare and stony, most people had nothing to lie on, and the few aluminium vessels they had brought with them looked just as forlorn as their owners in these alien spaces. Some of the tents were next to sewage ponds, and just after the rains, the slush was knee high. Camps like Gangalur, which were housed in schools, were a little better, with some semblance of 'relief' efforts like blanket distribution. By early 2007, these camps looked more permanent, with huts made of bamboo and thatch walls and tin or tiled roofs built very close to each other.

These villagers had no experience of living in tightly packed settlements. Gond houses are set in large courtyards fenced in with big wooden stakes, or, if the wood has run out, bamboo poles. Trees surround the houses. The yards are cleaned daily and used to dry forest produce. Many houses have wooden pigpens close by, and fowl cluck around in the yard. The hamlets of a village are often a few kilometres apart, separated by fields and forest; even within a hamlet, houses may be situated several metres away from each other. Dhurwa and Dorla houses in the plains are set closer together, but here again, each house has its own yard and kitchen garden.

The CRPF encampment and the police station were at the core of every Judum camp, ringed by barbed wire and sandbags. Armed SPO sentries perched behind the sandbags, manning the checkposts. UNICEF had placed its distinctive tents – white with a blue mother-and-child logo – in all the camps. But rather than being used for children, they were used by SPOs as places in which they could hide and take up position, if attacked, or hang out and play cards.

The government allowed people to cut trees close to the camp for fuelwood and to build houses. Forest land was allotted for resettlement. A number of trees were also cut by the Judum leaders and sold in Andhra Pradesh in collusion with the forest department and the sawmills. After the trees had been cut, the shrubs were cleared to ensure the Maoists could not creep through the undergrowth to attack camps.

Even after the houses became more pucca, sanitary conditions remained terrible, a far cry from the 'well-laid townships' the government claimed they had built in submissions to the Supreme Court. Women, in particular, suffered because, with the trees gone and so many SPOs and security forces roaming around, there was nowhere private even to defecate. In Errabor and Dornapal camps in April 2007, women said they felt scared to go out at night, and the only place they could bathe was at the hand-pump, which was not only public but also filthy. They said the camps smelt of shit. According to a local medic, malaria, tuberculosis, typhoid and scabies were widespread.

All through this period, visitors would be shown Kasoli camp in Bijapur, a model camp where inmates were provided vocational skills. This was under the control of Chaitram Attami, one of the RSS men originally behind the Salwa Judum. UNICEF also collaborated with the state government to showcase 'improvement' and 'uplift' of the adivasis. A 2007 UNICEF promotional film on the Judum camps describes the children as witnesses to a 'dance of destruction by Naxal terrorists' (there was no mention of Judum attacks) and the excellent work UNICEF was doing teaching the children and their parents about cleanliness (never mind that adivasi villages are spotlessly clean), including how to brush their teeth with foaming toothpaste. When challenged in court, the government relied on a UNICEF report to assert that conditions in camps were up to 'internationally accepted standards on most indicators'.[1]

It is hard to know what UNICEF was thinking of, since even the official data provided by the government to the Supreme Court revealed that the camps were not up to much. For instance, most of the 426 community toilets planned for over 50,000 people in 23 camps, according to a 2009 affidavit, remained at the 'sanctioned' stage even by 2011, when most people had gone home. The government claims to have spent Rs 33.58 crore on the Salwa Judum camps from 2005 to 2010, but the results were largely invisible.[2] Periodically, there was talk of turning the camps into permanent revenue villages.

Life on Rations

Each camp resident was supposed to get half a kilo of rice a day, apart from pulses, sugar, kerosene, soyabean, tamarind, potato, onion, ginger, salt, cooking oil, chilli, cooking vessels and blankets. But few got any of this.

Camp leaders and traders colluded to appropriate the difference between what residents were sanctioned and what they actually received. Camp leaders inflated the numbers in camp. The traders charged on paper for supplying the entire amount, and then undersupplied. Even some of this came back for sale in the black market. One trader told me that he had refused to supply rations to camps, for fear of alienating the Maoists on whom he depended for his trade in the interior. Those who did business in the camps became millionaires, but at a cost, because they could not travel around freely for fear of the Maoists and had to shift house to Jagdalpur.

Apart from the money officially sanctioned for camps, the rations meant for the public distribution system (PDS) in the villages, as well as funds for village infrastructure normally routed through the panchayat, were diverted to camps, as if those in the villages no longer had a claim to the state. For instance, in 2008 there were 2000 people from some 15 villages in Maraigudem camp. The population of these 15 villages would amount to 7000–10,000 according to the 2001 census. Rations meant for this much larger number were now restricted to a mere 2000 people.[3] On paper, several roads and ponds were built in these camps – sometimes more than once.

For the villagers, confinement in camps meant severe hunger. Since food supplies fell short, people often fought over rations. The SPOs also strictly rationed the amount they could buy, suspecting that camp residents were secretly sending supplies to the Maoists. In their own villages, people supplemented their grain with fruits, leaves and tubers, and also supplemented their income by collecting mahua, tora and tendu. But this was not possible in the camps. If their original villages were close enough, they might be able to go back during the day to collect tora, but collecting mahua was difficult since this is usually a predawn activity. Sometimes, as in Gangalur, the original villagers resented the outsiders collecting forest produce. But if food was in short supply, liquor was not: every camp had a shop selling pouches of 'foreign liquor' as it is locally called.

Even as early as 2005, many people were dependent on wage work, mostly road widening. For people used to a mix of livelihood practices – cultivation, grazing cattle, collecting forest produce and wage labour – it was difficult to survive on the same controlled activity every day. The limited work provided in the camps under the National Rural Employment Guarantee Act (NREGA) also did not always guarantee payment. In 2010, villagers in Konta camp told me that they hadn't been paid under NREGA for work done two years earlier, clearing shrubs 100 metres on each side of a 40-kilometre stretch from Konta to Dornapal. In camps along the Konta road, many of the youth migrated to Andhra Pradesh for the mirchi harvest or to work in the Bhadrachalam paper mills. Some widows survived by working as domestics in the homes of camp leaders, traders and officials, and a quiet supply of sex work also began. With so many policemen and security forces around, and such massive displacement, this was inevitable; rumours circulated of an AIDS outbreak.

Because of the fears that had been built up of Maoist attacks if people went home, the government sent camp residents back under armed escort in trucks and tractors to salvage what they could from their old houses in order to build their homes in the camp. They also gave them tin sheets for roofs. Many felt their only future lay in siding with the government. A group of young women and men returning to camp on one such truck told me: 'What have the Naxals ever given us? At least the government is giving us tin for our houses and rice.' 'What after that?' I asked. They had no real reply: 'Aise pade rahenge' (We will just lie around here like this).

There was enormous corruption in house building too. In 2010, residents of Dornapal complained that those building on government land got Rs 12,000 to build permanent structures, while those structures that came up on private land were deemed temporary and merited only tin roofs and Rs 1500. But many villagers saw neither the tin nor the money.

After a while, even though villages were dispersed, social visits took place between relatives and acquaintances from different camps and even from nearby villages. But following rituals or celebrating festivals in the camps was impossible and, inevitably, organized religions made converts here. The RSS was active in some camps in Bijapur. In Errabor and Injeram in Konta, thanks to the Naga and Mizo India Reserve Battalion's need for pastors, Christian evangelicals from the Global Missionary Society and the Macedonia Society managed to convert at least 100 people, especially after the flood of 2007 which devastated Sukma and Konta. War made bedfellows out of the RSS and the evangelicals.

The government also organized mass weddings in camps, which were conducted by the Gayatri Parivar, a Hindu revivalist sect. In 2006–7, officials told me, 161 weddings had been performed in Konta and Injeram, 36 in Errabor and 1010 in Dornapal. But people were scarcely in the mood for love and sex, and birth rates fell sharply.[4]

Divided Villages, Divided Emotions

> Earlier we had no problem with the dada log; now we have heard they are saying they will beat all those who went to camp.
>
> Camp residents, 2007

> If the sarkar is your mai-baap, why are you asking to come home now?
>
> A resident who stayed behind in the village, 2007

Surrounded by SPOs and paramilitaries and under the watchful eye of camp leaders, not knowing when they could go home, people were reduced to both anger and helpless, vacant despair. When I visited Maraigudem soon after it had been set up in 2007, I saw several men just sitting around staring in a sad, empty kind of way, with no work and no life. In the first year of the Judum, the police distributed bows and arrows, so young men roamed around aimlessly and angrily, waiting for the next Maoist attack, which they had been told to expect. In June 2007 when I met women in Dornapal camp, they gathered in a flash mob and started shouting that their husbands had been killed. Despairing at the loss of fields and homes, they were ripe to be incited by the Salwa Judum leaders and to turn their anger in whatever direction the camp leaders pointed them towards.

The camps were tinderboxes of confused emotions; for instance, villagers who had been forced into camps were upset with those who had not joined them. As one person told me, 'Either we should not suffer at all or we should all suffer equally.' They were convinced that those still in the forests were better off; and they longed to go home but were terrified that the Maoists would accuse them of collaborating with the government. One village militia commander I spoke to in a village across the Indrawati said that he kept writing to people in camps to come back, but the Judum prevented them from leaving.

But fears were hard to dispel; there were indeed some cases of killing of SPOs who had gone home, and Judum leaders kept up the narrative that it was dangerous to return. In 2008 in the Hirapur camp, across a bridge from Basaguda where 'Maoist territory' began, the perfumed, safari-suited leader of the camp insisted: 'If you go that side, you will be killed. Every day three or four bodies are thrown here.' The ordinary camp residents, however, were more shamefaced when we discussed the burning of Lingagiri and Korsamadgu:

> Villager: Those who burnt the villages were outside Judum people; no one from here did it. [They fell silent for a bit.]
>
> Me: How will there be peace?
>
> Villager: If the Naxals allow development funds and voting, then things will be okay.

> Woman teacher: They [Naxals] have lost people's confidence. [A pause.] No one gained from the Judum – they brought us and left us midway, *na idhar ke rahe na udhar ke*. (We belong neither here nor there now.)

In 2010, the residents of Errabor camp wrote to the Supreme Court: 'We wish to return to our villages and cultivate in peace and without any fear. There have been mistakes from both sides and now we want reconciliation and peace. There should be peace talks between government and Maoists.'

As for those left in the forests or those whose villages were repeatedly burnt, they resented the fact that while everyone in the area (including some Judum leaders) had been helping the Maoists, they were singled out and repeatedly attacked as Maoist supporters. In Meruwaya, a cut-off village at the beginning of the Marh across the Indrawati on the Maoist side, Deva talked bitterly of those who had left: 'Why would people living in camps come back when they get to eat for free there? Here they would have to work to eat.'

Death in the Camps

> We lived freely in our villages – here we feel bound and imprisoned. We don't even get food here. And we feel unsafe here. Here people keep getting killed.
>
> Camp resident, 2008

If the majority of people from a village had joined a camp, anyone not living there was suspect. For instance, Podiyami Bhima of Kattanad was living with relatives in Surapara village 3–4 kilometres away from Matwada camp and would frequently go to the camp to visit others from his village. Once, however, when he went to buy vegetables, he was caught by two SPOs who asked him why he wasn't living in camp. He was taken away and killed. This was not an isolated incident, and I was to hear similar stories again and again.

But even when living in the camp for a long time, life was no less tenuous. In March 2008, five men were killed in Matwada camp by SPOs; one man, Somdu, survived. The description here is based on the testimony that Somdu and the widows of those killed gave the NHRC in June 2008. In March 2008, unknown persons killed Baman and Unga, two headmen from Matwada camp who used to take people for the Salwa Judum meetings. As punishment, the SPOs gathered all the people from their village, randomly picked out 10–15 men from the crowd, tied their hands behind with cloth towels and told them to run. Madkami Sukko and Podiyami Maso who were in front were shot. Many of the Matwada villagers witnessed this, but could say nothing. About a week after this incident, three other men, Markami Mudda, Markami Deva and Madvi Hidma, were equally gratuitously killed by drunk SPOs. Mudda was near the hand-pump, so the SPOs asked him to work it for them to drink; when he bent to get a drink of water himself, they hit him from behind with a stick. Deva, Hidma and Somdu were returning from a stream when they were picked up. Somdu somehow managed to escape but the other two were killed. The CRPF saw all this from a distance but did nothing. Nobody from the camp was allowed to go near the men. The SPOs then fired in the air so that they could claim there was an encounter and left the bodies lying there. In the morning, when the families brought the bodies to Matwada camp and complained to the sarpanch and the CRPF commander, they said they could do nothing. The Salwa Judum leader Vikram Mandavi and the thanedar Markam advised them to say that the Naxalites had killed the men since they would get compensation. The family members refused. It was only because the NGO Vanvasi Chetna Ashram filed a case in the Bilaspur High Court on their behalf that the widows got compensation.

Former chief minister Ajit Jogi once described in a public meeting in Delhi how Congress workers had told him they had stopped eating fish from the Sabari river that flows past the camps in Konta because so many bodies had been dumped in the river. When one looks at the Sabari today – limpid, rushing past rocks and bends, fringed with trees like dark eyelashes, buffaloes buried deep in the sand, with red and cream boats waiting to take people across to Odisha – it is hard to imagine the horror.

From Human Shields to Re-establishing Human Relations

> We came back to our village in March this year to pluck mahua, leaves, etc. and have not gone back since then. But we do not know if we will be allowed to cultivate and whether the Salwa Judum will call us back to the camps. They hadn't let us cultivate in the past two years.
>
> Bogampad resident, 2008

> I do come back to the village and work in the fields, but I stay there for two days, and the next two days in the camp. I would like to permanently come back to my village but I don't, because I fear that the Salwa Judum and police will attack my family and me again.
>
> Cheruguda resident, 2009

People went back home in stages. On the Bijapur side, people started to escape in 2006 itself. Some left on the pretext of temporarily collecting mahua and stayed on, but were always worried about being summoned back. In some camps, after a year or so, people were allowed to cultivate their fields during the day, but had to return to camp at night. In other camps, one person from each household was retained as surety. Roll calls were taken. If a village was marked as a Maoist stronghold, the men were retained in camp while the women were allowed to stay at home to look after the cattle. When the *gaita* (priest) wanted to visit the village to conduct the necessary agricultural rituals, he was taken under police escort, lest he establish contact with the Maoists. The Judum leaders retained people as human shields, knowing that if the majority of villagers went home, they would be more vulnerable to attack in the camps.

On the Konta side, the first major exodus from the camps took place after November 2007, emboldened by the CPI's huge public rally against the Judum in Jagdalpur. In 2011, the government reported to the Supreme Court that the numbers in camp had come down by over half, to some 25,000. Sometimes, people managed to pay off the Judum leaders or SPOs to allow them to go home. For instance, the Koyapadu villagers paid Kiche Nanda Rs 3000–5000 per household to be allowed to leave Polampalli camp.

In some cases, however, villagers themselves did not completely want to sever all connection with the camps after returning home. In Dornapal camp, as long as rations were being handed out, households would send a family member back to collect them on a fortnightly basis. A house in camp became useful real estate. Since schools now only operated in camps, it was also convenient to have somewhere to stay if you had children studying.

It took a long time for people to settle back home. For one, the fields had compacted. For another, till all the villages in an area had come back, it was not possible to cultivate, since unclaimed cattle could damage crops. The Errabor people were keen to return to their regular homes, but could not till those from neighbouring Irla also returned and tied their cattle. In some places, the government provided seeds to people returning home, but more often these were purchased out of their own earnings from Andhra Pradesh or borrowed from neighbouring villages which had escaped attacks.

Re-establishing relations with villagers who had made other choices also took time. In Manikonta, where 13 men had been killed in a Maoist 'jan adalat' in 2006, different hamlets came back at different times between 2008 and 2011 – from the camps, from the forests with the Maoists and from Andhra Pradesh. In July 2012, they all held a meeting in the hamlet by the road and decided to bury the past. Everyone was happy to be back in the village, and even those who had been most vocal against the Maoists in camp earlier admitted that village life was infinitely better than being in camp.

The only people still unable to return home in 2015–16 are the sarpanches, SPOs and the families of Judum leaders. Moreover, Jagargunda camp continues to function and gets rations from the government which are provided under police escort every six months.

In the Crosshairs of the Conflict

> People are happy when we attack camps.
>
> Gudsa Usendi, Maoist spokesperson to ICI, May 2006

Even as the SPOs randomly killed people in the camps as a pastime, they were always on edge for fear of a Maoist attack. The government told the Supreme Court in February 2011 that the camps had been attacked 34 times since 2005. The attacks were usually made possible by informers in camps, sometimes Maoists turned SPOs who then escaped and rejoined the Maoists.

The Maoists initially described their attacks on camps as an attempt to liberate the people from 'concentration camps', as in the attack on Gangalur camp in January 2006 when seven SPOs were killed, and the attack on Injeram in May 2006 when four SPOs were killed. They claimed that camp residents had themselves pointed the SPOs out; this was a time when they wore no uniforms or badges. However, after an attack on Errabor camp in July 2006, where 32 people died, and one on Rani Bodli in March 2007, the camps became better fortified and the number of attacks went down.

In Rani Bodli, the police had set up their camp inside a girls' school and hostel. Newspapers reported that some 400 Maoists attacked the camp, killing 55 policemen, including 39 SPOs, in an assault that lasted for some three hours. The policemen were mostly drunk and sleeping. The three sentries who should have kept watch ran away and took refuge among the girls. Many of the SPOs who died in this assault were minors. Throughout the assault, the Maoists ensured that the girls were kept to one side and were unharmed. Six

Maoist cadre also died in that attack.[5] For a long time, Rani Bodli was emblematic of Maoist militarism till it was superseded by a larger-scale killing of CRPF jawans in 2010.

Life in the Forest

> All those who have stayed back in the villages are Maoists or sangham members.
>
> Chief Secretary, Chhattisgarh, to ICI, May 2006

> The revolutionary masses of DK, while taking up counter offensive operations did not neglect measures either for self-defence or production work. People of many villages have set up sentry posts along the four corners of their village to maintain a twenty-four-hour vigil. Some others constructed temporary shelters in deep forest pockets. People removed all their grain, livestock, money and other valuables to safe dumps in the forest. They are continuing their agricultural activities under the protection of the people's militia and other wings of the PLGA. It will not be an exaggeration to say that almost each and every village from Kattanad to Kunta have become bastions of mass resistance.
>
> *People's March*, January 2007

Choosing not to go to camp was not just a political choice – supporting the Maoists – but also an existential one. People said that they may have had nothing to eat at home, but they had more freedom, and at least they were in or near their own villages. The Maoist squads in the forest protected them. Such 'communities of resistance' are found across guerrilla conflicts, whether in Dantewada or El Salvador or Colombia.

The Maoists did their best to persuade villagers to stay. Deve of Vangeel was killed on 19 June 2010, defending the villagers while harvesting:

> During the Salwa Judum days she used to stay with the people of the village, did sentry day and night and she was always alert and ready to attack the Judum goons. Later Deve even did propaganda among the people who had gone to the *sibirs* (camps) and tried to make them understand who the real enemies were. She convinced them to return to their villages and was successful in many cases in making them return.[6]

However, everyone lived in constant fear of another Judum attack. Mothers recounted to me how they had to silence their children to keep the forces from finding them. Dogs and cocks had to be slaughtered to prevent betrayal. Initially, when the Judum was stealing bags and looting, the Maoists booby-trapped the houses. Because of this, the Judum then decided it was easier to just burn all the houses.

People survived on whatever little grain they had managed to rescue from the fire, tendu fruit and roots. The Maoists helped by sending grain from other villages which had not been burnt and sending teams of villagers to help rebuild houses. The party also arranged for some supplies from rice traders, or through networks of individuals who brought rice over from Andhra Pradesh for their relatives in the forests.

The food was just enough to keep people from dying. One family from Gangapadu whom I met in Andhra Pradesh recounted that the rations were 1 kilo of rice for 30 people every day, which barely allowed the adults to sip the cooking water. When even this ran out, everyone left for Andhra Pradesh. Typically, one or two persons in a village stayed back to keep an eye on the houses and fields.

Where the Maoists were strong, they ensured fields were cultivated. In villages where people had left for camp after the fields were sown, the squads supervised the cutting of their grain with sentries keeping a watch. Sometimes the grain was kept for the villagers in the hope that they would return, and sometimes distributed among those left behind, along with their cattle and roof tiles.

On the other hand, the Judum and police harvested lands that had been collectively sown under Maoist leadership to be distributed to poorer families, as in the government-owned Pamelvaya farm. And in an effort to starve people out, the Judum searched for hidden stocks of grain in the forest and burnt those too.

What It Means to Be an Unbreakable Arm of the Broken Indian State

Over time, the landscape across Dantewada changed. The highways became Judum territory, and the villages became Maoist country, so far as camp residents and forces were concerned. On their part, people began to barricade the approach roads to their village by felling trees and laying them across the tracks, cutting the paths and digging up the bridges. They dug neat square pits which were filled with bamboo spikes and *chhind* thorns and covered up with mud, so that unsuspecting CRPF men would step on these traps and get pierced. These were pitiable measures in the face of hundreds of troops and helicopters, but effective, nonetheless, in a small way.

Men grazing cows or children playing with catapults kept a lookout for troop movements. Sometimes the warning systems set up between villages did not work. For instance, villagers from Khumarpalli whom I met in Andhra Pradesh said they neither received intimation from the Judum to join their meetings or any warning that they were going to hold a meeting in their village. They heard that the Judum had burnt a neighbouring village, so they all ran away in anticipation; but the Judum turned back that day before they reached Khumarpalli. After two days they came again, and this time there was nobody left in the neighbouring villages to give information.

If the villagers in the forests were determined to keep the troops out, the Judum was equally determined not to let any of these villagers enter their area. The SPOs patrolled river crossings and checkpoints through which people might cross in order to access the markets or the limited health care available. The only people who crossed the barriers were the SPOs and troops when they went in for raids, and the tendu leaf traders.

On a trip to Meruwaya across the Indrawati in June 2009, I came across a three-year-old girl, Kope, who had fallen into the fire while her mother was cooking. Her stomach was badly burnt and her skin had peeled off and was bleeding. Both parents were sitting by her side utterly distraught; her mother was constantly fanning her and suckling her to comfort her when she cried. They had tried the local healer, but that didn't help. They couldn't take her to the Tumnar health centre across the river because the Judum wouldn't let anyone come peacefully from that side. They were only three and a half hours from help, and yet a whole world away. If you chose to live on the Maoist side of the river, the Judum insisted, you had no claims on the Indian state.

With half the population in camps, and the rest in the forest or in Andhra Pradesh, the traditional pattern of a cycle of haats in different villages in an area was also badly disrupted. Even as early as November 2005, the Sagkeli villagers had stopped going to haats, and relied on traders to come to their village to buy mahua which they exchanged for salt. Later, large groups of 130–140 women from Sagkeli started coming to Bijapur, leaving their homes very early in the morning. They sold 30 kilos of fuelwood for Rs 30 in order to buy rice; and as soon as they reached home around 3 p.m., they would have to start collecting again for the next day. Since the ration shops had been shut down for the interior villages on the grounds that they were deserted and everyone was in camp, they had to buy the rice on the open market.

People walked 40–60 kilometres to buy rice from ration shops or haats located in safer places like Orcha or in Andhra Pradesh, where they would not be recognized or accused of taking rice for the Maoists. The Judum taunted people from the forest villages: 'Don't the Maoists feed you, that you are buying rice from our shops?' In 2008, the Andhra Pradesh police stopped Chhattisgarh adivasis buying rice from markets in their state, and also forbade Andhra traders from taking rice into Chhattisgarh haats.

Morna – Cut Off from the Constitution

One of the first stretches along which Judum attacks occurred was the Bijapur–Gangalur road. We first visited Morna in 2005 to find it deserted, and the neighbouring village – tired of hiding in the jungles at night – ready to 'surrender' to the Judum. I went back in 2012. The forests had covered up any track of a motorable road, and the jeep had to skirt around tree trunks lying across the path. It was cloudy, and the area felt wild and desolate. There was no one to ask for directions. When we finally reached the first sign of habitation, we met some very young boys with catapults, sharp knives and a radio, who took us to a hut where we talked to some slightly older youth. They asked for the newspaper we had with us, saying they had been starved of any news for months. Morna is one of the many villages that chose to stay away from the camps, and suffered for it.

Out of the 75 houses in the village, 65 had been burnt in 2005. Five people were killed by the Judum and Naga forces that year: they had been picked up while they were harvesting grain and taken to camp to be killed. Two girls were raped and badly beaten.

After this the whole village fled and set up little huts in the forest. Even these were burnt at the beginning of 2006, and all the grain and clothes they had saved were destroyed. The village decided to send women to Bijapur to buy grain with whatever little money they had managed to save on their persons. When the women were returning, the Judum snatched all their grain and they came back empty-handed. So they went to neighbouring villages which had not yet been burnt (they were subsequently burnt in 2007) and begged for grain. Initially, the jan militia tried to protect them in the jungle but one day an entire company of police came and started firing, so they abandoned the attempt. The youth told us:

> The living conditions in the jungles were very hard: small children died of malaria; we had to treat snakebites with herbs found in the jungle; people fell and got lost while running in the jungle at night. On some days there was no food because we couldn't afford to light a fire since the police were patrolling. We lived like that for three to four months, and then we migrated to Bhadrachalam and to Uperu and Vadagunda in Andhra. After doing coolie work for four or five months, we all came back to the village in May–July 2007. Coolie life was very hard. If you fell ill and couldn't work, you starved. We decided we will die but will not leave our land again.

But after they came back, they were attacked again. The Judum and the Naga forces came in the 2007 monsoons and burnt around eight houses in one hamlet. Four people were killed, including one who, villagers said, was killed at the mother goddess shrine, and his tongue removed. In 2009, 14 persons were arrested and, as of mid-2012, were still in jail. On 22 May 2012, the forces took away two more persons to Dantewada jail. They claimed they found a gun, tiffin bomb and detonator in Budu's house, but the villagers insisted that there had been nothing there. Budu had been arrested in 2005, released in 2010 and then arrested again in 2012.

Even in 2012, everyone who was 14 years or older climbed the hills every single night to sleep, leaving around 5–6 p.m. after eating and returning at 8 a.m. Only old people were left in the village at night. In the hills, they had to shift spots every night in case the police found them, and sit up under umbrellas all night if it rained.

By 2012, the SPOs were allowing women to get rice from the Bijapur ration shop. The Morna school had been functioning till 2005. But after the police camped there four or five times, the villagers themselves destroyed it. After coming back from Andhra Pradesh, the villagers pooled money to pay Rs 600 to a boy, who had passed class 7, to teach smaller kids, but he was taken to jail in 2011. And that was the end of all the 'services' like health or education available to them.

8

Border Crossings

> If the Judum had simply said come to camp, I would have gone; but after seeing them burn houses, I preferred to run away.
>
> We are scared – both sides accuse us of joining the other. We will not go back even if called. We would rather die here.
>
> Displaced persons in Andhra Pradesh, 2007

Khammam, just across the border from Konta on the Andhra Pradesh side,[1] is flat and open, and much less forested. In the toddy season, you can see professional tappers out on their cycles with their knives in sheaths of wood and skin, and black coiled ropes which are tied around their waists when they climb. An occasional snake slithers across the road into the fields of red chillies, cotton and tobacco. The sickly sweet stench of the Ballarpur paper mills fills the area, and people have taken to growing eucalyptus in greenhouses on contract. Sometimes, you see forest department lands with a hammer and sickle where the CPI(M) and CPI(ML) New Democracy which are active in Andhra Pradesh had earlier helped farmers to take over land. The villages and towns are more prosperous, with clean toilets at the bus stand.

As far as adivasi culture goes, the border is an artificial one. The

Chhattisgarh Dorlas near the Andhra Pradesh border have marriage links, a common language and common customs with the Andhra Koyas (also called Koya Doras). The Marias, however, are seen as distinctively Chhattisgarhi, and called Gotti Koyas (archer Koyas) in Andhra Pradesh. They know how to make landa, which the Andhra Koyas do not, and where to get the best mahua from. For a while, Gotti Koya songs became the rage in the border villages. The Gotti Koyas, of course, all learnt Telugu.

There have been successive waves of migration over the decades, both seasonal and permanent, from Chhattisgarh to Andhra Pradesh. Much of the initial migration to Andhra Pradesh came from villages around Sukma, which first settled forest lands in Golapalli and Kistaram, before moving further afield to find fresh land in Andhra Pradesh. Networks of brokers developed. For instance, a Telugu Desam Party leader from Sarvel made Rs 5 lakh over eight years by settling 30 families from the Sukma area in his village. He promised to get them titles on government land but never allowed them to accompany him to government offices to do any paperwork. Finally, in 2006, the villagers gave up on him, and shifted to forest land on their own. Seasonal migration to work on the red chilli fields of Andhra Pradesh is even more common. The Gotti Koyas are willing to do jobs the locals will not do, and work at lower rates, leaving the latter free to work on the higher-paying work available under NREGA.

However, when the Judum started, the influx was unprecedented. People fled to places where they knew farmers who had hired them in the past, or where they had relatives. Sometimes they followed someone from their village who had migrated for land in the past. Many of those fleeing walked long distances to get to Andhra Pradesh. For instance, some families from Sambi near Usoor walked for two days to reach Cherla, the nearest market town on the Andhra side, and then another day to reach their current location, where they knew people from previous chilli harvest years. A fortunate few who fled before their village was burnt managed to pay for transport to bring along their household goods and cattle. Even though sangham members tried to persuade them to stay in the forest and fight, it became more difficult after the food started running out. Many had no appetite for struggle, and found it impossible with the daily combing operations. They hid their vessels and household items in caves in the forest, and their money beneath the earth.

The refugees, called Internally Displaced Persons (IDPs) in NGO and official parlance, set up small shelters wherever they could – sometimes just a small platform of bamboo supported by four poles, open from all sides, under which they could shelter from the sun, out on forest land, on the road or in ditches. Many farmers would not let them live on the fields where they worked, in case they stole. But other farmers agreed on payment, and even helped with tarpaulin. Slowly, the shelters grew walls and doors, but even after a few years, the settlements continued to look makeshift – a collection of huts with thatch roofs and a few stray chickens – a far cry from the tree-shaded, hill-surrounded villages of tiled roof houses from where they had come, leaving behind their gods. Cattle, pigs and goats were, especially in the early years, conspicuous by their relative absence, being far too expensive to purchase afresh in Andhra. However, some had managed to keep their cattle with relatives in Andhra, knowing how bad the situation in Chhattisgarh was. Water became a perennial problem, especially for those who lived out on forest land, far away from any regular settlement.

Relations with locals varied. Sometimes two or three IDP families were absorbed into regular villages, but more often, they settled on the edge of a regular village, on nearby forest land. I spoke to a settlement of 13 families in the Enkotur reserve forest who had fled from Kamlapadar when they saw neighbouring villages being burnt. They had walked for two days from village to village in Andhra, children in tow, before renting a room for Rs 50 per month from a shepherd. Three families lived in that room. Once settled, they hired a tractor owner to bring their grain and vessels from Kamlapadar, but had to sell most of their grain and a goat to pay him. Then they moved to Enkotur village, 10 kilometres away from the mirchi farm where they worked. There they got into a fight with a local Kamma farmer because their cattle ate his paddy. He accused them of bringing sangham members to defend them, so they moved to the reserve forest, where forest department officials came and threatened them for cutting trees. But they were convinced things would never get better in Chhattisgarh, and tough as it was in Andhra, it was safer than at home.

Later, as the Judum began cross-border operations and began to attack even the settlements in Khammam where people thought they were relatively safe, they burrowed deeper south in Andhra, going to places as far as Warangal, Adilabad and Karimnagar. Some went to Hyderabad where they worked as construction labour, and were easily cheated. Joga described how when a group of them got off at the station, an auto driver took them to a local paper mill. The supervisor of the mill then told the boys that the auto driver had taken their money and they would have to work free for him for a month. They were rescued by local NGOs after one of them managed to escape and seek help for the others.

In some places, the local farmers asked them to move on because of harassment by the police who were convinced that they were supply conduits for the Maoists in Chhattisgarh. Scared refugees also narrated stories of people being picked up from Andhra by SPOs and taken to Judum camps in Chhattisgarh.

The police are perennially suspicious of the Gotti Koyas bringing back Maoism to the 'disinfected' fields of Khammam, and use their presence to file 'bind-over' cases both on the Judum refugees and their hosts. These bind-over cases involve periodic reporting to the thana – sometimes every day, sometimes once a week – and even more conveniently, having to do free labour for the police, such as cutting grass, bringing water and cleaning the station. In the CRPF camps that have now come up across Bastar division too, conscripting village labour to work for free is common practice.

The Andhra forest department, for its part, reacted to

'encroachments' on forest land by burning the homes of the migrants and arresting them. However, those who came in search of land were determined to stick it out. Each time the department attacked, they would rebuild their houses. It takes four or five days to build a house, and one or two days to cut grass for thatch, apart from a few thousand rupees. In one village where the forest department had filed a case against six settlers, they managed to get out after posting bail of Rs 12,000. They raised the money from the local villagers by promising to pay their electricity bills at a later stage. They also had to pay lawyers' fees. But as one said: 'Having suffered the beatings and cut the land, why would I go back now?'

Things eased up after the Human Rights Forum (HRF) filed a case in the Andhra Pradesh High Court in 2007, which directed the forest department not to burn their homes, especially of those fleeing from the Judum. In one settlement in Warangal, which had been attacked by the forest department some 30 times, the foresters had given up in the face of their tenacity and started employing them to cut grass in its eucalyptus plantation.

I personally met only one family in Andhra Pradesh – among the hundreds who were fleeing Judum – who had left Konta because of Maoist threats. The man said the Maoists accused him of spending too much time with the police. His family had owned a mill and 50 acres in Bodaguppa, which was redistributed by the Maoists along with 300 sacks of rice.

The Fiery Harvest

The chilli harvesting season in Andhra Pradesh lasts from February to April, and is almost entirely run through migrant labour from Chhattisgarh. The wage rates have been steadily increasing (from Rs 40 in 2007 to Rs 100 in 2012), which makes it an attractive proposition for the Bastar adivasis, especially because there is no employment in their villages. They also get one basket of mirchi for every 12 baskets plucked, which is shared among the group of cutters. The work is not so hard, they say, but takes all day in the searing heat. After the chillies are plucked, they are spread out to dry, in big fiery-red lots.

Even after they returned to their villages for good, many people continued to visit Andhra Pradesh for the harvest. One evening in March 2012, sitting in Matpalli, I saw long lines of men leaving for work in Andhra Pradesh, carrying bundles on their shoulders, and another five or six men on cycles laden with sacks returning home from work in Andhra Pradesh. They said they call the farmers when they reach Cherla to enquire if they need labour, or learn where to go through bush telegraph.

Apart from the mirchi harvest, the Gotti Koyas also found agricultural work harvesting grain (from November onwards before the mirchi harvest begins) or picking cotton. The IDPs also sold firewood, ropes and bamboo mats. In March 2011, I met an old couple from Paledbanda village who had migrated to Andhra, along with their daughter who worked on the mirchi harvest. They survived by selling broomsticks in the Edguralapally haat, at Rs 4 apiece, every Friday. When I asked how much they ate every day, the old lady laughed and showed me a fistful of rice. Her husband wiped away a tear and said he missed his old village and wanted to die there. More often, the old people and animals were left behind in the Chhattisgarh villages while all able-bodied persons migrated, including children. These elderly residents would collect forest produce like mango, mahua or gum, which were then sold by their families in the Andhra markets. Women who did the market work had to walk from 6 a.m. to 2 p.m. to reach the Andhra markets.

There was a little more food in Andhra than found in the forests of Chhattisgarh, where, after a Judum attack, an entire village might have to subsist on a sack of rice for a month. In normal circumstances, a family of four or five persons would eat 2 kilos of rice each day; in Andhra, 10 people survived on the same amount. But even some years after they had been in Andhra, I found families where the adults were eating only once a day so that the children had enough to eat. The diet was also less varied than in their home villages. In 2009, a group of NGOs in Andhra Pradesh surveyed 482 refugee children and found that 76.6 per cent of them were in various stages of malnutrition, with 27.2 per cent suffering from third-grade or severe malnutrition.[2] All the money they made on the mirchi harvest was spent on food – they were unable to make any savings. Even broken rice cost Rs 12 a kilo on the open market in 2011, while dal was simply too expensive to buy.

The Long Road Home

The government of Chhattisgarh claimed, both in and outside court, that the IDPs had gone of their own accord to Andhra Pradesh in search of land, and not because they were fleeing from the Salwa Judum. In any case, they said, they were all Naxalites, implying the state was well rid of them. If they did want to come back, they told the Supreme Court, they would be put into 19 specially marked camps along the road. Little wonder that few refugees were keen to take up this generous offer.

However, some NGOs, notably the Vyavasayaka Mariyu Sanghika Abhivrudhi Samstha (Agriculture and Social Development Society, ASDS) and ActionAid in Khammam and the VCA in Dantewada persuaded a few villages to return. After the NHRC visit in June 2008, Himanshu Kumar of the VCA decided to adopt two villages, from among those who came to depose before the NHRC. In what was publicized as a 'human shield experiment', the VCA deployed some of its workers to live in Nendra and Lingagiri, and help rehabilitate people.

When I visited Nendra in December 2008, a small band of volunteers were camped out under a blue tarpaulin near the school. The road to Nendra was full of tall grass, which stuck to our clothes. But the villagers who had come back were relieved to be home – a small moment of hope and respite before it would all begin again. None of them had celebrated any festivals for three years. They had nothing to cover themselves with at night, and it was very cold. We huddled around a fire, one girl wearing a man's shirt to keep warm. The only consumer item I saw in all my time in the village was a cheap plastic mirror. The hand-pumps had been destroyed by the Judum, and the only source of water was a dirty pond. But slowly, life was being rebuilt – the women were starting to go again to the haats, selling gourds and fish, making baskets and cots.

In Lingagiri, ActionAid helped with some immediate relief like rice and clothes, while the Bijapur administration, under an earnest young Collector, Prasanna, worked with the VCA to provide seeds and tractors. Some kind of survey was carried out, but no one was given compensation. Once the villagers from Andhra returned, those resident in camps also followed. There was a reconciliation meeting in the village, after which they started cultivating collectively. In 2012, when I visited Lingagiri, en route to Sarkeguda where 17 people had just been killed by the CRPF, the whole area was traumatized again. It brought back memories of 2006 when the Judum had first attacked the village and four people were killed.

By far the most important factor in influencing people to return, however, was not NGOs but a big rally that the CPI held in November 2007 in Jagdalpur, which seems to have taken the edge off the fear somewhat. By 2008, many villagers were slowly beginning to return home on their own, as I show with the story of Cherapalli. But to this day, 2016, fresh attacks trigger new rounds of migration, making the border a zone of constant movement, and some families have decided never to return from Andhra even though many people from their villages have gone home and they are being pressed by their relatives to come back.

In 2015, I visited three settlements which were aspiring to permanence. The residents said there was work available in Andhra Pradesh, and it was safer than in Chhattisgarh. The houses had become more permanent, in some cases indistinguishable from older Koya settlements. People had acquired plastic chairs, cots, even a steel cupboard – and more importantly, ration cards and even voter IDs.

In one settlement, we saw a large herd of cows and goats, which had been brought over from Chhattisgarh. Some families had started their seed-sowing hunts in their new settlements, known here as *bhum pandum*, adopting either the existing mother goddess of the Koya settlement to which they were attached, or establishing their own devis, like Danteshwari. Some had also acquired a new religion. I met a plump evangelical pastor of the Bible Baptist Goodness Church, who ran a vigorous musical Sunday service. I left as the loudspeakers started blaring.

The Chronicle of Cherapalli

The road to Cherapalli crosses two streams, the sandy banks on either side shaded by trees, to arrive at what used to be a relatively large and prosperous settlement. Cherapalli has three hamlets. Before the Judum, its 160 houses all had electricity; there was a primary school and a panchayat bhawan; and houses with red brick tiled roofs stood next to leafy old trees of tamarind and mango. It was the sort of village one might be proud of coming from. The story of Cherapalli encapsulates the history of the region, especially over the last 10 years. Since the first attack in 2006, the villagers said the Salwa Judum had come through the village some 17–18 times; but four of these rounds were especially horrible.

In August 2008 when I first visited the village, people were slowly trickling back after nearly two years away. After the Judum burnt their homes in repeated attacks in 2006–7, most villagers fled to Andhra. A few, like the Kumhars – potters – had taken shelter with relatives up north. Now a wedding was being celebrated in the village for the first time since 2006, a small sign of normalcy. The groom's party had brought the bride home; all night, I could hear the drums and the girls dancing rhythmically, barely lifting their feet, swaying in perfect unison, singing. The Cherapalli villagers were giving shelter to 22 families from the neighbouring village of Tadvehi, who had also returned from Andhra. They wanted to go home but were nervous because the other Tadvehi villagers had spent the last two years in the Judum camps. Would each side be able to accept the other after the separation, which had been not just physical but also ideological?

As I walked around the village in the morning, people were surveying the damage to their houses, clearing out the burnt vessels and the heaps of ash. The brick houses could be repaired but the mud ones had blackened and fallen in the rain, and rather than live in these old houses, families built new structures next to them. Initially, there was a shortage of chhind leaves for the thatch and wood, so two or three families would live together till they were able to build separate houses for each one, over a period of two or three years. Now very few houses have tiled roofs, since the price of each tile has gone up from Re 1 to Rs 10. Luckily, their agricultural implements had been in the fields when the village was burnt, so most of those were saved, while the cattle, which had run away, had to be coaxed back.

The villagers gathered to meet me and we talked – of the past, of the Judum, of the future. In the 1990s, like many other villages in Konta, everyone in Cherapalli voted for the CPI. The sarpanch, Anda, had been active with the student wing of the CPI. When the Maoists were beginning to establish themselves, he complained that while the Maoists insisted on strict equality within the village, they placed no such restrictions on outsiders like the contractors. The Maoists broke his arm, and the villagers then quietly decided to go over to them. Like everyone else, they boycotted elections, formed a sangham and listened to what the dalam told them.

Cherapalli was one of the villages whose burning Mahendra Karma personally supervised.[3] On 15 April 2006, between 1 and 3 p.m., Karma and the Judum set fire to 127 houses in the *bade para* (big hamlet). Since the Judum had burnt Talamadgu on their way to Cherapalli, the villagers were forewarned and hid near the river. The Judum fired arrows tipped with chhind leaves and kerosene oil, aiming at the rafters because they knew grain was hidden there. Luckily, a big storm that night doused some of the fire, but the houses smouldered for many days after. A little rice was saved and, even though it smelled terribly, it was enough to survive on.

One of the villagers, Joga, told me that when he ventured out to see what was happening, he was taken to Mahendra Karma who boxed and slapped him. Then local Salwa Judum leader Ram Bhuwan Kuswaha hit him on the chest with a rifle butt and abused him for not coming to camp. He said the SPOs took him to Polampalli camp where he was tied up and left out in the rain all night. But one of the SPOs, Kiche Rama, had loosened the rope somewhat, so he managed to slip out around 7 a.m. and escape.

The villagers said the Judum burnt 42 houses on a subsequent visit in October/November 2006. Ten-year-old Bhima, with a close-cropped round head, was brought to see me. He stoically described how his father, Kalmu Waga, had been picked up by the Judum, beaten all the way to Toyapara and there tied to a post in one of the *ladis* – the open shelters constructed in fields – surrounded with dry leaves and burnt alive. His mother, Lakke, died some six months later, worn down with grief and desperation. She tried to hide her two small children from the constant attacks and look after them, but finally gave up. The family then split. Bhima's five-year-old brother was taken in by their maternal grandmother in another village, while Bhima continued to live in Cherapalli with a widowed aunt, who supported the two of them by selling mahua and tora. Incidentally, Kalmu Waga and Mahendra Karma shared the same grandparents.

At the same time as they killed Kalmu Waga, the Judum took away others. The 60-year-old patel, Dudhi Unga, was saved by the thanedar of Dornapal who told him to run away. Two teenage brothers, Hidma and Kosa, were picked up from their fields. Kosa managed to escape before they reached camp, on the pretext that he had to shit, but Hidma was in jail for two years. He had to pay Rs 8000 to the clerk, and give his land title as surety, to get out. Polampalli camp was established around this time, increasing the frequency of SPO visits.

In December 2006–January 2007 too, the SPOs burnt houses,

and killed a man. Sodi Masa's widow described how her husband had got caught:

> Thinking they had left, my husband and two others went to see the damage to their houses. They then drank water at the boring pump. Hearing the sound of the boring hand-pump, the SPOs came back and fired indiscriminately. Hunga and Manga managed to escape, but my husband was shot and died of two bullet wounds. Since he was carrying an election ID card, a patta and Rs 2500, the SPOs realized he was not a Naxalite and left the body lying in the village. They took away the money and documents. The next morning the villagers went in search, found the body and cremated him. We were too scared to file an FIR, and it would have been pointless since he had been killed by SPOs.

After a year or so, she said, when she came back from Hantapad village where she had taken refuge, and resumed going to Polampalli haat, she was able to get her husband's ID and patta back, through a man from the village.

In July 2007, the SPOs raped two girls. Fifteen-year-old Hurre told me she had recently returned from Andhra and was grinding grain at home, when five SPOs dragged her out, blindfolded her, tied her hands behind her back and told her mother they were taking her to Polampalli. They raped her en route, breaking her jewellery in the process. When I met her, Hurre had just had new jewellery made. Seventeen-year-old Bheeme said she had been living with her aunt in Kottapalli, having just returned to the village the week before. She described how she had been breaking tora in the courtyard of her house, when the SPOs came.

> They tied my hands and feet and blindfolded me and all four gang-raped me. They tore all my clothes and broke my jewellery. After that, I managed to escape on the pretext of drinking water and hid in a grain bin in someone's house. I recognize three of the SPOs

> – Rajesh (Oriya) from Polampalli, Kiche Soma of Korrapad and Linga from Palamadgu. Even after this incident they came to my house and threatened me. I was too scared to report to the police, and anyway, what would have been the point? I was even too scared to go to the market for fear of being caught and raped again. After being beaten and raped, my body was badly swollen. I also suffered a snakebite while running away that day. I could not go to a doctor and was treated with desi medicine.

The sarpanch, Anda, said he had been sitting with the officer in charge of the combing operations, when these rapes occurred. The SPOs phoned the officer, saying they were bringing two Naxalite girls. Anda recalled that the officer kept asking them why they were delaying.

Between the first few attacks, the villagers kept their grain in the school and panchayat bhawan to prevent the forces from staying there and the Maoists from blasting the buildings. They also blocked the road with fallen trees. It was only in 2008, when they came back, that they cleared the road so that mahua could be transported. All three times the houses were burnt, the Maoists sent teams of people from other villages to help them rebuild or at least provide immediate relief. But finally, uncertain what would happen next, everyone fled to the forest, living in makeshift huts under trees. No cultivation was possible that year or the next.

The entire village migrated to Andhra. But one or two villagers would come back occasionally to check on their land. Anda says he never really left but hung around close by, making sure that the gods were not neglected. Once some SPOs caught him fishing and told him not to linger lest the Mizo jawans took him for a Naxalite. They also confessed to him that they were unhappy with their jobs.

Through the testimonies – horrifying as they are – we get a glimpse of the contingencies created by civil war. Kinship with Mahendra Karma did not save Kalmu Waga, but on the other hand, sometimes the police or SPOs took pity on people they knew. ID cards and land titles served as tenuous indicators that someone was a civilian and not a Naxalite; on the other hand, ordinary village youth could be labelled 'Naxalites', and killed or raped. This was a war where everyone knew each other, but knowledge was never enough to decide on life or death.

By 2013, when I next visited, 129 out of 170 households in Cherapalli were back, while the Tadvehi vilagers had also returned home and reconciled with the others. Electricity was not restored. The school had officially started functioning again in the village since 2009, and was now housed in the panchayat bhawan, but the teacher lived in Polampalli and came only occasionally. The two anganwadis also functioned quite irregularly. The dalam no longer visited, but the poor continued to reap a portion of the fields of the rich. It was election time, and the villagers said they might even have considered defying the Maoist call for an election boycott, but since their polling booth had been shifted to the Polampalli Judum camp and they couldn't go there, the state had taken the decision for them.

In 2015, three boys from the village were killed by a joint team of the CRPF, the DRG and the Special Task Force of the Chhattisgarh police, in a so-called encounter. The Inspector General of Police (IGP), S.R.P. Kalluri, proudly announced that they had killed three 'Maoists'. Their relatives, however, said that the boys were picked up while on their way to get a drink. The force stopped one of the boys and started beating him, for no reason. When he tried to run away, he was shot. The policemen then asked the other two boys to carry the body of their friend to the Polampalli police station. They were shot en route.[4] Ten years on, nothing has changed in Chhattisgarh.

9

Notes on an 'Operation'

The CRPF ask us: 'Why do the villagers run away when they see us?' The villagers ask us, 'What else can we do but run away?'

Villagers in Lingagiri and other resettled villages tell us that they cannot go to the Collectorate to get seeds or even go to Mirtur haat: 'It is too dangerous.' The Collector says he cannot deliver anything to these villages: 'It is too dangerous.'

Field notes, 2009

The first phase of the Salwa Judum lasted from approximately 2005 to 2007. After this came a 'lull period' in 2008. Arson and killings continued, but people also slowly began returning home from the camps and from Andhra Pradesh. But in the meantime, the Maoist issue was acquiring nationwide dimensions. In November 2008, the Maoists ambushed the convoy of Chief Minister Buddhadeb Bhattacharya in West Bengal. In retaliation, the police went into nearby villages in Lalgarh, and indiscriminately beat up people, raided homes and molested women. Under the leadership of Chatradhar Mahato, the villagers set up a People's Committee against Police Atrocities (PCPA), blockaded the area, and for a brief period, ran a parallel administration. Earlier that year in June, the Maoists had attacked a boat carrying Greyhounds from Andhra Pradesh in the Balimela reservoir in Odisha, in which 38 commandos died.

In 2009, the central government launched Operation Green Hunt, which they insisted was just the name for a specific operation, but which caught on as a label for the war on Maoists across several states. In Bastar, what this meant was an intensification of combing operations by the CRPF. The war spread to new areas like Darbha block, in the east of Bastar district. The difference between killings in this phase and the Judum was that now there were fewer incidents, but more people were killed at one time. As Appendix I shows, after 2006–7 when the Judum peaked, 2009–10 were the bloodiest years in Chhattisgarh. The second difference was that now the deaths were justified as having taken place in 'encounters', whereas earlier the bodies had just been abandoned without any tally. The police claimed those killed were Maoists but made little distinction between ordinary villagers, poorly armed or unarmed Sangham members and professional guerillas. Maoist killings of 'informers' also increased in response.

From 2011 to 2013, there were three major incidents that caught public attention: 3 villagers were killed in Tadmetla and neighbouring villages in 2011, 17 villagers from Sarkeguda and neighbouring villages in 2012, and 8 villagers in Edesmetta in 2013.

Operation Green Hunt Begins in Darbha Block of Bastar District

During the peak of Judum atrocities in 2006–7, even as the villages of Dantewada district were being emptied out by the vigilantes and the police, people in neighbouring districts were both curiously ignorant and yet affected. The newspapers and television hardly carried anything on the Judum, and instead, repeatedly broadcast the crimes committed by the Maoists. In small urban centres like Jagdalpur, Dantewada and the administrative block headquarters, the media-consuming public was convinced, therefore, that the Maoists were simply irrational people who were against development. In the interior villages, on the other hand, news was spread by word of mouth from villagers fleeing the Judum. Maoist pamphlets and videos contributed as well. From 2007 to 2008, recognizing that they needed to expand to survive, given that their bases in the south were under attack, the Maoists had begun organizing in the villages further north, such as around Darbha block.

The year 2009 when Operation Green Hunt started was a bad one: there was no grain, not even the coarse variety grown on hill slopes; no mango and no tendu. Because CRPF combing operations had started everywhere and not just in the old Judum areas, people across the region stopped sleeping in the fields at night, leaving the crops unprotected from wild animals. Youth were scared to join migrant work gangs even though they needed the work, for fear they would be suspected of having joined the Maoists. The police were keeping tabs on everyone, using voter lists. People rushed to have photos and ID cards made at Rs 100 a shot, to prove that they were peaceful civilians and not Maoists. In Kalingaras, people put all their animals into a pick-up truck and took them to relatives in safer places. Women also stored their jewellery and valuables with relatives.

The only conversation across the region was of impending war. The CPI held meetings to warn the villagers to stay home after dark, and the Maoists argued that the CPI was creating an unnecessary fear psychosis. The CPI told villagers to stay put and face the police because they became even more suspicious and started to shoot if they saw people running away from them, while the Maoists told them to run away. The people did not know whose advice to follow.

When they first started working in the eastern belt of Bastar, the Maoists would call the villagers to meetings in faraway jungles. Villagers told me that men and women were asked to drop one twig each into different piles; the number of twigs provided a headcount of how many came. Many went out of curiosity to see what the Maoists had to say, and came back saying they didn't really want to take sides, but would have no option if the government tried to take away their land. There was a sense of looming horror – that Naxals would come and the police and the Judum would follow; or that industry would come and war would follow. *'Bhumkal vermo,'* I was told, 'the war to save the land, the *bhum*, is coming.'

There was also some excitement at being organized by the Maoists. The Dhurwas all agreed that they were cowards compared to the Gonds who always resisted authority, and they insisted that their villages would stay neutral even as they knew that the Maoists were nibbling away at this neutrality. Some youth from every village went off for a month's training with the Maoists, but came back without arms. They were potential militia members to be summoned when the need arose. Agricultural collectives were started, and lasted in some villages and flopped in others; sanghams were built and flourished in some villages, but failed in others.

In a conflict, the worst part is that one never knows who is who, and if you talk too loudly, the wrong people might hear. A sarpanch told me that she paid money in several instalments to men who came calling at night, saying they had been sent by the Maoists, carrying letters in red ink saying: 'Sarpanch ji, do you want to be silenced forever?' She stopped sleeping outside, and her husband left for the safer environs of Jagdalpur. They suspected that it was not the Maoists at all, but a former friend turned political rival, and put out feelers to the Maoists. The Maoists conducted their own enquiry to which they summoned the sarpanch and her husband. The Maoist leader said: 'We know and you know who took the money but we can't act unless you name him.' The sarpanch replied: 'Let it be then.' She told me that they could not and would not name the suspect because ultimately they all had to live together in the same village. The extortion stopped, but the perpetrator remained unpunished. Eventually, the Maoists beat him up, for some other reason.

In June 2009, the Dhurwa-Gond villages of Darbha and Tongpal blocks had their first taste of large-scale conflict-related deaths. It began with the Maoists warning a contractor not to build roads in their area. When he didn't listen, the Maoists burnt four of his trucks and one tractor. Two days later, on 20 June, CRPF men from

Sukma camp came to investigate. The Maoists set off an IED blast; five CRPF men died on the spot and four others died later. Enraged, the remaining members of the CRPF company started firing blindly. The Maoists ran away, but one buffalo was killed, two motorcyclists barely escaped and one cowherd was beaten unconscious. Seven other villagers, who had no idea what had occurred and happened to be cycling home through the area, were also killed.

Samlu of Soliwada used to sell *chindras* (date palm sap) at different haats. The trees belonged to a man from Kokawada, and every evening Samlu would cycle over to give the owner his money. Samlu was the first to be killed – around 5 p.m. After 15–20 minutes, Ram Vilas, who was cycling home to Kinderwada after ploughing his field in Badanpal, came in the line of fire. His bag containing mushrooms and an umbrella fell down. Wag and Lakhma were returning to Soliwada from Kokawada, where they had gone to buy vegetables, when they were shot. By now it was 6.30 p.m., and Dev, Sukalu and Sampat were coming back from the Bejaguda haat in Odisha, each carrying new fishing nets and a pump on their cycles, when they were hit. The CRPF fired indiscriminately all through the night. The next morning the police took away the bodies and announced they were Naxals killed in an encounter. The CRPF gave the Tongpal police Rs 3000 to cremate the bodies.

The deputy sarpanch of Tongpal visited the thana to inspect the alleged Maoists, and found the police trying to place bombs next to their bodies, and an ammunition belt on Samlu. He testified that they were all local Soliwada residents and insisted on having a post-mortem done. A boy who saw three abandoned cycles lying on the road with fishing nets informed Munna, the local CPI leader, and he too went to the police station and identified the bodies as local residents. After the post-mortem, the bodies were taken to their villages and the villagers discussed what to do next. On 22 June, 2000–3000 people met and decided to call a bandh to protest against fake encounters, under the banner of the Sarva Samaj, an umbrella body representing all the different Bastariya communities.

My informants told me that some 40,000 villagers attended the rally held on the 29th from all the surrounding villages. This was the first such mass protest. The Sarva Samaj questioned their MLAs as to what they were doing to protect the lives of the villagers from such fake encounters. Chief Minister Raman Singh promised to look into the deaths, but nothing happened. However, the experience of protesting gave villagers some confidence.

Bijapur, July 2009

In the old Judum areas, killings intensified again. In July 2009, I visited Bijapur along with two colleagues, J.P. Rao and Ajay Dandekar, and Kopa Kunjam of the VCA. We left our jeep at Cheruguda, one of the first villages after Mirtur camp, and walked to Vengaipadu, crossing the ruins of a blasted school, green fields and rain-soaked hills. We were now officially in Maoist land.

When we reached Vengaipadu, we found the village deserted. Slowly, the villagers who had run away on seeing us began to trickle back. There was clearly a Maoist squad present somewhere and they needed permission to talk to us. It began raining heavily soon after we reached, and we sat in one of the kothars. An old man, Chakko, described the previous week's attack, when some 100–200 CRPF jawans, policemen and SPOs from Mirtur thana had burnt 42 houses in the village. Everyone fled to the forest. The force found him and his 17-year-old daughter, Sukke, and dragged her away: 'There were 15-20 men', he told us. 'They took her to the other side of the Aajarev nala. We found her body three days later, covered with twigs and branches. She had been axed to death on the back of her neck, her face towards the ground. We cremated her the next day.' Another man, Kadti Somaru, described how his only son, 25-year-old Budhu, had been surrounded and shot by the security forces. Just like Sukke's family, Budhu's family too did not see any point in reporting the death.

By the time we finished noting down the losses of all 42 houses in

Vengaipadu and some in neighbouring villages, it was late afternoon. We were then summoned a little distance to meet two men and a woman. They evidently had some authority. One of the men spoke Hindi, and was very soft-spoken and polite. They asked us why we had come and noted down all our replies before letting us leave around 5 p.m.

When we returned to Cheruguda where we had left our jeep, we found that the SPOs and the Judum had taken away JP's mobile phone and charger. The villagers told us the SPOs had wanted to burn the jeep, but a Salwa Judum leader had warned against it. The ground had turned slushy after the rain, and our jeep got stuck. By the time we reached Mirtur thana, night had fallen.

When we were 100 yards away from the Mirtur CRPF camp, floodlights were trained on us, and when we stopped the jeep and got out, we were told to put our hands up. We walked the remaining distance like that. Our jeep was allowed to join us only a while later. We insisted that we be taken to the thana to lodge a police complaint about the stolen mobile and charger. The CRPF men accompanied us there in the pitch dark; it had also started raining heavily again. Once we were inside the thana, the police refused to let us go saying that they had instructions from their SP, Amaresh Mishra, to keep us there indefinitely. Our protests that we had informed the Collector of our visit cut no ice. We finally made it back to Dantewada only at 2 a.m. The next day, we filed a complaint with the Dantewada police about the theft of the mobile. They periodically sent JP summons to appear, which would only reach him after the date had passed; JP never got his mobile back.

The Konta Killings of September-November 2009

From September to November 2009, there was a fresh wave of killings in the Konta region, during combing operations covering several villages. Some of these were reported in the press and became quite well known. I pieced together my own narrative of what happened based on first-hand accounts from villagers who had come to Delhi to make their situation known, and interviews with IDPs in Andhra Pradesh.[1]

One of those I met was a young woman, Mooke, at her home in Andhra Pradesh. Mooke had narrowly escaped the attack on her village Gompad, where nine people were killed on 1 October. One woman, Sodi Seeta, was injured in police firing. Gompad is primarily a Dorla village and considered a Maoist stronghold. A force of about 200 CRPF and SPOs left for Gompad at night. One SPO, however, gave the force the wrong directions in order to delay them and meanwhile warned the villagers. Since the force reached at 5.30 a.m. instead of 3.30 a.m., most villagers managed to get away. Four of those killed were from one family. Forty-year-old Madvi Bajare was ill so he and his wife Subbi could not run away when the forces came. Bajare's two younger daughters, ten-year-old Bheeme and eight-year-old Mutti, were also at home, as was his elder daughter Kattam Kanni; she was visiting with her two-year-old son, Suresh. Everyone was dragged out of the house. The parents and their youngest daughter Mutti were stabbed and left by a mahua tree. The eldest, Kanni, was stripped, raped and then killed. In the process they also cut off three of her baby's fingers and put the crying baby on his dead mother's chest. His aunt Bheeme, herself a mere child, managed to seize the boy and run into the jungle.

Mooke started crying as she talked about the baby, rocking her own child in a cloth cradle while we talked. She then smiled weakly through her tears and said, 'But her baby is fine now, he is fine.'

The Tale of Tadmetla

On 6 April 2010, 76 CRPF men died in a Maoist ambush between the villages of Mukram and Tadmetla. Eight Maoists also died in the incident. Images of the 'Dantewada martyrs' lying in flag-draped, wreath-covered coffins were accompanied by headlines like 'The outraged nation', 'Government outraged over Maoist massacre – BJP wants fight to the finish' (*Hindustan Times*), 'War between India and the Maoists' (Times Now). Others emphasized the suffering and sacrifice of the soldiers: 'Country bids farewell to Dantewada martyrs' (NDTV), 'Amid heart-rending scenes 42 bodies reach Lucknow' (*The Hindu)*, 'Brave and helpless' (*Outlook* magazine).

The Maoists also memorialized their own cadre with a 15-foot-high red cement memorial in the open plains of Morpalli village close by. Their cultural troupe, the Cinem batch, composed a special song for the occasion. The photos of the eight Maoists who died were carried in their Hindi newsletter, *Prabhat*, in its January–June 2010 issue, while a Maoist press release noted: 'The heroic PLGA guerrillas led by the CPI (Maoist) have created history by wiping out an entire Company of the central paramilitary force in Dantewada district of Chhattisgarh.'[2]

The government ordered an enquiry by a retired Director General of the BSF, E.N. Rammohan, a handlebar-moustachioed, straight-talking officer. He blamed the CRPF leadership for sending out a deputy commandant unfamiliar with the area, and noted among other things that senior officers never participated in operations, merely helicoptering into the CRPF camps; that the camps themselves were not properly defended; and that standard operating procedures were not followed. DIG of CRPF Operations Nalin Prabhat, who ordered the combing operations, was initially transferred but got a gallantry award a year later.

The sequence of events that has emerged since is that Nalin Prabhat had decided, soon after taking charge, that the troops should conduct night area-domination exercises, to counter Maoist manoeuvres, which usually take place in March–April. Accordingly, the CRPF 62nd battalion set off from their Chintalnar camp on the night of 4 April. In the early hours of the 5th they camped near Mukram village and cooked khichdi, requisitioning firewood, water and utensils from the villagers. They returned to Chintalnar during the day, and set off again at night for Tadmetla. The Maoists had been keeping tabs on the CRPF troop movement, and had apparently even rehearsed the entire scenario days before.

An article in the defence analysis magazine *Force* cites an internal Maoist document saying four companies or some 500 men of the PLGA had been involved: 'Eight platoons were used for ambush, six for assault, and two were used as stoppers. The rest added to the numbers to get the psychological advantage.' Originally, the Maoists had planned another ambush site, but the CRPF spotted the Maoists near Chintalnar and started firing. The Naxalites then redeployed to successfully encircle the men from all sides. A mine-proof vehicle sent out from Chintalnar camp as reinforcement was also blown up by an IED.[3]

Three years later, the Maoists sent out a video of the attack to television channels, in which they were seen counting the weapons haul of light machine guns, AK-47s, INSAS rifles, mortars, grenades, etc., while the bodies of the cadre who died were covered with red flags. Inevitably, the television commentary on the footage spoke of Naxalite barbarity and speculated on their motives in sending such a video.[4]

When I visited Tadmetla in December 2011, I asked to be taken to the site of the ambush. The villagers were unhappy that it had come to be known as the 'Tadmetla ambush', and their village was consistently getting a bad name, when the fields where it happened were actually closer to another village. Three teenage boys who accompanied us, cycling so furiously through forest paths that they reached even faster than the motorbike I was on, said that had the ambush not happened when it did, the troops would have burnt Tadmetla in 2010 itself. (Eventually, the troops did burn Tadmetla in March 2011, along with Timapuram and Morpalli.)

As my youthful companions described it, the Maoists decoyed the troops with two boys who began to run on seeing the force. In running after them, the troops were lured for some 1.5 kilometres over open fields to another field. The Maoists had taken up position behind the trees on the bunds. My informants said the CRPF jawans jumped into a trough bordering the field to escape the firing and most of the bodies were found there. They also showed me the crater where the mine-proof tank was blown up.

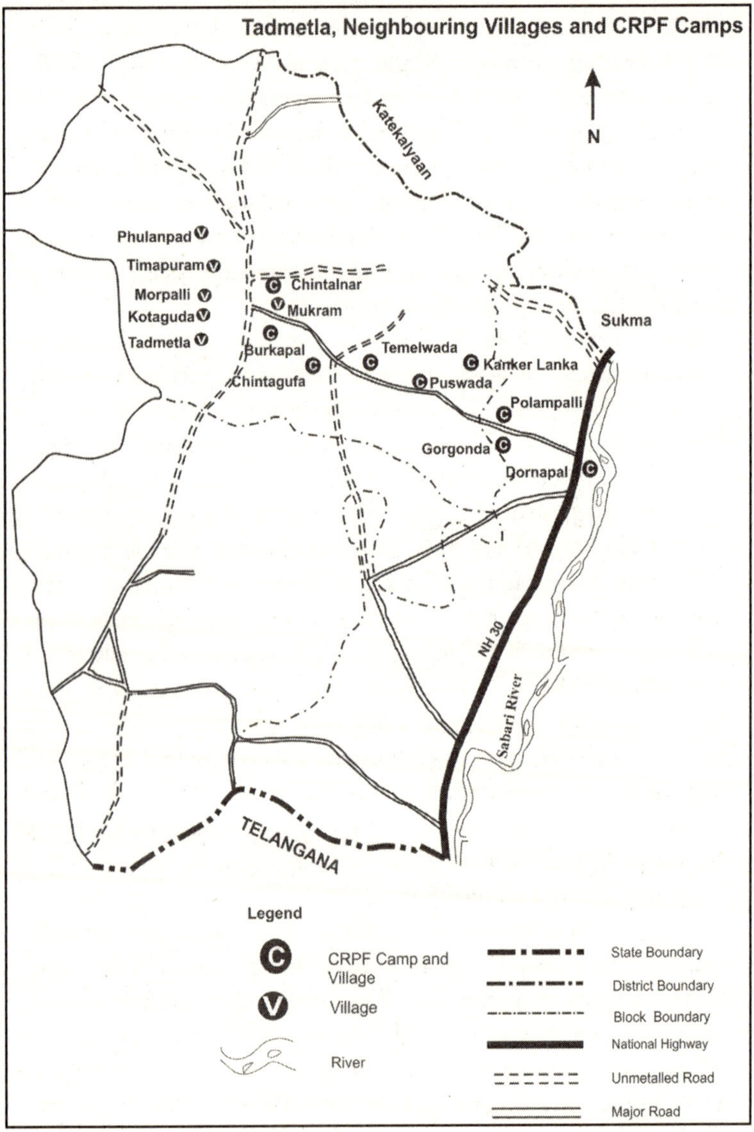

Tadmetla, Neighbouring Villages and CRPF Camps

300 Homes in Flames

On 14 March 2011, I was travelling along the Andhra–Odisha border interviewing IDPs. A sudden fragrance made me stop. My companion pointed to a tree with clusters of small white sweet-scented flowers – *kur mar* he called them in Koya. When we reached home, and turned on the TV, they were 'breaking news': the Chhattisgarh police announced that 36 Maoists had been killed near Chintalnar, and three SPOs and one policeman injured. Inured to boastful police claims, the Andhra Pradesh papers the next morning reported the news sceptically and said only three bodies had been found, including a woman's. They reported that the Senior Superintendent of Police (SSP) Dantewada, S.R.P. Kalluri, and the Koya Commandos, as the SPOs had begun to call themselves, had been intensively combing the area for 10 days on a tip-off that Maoist leader Ramakrishna was in the area.

As we later found out, the so-called 36 Maoists turned out to be one Maoist and three Koya Commandos killed in an encounter in Timapuram village on 14 March. There was nothing in the news or in the police press conference about the killings, arson and rapes that had preceded the encounter at neighbouring Morpalli on 11 March, and at Pulanpad, Timapuram and Tadmetla on the days following the encounter.

Morpalli, 11 March 2011

Morpalli has five Koya hamlets and two Dorla hamlets. The 15-foot high memorial to the Maoists who died in the 2010 ambush is located in Patel para, on a wide plain, with haphazardly arranged houses. Next to the memorial is a broken and abandoned school, and a hand-pump that is still in use. Even before the Judum, the teacher used to come only eight days a year; but after he was beaten by the Judum, he got a transfer elsewhere. This part of the district is scraggy and bare, an expanse of brown earth, though it does have some old trees here and there.

Sitting on a cot in the village, one might be forgiven for thinking it was one of the most serene places on earth. You can hear the wind rustle through the tamarind trees, cocks crow, the occasional voices of children calling out to each other. But it takes barely an hour for terror to strike and everything to be destroyed, the habitual peace making the terror seem all the more unnecessary and unreal.

People told me how the forces surrounded the village around 8 a.m. on 11 March 2011. First, they burnt Patel para, then Barse para, then Jonna para, stealing chickens, money and whatever else they could. Hemla Budri was pruning tendu bushes near her house, when the force caught her. They stripped and raped her as her three-year-old daughter looked on, and stole Rs 10,000 from a small pouch at her waist. Madvi Lalita was equally unlucky. She had gone to the river to wash clothes when she saw the force approaching. Lalita tried to run but was caught. Her father and brother came to the river to rescue her but were captured. The force beat up the father and son, asking them about the memorial, and took the family of three with them to Chintalnar thana. Lalita was separated from the men and raped. On reaching Bhanda Morpalli, the force saw Madvi Sula, who had climbed a tendu tree, and shot him. The villagers searched for him but found his body only two days later when they saw blood under a tree and looked up and saw his body hanging over a branch. On their way back from Morpalli to Chintalnar, the force burnt the house of Sodi Mase, which happened to fall by the road, and beat up Vanjam Aitu, returning home after pruning tendu. All in a pleasant day's work.

The Morpalli villagers had fled, but three old people were left behind in the village and the terror was so great that their relatives could not go back immediately to look for them. Other villagers warned them against venturing into the village. Nupe Rajulu's old wife, who had managed to run away, came back around noon the following day to find him dead at home. When Madkam Bhima came home on the 13th he found his mother, Madkam Mangdi, in the last stages. Madvi Joga of Patel para also died of starvation: on the 13th morning his son Mangdu found him lying under a tree, too weak to talk; he died a short while later. The houses of all three had been burnt, and there was nobody left to feed them or give them water. It was March, and the sun was harsh already.

This was not the first time Morpalli had been burnt. In 2007, the Judum had burnt 57 houses here, along with 66 houses in neighboring Kumadtong. At the time of the first attack, all the villages in the area left for Andhra Pradesh, coming back a year or two later with some vessels and clothes purchased from their mirchi coolie earnings. They continue to go there every year. But by 2011 Morpalli was completely pauperized. We tried to do a quick calculation of losses. The first time around in 2007, the richest household lost about Rs 1 lakh. In 2011, while the entire house was burnt, the losses per house amounted to only some Rs 20,000. There was barely anything left to lose. The money that some of them had buried below the ground to keep it safe from the Judum was too mildewed to use.

Pulanpad, 13 March, and Timapuram, 13–15 March 2011

On 13 March 2011, the forces came again, this time to Pulanpad village. They lobbed two hand grenades, injuring a man and a woman collecting mahua in the field. They also took away two men, Badse Bhima and Manu Yadav, even as Manu's wife ran after them up to the stream, clutching her baby and pleading with them not to take her husband away. She turned back only when they threatened to kill her. Since the SPOs were local, they would have known that Madkam Dodda, who goes around in tattered clothes, is a cattle trader, who also sells 25–30 quintal of grain every year. They ransacked his house and found Rs 4.5 lakh which he had been saving to buy a tractor.

In 2007 too, the Judum had attacked Pulanpad and pushed Aimla Sukka inside his house and burnt him alive.

The force halted that night at Timapuram where they spread out and built defence lines out of wood and bricks pilfered from the houses. All the villagers had fled to the nearby forest. The 350 Cobras and Koya Commandos gorged themselves on all the animals they found – chickens, goats and pigs. The next morning (14 March), the force left in the direction of Tadmetla, where they ran into the Maoists in a field outside the village. Three SPOs and one Maoist died in this encounter. A helicopter came and took away the SPO corpses, while the Maoists also took away their dead fighter. The forces then came back to Timapuram in the afternoon of the 14th and out of sheer bloodthirstiness killed Badse Bhima, who they had brought with them from Pulanpad the previous day. The villagers later found his naked body, face down, hands and feet bound, the axe still stuck in his back, amidst the ruins of burnt houses. The security forces spent the night dispersed in three hamlets, and left the next morning after gratuitously setting fire to 59 houses. They took Manu back with them to Chintalnar and killed him there, claiming they had got back the body of the Maoist killed in the encounter. The following day they set off for Tadmetla.

Tadmetla, 16 March 2011

Tadmetla is one of the larger villages in the area, with eight hamlets. A large pond in the middle separates some of the hamlets, surrounded by trees and a bund. On the morning of 16 March, the villagers of Tadin para, which is closest to the jungle, had just woken up. Some were sitting around a fire, easing themselves into the day with a little conversation or just silence. The more active women had begun to sweep their houses. They described how the force came from the jungle and started beating them, pushing them towards the middle of the village. They were beaten with rifle butts and sticks, and made to sit in a line:

> The CRPF shouted at us, 'When your *baap* [father, i.e. Naxals] come, you give them food and water, you give us nothing. Your house is now ready for you.' After three or four hours we were allowed to go back, and saw all our houses were burning.

Madvi Kusum, who spoke publicly about her rape at a meeting organized by the CPI in Jagdalpur, said she was sweeping her house when the force came. She tried to run, carrying all her valuables in a small bag, but two men caught her and dragged her into a clump of trees close by and raped her. They slashed her face, leaving a deep cut near the eye, so she could barely open it for days. A neighbour found her naked and unconscious. They also stole her bag, which contained Rs 8000 in cash, a gold necklace worth Rs 7000, nose studs costing Rs 2500 and earrings valued at Rs 3000.

The women named the SPOs they recognized from neighbouring villages. At least three gangs of Koya Commandos had been involved: the Kartam Surya gang, the Kiche Nanda group and the Madkam Mudraj group. It was a roll call of honour in the kill-your-own-people contest.

The village burnt for three or four days. After a couple of days, the villagers tried to put out the embers, but the blaze lingered on. Two hundred and seven structures (including sheds and pigpens) belonging to 160 families were destroyed in the attack. It had been a good harvest that year, so the villagers lost even more than usual.

As with Morpalli and Pulanpad, this was the force's second or third attack on Tadmetla; these were among the villages that had earlier given testimonies at Cherla. When I visited in 2011, a man dictated to me the following letter for the court:

> In December 2007, during the harvesting period, about 100–200 SPOs, CRPF and Judum attacked our village early in the morning. My brother, Sodi Nanda s/o Sodi Hadma, age approximately 35 years, was ill at home. We all ran away but he could not escape. There was a pile of big sticks for fuelwood stacked next to a tree

> near the house. He hid inside this pile to save himself. SPOs/Judum saw him go inside and set fire to the stack. He was burnt alive there. We thought he had managed to run away and searched for him in the neighbouring villages. After two days we saw his bones in the ashes and realized he had been killed.

The SPOs Resist Any Relief or Investigation

The attacks on the three villages might well have remained one of the hundred untold stories of this war had it not been for the former sarpanch of neighbouring Chintagufa, Podiyam Panda. Panda helped the villagers of Tadmetla douse the flames, and persuaded them to stay on in the village and not flee as they had previously. In the morning people went hungry, but by evening, neighbouring villages came with relief. Panda also alerted the press. The first ones in were Aman Sethi of *The Hindu* and Anil Mishra of *Rajasthan Patrika*, who had to take a roundabout route to get there, since the main road from Dornapal to Tadmetla was blocked by SPOs.[5] Sethi's detailed story of 23 March 2011 quoted senior police sources as saying that 200 SPOs or Koya Commandos and 150 Cobras had left the Chintalnar camp around 4 a.m. to destroy an arms factory at Morpalli. He then described how they ended up burning some 300 homes in the area and raping and killing villagers.

The very next day after reading the news, 24 March, the Dantewada Collector R. Prasanna ordered an enquiry and also sent relief trucks to the villages. This was the first time that any relief was provided in the immediate aftermath of an attack, whether by the government or civil society groups. The SSP, S.R.P Kalluri, on the other hand, 'dismissed the allegations as Maoist propaganda'.[6] The Chhattisgarh home minister and the Union Minister of State for Home Affairs dutifully supported the police version.[7]

Taking his cue from Kalluri, Kartam Surya, the leader of the 'Koya Commando gang' that ruled the area, stopped a truck carrying relief supplies and assaulted the driver. Surya, it must be remembered, had a non-bailable arrest warrant issued against him for rape, and was claimed by the police to be absconding.[8] The SPOs and the police also turned back the Collector and Commissioner, a Congress delegation, and journalists by using huge coils of barbed wire to block the road.[9] But what really captured public attention was a murderous assault on Swami Agnivesh and Art of Living representatives on 26 March by Judum leaders at the Dornapal relief camp, as they were trying to deliver relief. S.R.P. Kalluri was widely believed to have orchestrated the attack. In Swami Agnivesh's words:

> When we reached Dornapal (early morning), a motley crowd of 100–150 people led by some non-tribal looking, well built men, shouting filthy abuses in chaste Hindi, pulled all three of us out of the car. The driver was also threatened and the car tyres deflated. We had to face untold humiliation and unspeakable manhandling and pushing etc. This continued for nearly forty minutes or more.[10]

As Agnivesh and his companions turned around and fled, the crowd started throwing eggs at the car. Agnivesh then contacted Raman Singh who advised them to go again, this time offering an escort of 100–150 security personnel. Reassured, Swami Agnivesh and his companions set off again late afternoon. What happened next is best described in the FIR filed by Additional SP D.S. Marawi, who was in charge of his security:

> We had been previously informed that the families of people affected in Naxal violence were staging a protest 'Chakka Jam' at Dornapal – and this protest was being led by the leaders of Salwa Judum movement namely Dular Sai, Balwant Singh, Vijay Chauhan, Vijay Naidu, etc. I called all these leaders on the mobile who informed me that the protest would be peaceful. All the protestors would be waiting with their hands folded and would tell Swamiji about their woes. After this Swamiji could leave and visit the affected areas… I completely trusted the Salwa Judum leaders and accompanied Swami Agnivesh, Rishi Milind and Acharya Ajay to the area of Dornapal.

> There was a huge, boisterous crowd that had gathered. I went and started conversing with the protestors... Suddenly Dular Sai started shouting, 'Why should we allow the agents (dalal) of Naxalites to come tomorrow? We will not allow them to visit this area and will either force them to run away or murder them'... I recognized the other leaders who were shouting this – Balwant Singh, Vijay Naidu, Vijay Chauhan. Some 20–25 men (whom I can very well identify) started pushing the security forces and, hurling abuses, advanced towards Swamiji's vehicle, saying they would kill Naxalite agents. They then attacked Swamiji's car and also the security forces with stones which they picked up from the ground. They threw huge rocks at the windowpanes of the vehicles, shattering the panes, in a murderous attack. If the security forces had delayed their reactions by five or ten minutes, something very serious would have transpired that day. Somehow we managed to turn the vehicle around and left. After that, the crowd attacked the media persons present there, snatching away their cameras, IDs and microphones. The crowd then damaged the vehicles of the media persons too. In this grievous attack, three or four security men and some media persons suffered injuries. CG 18D – 1146 (Qualis), 1 Sumo car and 1 Sumo belonging to the media were badly damaged. This incident was also clearly telecast on TV channels. This untoward incident completely shattered my trust in the Salwa Judum leaders. The whole attack was a nefarious pre-planned act.[11]

On 28 March, once this news became public, the NHRC called for a report on police excesses, and the Congress boycotted the legislative assembly, demanding an enquiry into the whole affair. On the same day, we filed an affidavit mentioning the attacks on Tadmetla and neighbouring villages in our ongoing case in the Supreme Court which, later that year, ordered a CBI enquiry (see chapter 17).

On 29 March, responding to reports of starvation deaths in Morpalli, in an ongoing PUCL case on the Right to Food, the Supreme Court ordered its Commissioners to visit the affected villages. It was only after much delay, on 6 April, that Harsh Mander, Supreme Court Commissioner in the Right to Food case, was taken by helicopter to visit Morpalli. Mander reported starvation-like conditions. The police, of course, intimidated villagers and tried to keep them from talking; and after he left, the force stole a dance headdress with bison horns and cowrie shells, which had cost its owner Rs 50,000 the year before, and a hunting horn and arrows from another house.

In the meantime, on 2 April, Chief Minister Raman Singh, Governor Shekhar Dutt and DGP Viswaranjan flew down to Tadmetla and promised ration cards to 96 families, and jobs as schoolteachers and anganwadi to local youth. The Tadmetla women later told me that when they tried to tell the chief minister that Koya Commandos had burnt their village, the security forces accompanying him pointed their guns at the women and they fell silent. The jobs never materialized, the village remains without a school, and the volleyballs distributed by the chief minister's delegation disintegrated after three months of playing.

When It Becomes Dangerous to Celebrate Village Festivals

Although the Supreme Court judgment of 2011 provided a little respite, CRPF operations continued. In June 2012, I was attending a workshop in Bangalore when I heard on the television that 17 Maoists had been killed in Sarkeguda in Bijapur. Something sounded fishy about this story, so JP, Kopa and I visited the area on 3 and 4 July and brought out a small report on how 17 villagers were killed while planning for a village festival:

> The three villages of Sarkeguda, Kottaguda and Rajpenta merge into each other, and share a common earth shrine. The field where the firing took place is an open area surrounded by houses, some of which are in Kottaguda and some of which fall in Rajpenta. The villagers had returned only in 2009 after the Salwa Judum had burnt their

> village in 2005, and are still struggling to put their cattle together and rebuild all houses properly. The meeting on the 28th night was held to discuss how to help those without cattle and single women headed households, and also to plan the holding of the seed sowing festival. The villagers say that there were no Maoists present, and that the police were most likely injured in cross-firing. Had there been a squad in the village, there would have been sentries posted in the direction of Basaguda thana.
>
> Whatever the CRPF's claims, what is indisputable is that they knew they were in the middle of a village and yet did not use night flares or observe even the most basic precautions when firing. In all 17 persons have been killed, of which 7 are minors; 9 have been injured, and at least 5 women have been beaten/assaulted. One cow has died and one bull has been injured, and there are bullet marks on the houses. What is shocking is not just the massacre itself but the cover up that followed with the CRPF and Home Minister claiming that they had shot top Naxal leaders, when they could clearly see that they had killed villagers including small children, since 16 of the bodies were sent back that night.

By the time of the Sarkeguda and Edsemetta killings (a year later), civilian deaths had started getting media attention and judicial enquiries were ordered in all three cases. Unlike the initial period when villagers were scared to talk, by now they were eager to testify. The Judicial Enquiries by Justice V.K. Agarwal, a retired High Court judge, eventually found that those killed were indeed ordinary villagers and not Maoists, as the police claimed. The villagers were represented by JagLag, an organization of public spirited lawyers. However, the reports came out only in 2019 and 2022. In the meantime, the impunity enabled by these lengthy investigations and the lack of prosecutions emboldened the security forces to continue with their killings.

Mission 2016

In 2014–15, several factors came together to enable a new offensive. Following the NDA victory in Delhi, Ajit Doval, who had been the chief of the Intelligence Bureau when the Judum started and was a strong Judum supporter, was appointed National Security Adviser. The number of troops increased. S.R.P. Kalluri, who had been transferred out of the district after the Tadmetla burnings of 2011 and the attack on Agnivesh, was posted back in a higher position than before, as Inspector General of Police (IG) Bastar Range.

In 2014, the police once again started holding 'Jan Jagran' meetings and staging mass 'surrenders',[12] as well as reporting the arrests of '*inami naxali*' – those with rewards on their heads. Many of the villages targeted in the initial stages of the Judum were attacked again. Frantic family members who came to the thanas searching for their relatives were roped in to provide numbers for 'civic action' programmes. A police press release of 5 February 2016 claimed 'over 5000 tribal villagers have successfully participated in 11 sabhas organized as a part of a Janjagran Campaign, in which food was provided and civil action programmes were organized'.

When a friend and I visited Konta in January 2016, we found out what all this really meant. This is what I recorded in my diary:

> 24 January 2016: Woke up to find five or six shivering villagers from M. had come. The girl had a thin cotton lungi wrapped around her. They said the security forces had surrounded their village at 6 a.m., picked up 37 men and taken them to Chintagufa thana. In the afternoon, we visited M., and recorded the names of those arrested. The women from these families had already gone to the thana to try and get them back. Everyone was worried that Mulatong would be next, but we survived that night peacefully. The next morning on our way to the thana, we passed groups of men emerging from the forest, some carrying blankets, but most with nothing. Across the region, all the men are sleeping in the forests, because of the

> frequent raids. It is bitterly cold and they can't even light fires. At the thana, we found more groups of women from neighbouring villages had come in solidarity. One woman was crying, holding out her husband's election card as proof that he was not a Naxalite. We felt so helpless. The police would not let the women or us meet the men. All they would say is that they had orders from above and were 'investigating'. One of the policemen told the women to stop crying, they had organized a 'bhoj' or feast for them. Another told a woman with a suckling infant to get the baby checked by the CRPF doctor.
>
> On 29 January, the police put out a press release saying that they had conducted combing operations the previous day and arrested 12 men. [The law requires you to produce a person taken into custody within 24 hours; these men had already been with the police for six days.] They claimed that five were wanted for a firing on the police in June 2015, while another seven were implicated in a firing case from October 2014. Two days later, they claimed to have carried out another combing operation in M. village and arrested 13 more men. The police practice of registering FIRs against 'unknown persons' means that anyone can be easily slotted into an old crime. The police displayed the remaining M. men as having 'surrendered'.

These coerced 'surrenders' led to new tensions within the villages. In K. village, in Bastar's mixed Dhurwa and Gond belt, some 50 villagers surrendered after their names were discovered in a Maoist diary recovered by the police. They had been providing food and other kinds of help to the Maoists. The police followed up the surrenders by holding a meeting in the village at which they distributed saris and vessels; at this meeting some of the OBC households asked for a permanent police camp near their village. The Maoists took out their ire by beating up some villagers, including women. In May 2016, when we visited, two-thirds of the village was deserted out of fear of the Maoists. While some wanted a police camp, others were opposing it. In the neighbouring village, also under pressure from the Maoists for 'surrendering', the villagers had started patrolling to keep the Maoists out, laughingly calling themselves the '*tangiya* (axe) gang', because they used bows, arrows and axes. They said the officials had refused their request for a police camp, making them vulnerable in the first place and then abandoning them. It is hard to miss the parallels with 2005–6 and the rise of the Salwa Judum.

Along with surrenders and arrests, the numbers killed in 'encounters' increased exponentially in 2015–16. The police proudly announced that in the first three months of 2016 alone, they killed 55 'Naxalites'. Photos of the corpses circulated by the police show very few wearing uniforms; most were clearly ordinary villagers.

Sexual predation by the security forces is a constant fear. The campaign network Women against Sexual Violence and State Repression (WSS) reported that between 19 and 24 October 2015, 40 women of Peddagelur, Budgicheru and Gundam villages were sexually assaulted, beaten and stripped by the security forces; three women were gang-raped. On 12 January 2016, six women from Kunna village in Sukma district were sexually assaulted, and between 11 and 14 January 2016, 13 women were gang-raped in Belam Nendra village in Bijapur district. In all these cases, the rapes were accompanied by extreme physical and verbal abuse, including the squeezing of women's breasts to 'check' if they were indeed lactating mothers and not Maoist women cadre.[13] The women's groups managed to file FIRs but, predictably, very little happened after that, other than intimidation of the women themselves.

10

The Renegade and the Rifleman

> You listen too much to the soldiers...you should never trust experts. If you believe the doctors, nothing is wholesome: if you believe the theologians, nothing is innocent: if you believe the soldiers nothing is safe.
>
> Salisbury to Governor General Lytton[1]

While the Judum was a time of terror for most villagers, it was also a great opportunity for others, in particular, men who lived to make money, using their wits to think of underhand deals and ways of cheating the system. It was a time when men with criminal pasts were openly given arms and promoted, when informing on one's fellow villagers became the model to emulate, when excess was celebrated. All those whose exploitation of adivasis had been limited by their fear of Maoists now had state protection to do it freely. In selecting the SPOs (and later the DRG), the desire to take revenge on Naxalites was cited as the main qualification, enfolding vengeance and betrayal into the basic structures of policing.

But the village youth enlisted as SPOs, who were often the worst killers, were also at the bottom of the policing hierarchy, looked down upon by the security forces and the police, who resented having to fight this war. The best policemen are those who regard the war as an unfortunate evil, which they are duty-bound to prosecute, with the least damage to civilians. The worst are those who like killing for its own sake, and who make money off the war. The vast majority in between, especially the security establishment in Delhi and Raipur, are just indifferent and careerist, archetypes of what Hanna Arendt famously called 'the banality of evil', little men in their little cocoons of comfort. They try to convince themselves that the villagers support the Naxalites entirely out of fear, and they need 'rescuing' by the police, though in their hearts they know otherwise. They find comfort in claiming that there is a vast conspiracy afoot by human rights activists to defame the nation, without caring that it is they who have destroyed the Constitution from within.

The Tiger of Bastar

> For the elected governments, justice meant vengeance and memory meant disorder, so they dribbled holy water on the foreheads of the men who had waged state terrorism.
>
> Eduardo Galeano, *Upside Down*

Short, thickset, pugnacious and articulate, wearing the Indian politician's white kurta pyjama, with dark glasses and sneakers, Mahendra Karma, Congress MLA from Dantewada, became synonymous with the Judum. Listening to Karma, one would have thought the Judum was entirely his idea; he repeatedly claimed that he was the only politician willing to take on the Maoists. In 2006, he told the ICI grandiosely: 'I have one more strategy which I will deploy at the end: "Do or die."'

To illustrate his commitment to the anti-Maoist movement, Karma drew on not just the Jan Jagran Abhiyan of 1990 but also the anti-colonial Bhumkal of 1910. Adivasis are against any 'ism', he declared, and 'there is a limit to how long adivasis can live under terror'. His own family, however, was one of those that benefited from colonial rule and the suppression of the Bhumkal, when the pargana majhis were given greater political power. His father, Kalmu Boda of Pharaspal, the pargana majhi of Barsur, was a skilled tiger hunter – ironic that his son should take pride in being called the 'Tiger of Bastar'.

From 1980 to 1985, Karma was a fiery and dedicated member of the CPI. But the party was unable to give him the money and individual power he wanted, and he joined the Congress in 1986. For a brief period, he also stood as an independent. When I met him in 1991, he was supporting the Bodhghat hydroelectric project, which would have displaced large numbers of people, and opposing the demand to include Bastar in the Sixth Schedule of the Constitution. The Sixth Schedule is a step up in terms of powers from the Fifth Schedule under which the region is currently governed, and allows for the creation of autonomous district councils with powers to manage resources, administer justice, run schools and so on. This opposition to giving Bastar more autonomy placed him on the side of the BJP against the CPI and a faction of the Congress. In 2005, after the Judum started, despite officially being leader of the (Congress) Opposition in the state assembly, he was often referred to as the 13th minister in BJP Chief Minister Raman Singh's cabinet.

Between 2000 and 2004, Karma was the industry and commerce minister in the Congress government in Chhattisgarh and continued even afterwards to propagate the rights of big business. Karma saw nothing wrong in adivasis being reduced to manual labour on land they once owned. He told the ICI in 2006: 'Why shouldn't Tata, Essar and others be put on tribal land? Who can stop these big projects and why should we? ... Since tribals will consume any compensation they are given, they should be given work in ancillary industries. Instead of tractors, use them for land levelling.' As mentioned earlier, Karma was also charged by the Lokayukt with cheating both adivasis and the state in the malik makbuja scam.

One critical factor in Karma's support for big industry and the Judum was to maintain his patronage network and provide jobs for his constituents and factional clients, who were getting restive at the lack of employment in the area. Initially, most of the Judum leaders were Karma's '*khas aadmi*', that is, relatives or followers.

But Karma was merely the convenient adivasi face of a deeper counter-insurgency strategy for which the BJP government in Raipur and the Congress home ministry in Delhi were equally responsible. Even though, as chapter 4 showed, Karma attended more Judum rallies than any other politician, and was personally present when houses were burnt and people killed, the Judum and Operation Green Hunt went on even without him.

The Leader's Henchmen

> Whoever opposes us, whether in Parliament or outside, is a representative of the Naxalites… For all we know, Ajit Jogi could be a front for the Naxalites.
>
> Madhukar, Judum leader, May 2006

There were several teachers in the Judum campaign, most notably Madhukar 'Guruji', who was described by a local tendu contractor as the 'Boss of Kutru'. Of medium height and bearded, Madhukar roamed around with an escort of armed SPOs. Madhukar developed megalomaniacal political ambitions: he wanted to expand the Judum to cover the whole of Bastar and neighbouring Gadchiroli in Maharashtra as well. The newspapers reported that to celebrate the anniversary of the Judum in Kutru in 2008, Madhukar invited 90 MLAs. Being Karma's man did not extend, however, to being a Congress supporter – in fact, most Judum leaders mobilized votes for the BJP in camp. When we met him in 2006, Madhukar was contemptuous of Congress leaders like Ajit Jogi and Rajendra

Pambhoi who wanted the Judum to end, and strongly supportive of the BJP: 'Raman Singh has extended full support to the Salwa Judum, and if any party can support it, it is the BJP.'

Since all the schools in the Judum-affected areas were shut down and the teachers recalled to camp, it was a great opportunity for teachers with political inclinations. Occasionally, however, the government had to make a show of following procedure. Teachers like Madhukar in Kutru and P. Vijay in Konta said that initially the government encouraged them to participate in the Salwa Judum, but after getting complaints about their absence from school, suspended their salaries. Another teacher-turned-Judum-leader, Soyam Mooka, smelled a political conspiracy in the state's about-turn, suspecting that established parties were against his joining politics:

> Mukka told *The Indian Express* that he had received a notice from his department asking why action should not be taken against him for making 'political statements' at 'Salwa Judum' meetings and not attending to his duties. 'The department knows of my association with Salwa Judum for the last three years,' he added.[2]

But barely a year later, when Mooka was charged with rape, the police set aside all procedural niceties to ensure there was no conviction, claiming he could not be arrested because he was absconding. Mooka was too indispensable to the government. His father had been an MLA, and Mooka had started the Salwa Judum in the Konta area.

The Judum leaders have provided the police with deniability not just when targeting villagers, but also when they want to silence human rights critics. In 2010, Soyam Mooka under the banner of the newly formed Ma Danteshwari Swabhimaan Manch was seen heckling well-known social activists Medha Patkar, Sandeep Pandey and others in Dantewada. His gang threw garbage and rotten eggs at the activists before the police gently led Mooka and others away. As mentioned in the previous chapter, Judum leaders attacked Swami

Agnivesh in 2011. In January 2016, Madhukar led a mob against women activists who were trying to meet a visiting team from the National Commission of Women (NCW) to register complaints on rapes. It is not coincidental that the bulk of these attacks occurred under the watch of SRP Kalluri, who suffered from an obsessive hatred for human rights activists.

Many of the immigrant Judum leaders had criminal pasts. Ajay Thakur of Bhairamgarh, originally from Bihar, is alleged to have been a liquor bootlegger and murdered several people, including the principal of the school where he was studying. His lawyer was successful at getting adjournments in court. In June 2016, Subbarao, an active member of the Judum and subsequently of the vigilante organization Samajik Ekta Manch, was convicted and sentenced to a year's imprisonment for buying stolen jewellery. Ram Bhuwan Kuswaha, originally from Uttar Pradesh, the main Judum leader in Dornapal, is alleged to have couriered for the Maoists. But when he began extorting money in their name, they threatened to punish him, and he sought protection from the police. He was given an armed guard, but after the Congress government fell, apparently that stopped. He then got himself a rifle, became the leader of the Judum in Dornapal, and accompanied Mahendra Karma on his village-burning sprees. As camp leader, he allegedly amassed a great amount of money and built himself a huge house in Dhamtari, because it would be too dangerous for him to live in Dornapal. After 2008 he became so scared of Maoist retaliation that on the few occasions he came to Dornapal, he slept at different houses. These fears were not unfounded: many of the Judum leaders around Kutru are now dead; Mahendra Karma was killed in 2013.

Once the initial period of burning and looting villages had passed, the average day of a Judum leader involved driving around in an SUV acquired through money siphoned off from camp supplies, fixing deals and negotiating with government officers to give them contracts. Judum leaders bought expensive equipment like tippers and tractors, which they then hired out to the government. In 2007, I was sitting at a roadside shack in Chatti, on the Chhattisgarh–Andhra Pradesh border, quietly tucking into rice, when one of these SUVs drew up. Luckily, the Judum men were sitting on the other side of the bamboo screen at the eatery, and didn't see me. I overheard them discuss a road-widening contract – every approach road, one insisted, must be widened by 2 metres to prevent the Maoists hiding. A sub-inspector in Konta told me that there were two rival gangs headed by P. Vijay and Prasad Sharma. Both did their best to get government contracts and use the police to pull the other gang down.

While initially the Judum leaders came from both adivasi followers of Karma and upper-caste non-adivasi traders from Uttar Pradesh and Bihar, in 2015–16 most leaders of new vigilante groups like the Samajik Ekta Manch were non-tribal urban upper-caste immigrants, as even a casual trawl of their surnames, Parakh, Jha, Hemani, Mulchandani, Gupta, Tripathi, Awasthi, reveals. At one notable police-organized event on 6 January 2016, the wedding of two surrendered Maoists, the bride's and bridegroom's sides were represented by the Samajik Ekta Manch and the police. Needless to say, this benevolent cultural act had nothing remotely adivasi and everything Bollywood about it, with the groom and police wearing pink turbans, and a police band playing.

Foot Soldiers of the State

> I desperately want to go home. My brother and uncle are still in the village. The Maoists convinced me not to become an SPO. Now I am terrified they will kill me if I return. I regret joining this job, but now I can't leave it.
>
> SPO, 2010

Driving down from Sukma to Konta, outside the Salwa Judum camps in Errabor or Injeram, you see statues of sweet-faced youth in camouflage fatigues holding guns: Shaheed Veti Subah, Karam

Raju and Kawasi Kana. Years later, who will know the histories of these boys, foot soldiers in a war in which their roles were less than heroic, reviled by most of their own people?

Appointing SPOs from among those who had joined the Judum, and paying them Rs 1500 was an essential element of the Collector's 'Work Proposal' for Salwa Judum discussed earlier, 'because without an honorarium, nobody will want to put their lives at risk'. The government also knew that appointing untrained youth in counter-insurgency meant 'keeping aside rules' (Chapter 4, paragraph 3, Work Proposal). Under the 1861 Police Act and the Chhattisgarh Police Act of 2007, SPOs were meant to be a temporary supplement for the police during riots or other crises, not a cheap substitute for regular police forces in carrying out the dirty work of counter-insurgency.

In 2005, when the police sent out application forms to villages, many youth signed up, thinking that an SPO job might lead to absorption into the regular police. But what the police really wanted was not regular recruits but cheap and dispensable foot soldiers. In particular, they needed defectors from Maoist ranks, who could identify their comrades, track their routes and reveal their civilian contacts. As the Union home ministry wrote in 2011 to the Supreme Court, the SPOs were to be the state's version of the Maoist jan militias 'since the SPOs are also locally recruited and are familiar with the terrain, dialect and the local population'. To this logic, the Chhattisgarh government added the qualification that the SPOs should be 'the victims of naxal violence'.[3]

The police were not particular about age, and many of those recruited were barely 14–15 years, without even the first fuzz of a moustache. When questioned in court, the government claimed that all those protesting about using children in conflict were just culturally insensitive to how youthful adivasis looked.

In contrast to the Judum and Samajik Ekta Manch, the SPOs were mostly adivasi or dalit. Since dalits and non-adivasis tend to have other occupations besides farming and are less attached to land, they were more likely to sign up as SPOs. SPOs were often bound in patron–client relationships with the Judum leaders. For instance, many dalit boys worked with traders.

For a long time, I avoided the camps and SPOs: they had human rights activists in their sights. But in the summer of 2010, I had a research assistant, Sushant Panigrahi, interview some 42 SPOs; and later that year, I also interviewed five of the SPOs who had been set to guard me, to prevent me from visiting villages or talking to anyone.

The numbers of SPOs doubled from some 3200 in 2006 to 6500 in 2011 when they were officially disbanded.[4] By 2010, SPO wages had also doubled to Rs 3000. Many of the SPOs Sushant interviewed said, however, that they received only Rs 2150 and that it barely sufficed. Most SPOs sent money home to their parents. They also complained that while officially they were only supposed to put in four to six hours of work, in practice, they were made to work long hours, sometimes 16–18 hours a day, with no fixed times. Their tasks included accompanying the police on patrols and combing operations in villages (though they also carried these out on their own), road opening duties, forest watch duties and guarding the camps.

Initially, the SPOs were armed with an array of weapons – sticks, .303 rifles, an occasional self-loading rifle (SLR). They had no uniforms other than an armband and paper badges with numbers, and many refused to wear even these for fear of being identified by the Maoists. By 2007, they acquired more sophisticated weapons, black headbands and camouflage fatigues, but continued to wear civilian clothes when they wanted to, even as late as 2015.

Some SPOs were known to be bad apples – like Bodke Mutta of Matpalli, who allegedly stole a bull and molested a girl before signing up as an SPO. His father was too embarrassed to visit relatives or go to the market for a while after this. Markam Sannu from Gotagunda, who had already been an SPO for four years when I met him, said that the Maoists had accused him of being an informer since he never attended the village meetings they called, but he managed to run away before they could catch him. In the initial stages of the Judum, Karma and the police looked out for such characters so that they could spread the Judum in their areas – because all it took was a couple of SPOs to identify sangham members and force them to surrender, and then push the villagers into camp.

Several, including the women, joined because they needed a job. Soyam Naresh from Gorpalli told me he was 15 years old and had joined as an SPO after failing class 10 because there was no other work in the Judum camp. Karam Rava from Injinad who joined at the age of 17 said he enlisted because all his friends were doing so. In fact, almost everyone said that if they had had alternative employment, they would never have become SPOs, especially knowing that it meant one could never return home. Only a couple of SPOs had joined because of a genuine grievance, for instance, because the Maoists had redistributed their family land in the villages.

A large number of SPOs were sangham members who had been forced to surrender after the Judum attacked their villages. They were then conscripted as SPOs or '*gopniya sainiks*', literally 'secret soldiers', meaning police informers. Vetti Ram from Jagarmetla, one of those posted to guard me, said the Maoists used to frequent his school. Everyone there, including the teachers, attended Maoist meetings where they spoke of revolution and progress. They redistributed land and cattle. Some years ago, he was arrested when carrying oil and soap for the Maoists. The police recovered a letter from him addressing the shopkeeper as 'dear comrade'. After that he surrendered and became a 'special informant', spending his nights in the police station. According to the *Indian Express*, over '80 per cent of the 3,277 Maoists' who surrendered during 2000–13 had been attached to the police.[5]

The police worked on brainwashing these surrendered men into hatred for the Maoists, but since these men had worked closely with the latter, their anger was mixed with a deep admiration for their military prowess. Several SPOs told Sushant that it would take a lot of bloodshed and a long time to defeat them. Many remained secretly sympathetic to the Maoists.

For many of the young inexperienced SPOs, along with the money they earned, being an SPO was a way of becoming modern, learning new games like snooker, acquiring new goods like portable music devices and headsets, wearing fatigues, and acquiring fluency in Hindi which marked them out as 'national', educated and cosmopolitan. Some of them were personally loyal to local Salwa Judum leaders, forming gangs which ruled a particular area. But living conditions were hard. One SPO who was living in government-provided accommodation described a room with no ventilation, no water and barely any electricity even though a connection had been provided. They all missed their villages terribly, especially because they knew they couldn't return. Unlike the central forces, for whom some kind of entertainment was provided, most SPOs had nothing to do in their time off but hang out with other SPOs.

Many of the SPOs were deeply ambivalent about their roles. For example, Sushant recorded an SPO, Badru, as saying with no sense of guilt: 'I am proud of shooting a dozen Maoists.' Badru had been assigned an INSAS rifle with 100 rounds. But, Badru added sullenly, 'CRPF men are not good, they treat us like animals and inferior human beings.' Thirty out of the 42 SPOs Sushant interviewed echoed Badru's unhappiness at being treated as lesser citizens by the CRPF. Resentful at being posted in the jungle, far from city lights, where danger lurks around every tree and a man can be felled by malaria as much as by a land mine, the CRPF blamed the adivasi SPOs for their predicament, as part of a more general anger against the sheer impertinence of the resisting savage. The adivasi as Naxalite is savage and irrational, while the adivasi as SPO is 'poor material'.

Compared to women Maoists – many of whom joined in order to escape the drudgery of home – the lives of the few female SPOs were defined by patriarchy. They worked from 7 a.m. to 1 p.m., washing the clothes of the CRPF officers, cleaning the police station or barracks, and helping out in the canteen. They almost never went on patrols, and some of them were married to other SPOs or local constables. They were also vulnerable to sexual abuse by the police: in March 2007, two men from the Chhattisgarh Armed Forces

(CAF) were injured in a clash at Konta camp with SPOs protesting against women SPOs being molested. Among the female SPOs who formed part of my guard in October 2010, there was also a process of Hinduization – the senior ones were maintaining a fast. All of them hoped to get regular police jobs.

Killing former comrades, at least at the beginning, was tough. Karam Rava described to me – with a little sadness – how on a patrol with Naga forces they caught two Naxal women in uniform: 'They didn't see us – we hid and shot them. They were both local girls – one from Ipaguda and one from Bodaras. I recognized them because when I was studying they would visit our school and would tell me to join them after I had finished.' Some SPOs would warn their friends or relatives. Muchaki Raju, who was responsible for burning at least two villages and killing seven people, saved the lives of two girls who were in the Maoist cultural troupe, after they reminded him that he had been the one to recruit them in the first place.

The higher up the SPOs had been in the Maoist hierarchy, the worse they turned. For instance, Bhimu of Jonpalli, an SPO notorious around Konta for his harassment of villagers, used to be commander of the Nagaram dalam. He was sent by the party with Rs 15,000 to get some goods from Cherla in Andhra Pradesh. Instead, he went to Dornapal, surrendered and became an SPO. Then in 2006 he brought the security forces to Borguda and killed two dalam members. By 2013, Bhimu was well ensconced as the local SPO don, extorting money from villagers.

Over time, killing and raping became easier and almost casual for all SPOs. They were told they would be 'regularized' as constables after killing 10 Naxalites; and having killed they knew there was no return. Camp residents described to me how the SPOs, high on alcohol and drugs, would trade scores of how many people they had killed. Some of the SPOs were so cruel that even the police were moved to pity the villagers. More than one villager has told me how, after having been picked up by SPOs, they were rescued by the thanedar who told them to run away.

At the same time, attrition rates of SPOs were high. Vikram Mandavi, the Salwa Judum leader in Bhairamgarh, told Sushant in 2010 that of the 865 sangham members who had surrendered and turned SPOs, 205 had returned to their villages and rejoined the Maoists. Indeed, loyalties in this war have always been in question, with the newspapers reporting that the Maoist attack on Rani Bodli camp in 2007 was possible only because of help from within the SPO ranks. For a long time the government was reluctant to arm the SPOs for fear that the guns would find their way back to the Maoists. In August 2016, one of the Maoist jan militia commanders injured and arrested by the CRPF in Bijapur, Kudiam Panda, had earlier been an SPO.

SPOs were also killed disproportionately to security forces. While the compensation for SPOs who died went up from Rs 1 lakh in 2004 to Rs 5 lakh in 2007, it was nothing compared to the pension a regular policeman's family would receive.

Defending the Indefensible

> The SPOs work within the framework of law and SPOs abide by rules and regulations applicable to them. The petition seeks to eliminate SPOs so that Naxalites can pester and even prosper.
>
> Government of Chhattisgarh affidavit, January 2008

SPOs complained that they were always on call: they lived in fear of being sacked or having their salary deducted if found absent. All the cases of dismissal or suspension were to do with the dereliction of minor duties. In return, however, the police ensured there was no punishment at all for heinous crimes like rape, murder or loot. In fact, these were encouraged as part of a general design to create insecurity in the villages. The inferiority of the adivasi was underlined at every level: as menial SPOs they were low down in the police hierarchy, but yet armed with the power to kill other adivasis. The latter were completely outside the pale of state protection.

The government refused to entertain any complaints about SPOs. The first reaction was to dismiss the accusations as false. In the few cases where a public outcry made a blank denial difficult, cases might be registered, but the accused would be listed as 'unknown'. The villagers who complained would then have cases filed against them, accusing them of being Naxalites or sympathizers. Between 2005 and 2010, only two cases had been registered against security forces or police in Bijapur and Dantewada districts respectively. In Dantewada three cases were registered against Salwa Judum activists and none in Bijapur. Of 10 complaints received from the public against Salwa Judum activists in 2006–7, all were described as false, and in 2008, of the four cases investigated out of 44 complaints, all were again judged as false.[6]

The police bent over backwards to accommodate SPOs and Salwa Judum leaders. In an exceptional case, five young girls testified to rape before a trial court in 2009. This was possible because of the combined efforts of Podiyam Panda – the CPI activist who first persuaded the girls to tell their stories – the Dantewada organization VCA and Sudha Bharadwaj, PUCL activist and lawyer. The court issued arrest warrants for the SPOs whom the girls named but the police never acted on these, claiming they could not find the SPOs. All this while, however, the SPOs were living in police barracks. Inevitably, the matter ended with the SPOs threatening the girls and their families, and the girls retracting their charges.

One of these five was Markami Bode, who had been picked up by Salwa Judum leaders en route to visit her relatives and raped by SPOs in the Konta police station. We mentioned her case in an affidavit before the Supreme Court. The SP Dantewada informed the Supreme Court on 17 June 2009 that 'the police enquired about her', and 'nobody knows as to where she has gone away'. Incidentally, this was a day after she deposed in the trial court. As for the men he had 'enquired' from, these were the very people accused by her: Salwa Judum leaders Boddu Raja, Soyam Mooka and Dinesh.

New Avatars of the Old SPOs

By 2010, in a name that is widely attributed to the training they got from the Mizo Reserve Battalion, the SPOs began to call themselves Koya Commandos. Some, like Kartam Surya and Kiche Nanda – both of whom had been named in several instances of murder by villagers, and also had warrants against them for rape – became powerful leaders in their own right and not just subservient to the Judum leaders. They had their own 'gangs' of 20–30 SPOs who reported to them rather than to the police – like the 'Surya gang'. Kartam Surya also claimed to have direct access to S.R.P. Kalluri, SSP Dantewada.

A former DGP told me that Kartam Surya was an SPO out of 'conviction' because the Maoists killed his father. The villagers, however, argued that belief had less to do with his activities than the money he made and the power he enjoyed. He made money in every way possible – bringing people to Judum rallies and claiming higher numbers than those who actually came, extorting money from villagers, asking for a cut from ration suppliers and tendu contractors, demanding a percentage of every contract issued by the irrigation, forest or public works department. An acquaintance estimated that Surya made Rs 10 lakh per month, some of which was channelled upwards to senior police officers and some redistributed within his gang, while he retained a sizeable amount for himself. At the time of his death in a Maoist ambush in 2012, he was building an eight-storey house in Dornapal, something that would have been impossible for him before the Judum began.

By 2011, many of the SPOs who had been recruited in 2005–7 were married and living in more permanent houses in the camps. The Maoists repeatedly asked the SPOs to leave their jobs and come home. About one-third did, but 4607 stayed on with the police and were converted by sleight of hand into the Armed Auxiliary Forces,[7] in order to circumvent the Supreme Court's order banning the use of SPOs in counter-insurgency. Their salaries went up to Rs

9300, but the change of name made little difference to the danger they represented to the villagers or the danger they faced from the Maoists. In July 2015, for instance, the Maoists killed four SPOs turned assistant constables.[8]

In 2013, when the police created the District Reserve Guard, they followed the same logic: using combat forces willing to work on 'meagre salaries', who were 'familiar with the jungles', 'spoke the local language', 'knew the terrain', and had an 'interest in defeating the Naxalites' since they had either 'surrendered' or been victims of the Naxalites and wanted to return to their villages. The only difference was that they were better trained. Like the SPOs, the DRG were also involved in some of the most horrific events of counter-insurgency, such as the mass rapes at Peddagellur and neighbouring villages in Bijapur, in November 2015.[9]

Since the SPOs and DRG were local, the police often used them as decoys, making them pose as Maoists to trap the villagers, a common tactic in counter-insurgency. In 2016, IG Kalluri told PTI, 'Sometimes, it becomes impossible for villagers to identify the DRG as they belong to local area and clad in civil uniforms make them [sic] indistinguishable from the local armed Naxals.'[10]

In 2009, villagers in Jaipal told me how SPOs came to their homes at night wearing Maoist uniforms, asking for Masa, a sangham worker. They asked Masa, 'Didn't you get the message that we were going to attack Korku police station?' He denied knowing anything about it, so they asked to be taken to the sarpanch. The sarpanch told me:

> I had been to a cockfight that afternoon and was sleeping off my liquor. But when the SPOs knocked on my door at 3 a.m. claiming to be visiting Maoists from Jharkhand and ostensibly in search of Deva and Kiran, two squad members, I had the wit to deny knowing them. Then Masa innocently produced a Maoist pamphlet, saying, 'I have one, how come you don't?' Then I was taken out and saw a force of 150 SPOs. They started beating me, and when my old mother

> protested, they hit her with a rifle butt and broke her thigh. They dragged me to the school 1 kilometre away, and when Pramod and Hadma intervened, they hit them too. They took away the thousand rupees I had won in the cockfight. I fell unconscious from the beating and they poured four jugs of water to revive me and beat me again. They asked me which party I supported and said if you are with the CPI, we will not let you go. I said I was a Congress supporter, so they took me to Dulapara where there is a Congress leader and he confirmed that I was with Congress, so they let me go. That day they also beat up other people in the village.

These pseudo-Maoists also reportedly caught little kids and took down the names and villages of their parents, asking innocently if they had attended the last Maoist meeting.

A Method in the Madness

> If we imagine no worse of them than they of themselves, they may pass for excellent men.
>
> Shakespeare, *A Midsummer Night's Dream*

> The whole system is driven by distrust – the police distrust people, the people distrust the police, there is distrust within the system.
>
> SP in Chhattisgarh, 2015

The police stations in Bastar are so heavily fortified – with barbed wire, sandbags and turrets from which guns peep out through small chinks – that they resemble a force under siege rather than one set up to solve any local disputes that villagers may have, which is the routine work of policing. There are apocryphal stories of policemen who, finding themselves left out of the station by accident at night, are unable to get back in. Add to this the CRPF camps which have come up – which are equally ringed with concertina wire – and the overriding image of Bastar now is miles of forest interspersed with miles of barbed wire. In one village, the CRPF camp with its check post barriers was bang in the middle of the village, so anyone going from one hamlet to another had to go through the check post. While the forest roads are empty, except for the occasional cowherd or villager collecting mahua, there are now increasingly lines of CRPF men stretched out along the highways, monitoring road construction work and hiding behind trees along 'sensitive stretches'. Despite this overwhelming presence, Maoist posters mysteriously appear on trees, telling the police to go back home, or informing the villagers about some renegade who has surrendered.

Inevitably, many of my conversations with the police – even when I have tried to have a 'neutral' academic discussion – have been coloured by their perception of me as an adversary.

The View from the Top

> An officer, known for his ruthless ways of working…assured his top bosses present in the meeting that if the purpose of the anti-Maoist operation was to bring the Maoists then he could bring 'dead bodies' with some surgical operations.
>
> The Hindu, 15.10.2015[11]

My main encounter with senior police officers or retired army personnel has been in air-conditioned rooms at panel discussions organized by security think tanks, where I am always trotted in as the 'alternative view'. I am usually the sole woman. Another site, though a less common one, has been in the studios of television channels where my co-panellist was often the retired policeman Prakash Singh, well known for his public interest litigation (PIL) on police autonomy and a strong supporter of the Salwa Judum. The police narrative is quite standard: it is first a law and order problem and then a socio-economic one. Eventually, it doesn't matter that the socio-economic problem is never addressed so long as they get more resources to enforce law and order. Over time, even this narrative of development has stopped. 'Unless the cancer is cured,' one police officer asked me indignantly at a police academy talk in Hyderabad, 'how can there be any development?'

This pattern is echoed in interactions with senior officials in many spheres of governance. If one expresses doubts over the way land is being acquired, one is described as being 'against development', 'not wanting technology', 'keeping adivasis in museums', even 'not wanting cellphones' for them. If I say that I think cellphones are an excellent example of appropriate technology that has transformed people's lives, they look surprised – as if I had suddenly chosen a swastika over a red flag. Security experts bring up the question of Maoist financing, and talk of the need to choke off the taxes they levy. But when I point out that the problem goes much deeper because police and politicians also levy 'taxes' on every business in the area, they pretend I had never spoken.

In more private meetings, some officials claim that they used to be sympathetic to the Naxalites as youth, till they saw the light and cleared the civil service exams, the holy grail of all middle-class Indians. In 2005, a former senior officer in Raipur, who compared the Judum to the Vietnamese forces driving out the occupation army (here Maoists) from their land, proudly showed us his novel on Naxalites. His blog, complete with a photo of his long greasy hair framing his square face in the best traditions of visual romanticism, tells us:

> In spite of many challenging administrative assignments, Shri X is totally committed to the world of creativity. 'My commitment to creativity,' says X 'has strengthened my administrative convictions for justice and fair play'… Shri X has come out with his novel in English, 'The Revolutionary' written against the backdrop of terror and extremist violence. The story relates to two close friends who seek to change the world in favour of peace and non-violence. In

> spite of the extremist threat, they go ahead with their non-violent agenda. While one of the friends dies in the hands of the extremists, the other one resolves to go ahead with his anti-terror campaign in memory of his dear friend.

It is hard not to see shades of the peaceful, Gandhian Salwa Judum in its pages.

Initially, in public at these seminars, the police insisted the Judum was a spontaneous movement – at best, some would grudgingly concede that 'it was a good idea, but wrongly implemented', admitting it was a police idea in the first place. Or they insisted that the role of the police was only to 'provide security' to the Judum processions, as if there was nothing odd in the police providing security to people while they were burning, looting and killing.

In 2007, I met a senior official (SO) in the Naxalite Cell of the Ministry of Home Affairs:

> Me: This violence that is happening in places like Rani Bodli [where Naxalites attacked an SPO camp] is mainly because of the Salwa Judum.
>
> SO: From this statement I can tell you are biased. You have no objectivity. Basically you want us to hand over the place to Naxalites, and take a decision that on 31 March 2007, we handed over Dantewada to them. You can say that people are in the Salwa Judum camps involuntarily to socialites in Delhi but you can't tell me that – I have spent a lot of time talking to people and I know they have come on their own. If I want I will take my own team of people whom I consider objective – I can take good sociologists like Yogendra Singh [a senior sociologist who had retired from Jawaharlal Nehru University].
>
> Me: If there is nothing to hide, why not allow camps to be more open? How come even journalists are reporting that people are not there voluntarily?

> SO: People are scared. Naxalites send advance parties to scout the place.
>
> Me: There are reports of villages being burnt.
>
> SO: That is new data for me, but I can theoretically imagine that if so many people are there, they will be out of control. But I have been telling the Chhattisgarh police that they must appoint more police to supervise SPOs.

If one were to give them the benefit of the doubt, senior police officers helicoptering in from Delhi were likely to be exposed only to SPOs or Judum leaders, who convinced them that people were fleeing from the Maoists. But, in fact, almost all of them did know what was actually going on, even if all they were willing to concede was that 'some excesses *may* be happening'. In particular, the dismissive responses of senior officials at both the state and Centre, and their eminent legal counsel before the Supreme Court, showed they simply didn't care. In 2012, I interviewed a top security adviser on the sidelines of a conference in Australia, where distance and retirement enabled him to talk: 'When it [Salwa Judum] got out of hand, people realized that it was not a good strategy but because critics like you were taking it up, government had to defend it. Governments cannot easily publicly acknowledge their mistake.'

Over time, especially after the Supreme Court ban on the Salwa Judum in 2011, several thinking police officers owned it had gone wrong. For instance, in 2013, the same official who accused me of being biased and denied villagers were coerced – now softened and in a different posting – organized a 'dialogue' in the Institute of Social Sciences, where he invited several civil society representatives. His successor in the home ministry, however, chose the occasion to hector us, saying that civil society must tell the Maoists to give up arms, as if we had much say in the matter.

Like X, DGP Viswaranjan, grandson of the progressive poet Firaq Gorakhpuri, sought to portray himself as a literary man. He too appeared to mellow after retirement. When I interviewed him in June 2014, he sought to ascribe the Salwa Judum to his predecessor: 'I didn't believe that civilians could be used to dismantle Naxals but Rathore was convinced it would spread and Naxals would be driven out.'

In service, however, Viswaranjan did everything possible to defend the Salwa Judum. Writing in the *Pioneer* on 5 September 2008, Viswaranjan claimed that the Salwa Judum was subject to Goebbelsian propaganda: 'It is nearly two years since the Polit Bureau [sic] of CPI (Maoist) resolved to isolate Salwa Judum at all levels so that it can be crushed. The network continues its stepped up pressure tactics at every level. It petitioned the Supreme Court through Nandini Sunder and historian Ramchandra Guha [sic] to ban Salwa Judum.' After we challenged this description of us as Maoist stooges, he responded plaintively that policemen were mere 'Sudras' compared to powerful Brahminical forces like us.

Police officers in general, and not just Viswaranjan, are steeped in victimology – they like to portray themselves as misunderstood and misrepresented by a powerful network of left activists. Some also like to see themselves as messiahs, saving the nation from the Naxalites, even if it means breaking several laws and every norm of the Constitution in the process. S.R.P. Kalluri epitomizes the way these two aspects are often blended, the quintessential bully who claims persecution:

> Composite forces strike again in Bijapur district recovering a dead body of a uniformed male Maoist along with a 12 bore rifle, a bharmar, some tiffin bombs and naxal dump… The tally of Maoist bodies recovered this month has thus become 16 with no loss to Security forces… Fighting Maoism is an arduous and uphill task. But Bastar Police along with CPMF's [Central Paramilitary Forces] is highly committed to accomplish this what once appeared to be an impossible task. We face lot of criticism, negativity, complaints, cases, writs, bad publicity and foul mouthing by forces that are

antithetical to the unity and integrity of our nation and those who want to wreck our Internal security. We at Bastar Police very well understand these forces. We reaffirm our faith and commitment to free Bastar from the shackles of Maoism.

S.R.P. Kalluri, IG Bastar, Whatsapp message, November 2015

The Lower Rungs

Nobody wants to be posted to Bastar. When we joined, we just wanted a job, it didn't matter where – we had family responsibilities. We didn't set out to fight the Naxalites.

SHO in Sukma district, 2014

It will take 10 years, maybe 20 years, but in the end there have to be talks.

Constable, 2015

One more day has gone.

Sign in a Golapalli police station

I had less opportunity to interview policemen at lower ranks, but they were more varied in their attitudes than the senior ones. They were less sanguine that the government would triumph and less certain about the wisdom of the fight. A co-passenger on a bus ride to Sukma in 2007 told me that his life had been miserable, and he had left the district force to become a *shikshakarmi*, a contract schoolteacher. Excerpts from our conversation:

Ex-policeman: The force looks attractive from the outside, but it's not what you think it is. We had to patrol for days, sometimes five or six days at a stretch, eating whatever we got, without bathing, till our clothes and shoes stuck to our skin. It's not the fault of the police – it was the Judum people who burnt the houses. There were constant encounters. In three months last summer we shot 60–70 people on patrol in Bijapur.

Me: Were all these Naxalites?

Ex-policeman: Of course not. None of them were Naxalites. Sometimes an SPO would point out someone and tell us to shoot, sometimes we shot simply because the villager was running away and refused to stop when we called out. We called out in whichever language we knew – Telugu, Hindi, but the villagers didn't understand.

Me: Did you record these deaths somewhere?

Ex-policeman: [Sounding shocked] Our jobs would be in trouble if we did. We left the bodies in the jungles. We recorded it as an encounter only if someone was actually wearing a uniform or carrying a weapon. I personally never killed anyone, but if by chance my bullet hit anyone in an encounter, I hate to think of it.[12]

Some police and CRPF personnel I have met have even been sympathetic to our litigation, saying it was needed to check human rights abuses. But by far the majority have been unsmiling, unhelpful and hostile, determined to save their backs and advance their careers, regardless of the costs to the people and the place. This attitude is transmitted early on in training. One young recruit from Uttar Pradesh who I met near Jagdalpur, where he had come with his group to mine sand from the Indrawati, sounded indignant that one could even think the locals had any more right to the place than he had: 'It all belongs to the government,' he declared.

For the more seasoned ones, each day that passes is a relief. In many areas, the police have begun to wear civilian clothes when they venture out to the haat, leaving behind the uniforms that earlier gave them so much authority. Policemen complain that Maoists come into haats dressed as civilians and even as schoolchildren, and pick off the police. Some policemen have built good contacts in their villages, but complain that coordination with the CRPF is not always easy.

From Naga Freedom Fighters to Hindustan ka Phauj

> Me: How is support for the Naxalites different from Naga support for Phizo and the Naga National Council?
>
> Naga reservist (with pride): Phizo's was a freedom struggle. But we are Hindustan ka phauj [soldiers of the Indian army] now.
>
> Interview with a Naga IRB jawan, Dimapur, 2008

The Naga India Reserve Battalion (IRB), which was the main force in the initial years of the Judum, comprised young boys who had been unemployed in Nagaland. Naga newspapers reported that they were misbehaving in Nagaland as well, and Naga human rights groups protested at their being deployed in Chhattisgarh to oppress adivasis, when they themselves were oppressed by the Indian state.

The Naga IRB acquired a reputation for ruthless fierceness – and many accounts by villagers indict in equal measure the Judum and the Naga forces for the burning and the killings. In many cases, the Naga battalion seems to have gone on their own to attack villages. There were also dark rumours of the number of children being born with mixed adivasi and Naga features, and of the disappearance of dogs and pigs in the villages around the Naga camps. One person told me that the Nagas had offered Rs 100 for a dog and Rs 1000 for a woman. A newspaper article complained that the Nagas had killed more pigs than Naxalites. The All India Fact-finding team in 2005 reported seeing the Naga forces bring back a cow they had commandeered from Satwas, across the Indrawati, along with four prisoners. But given that Gonds also sacrifice cows, this was more of a scandal for small-time journalists and the administration than for adivasis, except that it was their cattle which were being stolen. Considering what the forces from mainland India have been doing to Nagaland over the years, the use as well as racist abuse of Naga forces seems doubly tragic.

By the time the Mizo battalion came in 2007, the everyday attacks on villages had passed; and I occasionally saw bored jawans emerge from their fortress camps to hang out in Sukma town. The newspapers occasionally reported IRB excesses against villagers – creating havoc in Mana airport in Raipur as soon as they arrived, eating the cattle and goats of Dhurli village without payment to the owners, harassing women in Chatti and looting a liquor shop in Konta.[13] The police tried to cover up the incidents, including when a Naga jawan killed a shopkeeper, Shekhar Shah, in Dornapal in October 2006. Shah made the mistake of asking for money for the goods he took. On 12 April 2007, the Thakurs of Nakulnar, who are a powerful lobby in normal times, held a 'chakka jam' in their village against Mizo jawans for getting drunk and molesting Thakur women. Adivasi women have, of course, always been fair game for the Thakurs themselves.

A Long Way from Home

> Nobody here is an ordinary villager – they are all Maoist.
>
> Special Task Force member out on patrol, 2015

> For some states, continuing Naxal violence is beneficial. It helps them get central funds. And then it's not their men who die but those from outside the state [central force personnel].
>
> Dilip Trivedi, Director General, CRPF, at his retirement[14]

The Naga and Mizo IRBs were replaced by the BSF and the CRPF, whose men came from all over India. I would often hear, when passing a CRPF camp, someone speaking Tamil on the mobile to his family, or see a man climb a small hill to catch a signal. In 2015, I found myself at a camp barrier, chatting to a kindly, homesick Sikh who had five years to retire, a thoughtful Kashmiri and a smiling Uttarakhandi. We talked of how Bastar compared to Punjab and Kashmir in terms of counter-insurgency. A stern Haryanvi who insisted that we could only talk of how well the government was doing soon pulled these men away. It is sad when an understanding of the cultural diversity of India develops under conditions of being occupier and occupied.

For several years, the entrance to the CRPF camp at Chintagufa retained a signboard erected by some ironic officer: 'Welcome to Heaven.' The camp is indeed located in a heavenly place, at a height overlooking a large lake with lotuses, against the backdrop of wooded hills. The name of the village means tamarind forest. But life is anything but heavenly for the villagers, and indeed, for the security forces as well.

There are two kinds of men among the CRPF: the first kind want talks and to get the hell out of a malarial, comfortless life in Bastar, where the only entertainment is devotional sessions in the camp or hanging out in the tea shack in some godforsaken village. The second type itches for a frontal fight with the Maoists. One of the former told me sadly: 'If we die, there will be more where we came from – our vacancies will be filled. And if they die, there will also be more where they came from. As long as the forces are constantly replenished the war will continue.' In 2013, *India Today* reported that 13,658 CRPF personnel left their jobs between 2009 and 2012, tired of their jungle postings, the malaria and the working conditions, among other things. Understandably, however, this is never given the publicity that Maoist surrenders receive; and recruitment continues to be high in these jobless times. Responding to a question in the Rajya Sabha on attritions in 2013, the then minister of state for home, R.P.N. Singh, said: 'The attrition of jawans of CRPF, BSF, ITBP & CISF on account of voluntary retirement and resignation from the service during 2013 is 1.34% only of the total sanctioned strength of the Jawans in these 4 Forces, which cannot be considered to be high.'[15]

One former CRPF commander said that he had sent out feelers to the Maoists saying his men would patrol in either direction for 2 kilometres and nothing should happen to them. In exchange, they would leave the Maoists undisturbed. Many of them, as trained fighting men, had also disapproved of the Judum, and were contemptuous of the SPOs, saying they used them only for cleaning. In 2016, one deputy commander told me he disapproved of his superiors' policies of mass arrests and fake surrenders but could do nothing. He said he felt pity for the villagers who were so obviously poor.

But on the other hand, there are plenty of men in the CRPF who felt sheer hatred for the Maoists and, by extension, for the villagers. They particularly resent the ambushes and IEDs. The anger escalated after the Tadmetla ambush of 2010, when 76 CRPF men were killed. A man from the ill-fated 62nd battalion told me a few months later, standing amidst schools which had been relocated from interior villages to Dornapal camp: 'Here we are surrounded by all *their* children' – as if village children were some kind of illegitimate Maoist spawn.

In January 2012, when the CBI visited Morpalli to investigate the burning of the village, on orders from the Supreme Court, they came accompanied by the CRPF. The CRPF took up positions inside the village – right around the memorial, next to the houses, under the trees. I was in the village then. It was the first time I had been so close to so many armed men, and my heart beat faster with anxiety. I could also feel the man sitting beside me stiffening with fear. Later, I wandered over to talk to some of the CRPF men who were looking at the memorial to the Maoists who died in the 2010 ambush.

The first jawan who spoke said, 'The forces must have seen the memorial and gone berserk. It was wrong to have killed the 76 CRPF men.' I replied, 'Yes, it was very wrong, but it was also wrong to have burnt houses and killed people here,' to which the jawan said, 'But they have got compensation.' I said, 'But all they have got is Rs 25,000 for burnt houses and some rations in relief.' Another jawan added, 'And out of that too, the Maoists have taken away Rs 15,000,' to which a third jawan said, 'But that is neither here nor there – the government has compensated them.' I asked, 'But hasn't the government also compensated the 76 CRPF jawans? Their families have got their pensions, these villagers have nothing.' To which the first jawan responded, 'Nothing can compensate for the loss of a loved one.'

Don't adivasis have loved ones too? Or can you throw some money at them and expect them to jump with joy at your 'civic action'? The conversation went on, with the CRPF jawan beginning to shout, 'We didn't burn houses or kill anyone. You are inciting villagers against us.'

~

This war is driving everyone crazy, especially those who are fighting without any ideals to sustain them. Those who are not depressed are angry, and others are angry and depressed by turns, and those who are neither depressed nor angry but complacent and careerist about it all are the most insane.

At least the victims have right on their side. The perpetrators have nothing. When they have cleared the land for the capitalists, they will go home and fight their own battles against land acquisition in their own villages, and take out their anger on their wives and daughters, in those 'civilized' parts of India where women are killed for marrying outside their own caste and community.

Necropolitics now defines the conflict. After an 'encounter' in West Bengal, the corpses of Maoist women were carried out on poles with their feet and hands tied together, like cattle being taken to a slaughterhouse; in April 2013, after an encounter in Puwarti village in Chhattisgarh, the police refused to let the family members of the Andhra Maoists take the bodies. On the other side, the Maoists would not let the police recover the body of a policeman they had killed in an encounter; instead, journalists were sent to recover the rotting corpse. In Jharkhand, the Maoists placed a bomb on the body of a dead jawan, so that others who tried to recover it would be hurt. The police have also been accused of being callous with the lives of their own men – with corpses being taken for cremation in garbage trucks.[16] Where even the 'martyrs' have no dignity, what can we hope for the living?

Part III

Institutions on Trial

11

Security or Development?

(T)he supreme government was affected by the poverty of the Indigenous peoples of Chiapas and endowed the area with hotels, prisons, barracks, and a military airport…

Chiapas loses blood through many veins: Through oil and gas ducts, electric lines, railways, through bank accounts, trucks, vans, boats and planes, through clandestine paths, gaps, and forest trails.

What does the beast leave behind in exchange for all it takes away?

Education? The worst in the country. At the elementary school level, 72 out of every 100 children don't finish the first grade.

One-and-a-half million people have no medical services at their disposal. There are 0.2 clinics for every 1,000 inhabitants, one-fifth of the national average.

Fifty-four percent of the population of Chiapas suffer from malnutrition, and in the highlands and forest this percentage increases to 80%.

This is what capitalism leaves as payment for everything that it takes away…

Subcomandante Marcos, August 1992, 'Chiapas: The Southeast in Two Winds – A Storm and a Prophecy'

The story of Chiapas, Mexico, is the story of Bastar – the story of all places where indigenous people give and keep giving, and are rewarded with mining dust, harsh and treeless landscapes, and the stink of death.

If you look at the list of legislation the Indian state has enacted to protect its scheduled tribes, its benevolence shocks and awes: the Fifth and Sixth Schedules of the Constitution allow for distinctive laws in scheduled areas; PESA 1996 requires the government to consult those whose lands are being acquired; the FRA 2006 aims to redress the historical expropriation of adivasis by recognizing their rights over their forests; and the SC/ST Prevention of Atrocities Act, 1989 punishes prejudice. Individual citizens are looked after: Article 15(4) and 16(4a) provide for quotas in education and government services; Articles 330, 332, and 335 for representation in Parliament and state assemblies. Article 275 (1) allows special central grants for ST welfare; Article 339 sets up the National Commission for Scheduled Tribes (NCST), and as the cherry on the welfare cake, an entire bureau, the Ministry of Tribal Affairs, exists to look after STs.

Why is it then that adivasis are the poorest section of India's population? In 2011–12, 45.3 per cent of adivasis, compared to the all-India average of 25.4 per cent, were below the Tendulkar poverty line of Rs 27 per day in rural areas and Rs 33 per day in urban areas. Why is it that when NMDC produces 20 million tonnes of iron ore annually from the Bailadilla mines alone, one of the biggest revenue earners for the state and for NMDC, people around the mines go to bed hungry? In rural India 40.2 per cent of men and 49 per cent of women STs have a body mass index less than 18.5, which indicates chronic malnutrition.[1] Why is it that the Governors in states with large populations of STs, who are supposed to play a special constitutional role in their welfare, are mostly chosen from the police, intelligence or defence wings of the state? It must be because the STs are inherently seditious.

Like everything else up for grabs in this civil war, the government's statements have vacillated over how best to pursue the war – from development *with* security, to *no* development *without* security, to no development, only security. The money tells us that the priorities were never in doubt. In 2014–15, continuing with the policies of previous years, the Ministry of Home Affairs reported the following allocations in its annual report, under 'The Government's strategy to combat LWE (left wing extremism)':

Security

- Rs 2 crore to fortify each police station under the Scheme for Construction of Fortified Police Stations.[2]
- Rs 5 crore per annum for anti-Naxal media propaganda
- Rs 19.3 crore per annum for the Civic Action Programme (to be spent by the armed forces to win over the villagers)
- Rs 207.08 crore as Security Related Expenditure (SRE) in 106 districts in 2014–15[3]
- Rs 445.82 crore for special infrastructure scheme for nine LWE affected states[4]
- Rs 7300 crore for 5477 kilometres under Road Requirement Plan I for 34 LWE districts[5]

Development

- Rs 2640 crore per annum across 88 districts for the Integrated Action Plan (IAP) started in 2009–10, to provide public infrastructure and services in backward districts[6]

But much of the IAP money also ended up in roads. Economist Kaveri Gill and others have found that: 'Around 40% of funds till September 2012 were spent on the construction of roads, while 8% were spent on education (through schools and *anganwadi* centres), and a dismal 3% was spent on healthcare.'[7]

Of course, the ministry lists roads and civic action under 'development'; and my list does not take into account the money spent on education, health, food supplies, etc. under the regular budget of the government. However, this is rarely pursued on a war footing, unlike roads. As of 2011, in undivided Dantewada, expenditure on drinking water was 0.81 per cent of funds available, and expenditure under the National Rural Health Mission for Bijapur and Dantewada districts was 1.18 per cent and 6.03 per cent respectively.[8]

On the security side, the balance sheet above does not take into account the money spent on deployment of central armed police. In November 2014, Chhattisgarh asked for a waiver of the Rs 2400 crore spent on CRPF deployment since 2007.[9] This is quite apart from what the state spends on its own police forces and other central armed police forces. The journalist Gautam Navlakha has estimated that 1.4 million out of a total of 2.5 million armed personnel are engaged in internal security in Jammu and Kashmir, north-east India and the central Indian states.[10] Both on the books and on the ground, expenditure on security trumps spending on development by a healthy margin.

The Judum permanently changed the landscape of the region in several ways. For one, the area became more urban because of the camps, and people fleeing to block headquarters. Many more immigrants came in. Sukma and Konta tehsils went from being negligibly urban to 21.5 per cent and 13.5 per cent urban respectively. In Bhairamgarh tehsil, the urban population expanded from zero in 2001 to 10.8 per cent in 2011, while in Bijapur tehsil, the increase was even more dramatic, from zero to 24.3 per cent. Of the urban population in Bijapur, 13.63 per cent was SC, reflecting the migration of Mahars and others from Gangalur and other villages after the Judum began. Following the Judum, Bhairamgarh in Bijapur district and Dornapal in Dantewada (later Sukma district) were declared statutory towns in the 2011 census. Both had been small, four-shop villages before the Judum camps were set up.[11]

Another major change has been the division of the revenue district of Bastar into seven smaller ones, including Sukma, Bijapur and Narayanpur, ostensibly because smaller districts enable more focus on development. Urban official infrastructure, with fancy collectorate buildings, has expanded greatly, while the villages remain without basics like schools, electricity and health centres. While, normally, police jurisdictions overlap with revenue administrative divisions,[12] in Bastar, the police districts of Bijapur and Sukma were formed earlier, showing the importance given to close policing over development.

A Battle about Roads

The government wants to build roads so that it can move troops around and take timber and minerals out, and the Maoists want to make the roads impassable to prevent this. Villagers say that they want good roads to make it easier to access markets and hospitals for emergencies, but this makes sense only if road construction is accompanied by better transport and health facilities. Less than one per cent of the villagers own cycles, and the vast majority walk to wherever they are going, even up to 100 kilometres. Villagers need roads, but also drinking water, irrigation, education and health. What they don't need are the only thing they seem to be getting in abundance: massive highways.

Over the years, I have seen the highways made and unmade, widened and slashed. In 2009, for the first time since 1990 when I began visiting Bastar, the portion of National Highway (NH) 30 that runs from Jagdalpur to Sukma was blocked. Villagers had gone at night during 'Martyrs' Week' to dig up the highway and lay trees across it. Further south on NH 30, the distance from Sukma to Konta that should take an hour now takes four hours, because the roads are potholed, cracked and bone crushing.

Periodically, the government puts out tenders in an attempt to widen or repair the highways; periodically, the Maoists burn the road rollers and dumpers, and periodically, urban residents sigh at the inconvenience. The government asked the Border Roads Organisation (BRO) – famous for their cheery signs: 'If you drive rash, you will end with crash' – to build the roads. But even the BRO failed in the face of Maoist determination. From 2014 onwards, the highways are being built under CRPF supervision with men patrolling each stretch, and armed men sitting on road rollers; huge billboards with images of sleek highways and expensive vehicles outside every CRPF camp exhort the residents to help in the construction of these roads.

But even if the roads were passable, travel would be unsafe. Initially, it was the Judum which made travel difficult. In 2006, when the Judum stopped buses on the road to Jagargunda, the bus drivers went on hartal. A truck driver I met on the Andhra Pradesh border told me, 'I used to do the Raipur–Madras highway route four times a month. Since the Judum started, we can't do the stretch between Dornapal and Konta at night any more – we get stopped by the SPOs and questioned. The frequency of buses has also come down.'

Since then, however, it is the Maoists whom the bus-travelling public perceives as the major threat. Jawans returning home for leave use passenger buses or private jeeps, thus putting everyone at risk. On several occasions, the Maoists have blasted civilian vehicles with IEDs, thinking they were carrying only soldiers. Their apologies for the 'mistakes' console no one. By 2015, burning passenger buses in protest against fake encounters or fake surrenders by the police seems to have become a major part of the Maoist repertoire.[13]

Schools, a Casualty

> These teachers belong to our government. We have kept them all together in one place. Those who don't join the Judum will get no school or be allowed to go to school.
>
> Basaguda camp resident, 2008

> Once you have the children, the parents will follow.
>
> Former DIG, Haryana, on tackling insurgency in Chhattisgarh by building schools in clusters, Forum for Integrated National Security meeting, May 2010

Even before the Judum began, teaching was erratic. In 26 years of visiting adivasi villages across India, I have seen schools which function as warehouses and liquor distilleries, schools where the teacher comes once or twice a month, and also some schools where the teachers are incredibly dedicated and know the family histories of every child.

But whatever the state of teaching, the important thing was that pre-Judum the government accepted the principle that every village should have its own primary school. When the Judum began in 2005–6, the government withdrew teachers from village schools in the targeted areas and ordered them to live and work in camps instead. Those villagers who had not joined the Judum were deemed to be with the Maoists and therefore undeserving of schools. In some cases such as Etrajpad, the village was burnt in 2009, but the teacher was shifted in 2006 itself. Since the Judum, many schools and ashrams have been running on paper alone; the teachers have got used to getting paid without teaching, and are reluctant to return to their village assignments, claiming they are scared of the Maoists.

Even otherwise, the Maoists have provided the excuse for teachers and others to renege on their work. In Polpadar village, the principal received a letter in red ink, purportedly from the Maoists, written in a style that the urban dweller fantasizes is Maoist (even though a threat is hardly likely to end with a red salute):

> Principal, correct yourself, or else you will regret it. You don't feel scared on hearing our name, but you will feel scared when you see us. I am giving you this last chance to correct yourself, if you do not do so now, you will not be able to regret it later. If you don't do as we say, you will die a dog's death. If you don't believe me, then eat this

> fruit (accompanied by a drawing of a crude grenade), the powder will make you fair. Send all the hostel children home, and keep the school closed for five months. If the school is not shut by Friday, you know what the consequences will be. Lal Salaam Lal Salaam Lal Salaam. (translation mine)

The writer turned out to be a disgruntled schoolteacher, upset with the principal's insistence that he come to work on time.

Apart from no teachers, there are now no buildings. When the war began, the security forces occupied schools since they were usually the only cement buildings in a village. The Maoists decided the schools had to be destroyed to prevent the forces staying in the village. Sometimes the villagers did it themselves; sometimes teams were brought in from neighbouring villages to do the job. Schools with trees growing out of blasted walls and half-collapsed roofs are a common sight across the district.

By 2011, in the worst-affected blocks of Konta, Bhairamgarh and Bijapur, barely half of the villages still had primary schools.[14] The situation was visibly different in blocks like Sukma and Chindgarh which had not been affected by the Judum. Literacy rates, similarly, reflect both war and decades of neglect. In 2011, literacy rates in Dantewada and Bijapur districts were the lowest in Chhattisgarh – a mere 42.12 per cent and 40.86 per cent respectively, compared to an average of 71.04 per cent for Chhattisgarh.[15] In 2005–6, because the conditions were so disturbed and schooling was difficult, the Collector, K.R. Pisda, issued orders that all the children should be automatically promoted. Ironically, the district got a Satyen Maitra literacy award in 2007 for its total literacy campaign.[16]

At the height of the Judum, a teacher in the Maraipalli hostel told me he never knew exactly how many children he would have to feed on any given night. Parents came and left their children in the hostel when attacks were on in the forest, and took them back when the situation became calmer or if they had decided to migrate to Andhra Pradesh. Many of the children I spoke to in Maraipalli had not seen their parents for months – indeed there had been an order that year (2007) that they should not be allowed to go home for the summer holidays. The situation was scarcely better for college students from Judum-affected areas, some of whom had not been home for four years by 2009. One student was doing a third MA, because a BEd was too expensive, waiting desperately for a shikshakarmi job.

While those who stayed in Chhattisgarh had no schools, those who fled to Andhra Pradesh found it equally hard to continue with their studies. In 2007, I met 15-year-old Lakshmi, in a bare, windswept hut on a hill in Andhra Pradesh. Lakshmi said she had been midway through her class 10 board exams in Basaguda when they heard that the Salwa Judum and police were 3 kilometres away in the neighbouring village. There was only time to climb into a tractor with the rest of her family, and flee. She wanted to study further but could not, because there were no Hindi schools nearby, and she had to work if the family was to eat. Another young Andhra IDP, Hadma, said his textbooks had been burnt in a Judum attack just before he was to write the board exam. When he went to Konta the following year to try to take the exams, he was accosted and beaten up by SPOs who asked him where he had been. Apart from loss of textbooks, many children suffered because they lost their caste certificates and school records.

The schools in the Judum camps disproved the claim that these were 'model' settlements. Even in 2015, many of these schools had no furniture, other than a jute runner on the floor for the children to sit on. In one boys' hostel, the beds double up as chairs and tables during the day, with the teacher perched on a bed at the far end of the room, giving lessons. The walls are cracking, water seeps in, and the primary impression is one of dereliction.

In Killeguda, near Sukma, the village had just acquired a new school when it was forcibly taken over by the CRPF. School staff recounted resentfully how the CRPF broke open the lock one Saturday afternoon and dumped all the school furniture into the old building. When I visited, the higher grades were having classes in the corridors, under cracking roofs. This was the story in several other villages. One teacher said that when he demanded to see the occupation orders in writing, he was slapped around by the jawans. The CRPF blame the administration for not building barracks for them, but even when these barracks are built, they continue to be located next to schools and hostels, effectively using the students as human shields. Despite the Supreme Court's repeated orders that schools should be vacated, many are still occupied by security forces.

Villagers are very keen to get their primary and middle schools restarted. The 2009 Right to Education Act also requires the government to provide every village with a primary school. It is the administration which is resisting, building huge 1000-seater hostels (Portacabins) next to Judum camps. The Portacabins are made of bamboo ply with tin roofs, and have colourful paintings on the walls. They often show the Hindu goddess of learning, Saraswati, but also maps, animals and trees. However, sanitary conditions are uniformly terrible. One principal of a new Portacabin announced cheerfully that she had 50 toilets for 524 girls. But when I exclaimed in surprise, she quickly conceded that none were working.

Initially started in 2008 as 'bridge schools' for children whose education had been disturbed, the Portacabins employ assistants, called *anudeshikas*, to identify such children and bring them into schools. Over time, however, the Portacabins have become the preferred mode of education, as everyone in the administration and the teachers themselves are firmly convinced that children will get educated only if they live apart from their Maoist/militant/illiterate/ backward parents. Several children, 'victims of the Naxalites', have also been taken away to hostels run by the Vanvasi Kalyan Ashram, a front of the RSS working among adivasis. The administration seems convinced that any schooling in the interior will only help the Naxalites. One former Chief Secretary of Chhattisgarh told me in all seriousness that if these children were taught chemistry, they would only learn to make bombs. In fact, they are learning how to make bombs even without the benefit of a science education.

The parents and children themselves are ambivalent about the Portacabins. They have internalized the idea of their own educational and civilizational inferiority. At the same time, they worry about their little ones who cry when they leave home. One parent told me he didn't know where to send his five-year-old son, since there was no school in the village. He would be lost in a 1000-seater Portacabin, and no relative could be charged with looking after such a small boy. The principal of a Portacabin told me that the children were happy in the school and didn't want to go home, but in the next breath she admitted that once they went, it was hard to get them back, and that many were very homesick after their parents visited. Like Australia's 'stolen generations' of aboriginal children who were taken away ostensibly for their own protection, India's adivasi children are being told they must choose between home and education.

School routines, both in the government schools and in the private schools run by the RSS, called Saraswati Shishu Mandirs, and the Mata Rukmini ashrams set up by the Sarvodaya activist Dharampal Saini, are designed to 'Hinduize' and 'civilize' the children, so that they forget their own languages and festivals. The children wake up at 4 a.m., do prayers at 4.30, and then clean the premises. School starts at 9 a.m. and finishes at 3 p.m., with a break for lunch. After 3 p.m., there is more cleaning up, sports, study and prayers again before dinner and bed. Children who come out of these schools are adept at diving respectfully at adult feet, singing bhajans and generally displaying all the markers of a good Hindu child. As one parent remarked, they are also turned into consumers: the scholarship money they get from government is spent on shoes, toothbrushes, papad, pickles – all things that are difficult to get in the villages. But while schooling creates a certain disposition, it does not necessarily offset all other aspects of their lives, including the rage they felt when the Judum burnt their homes. Children from such schools also join the Maoists. One elderly teacher I met who ran a Mata Rukmini ashram said his students had ended up in both camps – the Judum and the Maoists. Both were equally respectful when they saw him.

The Maoists claim to run their own schools; they also bring out some textbooks in Gondi; journalists who have seen these say they have chapters on local heroes as well as hygiene and basic science.[17] If the Maoists destroy government schools because the security forces occupy them, the security forces destroy Maoist schools for no other reason than they are Maoist. In June 2012, for instance, the CRPF destroyed a small school in Savapalli village, claiming it was being run by the Naxals. However, schooling is clearly not a priority for the Maoists, any more than it is for the government.

No Place for Health

The shortfall of doctors and surgeons in the tribal areas of Chhattisgarh is the highest in the country, with 170 doctors for 403 primary health care centres. Chhattisgarh's 84 community health centres in tribal areas have four surgeons and nine physicians.[18] Even if a health centre exists on paper, there is no certainty that it will be open or provide any treatment to people struggling with malnutrition, anaemia, malaria, cholera and dysentery.[19] In 2015, the government of Chhattisgarh decided to outsource recruitment of health staff to private agencies to draw on a wider pool than that available in the state. I met one of these newly hired nurses in a Konta village; he spoke no Gondi or Hindi and the villagers spoke no Telugu, so both were equally lost. Like the schools, the government has located health centres in clusters, ostensibly because of the war. For instance, the Mankeli panchayat sub-health centre is located 10 kilometres away in Bijapur, where there is already a district hospital.[20]

Despite the great need, the government has withheld medical care as an instrument of war. A block medical officer in Dantewada told me in 2006 that the CRPF had turned back one of his vehicles from the villages, alleging they were giving medicines to the Maoists. In July 2015, a villager informed me that he had gone to the health

Health Centres in Undivided Dantewada District

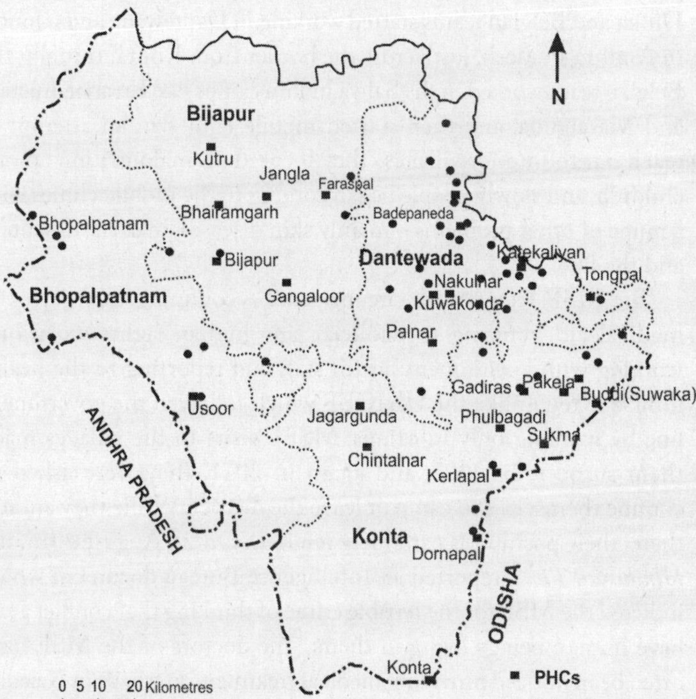

Source: www.jsk.gov.in/chhattisgarh/chhattisgarh_dantewada.pdf, based on 2001 Census

centre in Chintalnar, only to be directed instead to the CRPF camp where they were distributing medicines as part of their civic action plan.

The government has also made it difficult for international organizations like MSF and the International Committee of the Red Cross (ICRC) to offer medical relief in the interior. The MSF works primarily to provide health care in conflict areas. In September 2006, Dutch and Belgian teams started working in Dantewada and Chintur in Andhra Pradesh, just across the border from Konta. Initially, the Belgian team worked in the Salwa Judum camps like Errabor, Injeram and Maraiguda, and then started mobile clinics in an attempt to reach out to interior villages. They focused on malnutrition among children, and slowly people began coming to the mobile clinics with a range of other problems – mainly skin diseases, malaria, dysentery and the like.

The MSF teams were circumspect – confining themselves to medical aid, refusing to publicize any human rights violations, working with government health staff and reporting to the health ministry. Yet, unlike the UNICEF which followed the government line by working only in camps, MSF's visits to the villages made them suspect. In 2007, and again in 2011, they were asked to confine themselves to camp or leave the district. While they are still there, their position is extremely tenuous. On 24 August 2015, the *Hindustan Times* reported an Intelligence Bureau document which indicted the MSF for the terrible crime of thinking that conflict areas have human beings living in them: 'The doctors of the MSF have often been noticed providing medical treatment to tribals in Naxalite infested areas.'[21] The government also asked the ICRC, which was operating mobile clinics and primary health care centres in Kutru and Chintalnar, to leave in 2013,[22] worried that their presence would signal that the conflict in Dantewada should be counted as a 'non-international armed conflict'. Despite the use of paramilitary forces and sophisticated weaponry, the government has insisted that the war on Maoism is an internal law and order issue, to avoid following the

Geneva Conventions on non-international armed conflict, especially the involvement of outside observers.

The Maoists say they have never opposed medical relief, but in November 2010 they blew up an ambulance in Kandhamal and in April 2012 they attacked an ambulance carrying sick children from Chintagufa to Dornapal. In each case, they said they were targeting jawans who were travelling in these ambulances, in violation of operational procedures. But inevitably, civilians were killed, contributing to a general atmosphere of uncertainty over humanitarian operations.

Development as a Weapon

> Now that it is our [CPI Maoist] government, why should we let them establish their administration again?
>
> If we concentrate on ensuring transparency in the use of government funds, we will lose our struggle focus.
>
> Maoist leaders, 2012

> Behold, behold, where Madam Mitigation comes!
>
> Shakespeare, *Measure for Measure*

The IAP, which started in 2009–10, was much publicized as an effort to bring development to the Naxalite areas. The money was to be spent by a district-level committee consisting of the Collector, SP and Divisional Forest Officer. The Planning Commission wanted the funds to be routed through panchayats, but eventually the home ministry and its centralized approach won out. Not only was the Planning Commission itself jettisoned in 2014, but the CRPF managed to ease itself into the decision-making in the IAP. In 2015, the IAP was transferred, lock, stock and gun barrel, to the home ministry. It has since been renamed the Additional Central Assistance Plan.

In Dantewada, which was precisely the kind of place that the IAP was aimed at, the scheme was pointless because the district administration could only work through the sarpanches, and during the Judum most sarpanches in Konta, Bijapur, Bhairamgarh and other affected blocks had left the villages and come to live in camp. After that, no panchayat elections were held in the cut-off villages – the sarpanches filed their nominations and were elected unopposed in the camps. They worked with the district administration to create schemes on paper.

Several villagers in Konta – some of whom had been sarpanches earlier – told me in October 2011 that the idea of winning hearts and minds through the IAP would not succeed in their village because it was the Maoists who decided what kind of work would happen there. Maoist attitudes had hardened after the Judum. In 2012, I was again told that the Maoists had instructed people not to take government funds for anything other than schools (without concrete roofs), the PDS, anganwadi or pre-primary childcare centres and hand-pumps. Sometimes the dalam would agree to some works but then the village sangham would object, and they would have to stop. For instance, Kosa of Polampad said he had asked the Maoists for permission to build Indira Awas homes (low-cost houses for below-poverty-line [BPL] households). Everyone put in Rs 500 to open a bank account and the government put in the first instalment, but later the sangham members would not allow them to take it out. The sarpanches blame the local sangham members for this arbitrary enforcing of rules, as against the squads and top leaders who are seen as reasonable. They find it especially galling when the Maoist cadre are uneducated youth.

The Maoists have frequently debated the approach they should take to government funds: whether to agitate for implementation of works and ensure transparency or to completely oppose taking any funds from the government. The fact that the government specifically targeted Maoist stronghold villages for its schemes was seen as proof that 'development' was really just another means of war, or part of 'low intensity counter-insurgency'. The existence of the janathana sarkars finally decided the matter. The Central Committee issued a directive not to allow panchayat funds and to ask the sarpanches in their 'struggle areas' (areas where they were strong) to resign. The problem, as they saw it, was that the sarpanches were agents of the state inside the village, corrupting it and developing their own networks of clients, whereas traders and others who were also corrupt were not part of the community in the same way.

A local leader from near the Kanger National Park, where panchayats and elected sarpanches still functioned, told me that sarpanches were increasingly cautious about taking up works from the government. They found it difficult to meet both the officers' demand for a cut and the Maoists' insistence on transparency and high wages for the villagers.

The Maoists extend their autarkic beliefs to the PDS. One leader claimed that no one in the villages was dependent on rations – and that the rations were really there to serve government staff. But people walk long distances, 40–60 kilometres in some cases, to get rice, and without the PDS, even the Maoists would not have survived. In 2015, they attempted to ban PDS rice on the grounds that it was bringing in strange diseases but the village women protested and prevailed.

As for the CAPF's 'civic action programme' to win the 'hearts and minds' of the people, it is unclear what impact it has. On paper this involves training surrendered Maoists to become drivers or electricians (in practice they are given employment as police informers), providing some medical relief, and showing villagers films on India's great leaders and the eradication of social evils like dowry and child marriage (which don't exist in this area).[23] The CRPF distributes saris, transistors and footballs. Women in one Konta village described to me, laughing, how the jawans stood with a stick in one hand and a sari in the other, forcing them to take the clothes, and how the women threw them away as soon as they were out of sight. The main success of the civic action programme seems to lie, however, in inducing Maoist resentment. The Maoists then turn on the villagers, threatening and beating them for having accepted the benefits, and this in turn leads to disaffection with the Maoists.

The Maoists are not the only ones to debate the use of government funds as a proxy in the war. When a land rights movement allegedly close to the Maoists, Chasi Mulia Adivasi Sangh, won elections to several panchayats in Koraput, Odisha, the home ministry under P. Chidambaram wanted to deny them panchayat funds. This was fought off by the rural development ministry under Jairam Ramesh.

And where there are no Maoists, villagers repeatedly say that whenever they have asked the government for something – a road, a hand-pump, a school building – they get no response. CGNet Swara, a mobile radio news service to tap local information, carries stories from across adivasi India of missing schoolteachers, non-payment of wages for government public works, the absence of electricity, hand-pumps and so on. Between the government's cynical claim that they cannot carry out development because of the Maoists and Maoist hubris that they are capable of running a parallel state and therefore the villagers don't need government funds, the villagers continue with their subsistence lives.

Protection from Whom?

> It is denied that education of the children are affected in any manner due to occupation of school building by security forces [sic].
>
> Counter-affidavit by the government of Chhattisgarh in WP 250/2007

A 2013 letter from a headman in Narayanpur sent to the NHRC describes what it means to have the CRPF stationed in the village school:

> One night in April 2008 CRPF broke the lock of our school and forcibly entered and took control saying let us live here for only

one month till alternative accommodation is found for us. Neither was any gram sabha called nor was the permission of the sarpanch taken. It has been five years now and despite the Supreme Court orders, the CRPF has still not moved from our school, and has built a permanent building inside the school compound.

The coming of this outside force, CRPF, has had a devastating effect on our life. In the name of security the CRPF has cut the trees in our village, and even now for their cooking purposes they use threats to get us to cut new trees. The CRPF is stationed right where our village god lives – his name is Gusi Rav Devta. The CRPF does not let us worship there and as a result the village is suffering all sorts of illness and misfortunes.

The CRPF is an outside force and does not know about adivasi customs. This has had a very bad effect on the morale of the villagers especially women. The CRPF molest our girls, as a result of which they are suffering from mental tension and have been somewhat cured only by the siraha-gaita (folk healers) and by appeasing the gods.

I have complained about this situation many times to the sarpanch, but today every sarpanch in an adivasi village is rooted in corruption and has got support from the CRPF for this. With the help of the CRPF he is able to suppress all opposition from the village.

Earlier our adivasis used to make mahua liquor for their own use but now they are having to make it for the CRPF. Is this not ruining our culture? Some months ago a woman from K accused 4 men from the CRPF camp of raping her. But suppressing the complaint of an adivasi woman is no big deal for the CRPF and administration.

Sir, do you not think that the CRPF is in the schools and villages of Bastar for its own protection rather than for the protection of villagers?

12

The Amnesias of Democracy

> Democracy is afraid of remembering and language is afraid of speaking.
>
> Civilians fear the military, the military fears a shortage of weapons, weapons fear a shortage of wars.
>
> Eduardo Galeano, *Upside Down*

On 25 May 2013, 27 members of the Congress returning from a political rally were killed in a Maoist ambush near Jeeram village at the foothills of the Kanger forest, on the national highway running from Hyderabad to Raipur. The ambush was primarily aimed at Mahendra Karma, who had survived previous attempts on his life because he had the highest level of security detail ('Z plus') and pure luck. I was subsequently told by a member of a Maoist village militia that they had been informed about the plan 10 days in advance, but that the bulk of the actual killing was done by the PLGA while the militia simply watched. To make sure they got Karma, the Maoists had stationed a force on an alternative route as well.

Congress leaders and the media instantly described the ambush as a 'holocaust' and an attack on democracy, and went on to nominate Karma's widow, Devati Karma, as the party candidate in the state assembly elections in 2013 (she won) and his son Deepak Karma as the candidate for the national elections in 2014 (he lost).[1]

The Maoists responded by questioning the credentials of ruling politicians to talk about democracy:

> On May 17, when eight people including three innocent children were killed by police and paramilitary forces in Edsametta village of Bijapur district, then why did none of these leaders bother to think about 'democracy'?... Is your 'democracy' only applicable to the mass murderers like Mahendra Karma and ruling class agents like Nand Kumar Patel? Whether [sic] the poor adivasis of Bastar, the elderly, children and the women come under the umbrella of your 'democracy' or not?[2]

In December 2013, when I visited one of the villages whose burning Karma had personally supervised, we discussed his death. They said that because the Maoists no longer visited their area, they heard the news only many days later. 'But,' they said, not triumphantly, not angrily, but with a sense of quiet relief and closure, 'at last someone has heard us.'

The debate over democracy in the context of Karma's killing is emblematic of the polarized public discourse on this subject. The dominant position on Indian democracy – voiced by politicians, the mainstream media and the elite – is celebratory, resting on universal suffrage, federalism, subordination of the army to civilian rule, an independent judiciary and a broadly welfare-oriented economic regime. The second position is sceptical, pointing to the high levels of inequality and social discrimination, the long-term continuation of 'emergency' laws like the Armed Forces Special Powers Act (AFSPA) in the North-East and Kashmir which empower the army to kill on mere suspicion, and the frequent incidents of extrajudicial killings, rapes, custodial deaths, disappearances and torture by the police and armed forces.

When the Indian government and the media talk of democracy,

what they really mean are elections. There is, undoubtedly, relatively high investment in voting across India. However, if representation is meant to give people a voice and make governments accountable, why do places like Bastar fall off the map, and why do such high levels of violence and state impunity continue for so long in places like Kashmir, Manipur and Chhattisgarh?

The problem is not just the imperfect realization of democratic ideals – which is always work in progress – but the way in which India's mainstream political parties actively deploy electoral democracy as a weapon against dissenters. If democracy equals voting, any attempt to call for alternative democratic visions or a poll boycott is seen as undemocratic. The Maoists, for their part, are so blinded by the certitudes of their own revolution that they are unable to appreciate even the symbolic importance of elections as a moment of mobilization for popular demands or for the expression of popular anger, leave alone the necessity of working both inside and outside elected bodies. As Lenin famously argued in his tract, 'Left Wing Communism: An Infantile Disorder':

> How can one say that 'parliamentarism is politically obsolete' when 'millions' and 'legions' of proletarians are not only still in favour of parliamentarism in general, but are downright 'counter-revolutionary'!?... As long as you are unable to disperse the bourgeois parliament and every other type of reactionary institution, you *must* work inside them.[3]

Elections as Battleground

> **No** to the continuation of this semi-colonial, semi-feudal pseudo-parliamentary dictatorial system, **Yes** to genuine parliamentary system of the People's Democratic Federal Republic which serves the people and the country.
>
> Maoist press release, parliamentary elections, 2014[4]

The Maoists see electoral boycotts as a way of educating people about the hollow illusions of democracy. In their 'struggle areas', the boycott is near complete, and people escape into the forest to avoid being forced to vote. In 2004, I visited some interior villages with two members of the Chhattisgarh PUCL, Binayak Sen and Ajay T.G. Apart from a couple of roadside polling agents and some BJP and Congress flags, there was nothing to suggest it was election day. Off the main road, even the party flags disappeared. Village after village was deserted and none of the three notified booths we passed was open. One school had clearly not been used for several months except by goats, judging from the droppings in its veranda. Yet, we later found out, 'votes' had been cast from these booths, most probably by the security forces themselves.

The visit culminated in Gappapalli village, with sangham youth suspecting us of being police informers. Our efforts to explain that we were merely observing elections had no effect, and we were forced to leave behind Ajay's camera in case it had any incriminating evidence. We were told the dalam would adjudicate. Surprisingly, a month or so later, Ajay got a letter of apology from the Maoists, offering to compensate him in case his camera was ruined. (Four years later, the Chhattisgarh police used this letter to arrest Ajay on charges of being a Maoist, a claim that was farcical even by the Chhattisgarh police's own ham-handed standards.)

The Maoists insist their poll boycott is principled, regardless of who is contesting. Even in 2008, when a victory for Manish Kunjam of the CPI in Dantewada (where he was contesting against Mahendra Karma) would have clearly signalled that people opposed the Judum, they enabled the BJP to win. Poll boycotts in the adivasi villages (from where the CPI draws its bulk support) inevitably mean a win for the BJP or Congress. The BJP, in particular, with its trading base, dominates the small urban centres where the maximum voting takes place.

Though the Maoists claim rhetorically that they are against the 'fascist BJP and Congress', and will expose them 'politically', their main 'ideological' battle continues to be with the 'revisionist' CPI and CPI(M). Sometimes the logic is twisted: Konta villagers said they were told by the dalams not to vote for the CPI, because if they won, the elected representatives would go to Raipur (the state capital) and stop fighting for them as well as support Operation Green Hunt like all the other parties.

In 2008, in Nenduwaya village, I found the school walls adorned in red slogans in Hindi denouncing the Salwa Judum: 'Reject polls, beat and chase away any politician who comes to campaign'; 'Don't let adivasi murderers and Hindu fascist BJP into the village'; 'Chase away the Congress party which sent security forces for the Salwa Judum repressive campaign'; 'Reveal and reject the mask of the opportunist and reformist CPI'; 'Make the vote-seeking politicians stand before a people's court'; 'What have people got from democracy – lathi, jail and bullets', and finally, 'Teach the Salwa Judum politicians a lesson.' Some earnest Maoist wall writer had copied everything faithfully, including the instructions on what these were: 'Slogans related to poll boycott for posters, wall writing, etc.'

However, at least some of the so-called principled opposition to boycotts appears opportunistic. The party spokesperson, Abhay, conceded in an interview the Maoists released to the media in 2014: 'Depending on the concrete conditions, our tactics may vary to some extent according to the changing political formations at the all-India level and in the states, according to our strength and people's preparedness.'[5] It is widely believed that the Maoists helped the Congress come to power in 2004 in Andhra Pradesh in the expectation of peace talks. In West Bengal, Mamata Banerjee used the Maoists more than they were able to use her: after she came to power, those Maoists and PCPA members who were not killed or arrested joined her TMC. Political parties often try to mobilize Maoist support, or at the very least accuse each other of being close to the Maoists.

Even if the party principle on boycotts is well established, lower-level cadre may well help their friends and relatives:

> Pudiyami Linga, a Maoist recently arrested for the murder of a BJP leader, told the media before a CRPF and police superintendent in Dantewada that he had campaigned for BJP candidate Bhima Mandavi in the 2008 polls. Mandavi refuted this, but admitted that Linga had indeed campaigned for BJP candidate Dinesh Kashyap during the 2011 Lok Sabha by-polls that he eventually won.[6]

When Maoist leaders from Andhra Pradesh surrender, they often turn to political links established by friends and relatives, especially mainstream parties like the Telugu Desam Party or Congress who can help them with the police. They almost never join the parliamentary communists. Some of them, especially those who have no family support or land to fall back on, also join extortion gangs, working with builders and contractors.

Polls as a Form of Counter-insurgency

> When 119 special trains with 3,060 coaches speedily roll out, transporting millions of paramilitary, police and security forces, and dozens of helicopters join the operation performing hundreds of sorties, and eleven million people criss-cross from border to border, anyone would assume that India is at war...the difference is that this war is waged in peace time by the people themselves, not against an enemy but for the preservation of democracy.
>
> Former election commissioner S.Y. Qureshi,
> *An Undocumented Wonder*[7]

Despite Qureshi's claim that elections are 'a war waged by the people themselves', in places like Bastar or Kashmir where opposition groups call for poll boycotts, it is hard not to conclude that elections are war by other means. In the 2013 assembly elections, there was one armed security personnel to every 19 residents in Bastar.[8] No one asks why successive elections and democracy do not ensure a situation where there is no insurgency, a question that is glaringly obvious to soldiers on the ground. A CRPF jawan told the *Indian Express* correspondent Ashutosh Bhardwaj: 'You are spending hundreds of crores on us (additional forces) just for conducting these elections on a day. Why cannot you spend this money on people here? You won't need to fortify Bastar in the next polls.'[9]

High voter turnouts in Maoist areas showing the inefficacy of the Maoist poll boycott are extensively covered and cheered in the media,[10] with no one remarking on the fact that paramilitary forces are not used to coerce urban voters in areas of notoriously low turnouts, such as the rich residential areas of Mumbai or Bangalore.

The paramilitary presence is justified on the grounds that the Election Commission has to provide an opportunity for people to vote should they want to. At the same time, in 2014, several hundred booths in Bastar were relocated to the roadside on 'security considerations'.[11] Few citizens are enthusiastic enough to walk 30–40 kilometres to vote.

Left to themselves, of course, many more villagers, even in Maoist strongholds, say they would vote. And despite their claims that their poll boycotts are meant to ideologically awaken the villagers to the dangers of the parliamentary system, the Maoists have no compunction in enforcing their boycott militarily as well. In 2014, seven poll officials were killed in Bastar, along with five security personnel.[12] Electronic voting machines are often looted.

Mining and Money Power

In a sustained polemic on the election boycott in 2009, Maoist leader Azad writes: 'Never before had boycott become such a potent weapon in the hands of the people as during the Elections 2009. Hence the reactionary rulers had to spend hundreds of crores of rupees to refurbish the image of the rotten parliamentary system.'[13] Whatever the truth of this, what is undeniable is that money plays an important, if not the determining, role in Indian democracy.

The media has reported on the growing number of millionaire MPs who alone can afford the high rates of expenditure that campaigning involves; the phenomenon of 'paid news'; and the common practice of distributing liquor, cash or other goods to incentivize voters in the days, and especially the nights, before voting. In Chhattisgarh, it is an open secret that mining leases are given in exchange for election funding,[14] while the paying off of both media houses and individual journalists to ensure favourable coverage for the government is routine.[15] I was often told by journalists, starting from 2006, that Raman Singh had also managed to buy off the Congress leaders. In 2015, this long-standing insider knowledge came under public scrutiny when the *Indian Express* published tapes of conversations between Raman Singh's son-in-law and Congress's Amit Jogi over payments to persuade the Congress candidate, Manturam Pawar, to withdraw from the 2014 Antagarh by-polls, leaving the BJP candidate to win unopposed.[16]

This is not to say that elections are merely bought. In Chhattisgarh, BJP Chief Minister Raman Singh's successive victories have been attributed to his government's welfare measures like the Rs 2 rice scheme and the *mitanin* (village-level auxiliary health worker) programme, as well as the indoctrination and welfare work put in by RSS fronts like the Ekal Vidyalaya, Vaṇvasi Kalyan Ashram and Saraswati Shishu Mandirs. The Congress party has provided little opposition, being internally divided and depending on vertical patronage politics rather than cadres on the ground.[17]

People vote for all sorts of reasons. In the 2008 elections, Bhima Mandavi of the BJP, a former panchayat secretary, won the Dantewada assembly seat against Mahendra Karma and Manish Kunjam by activating a network of other panchayat secretaries. They are often the ones who manage the booths and polling. Sometimes, kinship also plays a role. The sarpanch of Dhurli had accompanied the CPI on all their election rallies because they were resisting land acquisition for Essar in Dhurli. But on polling day, he worked as a BJP poll agent, 'because Mandavi is a relative'. In 2013, in Antagarh in North Bastar district, everyone was all set to vote for the Congress, but the henchmen of the Halba Congress candidate beat up a Gond man during the elections. The entire Gond community then decided to vote for the Gond BJP candidate, the sitting MLA Vikram Usendi. One camp resident told me in 2008 that they had been threatened that if they did not vote for the BJP, their rice would be stopped.

The issue, however, is not just why individual parties win, but why electoral democracies fail to deliver on their promises to marginalized groups. In India, increasingly, regardless of regime, the government seems to work on the premise that what is good for business is good for India, and the only people worth engaging with are industrialists. One frequently sees photos of ministers socializing with industrialists and holding meetings with state police chiefs. Photos of a prime minister or chief minister meeting a victim of the security forces are hard to come by.

~

Since Chhattisgarh became a state in 2000, there has been one term of Congress rule under Ajit Jogi and three terms under Raman Singh of the BJP. The BJP swept most of the 11 assembly seats in Bastar in the first two terms (8/11 in 2003, and 10/11 in 2008), while the Congress recovered ground in the 2013 elections (7/11 seats).

Like Rajiv Gandhi (1984), Narendra Modi (2002), Mahendra Rajapakse (2010) and other leaders who have won elections after major massacres or war crimes on a wave of majoritarian triumphalism, Raman Singh has used his three-time electoral successes to claim that people supported him for his resolute stand against the Maoists.[18]

However, a closer look at the 2008 voting figures shows that this was not a result in which the victims of the Salwa Judum had a voice. The average turnout for Chhattisgarh was 70.53 per cent. In Bijapur, by contrast, 70 per cent did not vote, while in Konta nearly 60 per cent did not. It was largely the SPOs and their families who voted for the BJP since it was the one party that had fully justified their excesses. In Dantewada, where there had been no displacement, voter turnout was 55 per cent, much of which was accounted for by the urban townships of Bacheli/Kirandul, Dantewada and Geedam. While the Maoist boycott call was one reason for the low turnout in the affected districts, another was that a large number of people had fled as refugees to Andhra Pradesh. Controls over a not-unwilling media, a near-total blackout of the atrocities committed by the Salwa Judum and security forces, coupled with frequent coverage of Maoist attacks, meant that the violence committed by the Salwa Judum and the security forces was not an issue which bothered people living outside the conflict areas.

The state government has also cynically used the election to evade its responsibility to compensate victims. On 16 December 2008, when asked by the Chief Justice of the Supreme Court why it had done nothing for two months to fulfil its own assurances on compensation to the victims of the Salwa Judum, the counsel for Chhattisgarh gave the specious argument that 'the election code of conduct had come into play and they could offer no benefits'.

Responses by Political Parties

The Judum and subsequent operations are a rare example of inter-party collaboration by the main political parties in both Chhattisgarh and at the Centre: the BJP and the Congress. Between 2005 and 2015, there were hardly any questions in the state assembly on human rights violations by the security forces. One rare exception was the burning of Tadmetla in 2011. Questions are raised after major Maoist attacks, but these lead to further militarization, rather than suggest that the policy is simply not working. In Parliament, the CPI has been the sole exception to the general silence on the issue.

People often argue that the Maoists exist because there is a 'political vacuum'. Andhra Pradesh is variously held up as an example of the success of counter-insurgency operations through the Greyhounds, a specialized counter-insurgency wing of the Andhra Pradesh police, and of political mobilization by mainstream political parties to draw people away from the Maoists. In a conversation in 2010, S.R. Sankaran, former civil servant and peace negotiator, offered several other reasons too: some degree of infrastructural development like roads, schools, etc., stopping the harassment of ordinary villagers, strategic withdrawal by the Maoists after their leaders were killed, no active mobilization, and the autonomous dalit movement which weaned away many dalit Maoists. But, Sankaran said, support for the Maoists continues to be much deeper than is obvious on the surface.

As it often is on many questions, the Congress party has been divided on the Judum, and the anti-Maoist operations more generally. On the one hand, Mahendra Karma, as Congress MLA from Dantewada and leader of the Opposition, was the public head of the Judum. On the other hand, right from the beginning, several Congress leaders opposed it. Former chief minister Ajit Jogi was one of the first to write against the Judum, describing the mass displacement of adivasis as reminiscent of 'Hitler's "Lebensraum" – his effort to repopulate an area with pure-bred Aryans'.[19] Since 2011, after major incidents of human rights violations by the security forces (such as Tadmetla, Sarkeguda or the mass rapes in Bijapur in 2015), Congress politicians have been part of all-party investigative teams and opposed the violence. The Congress leadership also stalled Mahendra Karma's son Chhavindra Karma's attempts to revive the Salwa Judum in 2015.

At the national level too, Congress ministers like K.C. Deo and P.R. Kyndiah who were both in charge of the Ministry of Tribal Affairs, Jairam Ramesh and Mani Shankar Aiyar opposed the Judum. But they were countered from within the party by Prime Minister Manmohan Singh and Home Minister P. Chidambaram. Both strongly supported the BJP in its anti-Naxalite efforts, including the Judum. As for Shivraj Patil and Sriprakash Jaiswal, both in the home ministry when the Judum started, it is not clear they cared much either way. While Sonia Gandhi's and Rahul Gandhi's natural sympathies may have lain with the opponents of the Judum and Operation Green Hunt, they were ultimately happy to go along with the security establishment. At a private meeting at his office, Rahul Gandhi relayed to me the security view that the Maoists needed to be softened up with military operations before they would agree to talk.[20]

Resistance by the CPI

The CPI is the only party in Bastar led by adivasis themselves. Other parties field adivasi candidates in elections because these are reserved seats, but the decision-making and funding is controlled by non-adivasi upper castes. Even the Maoist leadership is non-adivasi.

In 2009, a Judum leader I met in Kutru cited the CPI as being the biggest obstacle to the expansion of the Judum, both in terms of its opposition on the ground and because it litigated against the Judum in the Supreme Court. The CPI under Manish Kunjam has indeed been the only open political force consistently fighting both human rights violations and land acquisition in Dantewada and Bastar, opposing the proposed steel plants on the grounds of both environmental damage and displacement.

They have suffered for this, with the police treating them as a front for the Maoists. The Maoists, as pointed out earlier, treat them as the main competition, and have undercut their cadre. If anyone is truly sandwiched in this war, it is the CPI. But having burnt its fingers supporting the JJA in the early 1990s, this time around the CPI was clear in its opposition to the Judum.

Now in his late 40s, but still lithe and fresh-faced, Manish Kunjam was a rising star in the early 1990s when I first met him. Having joined the CPI in high school in 1984, he was the youngest member of the legislative assembly for two terms from 1990 to 1998. In 1998, he became the district secretary of the Dantewada unit of the CPI when the district was carved out of Bastar, and in 2006 he became the national president of the CPI adivasi front, the All India Adivasi

Mahasabha. He has contested every election since 1998, but never won, in part because of the Maoist boycott, and in part because companies like Tata and Essar see Manish Kunjam as the biggest threat to their expansion, and every election time invest vast sums of money in ensuring that he doesn't win. Immigrants feel threatened by the CPI demand for the Sixth Schedule, which would give adivasis a deciding voice in governance; some years ago the CPI also earned the ire of Bengali immigrants for protesting about adivasi girls being trafficked with Bengali involvement.

As mentioned earlier, the CPI ensured that during the worst years of the Judum Sukma remained an oasis of normal administrative functioning. CPI activists often served, and still do, as the first port of call for desperate villagers. Even though he was unable to travel freely because his life was under threat from the Judum, police and industrialists, Manish Kunjam kept tabs on everything happening in the district.

When the Judum started, several CPI activists were beaten up by the Judum leaders for refusing to participate. Kartam Joga, a jolly man with a weathered face, had just returned home to Misma village one evening in February 2006 when he was told that the thanedar of Dornapal was looking for him. When he went to see the thanedar the following morning, he was beaten for three hours and hung upside down from a pole by Judum leaders for not coming as soon as he was called. After they let him go, he had to be hospitalized for 15 days or so. Along with Manish Kunjam, Kartam Joga was one of the three CPI members who petitioned the Supreme Court.

In dozens of villages I was told that the CPI's two rallies – in Cherla in June 2007 and especially the second one at Jagdalpur in November 2007, to which some one lakh villagers came – were major turning points in stopping the Judum, and giving people the courage to return home, or stop fleeing. No doubt, the large numbers were also because the Maoists had decided it would be a good thing to let villagers take part. From the end of 2007 to 2009, when Operation

Green Hunt began, the villages were slowly repopulated, as IDPs from Andhra Pradesh and camp residents came home. It was also the CPI which arranged for villagers to attend public hearings organized by the National Commission for Child Rights in December 2007, and by the NHRC in June 2008.

In 2010, S.R.P. Kalluri took over as SSP Dantewada, starting a conscious policy of wiping out any opposition to Operation Green Hunt. His first target, naturally, was the CPI, in particular all those local government elected representatives or activists who were influential in their areas. For instance, of the 10 CPI men jailed in 2010, Kartam Joga was then deputy president of the Konta janpad panchayat and member of the CPI State Council, Sudruram Kunjam was member of the Dantewada zilla panchayat and Kunjam Bhima was the president of the CPI student wing in Dantewada.

They were accused not only of attacking the Congressman Avdhesh Gautam's house but also of participating in the 2010 Tadmetla ambush. There was no way they could have been there or been involved. All of them spent two and a half years in jail before they were acquitted in January 2012. In jail too, the CPI prisoners fought – by going on a hunger strike for better conditions, against arbitrary arrests and demanding the release of prisoners who had been acquitted. Kopa Kunjam, an NGO worker who was in jail at the same time, later told me how Kartam Joga kept everyone's spirits up by singing and telling jokes.

With many of their leading activists arrested, and others under threat, the CPI found it difficult to keep operating as usual. During the Judum, one of their leaders in Bijapur went over to the Congress, and the party base there was virtually wiped out. Later, when Operation Green Hunt started, holding meetings in the villages became increasingly difficult as combing intensified, and any assembly of villagers could be fired upon on the pretext that they were holding a Maoist meeting. Yet, they continued to organize – for instance, holding rallies in Raipur in 2011 to demand implementation of the Supreme Court's orders banning the Salwa Judum, carrying out padyatras in 2013 through Konta and Dantewada to raise the question of the Sixth Schedule, and protesting against the Dilmilli steel plant in 2015, apart from several localized protests against encounters or rapes.

When Kalluri targeted the CPI, Podiyam Panda, the former sarpanch of Chintagufa and CPI district council member, was advised by the local police to 'disappear for a while'. In 2007, Panda had saved the lives of seven CRPF jawans who had been kidnapped by the Maoists when they were going home on leave, arguing with the Maoists all night to let them go. He also gave the CRPF rice from his own stocks, when their rations had not arrived. A gentle and sensitive man with a thin intelligent face, Panda is someone who commands instant respect from everyone who knows him – Maoists, police and villagers alike. During the worst years of the Judum, Panda ensured that the school in his village was not occupied by the security forces or demolished by the Maoists and that the haat as well as the PDS were functional. In 2010, when orders were issued to arrest them, both Kartam Joga and Podiyam Panda were working to get the schools relocated in the villages, back from the Salwa Judum camps where they had been functioning.

Since Panda has gone underground, the police have been trying to force him to 'surrender' as a Maoist. He refuses to do so on principle, since he is not a Maoist. Whenever there is a blast or an armed encounter in the area, they add Panda's name to the list of accused; the police constantly raid his house, destroying the grain and household goods, and beating family members, including his wife, Muye, who is now the sarpanch. In 2012–13 Panda's youngest son died of fever, and he was unable to do anything about it, forced as he was to live a peripatetic life in the forest. If and when peace ever returns to Bastar, on the ground and not just in the media, it will be because of men like Panda and Joga, and women like Muye, low key, rooted, brave and resilient.

Reneging on the Responsibility to Protect

The statutory institutions charged with looking after the rights of what are referred to as 'the weaker sections' of Indian society have a largely disappointing record. Under successive governments, these institutions have become sinecures for members or sympathizers of the ruling party. There may be an occasional chairperson or members who are genuinely knowledgeable and concerned about their field, but many have little experience or even interest in the assignments they are given. When researching the NCST in 2007, I found that one member used his tenure to travel to several pilgrimage sites – of course, on official duty. A member of an SC/ST employees' insurance federation described both the ST and SC commissions as 'tigers without teeth' since their usual practice is to forward every complaint to the state government or department concerned, and end the matter with that. To be fair to the commissions, they are almost purposely understaffed and underfunded by the governments whose work they are supposed to monitor and oversee.

In 2005–6, human rights groups wrote to the NCST begging them to intervene on the mass human rights violations, but they maintained an impassive silence. The only 'atrocity' the commission took note of was the Darbhaguda blast of February 2006, when villagers returning from a Judum rally were killed by the Maoists, asking the police what compensation they had been given. On the intervention of the former commissioner for scheduled castes and scheduled tribes, and architect of PESA, B.D. Sharma, the commission gave a hearing to Manish Kunjam and villagers from Dhurli, Bhansi and Lohandiguda who were being compelled to consent to steel plants at gunpoint, but they never visited the areas.

The NCW was marginally better in that they visited the camps for a day or so in December 2006, in response to pleas from women's groups. They noted that employing youth as SPOs was militarizing them and interfering with their studies, and would render them unfit to go back to the villages. They also visited female undertrials in Jagdalpur jail and recommended that they should get legal aid. But even this limited report was not acceptable to Mahendra Karma and the BJP, which called the report a farce and untrue, and said anyone opposing the Salwa Judum was anti-national.[21] And when in October 2008 another fact-finding mission by the Campaign for Peace and Justice in Chhattisgarh (CPJC) and women professionals from Andhra Pradesh led by sociologist Kalpana Kannabiran gave the NCW testimonies by rape survivors, they went silent. In 2015–16, both the NCST and NCW did visit Bijapur and Sukma districts to investigate the alleged mass gang rapes by the security forces, but the government is, as usual, ignoring the NCST's recommendations.

The NHRC was of course the first port of call for all fact-finding teams and individual complaints about the Judum and security forces. But all they did was forward complaints to the state government, and accept their butter-wouldn't-melt-in-our-mouth responses. In 2006, the ICI was given an appointment with the full bench of the NHRC. They listened, yawned, and ultimately ignored the photos of burnt villages, the lists of dead people and the stories of how ICI members were nearly lynched by the SPOs.

As for the State Human Rights Commission (SHRC), three of its six chaipersons to date have been police officers. The SHRC bestirred itself just once when it ordered an enquiry, after persistent lobbying by Subhash Mohapatra of the Forum for Fact-finding, Documentation and Advocacy (FFDA), in the Santoshpur fake encounter case in 2007, discussed later.

The only statutory institution that genuinely made some effort to address its mandate in Dantewada was the newly set up National Commission for Protection of Child Rights (NCPCR), headed by Shanta Sinha, whose PhD had been on the Maoists in Andhra Pradesh. An NCPCR team consisting of Sinha herself, former chief election commissioner J.M. Lyngdoh and Venkat Reddy of the MV Foundation visited Dantewada during 17–19 December 2007. They met government officials, visited the Judum camps and IDP settlements in Andhra Pradesh, and held public hearings at

Cherla in Andhra Pradesh and Kirandul in Dantewada. The NCPCR report was the first one by any official body to illuminate what was happening: 'Many participants in the public hearing had been hiding in the forests and trekked through the night to reach Kirandul. One woman had left her children under a bush, to be cared by others, to attend the public hearing.' After their visit, the NCPCR set up a programme of 'Bal Bandhus' to work with children in conflict, and monitored the situation of IDPs in Andhra Pradesh.

The big marker in terms of a sensitive 'official' response to the situation was the Planning Commission report of 2008, 'Development Challenges in Extremist Affected Areas'. Widely reported in the press, it brought in some breathing space on an issue that was rapidly being dominated by the security establishment. Headed by D. Bandyopadhyay, a West Bengal officer known for his work on land reforms, and consisting of people who had worked on the Naxalite issue for decades – such as K. Balagopal and Bela Bhatia – the report was forthright in its recommendations:

> Encouragement of vigilante groups such as Salwa Judum... delegitimizes politics, dehumanizes people, degenerates those engaged in their 'security', and above all represents abdication of the State itself. It should be undone immediately and be replaced by a strategy which positions an empowered task force of specially picked up responsive officials to execute all protection and development programmes for their benefit and redress people's grievances. This is the best strategy to eliminate the influence of radical left groups.

Not surprisingly, two members of the committee which drafted the Planning Commission report, former policeman Prakash Singh and intelligence official Ajit Doval, who promoted the Judum, dissented from this part of the report; on the left, Gautam Navlakha criticized it as being too paternalist and defining the 'problem' from the state's point of view.

~

Not only have India's democratic institutions failed to respond adequately to serious human rights violations, they are happy to cede the space to civil society. At a meeting on impunity, a former judge conceded the situation was bad, but said, 'At least the activists are there to take up the issue.' I have heard this from former bureaucrats too on other occasions. Activism is, indeed, a vocation, and sometimes also a profession. But the bottom line is that activists are not paid out of taxpayer money to save Indian democracy, while statutory institutions are, and activists are often vilified when they do take up the task.

13

The Rights and Wrongs of Human Rights

> The activists insist on talking of the 'root causes' of Maoism. The security experts brush aside any reference to 'root causes' and insist we talk of 'Maoist violence'. The academics debate what violence means, the journalists worry about their next big newsbreak. And so it goes on, this endless parlour game of seminars and working lunches and papers on the conflict. I can no longer see the child in the forest.
>
> Field notes, 2012

It is hard to say who the police hate more – Maoists or human rights activists. For many in the security establishment, the two are indistinguishable. After a Maoist attack in 2009 in which four Central Industrial Security Force (CISF) men were killed, the then home minister, P. Chidambaram, addressed the activists:

> What is the message that the CPI (Maoist) intends to convey? These are questions that we would like to put not only to the CPI (Maoist) but also to those who speak on their behalf and chastise the government… We think that it is time for all right-thinking citizens who believe in democracy and development to condemn the acts of violence perpetrated by the CPI (Maoist).[1]

A year later, Chidambaram again complained that the police forces were 'harassed by litigation' and demanded that 'civil society must answer for the deaths of innocents by outfits that do not respect democracy at all'.[2]

Large sections of the media are willing cheerleaders of the anti-activist brigade. Within minutes of any Maoist incident, whether the alleged sympathizers have adequately condemned and expiated for the attack becomes as critical to the framing of the news as the attack itself, with screaming headlines like 'Why are human rights groups silent now?' When activists do condemn Maoist atrocities, however, their statements are never carried. In fact, even their statements on state massacres receive little media attention. The aim of the exercise for both the media and the state is really to use activists as whipping boys.

In Max Weber's classic formulation of what it means to be a 'state' or government, the state is defined as having a 'monopoly over legitimate violence'. The reason why the state's violence is 'legitimate' is because it is employed to protect citizens. Internationally, human rights activism focuses on violations by the state, because anyone else who takes law into their own hands is already acting illegitimately and is liable to be punished by the state. The government, however, seems not to want to accept this grown-up and superior role, insisting truculently that human rights activists act as umpires and scold both sides equally.

However, the civil liberties movement has to take some responsibilty. In the post-Emergency phase, many groups sought to differentiate between revolutionary violence and other kinds of violence – caste, communal – terming the former legitimate and the latter illegitimate. Revolutionary violence, they argued, should be treated differently even in a liberal framework because, ultimately, it was aimed at implementing the democracy promised by the Constitution.[3]

Ultimately, all sides contributed to the simplification of an intricate issue. The state refuses to recognize critical voices within its own ranks and reduces all opposition to the Judum and Operation Green Hunt to the work of Maoist sympathizers. Maoist sympathizers adopt an equally stringent 'with us or against us' attitude. Sections of the professional human rights community choose to focus on celebrity cases at the expense of the larger conflict. Finally, the media, with its desire to reduce all complex problems to a prime-time talk show, is also complicit in the reductionism. In the process, there has been little justice to the serious human rights violations of ordinary adivasis, and 'human rights' itself has become the object of government attack.

Civil Society Advocacy *against* the Judum

Starting from the independence movement, when the Congress undertook 'fact-findings' into colonial atrocities, massacres have become important sites for the forging of democratic citizenship and a pan-Indian consciousness. Human rights groups and political parties conduct investigations in different parts of the country, hold press conferences and publish reports. There are also moments of solidarity at 'public hearings' or 'people's tribunals' when witnesses from across the country congregate to share their experiences; sometimes, though more rarely, victims visit each other's areas. Members of two village Joint Action Committees from Manipur came to Dantewada in the summer of 2008 to find out what SPOs did, since the Manipur government had deployed the Chhattisgarh model of arming villagers to fight the 'underground', as the Manipuri armed resistance groups are called.

Despite this tradition, for nearly six months after the Judum started, there was no detailed civil society investigation, and the national media took even longer to visit. This was an indication both of how cut off Bastar was from national politics, and the degree to which the administration was successful in repressing all news.

The first investigation revealing the scale of the killings was by the CPI in November 2005, written in the form of an open letter to the President.[4] This was followed by a short fact-finding report by the Human Rights Forum of Andhra Pradesh in July 2005.[5] Between 28 November and 1 December 2005, a 14-member fact-finding initiated by the PUCL, Chhattisgarh, but comprising five different organizations, visited Dantewada. Its immediate press release generated some attention, but also the usual charges of being sympathetic to the Maoists.[6] In May 2006, the Independent Citizens' Initiative, a group of six individuals who came together to understand the Salwa Judum, visited the area. The veteran journalist B.G. Verghese was, at 79, the most senior member of the group, which also included the retired civil servant E.A.S. Sarma from Andhra Pradesh, Harivansh, editor of the *Prabhat Khabar* newspaper, the historian Ramachandra Guha, the feminist writer and activist Farah Naqvi and me.[7] No one could accuse the ICI of being Maoist spokespersons; the stature of some of the members also enabled the ICI to meet the full bench of the NHRC, the Planning Commission, the prime minister, the home minister and various MPs. By the end of 2006, everyone responsible in Delhi knew what was happening in Dantewada, even if they chose to feign ignorance.

Between 2006 and 2008, several other fact-finding reports followed, painting a grim picture.[8] Inevitably, most of these investigations were limited affairs, constrained by the time and resources of the groups doing the fact-finding, hemmed in by the Judum and security forces, and prevented from accessing the villages. There was also a noticeable divide in the reports coming out of a democratic rights tradition – which thought the focus should be primarily on the Salwa Judum as a war on people – and the 'professional' funded human rights groups, like Human Rights Watch, who were less interested in the historical and political context of the conflict, and were more willing to critique Maoist violence on the same terms as state violence. But taken together, they were more honest than the investigation carried out by the statutorily mandated NHRC. The NHRC had both resources and access, but chose to deploy these in the service of the state.

Civil Society *for* the Salwa Judum

Like the Salwa Judum which armed civilians to counter the Maoists, the security establishment promoted its own fact-findings to counter those conducted by the human rights groups. They even appropriated the language of civil society such as the label 'people's movement', and their reliance on the credentials of 'independent' citizens. The home ministry, then under the Congress-led UPA, worked closely with the RSS, using its members as 'academic advisers'.

The RSS, through its related think tanks like the Forum for Integrated National Security (FINS), the Rambhau Mhalgi Prabodhini (RMP), the Vivekanand Foundation and the Surya Foundation, organized meetings and published reports to counter the critiques of the human rights groups. Some of the diagnoses was common. For instance, an RMP report based on a 'study tour' in 2005, led by a retired colonel and the joint director, War Studies, Ministry of Defence, Dr Anil Athalye, recognized 'inadequate public services, distrust of police, utter disregard to development and the fact that the naxalites helped restore adivasi self esteem' as causes of Naxalism. Yet, they strongly supported the Salwa Judum.[9]

Like the Left, the RSS and BJP meetings usually preach to the converted, except that they are able to summon a whole range of retired and serving army officers, police and administrative personnel to their meetings. Like human rights activists, the RSS organizations also bring 'victims' to testify at their meetings. In February 2007, Salwa Judum leader Madhukar and several women SPOs came to an RMP meeting in Delhi and spoke of Maoist atrocities. RSS leader Bal Apte described 5 June, the Salwa Judum's official starting date, as a *punya tithi* (auspicious day) since it was the death anniversary of the RSS leader Golwalkar.

Three years later, at a FINS meeting in May 2010 held in the Constitution Club in Delhi – which was attended by BJP leader Sheshadri Chari, retired Air Marshal R.C. Vajpayee, B.R. Ranjit, a retired DGP from Haryana, and RSS leader Indresh Kumar among others – speakers again raised the spectre of the enemy within and abused human rights activists. They portrayed the BJP-ruled state of Chhattisgarh as the helpless victim of separatist and 'imperialist' forces (read Christian missionaries) who wanted to break the country up into small pieces. Indresh Kumar insisted that Salwa Judums were needed all over the country to separate people from the Maoists.

Human rights activists argue that it is the threat of displacement which explains people's support for Maoists in mining areas. The Maoists keep the companies at bay. The government, however, turned this argument around to claim that the Maoists are in these poor but resource-rich areas to make money off mining. Chief Minister Raman Singh, in his trademark white safari suit and white shoes, declaimed at the FINS meeting: 'The Maoists are in place wherever the minerals are. This shows there is some power behind them which wants to capture India's wealth.' The same link between Maoists and minerals was reiterated by former Chhattisgarh Governor Shekhar Dutt at a Surya Foundation meeting in 2015.

The Indian security establishment has fully appropriated the language of human rights, speaking with great felicity of the need for 'training' to 'sensitize' their men to the dangers of human rights abuses; and of the civic action programmes they are carrying out to 'win over the hearts and minds' of the public. But this rarely extends to any justice for the civilians they may have killed, whose deaths are seen as mere 'collateral damage'. By far, the main interest of the police and paramilitaries is in promoting the idea that it is their human rights which are under the greatest threat.[10] In 2015, the Indian government decided to make 'official' its practice of calling security personnel killed in internal security operations *shaheed* – martyr.

The Struggle to Provide Relief

Between 2005 and 2007, when the Judum was at its height, there was no attempt by domestic civil society groups to provide relief to those displaced by the Judum. In part this was because of the difficulty of accessing villages, and in part because any such attempt would have been seen as material support to the Maoists, punishable by several years in jail under Chhattisgarh's draconian CSPSA. The only ones helping the villagers with immediate provisions when their villages were burnt were the Maoists.

It was left to international organizations like the MSF and ICRC to provide some humanitarian assistance, even though since the conflict started, a whole range of NGOs also set themselves up. Some of them are known professional NGOs like the Nandi Foundation and PRADAN, engaged in community development, creating self-help groups and the like; many are dubious, like Bastar Bandhu, the NGO which ostensibly helped in mobilizing villagers to join the Salwa Judum or the Jai Johar Seva Sansthan run by one Pawan Dubey and funded by Essar out of its CSR funds, allegedly to pay off the Maoists.

In the early 1990s, when Himanshu Kumar and his wife Veena started the Vanvasi Chetna Ashram (inspired by Vinoba Bhave and his Sarvodaya philosophy), they were perhaps the only NGO in the area. They chose as their base Kawalnar, 11 kilometres out of Dantewada, close to Mahendra Karma's village, Pharaspal. Every government project in the area that required NGO outreach – sanitation, health, literacy – was routed through the VCA, whose sizeable campus housed training centres, a dormitory and several vehicles. In his obituary of Karma, Himanshu Kumar writes of their intimacy: 'When Chhattisgarh became a separate state in November 2000 Mahendra Karma became its industry minister. My friendship with Karmaji was getting ever deeper. The administration would nominate me to every committee in the district. So much so that BJP leaders started calling me a Congress man.'[11]

Initially, when the Judum started, the VCA was not involved, other than helping visiting human rights groups with translators. None of the VCA workers were sympathetic to the Maoists; some may also have been informing on the human rights groups to the Judum. Since Himanshu was close to Karma, the Judum leaders did not bother him. However, slowly the war began to creep up on him, till a position of neutrality could no longer suffice. When it came to the crunch, Himanshu cast in his lot with the adivasis rather than their tormentors. Over time, social media savvy, networked, expansive and hospitable, Himanshu became one of the main points of contact for journalists, visiting activists and student interns interested in helping out.

By 2008–9, though the VCA's government programmes were still going on, Himanshu was becoming a full-time human rights activist. He started a legal aid cell which recorded losses by villagers; they also filed cases on behalf of women in Matwada camp whose husbands had been killed by the CRPF and SPOs, as well as in two major incidents in Singavaram and Gompad, where large numbers of civilians were killed. However, VCA's July 2008 attempt to 'adopt' villages for rehabilitation was derailed a year later, in June 2009, when the Maoists kidnapped and murdered Punem Hunga, a sarpanch accused of being active with the Judum. Hunga had forced a reluctant Kopa Kunjam, one of the lead workers of the VCA, to give him a lift on his motorcycle when they were stopped by the Maoists. They took Hunga away. Kopa was accused of being complicit with the kidnapping, and was jailed for two years.

Himanshu's crusade was a red rag to the government, and retribution followed. In May 2009, the district administration bulldozed the VCA campus, claiming it encroached on forest land. The VCA had papers showing it was land donated by the villagers (and when the land records went online in 2022, they showed the land in VCA's name, making the demolition illegal). One of the outside volunteers present during the demolition described what happened:

> At around 5 a.m. a huge force of around 500 CRPF, STF, Chhattisgarh Police and SPOs (the contingent included 100 policewomen), landed at the campus of VCA at Kanwalnar and began cordoning off the entire area by posting para-military personnel in every direction…
>
> The SDM, Mr Ankit Anand, then informed Himanshuji (at 7 a.m.) that he and his family and staff had one hour to remove all their personal belongings, official papers, etc. At 8 a.m. around four or five bulldozers began rolling into the ashram premises and within the next few hours they had razed the entire campus (including training halls, staff quarters, the main office building, and residential area) to the ground, not even sparing the tubewells and an open well which had been constructed by the government. The boundary fence of the ashram, the boards on the road leading to the ashram were also twisted and uprooted. All this continued for four hours.

Despite this direct attack, Himanshu stayed on in Dantewada till January 2010. If anything, the demolition made him even more vocal. He invited then home minister Chidambaram for a *jan sunwai* or public hearing in December–January 2009–10. Chidambaram didn't come. This was a doomed project – for the government, Himanshu was too pro-Maoist; on the other hand, the Maoists have a general disdain for NGOs. Soon after this, fearing imminent arrest, Himanshu left Dantewada.

~

Though 'development' came to the adivasi areas of Khammam to wean them away from Maoists, the Andhra Pradesh government's Integrated Tribal Development Agency (ITDA) has done a much better job than similar tribal sub-plan schemes in Chhattisgarh. Maraigudem village which has an Andhra Pradesh half and a Chhattisgarh half is a model advertisement for the Andhra government – with lighting, shops and usable roads, compared to a dark, potholed, dangerous Chhattisgarh. The roads of Konta and Khammam are also a study in contrasts. Andhra/Telangana historically also had a far more active civil society than Chhattisgarh, especially with groups like the Andhra Pradesh Civil Liberties Committee (APCLC) and HRF, as well retired civil servants who took up public issues.

In 2007, when sociologist and long-time adivasi rights activist J.P. Rao and I spoke to the head of the Khammam ITDA, he conceded that they were torn between providing humanitarian relief and refusing to legitimate the presence of the IDPs in Andhra Pradesh. JP responded by getting clothes from Chennai from the NGO Goonj and involving local NGOs in their distribution. Andhra NGOs, such as the Vyavasayaka Mariyu Sanghika Abhivrudhi Samstha (ASDS) led by Gandhi Babu, mobilized to provide relief to the refugees who had fled from Chhattisgarh with some help from the ITDA, Action Aid and the others. They identified IDPs, got them ration and job cards, ran schools in the forest settlements as well as 'residential bridge course schools' which helped older children transition to regular Telugu government schools. Many of the workers employed by ASDS were IDPs themselves, like the wizened and dedicated Dodda, who had been Patel in a forest village in Kistaram range, and had left for Andhra rather than take his village to the Judum camp. He worked on road construction for a while, before being employed as a teacher and then an organizer with ASDS. By 2015, however, funding for ASDS was drying up.

The Good Doctor

At a time when fact-findings were small drops in the ocean, and the Supreme Court had just begun its critical journey on the Salwa Judum with the first hearing in May 2007, civil society's major engagement with Chhattisgarh's conflict centred on demanding the release of Dr Binayak Sen, a paediatrician and vice-president of the Chhattisgarh PUCL.

Binayak Sen had first arrived in Chhattisgarh in the 1980s to work with the visionary trade unionist Shankar Guha Niyogi in setting up the Shaheed hospital for workers in the iron ore mines of Dalli Rajhara. Along with his wife Ilina, the well-known feminist who ran the NGO Rupantar, he was involved in practically every cause in the state – preserving seeds, nuclear disarmament, women's rights, etc. Sen also ran a weekly clinic in Bagrumnala near Dhamtari, and was an active member of public health platforms like the Medico Friends Circle.

Binayak Sen was arrested on 14 May 2007, and was in jail for two years. The essence of the police case is that Sen was a courier between the Maoist leader Narayan Sanyal, who was incarcerated in Raipur jail, and a tendu leaf businessman, Piyush Guha, acting for the Maoists. The defence case was that Binayak Sen was involved with Narayan Sanyal only to the extent that he was a doctor, and helping prisoners with their cases is part of the long-standing and legitimate activities of PUCL. The Chhattisgarh government, helped by the local media, went all out to defame Sen, even claiming that he was a fake doctor because no stethoscope had been recovered from his house! The trial culminated in a life sentence for sedition in December 2010. Given the atmosphere in the state, the high court denied him bail and it was left to the Supreme Court to grant him bail in 2011. The alleged crime by itself hardly warranted the application of Section 121 A (waging war) and Section 124 (sedition) of the Indian Penal Code. Indeed, sedition and waging war are the last clauses one should apply to activists, when only a deep patriotism compels them to give up the comforts of a self-interested life and take on the state's failings.

The CSPSA of 2005, however, under which too Sen was charged, was precisely devised to cast a wide net with its sweeping definition of 'crime': 'Whoever commits or abets or attempts to commit *or plans to commit* any unlawful activity in any specified area shall be punished with imprisonment for a term which may extend to seven years and also be liable to fine' (Section 8.5, emphasis mine). Those arrested and convicted under CSPSA included two Sindhi cloth merchants who sold yards of camouflage khaki to what they thought was a security company, and a tailor who allegedly stitched uniforms for the Maoists. In 2006, the PUCL filed a case in the Chhattisgarh High Court challenging the constitutionality of the CSPSA, which was rejected in 2014.

Apart from Binayak Sen and Ajay T.G., the police arrested a third PUCL member, freelance journalist Praful Jha, along with his transporter son Prateik. Prateik's friend and travel agent, Siddharth Sharma, as well as two women, Malti and Meena Chaudhury, were also arrested in January 2008, in what the police described as the biggest catch of the Maoist urban network. The *Indian Express* journalist Ashutosh Bhardwaj who was the only one to cover the Jha case in any detail, quotes the police as conceding that Praful Jha was not involved, but that his arrest was necessary to 'teach others a lesson'.[12] All five were given seven-year terms and released only in September 2014.

The campaign for Sen's release touched many chords. Bearded, with heavy-lidded eyes, wearing a khadi kurta and carrying a jhola, a photo of Sen behind bars became an iconic image of injustice. Ilina Sen's foreword to Minnie Vaid's *A Doctor to Defend* lists the range of individuals and organizations involved in the campaign to release Binayak Sen, as well as some of their activities: protest meetings in all the major Indian metros organized by civil liberties and democratic rights organizations like PUCL, PUDR, the Association for the Protection of Democratic Rights (APDR), etc., Mumbai and Delhi committees for the release of Binayak Sen, international networks like Amnesty and Human Rights Watch, as well as what came to be known as the Raipur Satyagraha – a rally that was held every Monday between March and May 2009 to demand his release.[13] While Sen was arrested for his human rights activism on behalf of the prisoner Sanyal, what captured public attention was his role as a doctor – a doctor who had given up the comforts of an urban practice where he could have made huge amounts of money to work in a poor rural area. Binayak had studied at the Christian Medical College, Vellore, and its alumni were actively involved in writing letters and petitions, and lobbying with influential people. A group was formed called 'Doctors in Defence of Binayak Sen'. The Indian Academy of Social Sciences and the Global Health Council gave him the R.R. Keithan and Jonathan Mann awards in 2007–8, while a group of Nobel laureates wrote to the Indian authorities asking for his release to collect the Jonathan Mann award.

The PUCL argued that Sen's release was the most important cause before the civil liberties movement because his arrest had intimidated other activists in Chhattisgarh, preventing them from speaking out. It is true that the charges against him did have a chilling effect on PUCL and its associates, but the documentation of the ongoing killings, relief to the IDPs, the litigation in the Supreme Court and protests on the ground by the CPI and others went on in parallel, independent of the Sen campaign. Though focused on the release of an individual, what the Sen campaign did was to put the Salwa Judum on the public map.

Predictably, for the BJP government and Chhattisgarh media, the Sen campaign became a case of outside activists intervening in the internal affairs of the state. There was much applause at the FINS meeting in Delhi in 2010 when Raman Singh said, 'Where are these human rights activists who hold candlelight vigils when civilians are attacked, when jan adalats happen and people are killed… Why are there no candlelight vigils when CRPF men are killed?'

After Sen's release on bail in 2009, energies were briefly transferred to issues like Operation Green Hunt and the need for peace talks, but activist space was again taken over by the Free Soni Sori campaign in 2011. Two successive cause célèbre campaigns centred on individuals are quite unprecedented in Indian activism; the second succeeded in part because of the networks put in place by the first.

The Birth of an Activist

In 2009, the police tried to get a young Gond man, Lingaram Kodopi, to join them as an SPO because he came from an influential Congress family. Linga, tall and gangly with curly hair and an engaging manner, told me that he used to run a jeep-taxi from his village, Palnar, to Bacheli. In the course of his work he had to deal with both the Maoists and security forces. When he got a contract to build toilets in his village, the local traders became jealous and complained to the police that he was a Naxal supporter. The police arrested him, putting pressure on him to name the sangham members in his village. Helped by Himanshu Kumar, Linga's family filed a habeas corpus case in the Chhattisgarh High Court. After his release, Linga went to Delhi and joined a journalism course, arranged by CGNet founder Shubhranshu Choudhary in an attempt to promote local journalism in Chhattisgarh. Linga also helped out during this period with the Delhi campaigns against Operation Green Hunt.

In the summer of 2010, after the Maoist leader Azad had been killed, the SSP Dantewada, S.R.P. Kalluri, publicly declared that Linga was now the second-in-command of the Maoists. It was absurd to think a 19-year-old, whom the Maoists themselves called a 'lumpen youth', could replace a senior leader like Azad, but Kalluri has never been embarrassed about making preposterous statements. Kalluri also claimed that Medha Patkar, Arundhati Roy, journalist Javed Iqbal and I, along with Linga, had been 'masterminding from Delhi' the Maoist attack on the house of Congressman Avdhesh Gautam.[14]

Avdhesh Gautam became a very useful agent for the police, since all those whom the police wanted to arrest were allegedly involved in the attack – ranging from CPI activist Kartam Joga to Lingaram Kodopi, his aunt Soni Sori, a schoolteacher and hostel warden in the Jabeli ashram school, and her contractor husband, Anil Putane. In a conversation with me, Soni attributed her entanglement in this case to Avdhesh Gautam's jealousy at contracts to build schools which had been given to her and her husband. The acquittals of the CPI activists were delayed for two years because Avdhesh Gautam refused to come to court to testify and the police, of course, were in no hurry to ensure his presence.

In September 2011, when the Chhattisgarh police first attempted to arrest Soni Sori for acting as a courier between Essar and the Maoists (they had already picked up Linga in the case), Soni escaped to Delhi. With the help of her mentor Himanshu Kumar and the magazine *Tehelka* she conducted a sting operation on a policeman, to prove her innocence. This enraged the already rogue Chhattisgarh police, for whom it became a point of prestige to arrest her from Delhi. Soni alleged that while in police custody, she was stripped and tortured, and had stones inserted in her vagina, on the instructions of Ankit Garg, the Dantewada SP. She spent two years in prison, before being released on bail along with Linga. (Both Sori and Kodopi were acquitted of all charges in 2022.)

Soni became a cause célèbre among women's groups and rights activists, the Rigoberta Menchú of Bastar. Amnesty International declared her a 'Prisoner of Conscience' like Binayak Sen, claiming that Soni and Linga Kodopi were arrested because they were vocal about the violation of human rights. Human Rights Watch chipped in. Her cause was part of the international One Billion Rising campaign against violence on women. Much of the tone was set by Shoma Chaudhury's article in *Tehelka* immediately after her arrest, claiming that Soni and her nephew Lingaram Kodopi were the 'last people left standing' for the rights of the adivasis in Dantewada, and that she, Linga, 'and in this instance Essar' were being framed by the police:

> They fought to get minimum wages of tribals raised from Rs 60 to Rs 120; fought for the rights of mine workers; and kicked up a row about senior police officials pocketing huge money from the illegal teak trade, generated in the name of 'jungle clearing' to thwart the Maoist movement.[15]

In reality, Soni Sori was not known for any human rights or political work before she was arrested. It should have been possible to celebrate her courage in speaking out about her own arrest and torture, through her letters from jail, without turning her into a lone crusader for the rights of others in Bastar. As she herself told a reporter in 2015, she had been transformed into an activist by her incarceration and the support she had received from outsiders.[16] Hers is a classic reprise of what Clifford Bob described in the Rigoberta Menchú case, where 'obscure individuals may also be thrust into leadership roles through outside acclaim'.[17]

Having become a visible emblem of state repression on women, Soni Sori was given the newly formed Aam Aadmi Party (AAP) ticket to contest the Lok Sabha elections in 2014. Apart from AAP supporters, several other activists flew in or donated to help her cause. Some even castigated the CPI for contesting elections and thus denying Soni votes, despite the fact that the CPI had been the only party fighting against human rights abuses and mining-induced displacement in Bastar till then.

Since 2014, Soni Sori has grown into her reputation. She used her own experience as a woman prisoner, her celebrity status and urban activist contacts to raise the issue of prisoners, fake encounters and assaults on women, providing a public face to the large numbers of women who have traditionally gathered outside police stations to protest against police excesses or arrests of their men. She worked closely with JAGLAG, a collective of metropolitan English-speaking fresh law graduates. Shalini Gera, Isha Khandelwal and Parijat Bhardwaj started JAGLAG in 2013 with the intent of addressing the lack of legal aid for adivasi prisoners, but soon found they were being called upon for a variety of issues relating to police atrocities. Together with former-ICRC-employee-turned-journalist Malini Subramaniam and researcher Bela Bhatia, who settled in Jagdalpur, they set the stage for a new phase of locally based activism, taking up fake surrenders, rapes and encounters. The Chhattisgarh

Bachao Andolan, a platform of groups defending community rights to natural resources, had also become active by this time.

As the war aggravated in 2014, and given Kalluri's antipathy to any kind of criticism, all these activists came under attack. First, the police fanned resistance among the Jagdalpur and Dantewada legal fraternity who objected to JAGLAG's practice. Then, in 2016, police-supported vigilante organizations like the Samajik Ekta Manch and Mahila Ekta Manch demonstrated against all the activists, burnt their effigies and called them Naxalite supporters. Subramaniam's car was vandalized and sewage was thrown into JAGLAG's compound. Above all, the police intimidated their landlords, so that Gera, Khandelwal and Subramaniam were forced to leave Jagdalpur. 'Unknown assailants' attacked Soni Sori, blackening her face and causing substantial burns. All of this, along with the arrest of four journalists in 2015–16 crystallized new campaign networks across the country.

The Limits of Cause Célèbre Campaigns

In his book *The Marketing of Rebellion*, Clifford Bob provides a number of reasons why some campaigns become more successful than others. These include the innovation and energy with which certain campaigns are run, what he calls 'local matchmakers' or NGOs who identify suitable causes, the degree to which they are endorsed and taken up by important gatekeeping organizations, as well as the degree to which they match with the organizational goals and cultural expectations of international NGOs. While the campaign for Binayak Sen appealed to middle-class sensibilities and respect for the medical profession, Soni's status as an adivasi woman gave her a greater degree of authenticity for international and national publics. What was also important, however, was her articulacy in Hindi and the involvement of urban activist groups, especially women's groups, in her campaign.

There are local reasons as well for why these campaigns succeeded, even as mass violations by the security forces and the Judum went relatively unaddressed. Civil and democratic rights organizations in India tend to work in reactive mode, attaching a greater value to the state's – often erroneous – assessments and opinions than to their own analysis. Being targeted by the state becomes a badge of heroism. This obscures the fact that in places like Bastar, anyone can be arbitrarily arrested and tortured.

In the absence of a clear stand on Maoist violence, it has been much easier for civil society to take up individual cases. Moreover, since the 1990s, single-issue centred, personality-driven 'new social movements' have gradually overtaken political parties, and the influx of funds and terminology like 'human rights defenders' have so transformed the human rights movement that the defenders become more important than the cause they are defending. Till at least 2012, there was hardly any focus on prisoners beyond Sen and Sori, despite the high rate of incarceration and the terrible conditions of jails. The vast majority of Sen's supporters fell silent after his release, as if that was all that mattered.

The Maoists and the government too are not averse to personality-centred campaigns, the former because they don't challenge Maoist ownership of the issues. Though the Maoists had an uneasy relationship with Soni Sori, accusing her in a jan adalat of being too close to the CRPF, and shooting her father in the foot for usurping the land of others, they were happy to use her and Binayak Sen as symbols of government repression. The government is also not unhappy with individual campaigns because it enables them to sidestep the horror of what they are doing to vast numbers of people, and the structural nature of their violence.

But it is not always easy to identify the people or causes behind a celebrity campaign. In the rhizomatic spread of information in the internet age, campaigns follow the flow of media networks, different groups bring different agendas to them, and once a certain version is out, it becomes easier for others to repeat it, if only because more information on that case is available. Moreover, the police have made Bastar very difficult to visit.

Of course, celebrity campaigns have important uses. The ability to put a face to a cause is useful as a communication technique, and such campaigns bring attention and recruits to an issue that might otherwise have been completely forgotten – even if in this case, the horrors of what was happening across a huge tract came to be, at least till very recently, metonymically captured by and limited to Binayak Sen and Soni Sori. Sometimes, as in the 16 December 2012 gang rape case in Delhi, they may also lead to significant changes in law. Or, as in Soni's case, they may have the effect of driving the activism of the celebrity herself.

At the same time, celebrity campaigns obscure politics on the ground, and rewrite history. A quick Google search on 11 April 2015 showed the following number of times a person was mentioned: Binayak Sen – 1,42,000, Soni Sori – 67,700, Lingaram Kodopi – 11,300, Manish Kunjam – 4,770. Future historians of the conflict in Dantewada, for whom the internet will form an important archive, will write that it was Binayak Sen and then Soni Sori who led the fight against the malik makbuja scam, the Salwa Judum, Operation Green Hunt and corporate mining in Dantewada. Names like CPI's Manish Kunjam and Podiyam Panda – as well as the many Maoist cadre who helped people after Judum attacks – will be consigned to oblivion. Manish Kunjam is known in cyberspace primarily as the man who delivered medicine to Alex Paul Menon, the Sukma Collector kidnapped by the Maoists, rather than as the man who most openly took on the Salwa Judum as well as corporates in the district.

Some of this is of course the CPI's own doing. The parliamentary Left nationally tends to be insular, has no media skills and never bothers to publicize the work they do on the ground. The outrage expressed by the media and the 'Independent Left' over forcible land acquisition and the use of vigilantes by the Left Front government (in which the CPI was a junior partner) at Nandigram and Singur in West Bengal also translated into negative publicity for the CPI in Chhattisgarh. They were accused of double standards in protesting acquisition in Bastar.

Some of the Dantewada CPI's refusal to engage in media campaigns was principled – for instance, they did not highlight the arrests of their own activists, since focusing on a few at the expense of the large number of ordinary villagers who had been arrested would alienate them from their base. (The Maoist ideologue Ganti Prasad took this to another level. When the Maoists sought his release in exchange for Collector Vineel Krishna who they had kidnapped in Odisha, Ganti Prasad said he would 'like to remain in jail despite getting bail till all 627 tribals were released from prison'.[18]) At another level, Manish Kunjam and others were just too busy fighting for survival for themselves and their people to care about national coverage or links. Not only were the CPI activists attacked on the ground by both the state and Maoists but they got none of the outside support and encouragement that might have enabled them to grow.

Reading the national and international campaigns around individual 'human rights defenders' one might well be forgiven for thinking that everyone else in Dantewada was either simply a voiceless victim, or used the language of arms. In fact, however, right from the beginning, several people took a stand even at considerable personal risk. Even if their voices were never amplified, their actions were important for local morale; they also counter the impression promoted by the state and Judum leaders that all opposition to the Judum, Operation Green Hunt or land acquisition comes from urban intellectuals and human rights activists, who are willing dupes of the Maoists.

Apart from resistance by elected representatives, both Congress and CPI, and locally influential people both in Bhopalpatnam and Sukma, which prevented the Judum from spreading, there were other voices too. On 15 October 2006, a local Bastar newspaper, *Highway Channel*, reported that the Chhattisgarh SC/ST students union had demonstrated at Jaistamb Chowk in Raipur and were planning a statewide signature campaign asking the authorities to close down the Judum, and stop killing innocent people. Three weeks later, a group of children wanted to appeal to President Kalam to stop the Judum: '12-year-old Soyam Sandhuri, a resident of Errabore Salva Judum camp…wants to tell President APJ Abdul Kalam that Naxal violence should end and blames the government-initiated movement for driving her family out of their village.'[19] Not surprisingly, however, the children were stopped from meeting the President.

In August 2006, Pratap Agarwal, an elderly lawyer in Jagdalpur, filed a writ in the Bilaspur High Court. Pegged on the 2006 Maoist attack on Errabor camp, it pointed out that the state had failed in its duty to protect the lives of the residents of Bastar. He also noted the horrible conditions and corruption in the camps and asked that camp residents be enabled to go home. Unfortunately, nothing came of this.

By 2009, apart from localized protests when people were killed or arrested (for instance, the Soliwada protest of June 2009), there were some public meetings, like one in Jagdalpur organized by the Bastar Sambhag Kisan Sangharsh Samiti, attended by around 20,000 people, to protest against steel plants and mining projects. However, unlike the ease with which the Salwa Judum or the equally state-sponsored Samajik Ekta Manch rallies obtained permission, an independent initiative of this nature has to try for months before the administration clears it.[20] On 8 March 2013, I attended an International Women's Day meeting organized by the Sarv Mool Samaj, an umbrella body of different adivasi organizations (not to be confused with the more establishment Sarv Adivasi Samaj) on the outskirts of Jagdalpur. Not only did the CRPF keep a close watch on this meeting, but the local administration also hijacked some of the vehicles carrying women to this meeting and took them off to swell the ranks of the official function that day.

In the complicated world of today, the structure of emotions is determined by how an incident is reported in the media. But this is also a moment where cellphones are giving villagers some small access to media space. Ultimately, when you take away the funding, the conferences, the media and the law, the idea of human rights is produced whenever people feel they can't take it any more, when one brave resident is willing to serve as a guide to the site of a massacre, and above all, when the desire to let the world know their story overcomes people's fear of telling it. It is the people of Bastar who have been and will be their own and bravest human rights defenders, long before the rest of the world recognized them, and long after everyone forsakes them. Living in their villages, refusing to inform on their sanghams to the state, despite knowing they might be randomly arrested, means that the vast majority of those in the jails of Bastar and Dantewada, are 'prisoners of conscience'.

14

To Talk or Not to Talk?

> True peace is not merely the absence of some negative force – tension, confusion or war; it is the presence of some positive force – justice, good will and brotherhood.
>
> Martin Luther King, *Non-Violence and Racial Justice*, 1957

Over the years, several attempts have been made at initiating dialogue and raising the question of peace talks, but almost as soon, these attempts have petered out. In 2006, fresh from the experience of the Andhra peace talks brokered by the S.R. Sankaran-led Committee of Concerned Citizens, K. Balagopal and others from the HRF in Andhra Pradesh visited Chhattisgarh to propose a similar process. But there were no takers. However, in the same year, some predominantly Delhi-based organizations and individuals formed the Campaign for Peace and Justice in Chhattisgarh (CPJC), which met periodically to discuss what was happening, organize public meetings in Delhi to publicize the Salwa Judum's atrocities, and help fact-finding teams visit the area.

The first major dialogue on the Judum was in January 2007, when the Nelson Mandela Centre for Peace and Conflict Resolution at

Jamia Millia Islamia organized a meeting and invited representatives of the Chhattisgarh government and the Union home ministry, retired bureaucrats like S.R. Sankaran, B.N. Yugandhar of the Planning Commission, representatives from the NCW, international organizations like the MSF and UNICEF, Essar Steel, and civil society organizations like the CPJC, PUCL and the Revolutionary Democratic Front. A press note on the conference summed up the proposals that emerged, none of which were in the least seditious:

> (1) Dantewada should be declared a zone of peace, or in other words, there should be an immediate ceasefire; (2) There should be a joint determination of facts regarding human rights violations by the Chhattisgarh government and independent observers; (3) Policing should only be carried on by the regular state police and not through special police officers; (4) A process must be set in motion whereby villagers could return home and start cultivation once again; (5) A policy on internal displacement should be created to deal with such situations.

But, as the *Telegraph* reported, even these innocuous proposals were too much for a paranoid home ministry:

> A crackdown that might have been labelled 'India's McCarthyism' was about to unfold early this year but for a 'top-level intervention'... A section of the home ministry officials, advocating a tough line against 'overground' sympathisers of Naxalites, raised the pitch after arming itself with a report on a seminar held in January on the campus of a university in Delhi. The report, drawn up by home ministry officials, said the tenor of the seminar was 'pro-Naxalite'. The participants, who included bureaucrats, academics and students, engaged themselves in 'anti-state' discussions that seemed to justify armed uprising, it said. By February, the officials behind the initiative had begun to discuss specific punitive measures that

could be taken against the 'sympathisers'. Penalties put on the table included shunting officials to nondescript areas and cutting down retirement benefits.[1]

The next attempt at demanding peace came with the formation of the Citizens Initiative for Peace (CIP) in 2009. A number of prominent people had signed on to this initiative, including the former speaker of the Lok Sabha, Rabi Ray, former Justices P.B. Sawant and Rajinder Sachar, the writer Mahasweta Devi, the senior journalist Kuldeep Nayar and others. A meeting was held at the Constitution Club on 20 October 2009; representatives from several states spoke – on mining, fake encounters, and all the problems faced by villagers caught up in conflict. Some of the Gompad victims came to this meeting, including Sodi Seeta, who had been hit by a bullet and was dramatically brought on a stretcher. Since Operation Green Hunt had just started, and the home minister sent a letter to Rabi Ray expressing his willingness to talk if the Maoists 'abjured violence', the event received more media attention than it might otherwise have. The CIP demands focused on a ceasefire and access to the area for independent observers, as well as the right of people to control their own resources and livelihoods.

Throughout, however, more radical groups kept up their own meetings. Unlike the CPJC or the CIP, they did not ask for both sides to engage in peace talks, but only for the state to withdraw its 'war on people'. Eventually the CIP petered out, because of the ambivalence of some key members and a lack of proper organization.

Another critique came from groups who argued that the CPJC/CIP focus on peace talks and human rights did not address the 'real issues', the activities the Maoists were keeping at bay – land acquisition and mining. In April 2010, the NAPM, with the help of the lawyer Prashant Bhushan, held a meeting at the Constitution Club named the 'Independent People's Tribunal on Land Acquisition, Resource Grab and Operation Green Hunt in India'.

Soon after this meeting, again as part of an NAPM initiative, some 50 people marched from Raipur to Dantewada and back, between 5 and 8 May 2010. The group included a large number of Gandhians like Bhanwari Lal Sharma of the Azadi Bachao Andolan, the noted educationist Yash Pal, the chancellor of the Gujarat Vidyapeeth, Narayan Desai, Thomas Kocherry of the fishworkers' movement, Radha Bhatt, president of the Gandhi Peace Foundation, and Swami Agnivesh, an Arya Samaj priest known for his work on bonded labour. They appealed to all sides to engage in dialogue. Their press note speaks of the attempt to paint anyone who spoke of peace as Naxalite agents, and the constant heckling and harassment (abetted by the police) that they encountered:

> In Raipur, Jagdalpur and Geedam, a handful of people held demonstrations against the March shouting slogans 'agents of naxals, go back'. Demonstrators were youths belonging to Congress, BJP and business community... In Jagdalpur, similar demonstrators, about 30 in number, shouted slogans and abuses outside the Press Conference hall. The interesting thing was that the police was standing but not intervening... When the SP Jagdalpur reached the spot, he intervened and more than a dozen demonstrators sat with the marchers and talked for more than an hour. All their questions were answered forcefully and they were silenced. But after going out on the road, they started again slogan shouting. On May 7, while proceeding to Dantewada, 5–6 youths on motor cycles with golden chain round their neck came in front of our bus and started slogan shouting: 'Go back'.

The reaction to both the Jamia meeting in January 2007 and the Gandhian peace march in May 2010 makes it clear that the state has no time for non-violent dialogue, even if it keeps insisting that Maoist 'violence' is the issue. Raman Singh invoked the usual 'Where were you argument' to ask why the peace march had not come earlier when jawans were killed, even though the marchers paid homage to their memory. And as usual, the SPOs, Judum leaders and non-adivasi lumpen youth from the Congress and BJP claimed to represent the indigenous voice of Bastar against the allegedly pro-Maoist, peace-demanding outsiders.

The final nail in the coffin of peace attempts came when Maoist leader Azad (Cherukuri Rajkumar) was killed in July 2010 while carrying a letter on talks from Swami Agnivesh, on behalf of Home Minister Chidambaram, to his comrades inside the forests. Azad and an accompanying journalist Hem Chandra Pandey died in what the police claimed was an encounter, but the Maoists allege was a staged killing. Had the home minister been genuine about peace talks, he would at least have ensured the safety of his messengers, or ordered a proper enquiry if there had been crossed wires.

Hostage Mediations

Between 2009 and 2012, after the start of Operation Green Hunt, the Maoists resorted to a number of kidnappings – of policemen (in Jharkhand in 2009, in Bihar in 2010 and in Chhattisgarh in 2011), Collectors (in 2011 and 2012 in Odisha and Chhattisgarh respectively) and even two Italian tourists in Odisha, along with an adivasi MLA, Jhina Hikaka (in 2012). In the case of policemen Francis Induwar and Lucas Tete who were abducted and killed in Jharkhand and Bihar, the media made much of the fact that it was adivasi policemen who had been singled out for killing, while the others who had been kidnapped along with them had been spared ostensibly because they belonged to the same castes as their captors.[2]

In the two cases involving the Collectors, Vineel Krishna and Alex Paul Menon, in Malkangiri (Odisha) and Sukma respectively, the national print and television media camped for days at what they liked to describe as 'ground zero'. In Sukma, the Congress and the BJP organized processions of local townspeople, especially schoolchildren, to show what a popular collector Menon was; his family and friends were interviewed, and much was made of the fact that he was a dalit. The two bodyguards who had been killed during his capture naturally received little attention. While they were captive, the media focused on what good Collectors these two were, men who risked their lives by visiting villages in their district rather than sit comfortably in their offices. It also helped that both men were tall, young and handsome. For instance, the *Times of India* titled its story: 'With Che as hero, Alex Paul Menon roamed the badlands'.[3] On the other hand, once Menon had been released, the right- wing Chhattisgarh media also implied that he had somehow been involved in his own kidnapping by taking unnecessary risks, and was perhaps even in collusion with the Maoists. The media appealed to the Maoists to release Menon on 'humanitarian' grounds, since he was an asthma patient and his wife was pregnant. But later the Chhattisgarh media also suggested that Manish Kunjam, who had declined to be a mediator but agreed to deliver asthma medicines to Menon at the chief minister's request, was somehow a Maoist agent for being named at all. Had even one-hundredth of an ounce of this media attention been focused on the inhuman arrests and killing of ordinary villagers, including pregnant adivasi women, it might have served more purpose, as a pre-emptive step in this desperate conflict.

G. Haragopal, professor of political science at Hyderabad Central University, who mediated in both cases, has written extensively on the process, describing how indifferent the Chhattisgarh government was, compared to the Odisha government, when it came to procuring the release of their respective officials.[4] It was only due to the insistence by the mediators, Haragopal and B.D. Sharma, that the Maoists gave in and released Alex Menon. Inevitably, the media gave all credit to Chief Minister Raman Singh, talking about how he stood firm against negotiations over kidnapping. In the case of five policemen who were kidnapped in Narayanpur district in Chhattisgarh in January 2011, the state displayed even more apathy and disinterest in getting them back, and there was less media attention. The Maoists were finally forced to release them to human rights groups led by Swami Agnivesh.[5]

In exchange for their prisoners, the Maoists demanded the release of some of their leaders, as well as ordinary adivasis who were being arrested on false charges, an end to Operation Green Hunt, and the withdrawal of various MOUs and mining leases with multinational corporations. But in Malkangiri, they also asked for:

> declaring Nooka-dora, Konda Reddy communities as scheduled tribes; stopping Polavaram project; issuing of pattas to the tribals of Koraput, Malkangiri, Narayanapatnam and Vishakapatnam areas; constructing a canal from Kotapalli to Maneguda; paying compensation to the families of Tadangi Gangulu and Ratana Sirike, who died due to torture in the jail; payment of compensation to farmers of the cut-off and submerged areas of Balimela reservoir and providing alternative facilities to the project-affected persons; justice to the displaced persons of Nalco project in Damanjodi; and withdrawal of the cases against the tribals and Chasi Mulia workers in Koraput and Malkangiri jails.[6]

In the Narayanpur policemen's case, the Maoists also asked for implementation of the Supreme Court orders asking security forces to vacate schools.

Which of these demands, other than the release of their leaders, could be termed illegitimate or not in keeping with the Constitution? What did not bother the media at all was why such problems had been left unaddressed by elected governments. Follow-up on the government's promises is also rare. Though the Chhattisgarh government set up a committee under former administrator Nirmala Buch to look into prisoners' cases as part of the negotiations over Alex Paul Menon, few have been released on bail even on its limited recommendations, and many more have been arrested since.[7]

The kidnappings left human rights activists and groups in a difficult position. On the one hand, they did not want their mediation to be interpreted as an endorsement of the practice of kidnapping. On the other hand, they were confronted by the testimonies of people whose plight the kidnappings highlighted, even if momentarily.[8] What is ironic, however, is the pressure exerted on human rights activists to mediate by the same governments that are otherwise busy condemning or even arresting them as Maoist sympathizers. Indeed, it is their very positioning 'between' that the state makes use of in times of crises. There is a tacit acknowledgement at such times that human rights activists are not only distinct from the Maoists, but fair in their efforts. However, the state has never extended this acknowledgement by listening to them on other aspects, including finding a lasting solution through peace talks.

The Debate on Violence

> Despite everything, in the popular imagination, the Maoist party stands for something that has changed their [the people's] lives for the better.
>
> S.R. Sankaran, 2009

Between 2008 and 2011, the PCPA was developing an alternative model of development in Lalgarh, West Bengal, the Chasia Muli Adivasi Sangh was struggling for land rights in Koraput in Odisha, and the Maoists were active in Jharkhand. There have been efforts by radical groups to highlight these as alternative models of development. However, much of the struggle between human rights voices (broadly defined) and the state, as well as debates between independent voices and the Maoists, has been over definitions of violence, attributions of violence and justifications for violence.

As far as villagers are concerned, the Maoist use of weapons is not the central question by which to evaluate them, as long as the guns are primarily aimed at their oppressors. However, it is by no means glossed over in their understanding, especially when the same violence is used against them, albeit in the name of killing 'informers'. As K. Balagopal wrote, 'Violence may be good or bad, necessary or unnecessary, but it is always crude.'[9] The parallel perhaps might be the way in which large sections of the middle class were willing to overlook Narendra Modi's culpability in the anti-Muslim pogroms of 2002 because they felt he would bring 'development'. For the villagers, it is the Maoists who have brought them economic empowerment.

The government, however, is keen to make violence the central issue, even if, as a former security advisor conceded to me, the Maoists were described as the 'biggest security threat facing the country' not because they were powerful militarily but because they were the only group ideologically challenging the status quo. As far as the government is concerned, what it does itself – even if it involves killing little children and burning old men alive – is not 'violence'; it is simply what is required to keep the state intact, in the way that 'reasons of state' and 'security' have been used the world over to justify the suspension of basic rights. When the state talks of violence, it does not mean the violence of a system which causes people to go hungry or enables corporates to displace large numbers of people for their own profit, or the government's own barbaric acts of custodial and militaristic killing. The government can thus claim it is interested in peace, while conducting war.

The Maoists are also keen to make violence an issue. Their fetishization of 'armed struggle' as a strategy superior to non-violence goes well beyond a defensive response to the 'structural violence' of the state. In 2006, the ICI wrote open letters to both the Maoists and the state, but only the Maoists replied. In response to the ICI claiming that non-violent methods would have served the adivasis better, the Maoists replied: 'Can you show us one instance from the pages of Indian history where the rights of the adivasis were ensured through non-violent and open means? And not just in India but anywhere in the world for that matter? What have the tribals of Kalinganagar received for their peaceful protest against Tata Steel?'[10]

One might well turn around and note that what the adivasis of Bastar had received for their armed struggle was permanent occupation by CRPF camps, and thousands of deaths, rapes and arrests. On the other hand, it is true that had they not resisted, the area would have been occupied by mines, steel plants and dams at a faster rate. Either way, it is a question of the pace and intensity with which occupation takes place, not whether it will happen. The question of efficacy and consequences is not something to which existing history has empirical answers, to justify a stand either way. Nor is it clear why one must choose between only violence and non-violence, instead of a range of actions, each of which has some small impact.[11]

Like the state and the Maoists, the civil liberties groups are also concerned with the question of violence, though in a more conflicted way. Indeed, this is the question that initially divided the movement. K. Balagopal, who founded the HRF argued that if the civil liberties movement truly wants to side with the oppressed, it must distinguish their needs from those of the revolutionary organizations which claim to represent them: 'It can do this only if it speaks with its own voice and not the voice of the political movement in question. And only if it speaks in terms of values and ideas and not in terms of the political ideologies and strategies of the movement.'[12]

Dithering over Dialogue

> At one level, I was personally very disappointed about the breakdown of the talks, but at another level, talks have changed the situation a little bit for the better. The party has become a bit more democratic and government also has had exposure to some of these ideas... Government ignores you and makes you feel unwanted. The Maoists want to take you over.
>
> S.R. Sankaran, 2009, on his own role in peace dialogues in Andhra Pradesh

Like their differing positions on violence, the government, Maoists and civil society activists each have their own stand on dialogue. The government has never wanted peace talks, though in a democratic set-up it cannot fully afford to be seen as letting that possibility go. Successive home ministers insist that talks are only possible if the Maoists give up arms, though the government's record of talking to peaceful protesters is even more dismal than its policy on armed groups. The government's indifference to Irom Sharmila's 16-year fast is a glaring example. The police sell the view that talks are merely a tactical line to give the Maoists breathing time to regroup. Since the state has endless money and time to continue holding operations in these areas and since all political parties are united on a militarist approach, there is absolutely no political pressure to act for peace. Welfare schemes give political parties in government a veneer of legitimacy, while the expansion of paramilitary and police jobs buys them support among youth.

The Maoists, like the government, have not been keen on peace talks. In the past, peace talks have proved fatal for Maoist presence and organization, not just in Andhra Pradesh and West Bengal – where talks led to police infiltration of ranks – but also in Nepal, where the Indian Maoists argue that parliamentarism wiped out the revolutionary nature of the Nepalese party. The Maoists also say that there is nothing to talk about, since the government will not give in on mining or land rights. But at the same time, they have to appear willing to consider peace talks because their constituency of villagers needs it and a liberal democratic audience demands it.

While all activists claim they want peace talks, in practice they have provided the following range of reasons for not pursuing this demand vigorously: 'Since we can't prevent mass arrests or mining, why stop the Maoists from continuing their fight'; 'Unless we get assurances on all the issues that affect villagers – forest rights, land rights, mining – we are not asking for a just peace'; 'After the killings of (Maoist leaders) Kishenji and Azad, there is no point –

talks will only endanger Maoist leaders'; 'One has a right to be a Maoist sympathizer – so long as one is not engaged in criminal acts'; 'The main problem is criminalization of dissent'; 'The real issue is Operation Green Hunt, not Maoist resistance'. Under the Modi regime's onslaught on rights and resources, talks seem even more unlikely to lead to anything productive.

Whatever one may think of opinion polls, an August 2010 survey by *The Week*–CNN–IBN–CSDS, across the 'red belt', showed that the public at large believes in unconditional dialogue, developmental solutions over military ones, and reform of the existing political process. Another 2010 *Times of India* poll in Telangana showed that 58 per cent felt the Maoists were good for the area, 65 per cent said that government killing of the Maoists was unjustified, and 60 per cent did not believe the government on claimed encounters.[13]

There is an argument to be made for talks as a way of providing breathing space for people who have lived with combing operations and violence for far too long, and for some progress on the mining issue. But there are few takers for measures which are clearly palliative and reformist. The choices we are offered instead are the impossible dream of armed revolution or the soul-numbing acceptance of armed repression.

15

The Propaganda Wars

The front page reports
120 soldiers were killed

the war was long
you get used to it

right next to this news
of a spectacular crime
with the killer's photo

Mr Cogito's gaze
moves with indifference
over the soldiers' hecatomb
to plunge with great relish
into the quotidian macabre

a thirty-year-old farmworker
in a state of manic depression
murdered his own wife
and two small children

we are told the exact
way they were killed

the position of bodies
and the other details

it's no use trying to find
120 lost men on a map
a distance too remote
hides them like a jungle

they don't speak to the imagination
there are too many of them
the numeral zero on the end
turns them into an abstraction

a theme for further reflection:
the arithmetic of compassion

Zbigniew Herbert, 'Mr Cogito Reads the Newspaper'

Lying in bed at night, lazily switching channels, the average viewer will sometimes see the ticker below the main frame announcing '3 Maoists killed in Sukma' or '4 CRPF men killed in Bijapur'. If it is a major attack, she might find the channel running several talking heads in different frames, shouting at each other, the anchor shouting at them all. The civil war 'out there' in the killing fields of Bastar is replicated in the studio. In the midst of the melee, it is impossible to know what the real war is about – or even care. What she will learn is that the Naxalites are irrational at best, and terrorists, extortionists and inhumane monsters at worst, holding back the development of the country. If the government is at fault, it is only because, as the Opposition spokesperson has just pointed out, they have not sent in sufficient troops or the troops did not follow the standard operating procedure, laying themselves open to an ambush. There may be one lone voice saying something about adivasis and the need for peace talks, but the anchor will not let her speak, and anyway she is probably anti-national, so it's a good thing. After five minutes, the average viewer switches off the TV and the light, and falls asleep.

As the media never tires of reminding everyone, it is the 'fourth estate' of democracy, a neutral recorder of events and watchdog rolled into one. Over the years, media critics have questioned the watchdog label, arguing that they are more like the 'guard dogs' of the establishment, saving it from harm. Even when the media is not directly a mouthpiece of the government (as many channels became post 2014) but filters the news through its organizational requirements, it ends up supporting the dominant order.[1]

Silence on the Judum

In the first year of the Judum, I can count on the fingers of one hand the newspaper articles that were written on it in the national press. The local press largely followed a pattern of embedded journalism, with several Chhattisgarh journalists being flown from Raipur to Dantewada in state helicopters. They were also whisked off to Goa and Hong Kong on paid holidays. Over the years, the Chhattisgarh government has actively and consistently bought off the press.[2]

Since the mainstream media did not report what was happening, the major source of news on Chhattisgarh was a Google group and website called 'Chhattisgarh Net', more commonly known as 'CGNet', set up by the journalist Shubhranshu Choudhary and his wife Smita Choudhary in 2004. It aggregated all the news published on Chhattisgarh: individuals posted their own information, and at least for the first few years it was a site of lively discussion on the conflict.[3]

The first news stories indicating any conflict came on 22 June 2005, reporting that the Naxalites had attacked villagers in Dantewada. A couple of other articles followed giving the government version of a tribal uprising against Maoists. Some of the stories were so fanciful that even the government had to later deny them:

> The extremist Communist Party of India-Maoist (CPI-Maoist), which has virtually ruled the Bastar region of Chhattisgarh in south-

> central India for 15 years, is fighting to save its fiefdom against a gastronomic offensive by the state government. For the first time since the early 1990s when Maoists gained ground in Kanker, Bastar and Dantewada districts, the rebels have been facing a serious revolt thanks to the pizza and Pepsi showered by the home department in poverty-stricken Maoist bastions. And it is working far better than the various strategies and millions of rupees invested in tackling the menace… The official sought to link the 'change of heart' of some former Maoists to the fact that they were well fed.[4]

The first critical story appeared on 29 June 2005 on Sahara TV: Ruchir Garg, a seasoned reporter on Naxalite issues, compared the anti-Naxal protest to the 1990 Jan Jagran Abhiyan, pointed out that there was heavy pressure on roadside villagers to join, and connected it to the entry of the Tatas. On 2 August, K. Srinivas Reddy of *The Hindu*, another long-term observer of the Naxalites, reported the Maoists as saying they would oppose the JJA. There was nothing on the scale of killings by the Judum. On 9 August, Alok Putul of the BBC, reporting on a Naxal attack on Mahendra Karma's house, referred to the Salwa Judum in terms of forced mass surrenders, Naxal retaliation, people fleeing to camps, etc. This was pretty much all there was.

In September 2005, the Bastar MP Baliram Kashyap said journalists should be jailed for glorifying Maoists, though no journalist had done anything of the sort.[5] Soon after, on 8 September, the government enacted the Chhattisgarh Special Public Security Ordinance (which became an act in 2006), which would indeed make it possible for the government to jail journalists at its discretion.

In early September 2005, Shubhranshu Choudhary reported getting calls from Dantewada about atrocities by Naga forces, followed at the end of the month by reports from Nagaland that the Nephiu Rio government was facing flak at home for sending Naga youth to malarial, illness-prone Chhattisgarh. However, positive stories spun by the government continued, including in journals which prided themselves on being anti-establishment, such as *Tehelka*.[6]

The first indicator that there was a humanitarian crisis came only four months after the violence and evacuation of villages began, with an email sent out to the CGNet group on 3 October 2005 by Mohuya Chaudhuri of NDTV, known for her reporting of rural issues. She described the fear on everyone's faces, an attack by the Naga battalion and the awful conditions in the camps. The All India Fact-finding team's press release from Raipur on 5 December generated some negative coverage of the Judum, but between January and April 2006 the media went back to reporting Naxalite attacks, and the steely determination of the Salwa Judum and SPOs to fight the Maoists.[7]

In April–May 2006, the first critical stories begin appearing in the international press, much before most of the Indian press.[8] This was, however, driven by the familiar trope of third world inequality, highlighting the contradictions between India's high economic growth and a seemingly anachronistic Maoist movement.

Context for Local Reportage

There are several reasons why there was so little coverage of violence by the Salwa Judum and security forces under Operation Green Hunt, and why the media predominantly reflects the government version of events. To begin with, there is the generic aspect of all news, especially news to do with law and order. The organizational requirements of a newspaper or TV channel include the need to get news out fast, which involves relying on an 'authoritative' source. When it comes to crime, this means reproducing the police narrative.[9]

Media distortion of facts is a widespread problem the world over.[10] In the case of the Maoist conflict, this is evident in a number of ways – for instance, sporadic, decontextualized reporting; blaming the Maoists alone for the lack of education or development in Dantewada despite the lack of development in places where there are no Maoists;

and following the government line on Maoist 'extortion', ignoring the fact that the media themselves periodically report governmental corruption or extortion.

But there are additional reasons why the war was covered – or rather, initially not covered – the way it was in Chhattisgarh. Because the states of Jharkhand and Chhattisgarh were formed only in 2001, and are not major markets for the advertisers that drive the Indian media, neither the national English print nor television media had full-time reporters stationed on the ground. At best, the *Indian Express* and *Hindustan Times* had correspondents in Raipur, and Dantewada was a long way away. There were also few organizations to feed the media any alternative perspective. In contrast to the Salwa Judum, both Nandigram and the Gujarat massacres of 2002 became front-page news, in part because they were located next to major cities with concentrations of journalists (Ahmedabad and Kolkata), in part because of the presence of middle-class local activists, in part because the issue was taken up by parliamentary parties. Chhattisgarh, on the other hand, lacks a tribal middle class or a density of civil/political society organizations; and both the Congress and the BJP were jointly executing the counter-insurgency.

Media owners are generally reluctant to confront governments on whom they are dependent for advertisements or contracts. For instance, *Dainik Bhaskar*, one of India's largest circulating newspapers and the leading daily in Chhattisgarh, is deeply invested in mining, real estate and other businesses. The government on its part blatantly justified payment to influence coverage of the Maoist issue as legitimate counter-insurgency:

> Referring to TV channels being funded for some of their Naxal reports, Kumar [Officer on Special Duty to the chief minister] said this was required to counter Naxal propaganda. 'The urban network of Naxals is able to use the media to support them and their ideologies. Human stories of Naxal violence and efforts of government officers often go unreported, so we get these done,' he said.[11]

Not surprisingly, anything that helps the Chhattisgarh government makes headlines, and anything critical is relegated inside. When the NHRC gave its report on the Salwa Judum in 2008, some national newspapers and all the state newspapers made the 'NHRC clean chit' front-page headlines, while the fact that the NHRC also recommended compensation to all those affected made a small back-page item.

The world of Hindi journalism is quite different from that of the national English dailies.[12] Many of the journalists writing in the local Hindi press are stringers who get paid very little, and have to make the bulk of their income on commissions for advertisements. A sarpanch told me how he was forced to put out an advertisement for Rs 20,000 by a 'journalist'. As several Bastar-based journalists have told me, they have no money for news gathering, and visiting interior villages is both difficult and expensive. As a result, even in predominantly rural and forested Bastar, the bulk of the stories tend to come from an urban beat or easily accessible villages.

There are also factors unique to Bastar: there are almost no adivasi journalists in the area, and almost none of the local journalists know any of the adivasi languages. Unlike traders who need to learn the language of the interiors they visit to buy and sell minor forest produce, language skills have never been seen by journalists as essential to their work. When the Salwa Judum started, many local journalists were not unhappy with it. They felt it made the adivasis 'more like them'. Subsequently, a certain resentment also developed among local journalists, strongly fanned by the police and politicians, about the view from Delhi – allegedly led by the naive urban pro-Maoists – being quite different from the view from Bastar. What they don't acknowledge, of course, is that this is a view from urban non-adivasi Bastar.

Sadly, the whole structure of news – paid news, lack of trained journalists, self-interested media owners and vulnerability to police power – has meant that the most elementary professionalism is sacrificed. To be fair to local journalists, many of them are handicapped by laws like the CSPSA and the Unlawful Activities (Prevention) Act, and intimidated by the administration as well as by the Maoists. Sometimes, dedicated local journalists pass their stories on to the correspondents of national dailies to ensure they get covered. And many do display remarkable bravery.

A Dangerous Occupation

One of the first journalists to become a victim of the civil war was 27-year-old Kamlesh Paikra from Cherpal village. Small, round-faced and with a ready smile, Kamlesh worked as the Bijapur correspondent for the *Hindsatt* coming out of Jagdalpur. He also ran a fair price shop. On 8 September 2005, Kamlesh wrote of the burning of 50 houses in Mankeli village, which then prompted the CPI to visit the area. Kamlesh's permit for the shop was cancelled; and his brother, who worked in the Cherpal high school, was arrested on charges of possessing Naxalite literature. By the time the All India Fact-finding team visited in November 2005, Kamlesh was already a marked man. The Chhattisgarh Shramjivi Patrakar Sangh (Working Journalists' Union) as well as the members of CGNet petitioned the Collector, chief minister and Governor on his behalf, but eventually he was forced to leave Bijapur for Dantewada where he got a job with the MSF.

The second journalist to be targeted was Mohammad Afzal, a well-respected, grey-bearded journalist in Bhopalpatnam, who also worked for the *Hindsatt.* When the Judum held its first meeting in Bhopalpatnam, they called various dignitaries on stage, even as they were beating up suspected sangham members backstage. When Afzal protested, they assaulted him, fracturing his hand in the process. Fortunately, the Judum never took off in Bhopalpatnam, and Afzal was able to continue working there. In conversations with him over the years, I found him critical of both the Maoists and the state, and deeply concerned about the situation of ordinary villagers.

But perhaps the saddest case was of Sai Reddy, who was arrested by the police in 2008 for having Maoist links and then killed by the Maoists in 2013 for working for the police. I met him at his home in December 2008. He was then a sallow-faced 49-year-old, who had just spent four hot summer months in jail. Sai Reddy was born in Basaguda, and had started off as a trader in minor forest produce, working the weekly markets. He wrote for *Navbharat* on local developmental issues. For some reason the Naxals told him and his entire extended family of four or five households to leave, so he went to Andhra Pradesh. But he came back after a few months, because the children had problems studying in Telugu. Initially when the Judum started, he said he kept himself neutral, but after a while he got involved when people approached him for help to return home from the camps. The SPOs, who hated seeing anyone leave the camps, accused him of smuggling rice to the Maoists from his wife's fair price shop. He told me he had sent his whole file to DGP Viswaranjan even before he was arrested, but the DGP did nothing to help. It was other journalists, in particular N.R.K. Pillai, a senior, balding Malayali journalist, leader of the local journalists' union, who helped to get him out of jail; part of the help was ensuring that reporting of his case was muted.

When the Sai Reddy killing was challenged by civil liberties organizations, and local journalists vowed they would not report any Maoist press releases, going on a week-long padyatra to protest, the Maoists responded by providing a convoluted and self-serving history of how his killing came about:

> For about two decades Sai Reddy had been taking up anti-people and anti-movement activities even while being a journalist. So the party's South Bastar Divisional Committee (DVC) decided to punish him and accordingly a PLGA unit attacked his house once. But he escaped in that attack. In 2008 he was arrested by the Chhattisgarh police under Chhattisgarh Special Public Security Act on a false

> accusation that he was a Maoist supporter and put in jail for one year. However, there were other reasons for his arrest. But with this arrest his image turned into one who opposed the government. In this backdrop the DVC stalled the decision to punish him. However this decision was not passed on to the lower ranks properly. As a result, this happened.[13]

A similar story of crossed wires between higher ranks and lower-level cadre was narrated to me by a knowledgeable villager from Tongpal as an explanation for the killing of Nemichand Jain on 12 February 2013. Jain was a stringer for *Haribhoomi*, *Nayi Duniya* and *Dainik Bhaskar*. According to my source, Nemichand had been taking the Tongpal thanedar, Surjan Singh, into the interior villages, ostensibly to show him the local culture and customs. On 8 February 2013, a Maoist squad warned Nemichand not to show the police around, and to refrain from visiting the villages for six months. But overconfident because of his long years in the area as a journalist, Nemichand ignored them. A day later, he brought three other men dressed in safari suits, riding on two bikes, and asked where the Bhumkal Divas (Maoist commemoration of the 1910 Bhumkal on 10 February) was being celebrated. When one of these safari-suited men reached for a cigarette, the villagers saw that he was carrying a pistol. The men left, but Nemichand stayed on in one of the villages, spending the night drinking. On the 12th, he went to Soutnar haat, and while he was returning, one of the sanghams killed him. They were scared that he would identify them to the police. The dalam did not get to know till much later, and while they censured the sangham, they could not punish them harshly because, after all, Nemichand had ignored their warnings.

This story is plausible because it has all the hallmarks of local power relations: immigrant men, journalists included, spending nights in adivasi villages in order to drink, claiming to be 'familiar' with adivasi life; a growing discomfort among the villagers about such familiarity in times of war when outsiders were potential informers; a panic attack by the local sangham; and the routinization of killing. The Maoists apologized, but the damage was done.

In 2015, two reporters, Somaru Nag and Santosh Yadav of Darbha block, working for the *Patrika*, and *Dainik Navbharat* and *Dainik Chattisgarh* respectively, were arrested on charges of working for the Maoists. Journalist Chitrangada Choudhury describes the unlikely charges: Yadav's 'name was subsequently added to a case where 18 villagers are in prison, charged with an encounter on 21st August during a road-opening operation by the security forces in which a Special Police Officer was killed' while Nag 'has been charged with keeping a look out on the movements of the police while a group burnt a crusher plant employed in road construction in Chote Kadma on 26th June'.[14] The Chhattisgarh journalists organized to get them released, demanding a special law for the protection of journalists.

Days before the journalists were to hold a *jail bharo andolan* in Jagdalpur on 21 December 2015, the police engineered a split among them, with IG Kalluri announcing on Whatsapp the formation of the Bastar Division Journalists' Association, and the decisions they had taken, including not to participate in the journalists' rally. Just like the 'people's movement' that the Salwa Judum supposedly was, purportedly independent journalism is now being openly run from police headquarters.

In March 2016, two more journalists, Prabhat Singh and Deepak Jaiswal, were arrested, the former after he accused others on a Whatsapp group of being too close to Kalluri. All these arrests, together with the eviction of Malini Subramaniam who was reporting for Scroll, a national news portal, finally moved the Editors Guild to send a fact-finding team to Bastar. The team reported a sense of widespread fear among journalists, pressure from both the Maoists and the government, and a sense of being under government surveillance at all times.[15]

Cycles of Reporting by the National Media

> Outside the sphere of the media there is only political marginality.
>
> Manuel Castells, *Power of Identity*

For a long time, as mentioned earlier, the national media more or less ignored the conflict. In the summer of 2006, I personally contacted several editors of both the print and television media in Delhi with photos of the Judum's devastation, and lists of people who had died, asking them to do their own investigation, but there was no interest. This is not to say there were no critical opinion pieces; the ICI received considerable coverage of its report, apart from the articles written by individual members. After Supreme Court hearings in May 2007, and again in March 2008, there were also a number of critical editorials in the English press saying the government must cease arming civilians. However, these were merely opinion pieces. The bulk of the news coverage and terminology used there – which is what defines the news for the average reader – iteratively reflected the government standpoint on the Salwa Judum as a 'people's movement' and 'peaceful campaign', and downplayed any killings by the state. On the other hand, what did get reported were the gruesome Maoist attacks on SPOs, camps and security forces. These attacks naturally exercised a strong hold on the popular imagination, without a parallel revulsion being created towards state violence. The only Indian journalists who reported the conflict in any depth in 2006 were Smita Gupta in *Outlook* and Maureen Mitra in *Down to Earth*.[16]

Even when the press did report the conflict, the decontextualized presentation played a critical role in reproducing the status quo, providing no background to explain the rise of Naxalism in the area. Media reports on poverty stories are largely in human interest mode: villager-as-victim makes good reporting, while villager-turning-violent to defend her or his rights is less appealing to the credit ratings. Except, of course, when it serves the media to focus on the 'threat' posed by India's 'red corridor'. Even when the Maoists provided their own guided tours to reporters, the latter invariably highlighted the rivers they crossed and the long treks they took in the forests to reach Naxalite strongholds. The media was more interested in reporting on the Maoists' marital and sex life than on the conditions that drove them to fight, or the sufferings of ordinary villagers. When one lakh people marched 200 kilometres and several days, in November 2007, to demand an end to the Salwa Judum and the opening of dialogue with the Maoists, it did not make national news, since they did it peacefully – and stories coming out of Naxalite areas must have blood and gore.

In the case of TV, the bias against providing context is even more pronounced. The visual nature of the medium ensures that news is 'event-centred, action-centred, and person-oriented'.[17] Large military attacks by the Maoists or police thus inevitably dominate TV news, to the exclusion of everything else. The standard television frame is to describe the Maoists as terrorists and the security forces as martyrs, to talk in apocalyptic tones of shock and horror, and to naturalize the dispossession of people as 'development'. This is supported by an analysis of the media coverage of two major attacks by the Maoists.[18] Such coverage, however, can also be a double-edged sword, because it gives an impression of Maoist strength. By 2011, stories on the Maoists started petering out, primarily because the government decided that the media commentary on the war was helping the Maoists.

Naveen Mishra and Pradeep Ninan Thomas, based on content analysis of major English language newspapers in 2009 and 2012 respectively, also confirm the overwhelmingly state-driven nature of reportage on the Maoist conflict. Naveen Mishra points out that 91 per cent of the sources were government or police, with the police/security establishment being dominant; while coverage of the causes of insurgency, like land or forest issues, was almost negligible.[19]

~

For a brief period between 2009 and 2011, there were some challenges to the one-sided nature of media discourse. Not totally, of course, as the Mishra and Thomas essays show, since the majority of the stories continued to relay what the government wanted reported. There were several reasons for this, of which the most prominent was the government's own grandiose announcement in 2009 of Operation Green Hunt against Maoists across the country.

The Maoists had also started fighting back with some spectacular victories, such as the 2010 Tadmetla ambush, which no television or print channel could afford to ignore. In Lalgarh in West Bengal, the media-savvy Maoist leader Kishenji routinely gave interviews to the media before he was killed, a red checked towel facing the camera. By this time, the Binayak Sen campaign had also caught on in the media. For many people, however, especially those outside India, it was Arundhati Roy's essay 'Walking with the Comrades' published in 2010, and her subsequent interviews, which acquainted them with the Salwa Judum and the Maoists.[20]

Around 2009, a number of national newspapers posted journalists to the area, and front-paged their stories. These were young, talented men and women, with empathy, an ability to capture pain in a photo, drive motorcyles and file stories in difficult conditions. They wrote movingly of civilian deaths and rapes, and for the first time, readers across the country were exposed to the scale of the war in real time. Many of these reporters went on to get awards for their stories.

But some of them were also filled with a competitive instinct to be the first to get a story, and it is this – regardless of danger to oneself, to local informants, or even to the victims themselves – which led to the death of Tarun Sehrawat, a photojournalist with *Tehelka*, who died of malaria after visiting the Marh. *Tehelka* in particular became known – and popular among the radical crowd – for its dramatized description of the violence, but this included a bad case of reporting on rapes, where the photos of the survivors were so thinly pixelated that it helped the SPOs identify and threaten them.

~

As with roads, trees, schools and electoral booths – all of which have become sites of conflict – the war ranges back and forth across the terrain of media coverage: more news, less news, propaganda. The 'truth', whatever it is, is an object of war.

The police often inflate figures of Naxalite losses, or try to pass off killings of villagers as Naxalites to reduce the morale of the rebels. For instance, in May 2006, the CRPF commander leading the operation clearly told the ICI that only one woman Naxalite had been killed; the rest had fled. We saw the body they brought to Dornapal camp. But the IG's press release claimed that three Naxalites (one woman and two men) had been killed, and the Naxalites had dragged the other two bodies away. Surrender figures are similarly inflated as part of a psychological war to bring down Maoist morale. Even though the local media know that the spate of surrenders from 2014 onwards is coerced, they are obliged to carry the police press releases faithfully. The national media have been more openly sceptical on the surrenders issue, but to little effect.

Between 2012 and 2015, there have been brief flares of media interest whenever the Maoists have mounted a major operation – like the kidnapping of the Collector of Sukma, Alex Menon, in 2012 or the killing of Mahendra Karma and other Congress leaders in 2013 – but these have soon died out. There appears to be a general acceptance that this will be a long-drawn-out war, with 'collateral damage' among civilians. Among concerned citizens too, there is a dulling of senses, with repeated exposure to horrors. Even front-page news of rapes by the security forces appears to make no difference to the government. The media ownership scene also changed by 2014, with takeovers by corporate houses close to the new BJP government.

In the Iraq war, between 2003 and 2007, the US media coverage of bad news declined as its novelty value wore off and particular attacks or casualties were reported as discrete, unconnected events. The US administration's claim to be succeeding, or at least the idea that there was light at the end of the tunnel, received far greater prominence. Any attempt to suggest that the policy was not working was met with stern warnings of the dangers if the US did not stay the course. Thus an 'accountability gap' came into existence.[21] A similar accountability gap is visible when it comes to the Maoist conflict. The media rarely questions the government on its overall policy, even when home ministers like P. Chidambaram and Rajnath Singh announce every four years that the Maoists will be finished in the 'next two or three years'. They even report, without seeing any contradictions, these comments regarding an imminent finish together with scare scenarios like that relayed by G.K. Pillai, a former home secretary, who talked of the prospect of a Maoist takeover of India by 2050.[22]

Unlike the US war on Iraq, here those killed on either side are citizens of India, for whose security the government is responsible. However, the targeted killings or rapes of ordinary adivasis by the security forces, if exposed, are rarely, if ever, attended by direct calls upon the home minister to condemn or compensate for each such incident. This is quite different from the manner in which television anchors make human rights activists answerable for every action of the Maoists. This easily summons to mind Herman and Chomsky's distinction between 'worthy and unworthy victims' as part of what they call the media 'propaganda model'.[23] While news coverage of the worthy is replete with detail, evokes indignation and shock, and invites a follow-up, unworthy victims get limited news space and are referred to in generic terms; there is also little attempt to fix responsibility or trace culpability to the top echelons of the establishment.

In 2016, with several journalists arrested, and attacks on middle-class activists, media interest in Bastar has revived again, especially among young reporters. The proliferation of Internet-based media sites like The Wire and Scroll has certainly helped to ensure that some human rights violations are covered, as has the growth of social media. On the other hand, the BJP, the RSS and the security establishment have been equally, if not more, successful in mobilizing both the mainstream as well as social media for counter-insurgency, including to malign anyone critical of the government. Since 2014

I have been on a Bastar Whatsapp group run jointly by police and journalists. Whenever the police post photos of bullet-riddled bloody bodies of alleged Maoists allegedly killed in an 'encounter', some journalists punch victory signs. In 2016, these same journalists faithfully reproduced in their newspapers and channels what they knew was a police-fabricated complaint, ostensibly from villages in Darbha block, claiming that a group of researchers of which I was a part had threatened the villagers with Maoist retaliation if they supported the police. This was nationally relayed by the rabidly right-wing Zee channel, owned by Subhash Chandra, an MP backed by the BJP.

The Poster Competitions

Apart from the mainstream media, the government has also invested money in other kinds of messaging to spread its word. At one annual Dussehra exhibition, where each government department showcases its wares, the police had put up large comic posters showing how uniformed Maoists were holding back roads and development, while the police were helping villagers. In 2014–15, the central government allotted Rs 5 crore to creating radio jingles and short films, as well as organizing tribal youth exchange programmes, to convince people that the Naxalites were impeding government schemes.[24]

In 2015, just outside Jagdalpur, I came across a large hoarding with photos of two surrendered Maoist couples – in both cases, the man was from Andhra and the woman a local adivasi. The police had written: 'These outside Naxalites don't let adivasis surrender or get married, but themselves surrender and take all the benefits. These characterless and opportunist Naxalites live in comfort while they force adivasis into antisocial activities which land them in jail.' Given how few of the top leadership had surrendered, and after much wrestling with their conscience, to humiliate them in this manner seems hardly conducive to more surrenders. But both in Odisha and Chhattisgarh, the police have tried hard to play up the regional differences between the Telugu leadership and the rank and file of cadre who are local.

On the side, the police had listed the rewards for surrendering weapons – for example, Rs 4.5 lakh for a light machine gun, Rs 3 lakh for an AK-47. Smaller posters declaring rewards for IEDs by the kilo are also pinned to trees across the district. Kalluri also personally conducted active propaganda through Whatsapp messages, circulating photos of Maoists' corpses, those surrendering and anti-activist media reports.

~

The Maoists also attempt to carry out their own poster campaigns. The cadre write slogans on schools and on the roads – 'Salwa Judum Murdabad', 'Boycott elections' – addressed to the security forces, since they are the only ones likely to read these. Long stretches of apparently deserted forest have trees with posters pinned to them. Sometimes these are printed, but often they are painstakingly handwritten. The messages vary from the deeply local – condemning a particular informer or someone who has surrendered and run away with money – to wider demands for the release of political prisoners and the removal of the troops.

The Maoists produce a number of different journals to cater to different sections locally, such as *Pituri*, *Bhumkal*, *Pordu* and *Prabhat* (referring variously to uprisings and new dawns). Lachanna told me that each division had its own newsletter, and state committee members were tasked with writing one article about struggles in their own areas for each issue. But many failed to do so, and eventually a few people had to do all the writing. The readership consisted of people with some elementary education in the villages, teachers, etc. Before computers came in 1996, they used cyclostyling. The computers were run on kerosene generators and solar-powered batteries. There were 25 people in the press unit, and they used horses to carry around the heavy generators. In mid-2008, the Salwa Judum and CRPF raided a press camp and took away the horses and generators. The Maoists have also deployed Gondi songs with great effect, since they have a reach far beyond their committed constituency.

But the Maoists are also aware of a national audience. The name Gudsa Usendi – taken on by a succession of party spokespersons – has become familiar to everyone who has reported on Dandakaranya. There were shades of the communiqués by Subcomandante Marcos of the Chiapas struggle in Mexico, as Gudsa Usendi would call or email journalists owning responsibility for some major attack, or informing them of massacres of civilians by the security forces. Maoist press statements and interviews also make their way into websites such as Banned Thought.net, though frequently URL links are snapped as a result of the home ministry's blocking attempts. The Maoists have also employed more ingenious ways of getting their message out, even if the capacity of their target to hear the message is restricted. In 2005, at the height of the Salwa Judum campaign, the Maoists distributed CDs containing footage of burning villages to the houses of a number of MLAs. Nobody was concerned with the horrifying images these videos contained; instead, the legislative assembly in Chhattisgarh chose to fret that the Maoists were 'close enough to the state capital to distribute CDs to MLAs'.

16

Praying for Justice

> The average intelligent Indian thinks of PIL as the modern equivalent of the bell which the better kind of king is reputed to have strung outside his palace for the desperate citizen to tug at and get an instant hearing and instant justice. The average intelligent Indian also thinks that all the limitations of judicial power that he or she is otherwise familiar with vanish when the Courts sit to hear PILs, namely that they become benign despots who can set every wrong right by passing a condign order. Desperation can be the only reason for these illusions.
>
> K. Balagopal, *Beyond Violence and Non-Violence*

This chapter is an account of such desperation. Every time the case we filed against the Salwa Judum in the Supreme Court was listed for hearing, I made offerings at the tomb of a medieval 'judge saab' in the scrub jungle near my home in Delhi, to give the judges wisdom and our lawyers strength. I clasped my hands together in prayer when arguments were about to start. I put aside all my agnosticism and social science cynicism. But later, when the case went cold, it was social science and not supplication that came to my comfort. As I learnt when I read Gerald Rosenberg's *The Hollow Hope*, across the world there are limits to the interventions that courts can make on social issues.[1] My narrative here chronicles the passage from faith to sociology.

In the 1970s, the Indian Supreme Court fostered a remarkable innovation: public interest litigation. It devised procedures to make justice accessible to the ordinary citizen, including waiving locus standi, so that any concerned individual – not just one personally affected – could approach a court directly on the violation of fundamental rights; commissioning enquiries of their own rather than relying on the litigators to produce evidence; and constituting committees to monitor the implementation of their judgments.

Like any mechanism that makes space for the poor, PILs have invited flak for using up precious court time with 'frivolous litigation'. True, some PILs are absurd and filed by cranks of which India has no shortage, or by corporates in order to beat their competition down. However, PILs were barely 1.3 per cent of the total cases disposed of by the Supreme Court between 2007 and 2011.[2] Moreover, even genuine PILs necessarily involve cross-class alliances. Despite pro bono lawyering which is another hallmark of PILs, all that is involved – briefing lawyers, translating all documents into English for the Supreme Court, the need to be present in Delhi for hearings which may or may not happen – means that ordinary adivasis have no real access to court. Those who do come to court, even state high courts, manage only because their cause has been taken up by NGOs, civil society activists or concerned individuals. As one lawyer with experience of fighting many pro bono cases put it, the new model is for industry to forcibly acquire land at low rates, and then pay corporate lawyers huge sums to defend them in court against poor litigants.

In 2007, we filed two PILs or writ petitions (WPs) against the Salwa Judum. The first one, WP (Civil) 250/2007, *Nandini Sundar, Ramachandra Guha and E.A.S. Sarma* v. *State of Chhattisgarh*, heard in May, was an outcome of the ICI. The second one, WP (Criminal) 119/2007, *Kartam Joga, Dudhi Joga and Manish Kunjam* v. *the State of*

Chhattisgarh and the Union of India, was heard in October. The Union or Central government was implicated for funding the SPOs and also supporting Chhattisgarh's policy on the Salwa Judum.

Deciding to Litigate

It took time to decide whether and where to litigate. Civil liberties groups were reluctant to go to court on the Salwa Judum perhaps for fear that the courts would legitimize it. I felt, however, it was necessary to cover all avenues. In any case, the court could not make the situation worse than it already was.

Fortunately, other members of the ICI were equally disturbed by what they saw, and agreed to explore litigation. Their individual reputations were useful in dispelling the idea that we were Maoist agents. Ramachandra Guha is well known as a historian and columnist, especially as the author of *India after Gandhi*, while E.A.S. Sarma has held responsible positions as a civil servant including as Secretary or the top official in the ministries of power and finance. They helped out with the case whenever they could, and together the three of us put out letters whenever there was a major Maoist attack, or conversely, an attack by the security forces on civilians.

After six months of discussion with a senior Bilaspur High Court advocate, Kanak Tiwari, we decided to approach the Supreme Court instead. Friends introduced me to former Solicitor General T.R. Andhyarujina. He readily agreed to take on the case, in part persuaded by his junior, Ashish Chugh. Ashish drafted the first petition, based on fact-finding reports, and got a friend of his, Pragya Singh, who worked for corporate law firm Karanjawala and Co., to file it, as the advocate on record (AOR). An AOR is one's official address as far as the court is concerned, and all filings are done through an AOR, who has to pass a special exam to be eligible. Andhyarujina had himself been a junior to H.M. Seervai, the famous constitutional lawyer, and photos of him and other legal luminaries lined the stairs to his book-lined office facing a large terrace. Every time I went for a briefing, I came away in despair, convinced he did not appreciate the enormity of what was happening, and every time I heard him in court, I was amazed at how succinctly he got to the heart of the matter. I learnt the difference between the kind of details that interest anthropologists, and those that a lawyer needs to know.

The case was filed at the end of April 2007 and heard two weeks later, on 17 May, days before the court closed before the vacation. I was in a meeting of a committee chaired by S.R. Sankaran to frame the rules of the 2006 forest act when Pragya messaged me that the court had 'issued notice', which meant that the court had taken note of the matter. That evening, I also heard the news on the radio. For some years now, Supreme Court hearings had become newsworthy; there is always a large bank of television vans posted on Bhagwan Das Road, particularly on days when important judgments are expected. All our efforts as activists over the last two years had not worked as effectively to highlight the case as this one court 'notice'.[3]

Soon after that, I travelled to Sukma, where Rama Sodi of the CPI showed me the testimonies regarding the Salwa Judum's atrocities which had been given to them at the Cherla rally (see chapter 6) and suggested we use them in court. In Delhi, Comrade A.B. Bardhan, general secretary of the CPI, thought it was a good idea. The district party chose people who were victims as well as elected representatives to put their names to a petition. Given the atmosphere of the time – when villages were still being burnt on a daily basis and hundreds of people were being randomly killed or arrested – a braver set of men would be hard to find. Kartam Joga was a member of the zilla panchayat, and had been severely beaten by Salwa Judum activists and the local police. Dudhi Joga, Petitioner No. 2, was a resident of Arlampalli. The entire village, including his own house, had been burnt down by the Salwa Judum in the presence of Mahendra Karma. At the time the petition was filed, Dudhi Joga was taking refuge with relatives in another village. He was also an elected member of the janpad panchayat. Manish Kunjam, Petitioner No. 3, 'is the president of the All India Adivasi

Mahasabha, and a former MLA of Konta. He has barely escaped being assaulted by the Salwa Judum and has personal knowledge of several of the incidents mentioned.'

A hectic summer followed, during which, with the help of two students, the testimonies were translated into English and the names of people killed and raped culled. 'Kartam Joga and ors' was filed around the end of August, but the first hearing took place only on 12 October 2007, after three delays. This time the court not only gave notice but fixed an early hearing. From this time on, both cases were clubbed together and argued as one, with Sumita Hazarika acting as AOR for both.

It was from the summer of 2007 that I got to know two spaces particularly well – Nitya Ramakrishnan's office in central Delhi and Ashok Desai's office in the basement of his house. Nitya's office is a set of small rooms leading into each other. When you walk in, there is always an intern working at something, and people frequently drop in – friends, clients, or younger lawyers wanting to brief her. For one of the most reputed criminal lawyers in the country, with a string of acquittals and death sentence reprieves to her credit, her office is remarkably homely. Nitya herself is tall and striking, fanatical about mathematics, cricket and crosswords.

Ashok Desai's office is more imposing, with a separate room for his clerks and files, and a waiting chamber for clients. A former attorney general, he is one of the most senior and respected advocates practising in the Supreme Court. In 2017 he will complete 60 years of practice, but his steady fund of funny anecdotes, wide reading and keen interest in everything around him make him forever young. When Nitya, her juniors and I were ushered into his office, he would look up from whatever he was doing and say kindly, 'Come along now,' and after some small talk, we would set to reading the files.

All the lawyers, both senior and junior, who have worked on this case, have done so pro bono, over several years, leaving aside other lucrative cases, sometimes sitting late into the night drafting notes and formatting affidavits. I often wondered at their dedication. They had no personal connection to Bastar, and are not activists in the narrow sense it has come to be understood, but they do identify with the issue as legal professionals and, above all, as citizens.

The Setting

The impressively domed Supreme Court building, inaugurated in 1958 on 17 acres in the heart of Lutyens' Delhi, was designed as a balance with a pair of scales.[4] Court 1, where the Chief Justice sits along with two others, occupies the central portion of the beam, opposite the front lawns. Two doors on either side lead into the visitors' galleries, while lawyers enter from the middle door. The walls are wood panelled, the ceilings high, with fans suspended on long stems, though there is air conditioning as well. The judges enter from the back on to a raised dais. Attendants clad in red and white livery, with starched white turbans, stand behind each judge whenever they enter and exit. The three judges sit behind a table, on high-backed red plush chairs with an Ashoka Chakra emblem, symbolizing truth, embossed on the back. Behind them is one Ashoka Chakra high on the wall. Opposite them, above the entrance, is a large wall clock, and on both sides full-length oil portraits of former Chief Justices. The 'Court Masters', as the clerks are known, sit in front, just below the judges, at facing tables. There are mikes and amplifiers throughout the room, but the judges never seem to use them so it is a strain to hear what they say, and when they pass an order, the Court Masters have to stand up and take notes. A few library attendants in blue-grey uniforms scurry around before the judges enter, making sure all the files and law reporters are present. When they are done with a case, the judges throw the file down on the desk, from where it is whisked away to the registry below.

Courts 1–5 are in front, and the rest are on the right through a narrow corridor. Except for Court 7, these are small courts without a separate visitors' gallery. From 2007 till July 2010, we were in Court 1, but after that we moved to one of the side courts, which was a relief since this allowed me, as a litigant, to sit next to the lawyers while they argued. In general, the petitioners sit on the left and respondents on the right. There are bookshelves along the sides as well as narrow ledges on which one can perch one's files.

To one side, below the judges' desk, is an electronic display of the case being heard in each court so that lawyers can track the progress of their cases. In addition, a small electronic board outside each court and the Supreme Court website displays the 'item number'; thanks to computerization, lawyers can also access this in their offices. However, because the time that each case takes is unpredictable, a junior is often parked inside the court to quietly message the senior advocate on the status, or if the matter suddenly comes up, to jump up and ask for a 'passover'.

Outside each court, there are also paper lists pinned up in a wire cage from an earlier era, and two guards who frisk you and check the passes of those going in. The 'pass office' is at the entrance of the court premises. The most stomach-wrenching part of litigation was wondering whether the senior advocates would be free on the date of the court hearing, since cases run over to the next day, lawyers ask for adjournments, and as a result, cases constantly clash. You know whether your case will be listed only at 6 p.m. the previous day, and even then, there is no saying when it will come up. Sometimes our advocates would sit long hours in court waiting, but in vain as earlier matters would exhaust all of the court's time. Often, they would come fully prepared and the lawyers for Chhattisgarh would ask for time. The state of Chhattisgarh also tried to make things difficult for us by always giving us a copy of its affidavits at 5 p.m. the day before a hearing in the hope that we would ask for time to respond, but we never did.

The language of the courts was unfamiliar but interesting: 'giving appearance' means signing an official attendance sheet for advocates; 'settling cases' refers to seniors signing off on drafts that juniors prepare. I learnt to walk backwards when leaving the court so as not to show my back to the judge, though it was hard when one was staggering under a pile of files. I was in shock when I first heard a lawyer get up and say, 'I have murdered my wife,' and another one say, 'I am in jail for criminal fraud,' till I realized they were representing their clients quite literally. I always marvelled at how the judges sat so patiently through case after case on diverse subjects.

The experienced lawyers know when to stop – because occasionally the judges will whisper among themselves – and when to proceed and respond to the cues the judges hold out. Much depends on what transacts in court, regardless of what the files contain. Time is of the essence, and the slightest fumble in turning to the right page or the slightest error in the files can ruin even a solid case. Usually the lawyers only argued from the latest submission, but sometimes the opposing lawyer would read from an old file, and if we didn't have our own copy, we would be at a loss. So we took to bringing all the files to every hearing. Over the years, the files grew more and more voluminous, weighing several kilos, and needing several bags. Friends, the junior lawyers or the clerks would often help, but getting the files to court was always a big worry for me.

A typical court day starts with 'mentioning' before the judges – when lawyers mention cases which need an early hearing, or ask for a change of date. Mondays and Fridays are termed 'miscellaneous days' and are like a marketplace; the judges hear hundreds of cases on these days before deciding which ones to take up (though a case can go on for years without being formally 'admitted'). But on regular hearing or non-miscellaneous days, a single matter can take all day or even all week, while other lawyers wait their turn. In November 2009, several important matters, including ours, were put on hold for weeks while the Chief Justice's court heard the dispute between the two Ambani/Reliance brothers. When senior lawyers argue important cases, there are often lots of junior ones who come to listen, and often it is a mad run through a crush of lawyers and reporters when one's case is called.

The most unfathomable part of the court system, however, is the registry. Court dates can be tracked on the website of the Supreme Court, but they frequently appeared and then disappeared. The sequence of the case through 2009 – based on a list of dates I kept – shows how, between the registry dates, the need to be heard on non-miscellaneous dates so that we would get sufficient time to argue, and adjournments, a whole year passed without any actual hearing. The next proper hearing after 16 December 2008 was 18 February 2010!

The registry also houses the files which are piled on shelves and overflow into the corridors of the basement. The staff told us that they are able to retrieve the files required on any particular date only through sheer experience. Sometimes, the files get lost in transit between different judges; it is the AOR's task to ensure they are all there, as it is to ensure that five sets of every affidavit are filed each time, with the proper font and margins. The photocopiers in the court premises have acquired such wizardry in their craft that they are able to photocopy, straighten, compile and bind papers into finished 'paper books' in a matter of minutes.

The Life History of the Case

There have been five stages to our petition so far: the first phase before the Chief Justice which began in April 2007, consisted of our initial filings and hearings, and culminated in the order to the NHRC to investigate on 15 April 2008. In the second phase, both sides responded to the NHRC report, lasting from August 2008 till mid-2010. During this phase we also prepared a rehabilitation plan, and came close to securing a monitoring committee. A third phase spanned the period from July 2010 to July 2011, when the case came before Justices Reddy and Nijjar. The focus in the latter half of this phase shifted to SPOs. The fourth phase included a 'revision petition' by the Union of India challenging the July 2011 order, and our 'contempt of court' petition in March 2012 for violations of the order. The fifth phase, especially since early 2014 after Justice Nijjar retired, has been one of 'non-hearing' of the contempt case, in both the literal and metaphorical senses.

The synopsis and list of dates provided at the beginning of a litigation give a sense of the issues at stake. What we were asking for was 'an appropriate remedy to acts of systematic human rights and humanitarian law violations committed by an organized group called the Salwa Judum, with the active connivance and participation of agents of the state, the state police and paramilitary forces'.

The Kartam Joga petition attempted to put a number to those killed and houses burnt, based on the testimonies:

> Between 2005–2007 at least 33 children, 45 women, 416 men and 43 unnamed persons have been killed by the Salwa Judum from June 2005 till the present. In all reported deaths amount to 537 persons, and this is a small fraction of the likely killings, most of which have gone unreported... Between June 2005 and 2007 at least 2825 houses have been burnt in the undivided district of South Bastar (Dantewada), 1733 houses in Bijapur district and 1092 houses in Konta tahsil of Dantewada district.

In both the petitions, our 'prayers' included a ban on the Salwa Judum, the practice of arming civilians and state support to vigilantism; a stop to appointing minors as SPOs and the disbanding of the SPOs. We requested an independent enquiry into killings, rapes and arson by all parties, whether the Salwa Judum, SPOs, security forces or Naxalites; directions to the state to rehabilitate and compensate victims, to disband camps and to bring back refugees from Andhra to their own villages. We also wanted the state to register FIRs and prosecute all those responsible for human rights violations.

At the time of the first petition, the material available included, apart from fact-finding reports by human rights groups and some newspaper reports, government documents which revealed state support for the Salwa Judum.[5] The state's first response was to claim these were official secrets despite the fact that the government had put them on its website and freely distributed them. The second petition relied primarily on the testimonies from 110 villages in two volumes, collected from the Cherla rally of June 2007. From time to time, we annexed more testimonies, the stray official report critical of the Judum or other kinds of evidence, such as photos of the police memorials to SPOs killed in a Maoist attack at Rani Bodli camp. These gave the actual ages of the SPOs and showed that they were minors when they were killed despite the police claim that they were all adults.

~

Our strategy in court, in as much as we had any beyond presenting the evidence, was to contest the politicization of the case, list the legal principles involved including international law from the Court of the Americas, and highlight the humanitarian aspect. Ashok Desai repeatedly argued that this was not an adversarial petition, and that the government should be as concerned as the petitioners to find a solution, since it was constitutionally mandated to protect adivasi interests.

The Chhattisgarh government strategy, on the other hand, was to reduce the case to politics and to divest it of any legal principles. The central thrust of their response was to claim that the petitioners were fronts for the Maoists and that the state's actions were justified because of Maoist attacks: 'The writ petition indirectly trenches upon eulogizing the ideology of Naxalism' (January 2008); 'It is reiterated that the petition eulogises the Maoist activity and is not to combat Naxalite violence or to alleviate the suffering of people' (July 2010).

Mukul Rohatgi, appearing for Chhattisgarh, even called Ashok Desai a Maoist at one point. In early 2008, Rahul Sharma, SP of Dantewada, and DGP Viswaranjan created a photo of me posing with armed women cadres, which they displayed to visiting journalists and others as evidence of my partisanship. After I sent them a legal notice for defamation, Rahul Sharma replied saying that the photos had been of a 'scholarly looking lady', who turned out on police investigation to have been one Ms Jeet, and that I should thank the police for stemming further misconceptions. Nothing was ever heard of this Ms Jeet before or after, but in the meantime, I had spent sleepless nights worried that the judges would not understand Photoshopping. I even printed out images of Osama and Bush together as a pre-emptive strategy.

While we continued bringing evidence, the Chhattisgarh strategy was to refuse to engage with any facts at all. They kept producing exactly the same documents – on the number of FIRs registered and the conditions in camps – but giving them different dates and headings, to give the impression that they were providing new information as and when demanded by the court. Chhattisgarh simultaneously claimed they were in control of the situation – hence there was no need for any independent monitoring committee – and also that they were helpless before the Naxalites and therefore could neither register FIRs nor carry out any development.

Both inside and outside the court, the state government insisted that the Salwa Judum was not state sponsored, and was a 'peaceful people's initiate' (sic). In the same breath, however, they argued: 'The State is committed to resolve the problems of Naxalism and any peaceful movement, which resists the violent methods, definitely gets support of States [sic]' (January 2008).

The Union of India also played a double line. In court they claimed that they could not interfere because law and order was a state subject, and their own role was limited to providing funds under the security expenditure scheme. But at the same time, they made their support for the Chhattisgarh government quite clear. In April 2008, Additional Solicitor General Gopal Subramaniam even argued that the state government was forced to arm civilians since policemen were unwilling to fight Naxalites and there were 17,000 vacancies in the police forces.

Outside court, of course, the UPA-controlled home ministry stood solidly behind the BJP-ruled government of Chhattisgarh. In fact, it was the home ministry that had initiated both the idea of 'local resistance groups' (Salwa Judum) and Operation Green Hunt. When the ICI met Shivraj Patil in 2006, he gave us a patient hearing but said he could do nothing as it was a state issue, and that the families of the victims should register FIRs. Our contention that they could not – because the very people who were supposed to register the FIRs, the police, were the ones doing the killing – had no effect. As for the Fifth Schedule of the Constitution, under which the Governor should have intervened to protect the adivasis of Bastar, both the state and Union pretended it didn't exist, with the Union telling the court in April 2008, 'Recourse to the provisions of the 5th Schedule is not warranted or necessary in this context.'

On 31 March 2008, Chief Justice Balakrishnan remarked that arming civilians who committed murders amounted to the state abetting crime. Responding to the tone of this hearing, all the national English dailies published editorials critical of the Salwa Judum. The Chhattisgarh press, however, was silent. The court allowed us to file an application for an independent investigation. Accordingly, we suggested several names who could be part of this: retired judges, senior bureaucrats familiar with adivasi issues, and eminent women with experience of conflict issues. All of them generously gave their consent to be part of any such process. However, on 15 April, the court tasked the NHRC with appointing 'an appropriate fact-finding committee with such members, as it deems fit and make available its report to this court within eight weeks'.

The Union of India and the State of Chhattisgarh, which had vigorously opposed any independent investigation up till then, readily agreed to this proposition in court; in retrospect it is not surprising why. I cried for a long time that evening, remembering all the times we had approached the NHRC in the past, to no avail. In fact, on one of my frequent trips to the NHRC in the summer of 2008, I discovered that they had closed the ICI's 2006 complaint without informing us, after the SP Dantewada and DGP Viswaranjan denied all our allegations.

Betrayal by the NHRC

The only 'appropriate fact-finding committee' that the NHRC 'deemed fit' consisted entirely of police personnel drawn from its investigation wing. As a great concession to the repeated demands from the petitioners and NGOs that the team should include a woman to investigate rapes, an SSP, Mamta Singh, was included. However, in the one case of mass rape that she investigated, she used minor discrepancies among the young girls to discredit their evidence. Justice Rajendra Babu, who was heading the NHRC, also broke his promise to women's groups to organize a hearing specifically on rapes.

At one meeting with Justice Babu, I showed him the photos I had taken of Muchaki Mutti from Nanduwaya who had fled to Andhra Pradesh with the bones of her husband and son; they had been killed by SPOs in the Errabor Judum camp for allegedly passing on information to the Maoists. Painfully emaciated, Mutti dug the bones out from the ground and placed the small cloth bundle before me. 'How do we know they are the bones of her relatives and she is telling the truth?' Justice Babu asked me, as if women in India are in the habit of carrying the bones of their relatives around, like vegetable shopping.

Before the investigation started, several of the 'Core NGOs' associated with the NHRC – such as People's Watch, the Commonwealth Human Rights Initiative and Jan Swasthya Abhiyan – volunteered to accompany the NHRC team. Several people like the Indian Administrative Services (IAS) officer turned activist Harsh Mander and then right to information (RTI) activist Arvind Kejriwal also interceded to try to ensure a fair hearing. As petitioners, Manish Kunjam and I wrote to and visited the NHRC several times, offering help, providing depositions and, as the investigation wore on, complaining that people were being intimidated. However, the state of Chhattisgarh and the Union of India were clearly more influential, because at a meeting on 21 April, Justice Rajendra Babu said he already knew everything, based on a two-hour briefing by Chief Minister Raman Singh.

At a meeting on 6 May, DIG Sudhir Chowdhury, who was heading the NHRC team, twice asked us, 'Wasn't Salwa Judum a well meaning plan to begin with?' His boss at NHRC, Director General Sunil Krishna, also a police officer, had equally made up his mind, telling me a week later: 'We are not going to use the lathi against the police,' and then after a long pause, 'nor against you.' He asked to see the Planning Commission report and then remarked, 'Very interesting committee, they have policemen also on it.' The NHRC's police investigating team was quite clear with whom their loyalties lay.

In Dantewada, the NHRC team stayed in the police mess; they employed Salwa Judum leaders, such as Ram Bhuwan Kuswaha, who had been accused in many of the testimonies, and some of the more notorious SPOs as translators. The SP of Dantewada also accompanied them to the villages around Jagargunda. The NHRC convoy consisted of 10 four-wheeled drives and an anti-mine vehicle with gunners on top. A road-clearing exercise ordered by the SP the previous day resulted in the Naxalites attacking the party. There was another instance of firing, but this, we were reliably told, was engineered by the police themselves. The NHRC team justified the armed convoy saying that since they were senior police officers, their security was under threat. As we wrote to the NHRC, this was all the more reason that people perceived as neutral should have been sent. Photos of the NHRC visit taken by local photographers show SSP Mamta Singh taking notes as a uniformed SPO talks volubly, and an unidentified photographer in plain clothes records a video on a handycam. The man they are focused on, a skeletal villager, stands by silently and nervously in the presence of these armed men. The local press also reported that after the NHRC team visited Chintalnar, the Salwa Judum cut off all rations and road access to the villagers in retribution for testifying against them. Little of this made any difference to the NHRC.

We had repeatedly begged DIG Sudhir Chowdhury to inform us in advance of any public hearings, since it took time to get messages out to the villages. But on 19 May they told us they would hear testimonies the next day in Sukma, and a day later at Cherla in Andhra Pradesh. After some international organizations also complained about the use of SPOs as translators, the NHRC agreed, as a great concession, to hold a public hearing at Dantewada on 10 June. The Maoists did their bit to ensure the process was a washout by blowing out transformers, which plunged the entire district of Dantewada into darkness for 10 days. The NHRC team had to record some of its depositions on 10 June by candlelight.

A group of students from the Tata Institute of Social Sciences, Delhi University and NALSAR, the law university in Hyderabad, came to help out in this public hearing, going to the villages to inform victims and recording statements with the aid of the VCA staff. The CPI brought a large number of witnesses from Konta, while the Andhra organizations persuaded witnesses to come from Andhra Pradesh. It required singular courage on the part of everyone who came, which made the NHRC betrayal even worse.

On their way back to Andhra, one group of refugees from Nanduwaya, accompanied by NGO staff, were stopped by the Konta police and Salwa Judum leaders P. Vijay and Soyam Mooka. The villagers were slapped around; the police took copies of the statements they had submitted to the NHRC, and also made them sign fresh statements on stamp paper.[6] We appealed to the NHRC SSP S.P. Singh, who said it was not their responsibility to protect witnesses. Later, in the annexures submitted by the NHRC to the court, I found a letter from the Chhattisgarh DGP to the NHRC – which they had apparently accepted at face value – denying that the witnesses had been forcibly detained and claiming instead that Soyam Mooka had merely invited them for a 'friendly chat' over tea. The Salwa Judum and the police followed up this friendly gesture by going to Nanduwaya on 15 June 2008 to burn houses and beat up villagers.

The NHRC filed its report in a sealed cover to the Supreme

Court on 26 August 2008, refusing to share it with us. However, on the morning of 26 August itself, before the court had seen the report, the *Economic Times* published a report by Devesh Kumar headlined 'NHRC gives thumbs-up to Salwa Judum movement'. The Chhattisgarh press, of course, instantly picked it up, with front-page headlines in all the papers: 'NHRC gives clean chit to Salwa Judum'. Devesh Kumar told me he got the report from a source other than the NHRC; his source was most probably the Union home ministry, which is also the nodal ministry for the NHRC. In litigation against the government, there is no level playing field – not when they can arrest the petitioners (as they did with Kartam Joga in 2010), tap phones and even manipulate statutory institutions. An Australian film-maker who happened to be in Bastar when the NHRC team was visiting and shot film on the convoy was later denied a visa to India.

NHRC Findings

The manner of the NHRC investigation gave us some warning of what was to come. But I had not expected quite such a venomous interpretation of our motives. The report stated that our allegations were based on hearsay (NHRC report, para 6.23), that we were unable to coach witnesses sufficiently (because the testimony of rape victims differed somewhat), and even that Dudhi Joga was unreliable because he was no longer a refugee as stated in his first affidavit but back in his own village – no matter that a year had passed since then. The strangest charge was that we had mistaken the annual *jatra* roadblocks in summer, when villagers stop passing traffic and demand money for their seed-sowing festival, for unauthorized checks by SPOs. Presumably policemen visiting the district for the first time had more ethnographic knowledge than three adivasi residents of the district, and an anthropologist of some 20 years' standing. While treating the petitioners as if we were the ones accused, the NHRC team made no effort to question Mahendra Karma or any other Salwa Judum leader.

Hierarchy of Truths

The NHRC report established a hierarchy of truth: the greatest veracity was attributed to the police and their records (despite the NHRC team being provided such hilarious compilations as a list of 'naxalites killed by naxalites' as if they were some kind of auto-cannibals). SPOs came next in the list of trusted sources, followed by Salwa Judum leaders, camp supporters, and finally, those continuing to live in their own villages. The testimonies of IDPs in Andhra Pradesh were totally discounted, presumably on the grounds that anyone who was not in a Judum camp was a Naxalite. Two examples – from Santoshpur and Lingagiri – show how shoddy the investigation was, and how the NHRC went out of its way to deny evidence, including what they saw with their own eyes.

On 31 March 2007, seven men were killed in Santoshpur village, in Bijapur district. The Santoshpur villagers told reporters they were just waking up after a night of wedding revelries when they found the police and SPOs in their village.[7] They saw another police party bringing six men from nearby Ponjer. The Ponjer villagers corroborated this, saying they had been rounded up early in the morning, and six men had been taken away. Later, the Santoshpur villagers found seven bodies in the forest, axed to death. Of them, only one, Kudiyam Bojja, had anything to do with the Maoists. Bojja was betrayed by his own brother, Kudiyam Sannu, who had become an SPO. The police initially tried to claim nothing had happened, and then said they were Maoists killed in an encounter. Finally, in early May, given the media exposure, they were forced to conduct an autopsy, register an FIR and order a magisterial enquiry.[8] As usual, however, the police listed 28–30 'unknown armed men' as accused, their standard terminology to confuse the issue by implying the killings could also have been carried out by the Maoists. On 26 May 2007, at the instance of Subhash Mohapatra of the FFDA, the SHRC ordered an investigation into the killings. The NHRC, however, blithely ignored all these contemporaneous media reports based on video interviews with the villagers, in which they say clearly that Bojja was killed by the SPOs. Instead they recorded: 'The villagers confirmed that one Kariyam/Kodiya Bojja had been killed by some unknown people in March 2008. As per police records, he was killed by Naxalites and Case FIR No. 50/07 PS Bijapur has been registered in this regard. His NOK have also been given compensation by the Government' (6.37.4). They tried to attenuate this nonsense by recommending further enquiry into the killing of the six Ponjer villagers.

Despite Supreme Court orders saying that all victims of conflict must be given compensation, the state government has persistently given compensation only to alleged victims of Naxalites. If under pressure for any extrajudicial killing, the police get the families of the victims to take compensation and then record it as a killing by Naxalites. This also helps thc police to inflate figures of Naxalite killings, which in turn keeps their funds for security-related expenditure flowing. Despite this being pointed out to the NHRC, the complicity with false police records is evident across the report in case after case.

The most shocking example, however, of how cavalier the NHRC was, comes from its investigations on Lingagiri village in Bijapur district:

> Some tribals from village Lingagiri...gave a written petition to the team during the public hearing held at Cherla in Khammam district. They alleged that Salwa Judum activists and the police used to harass and assault them as they did not attend the Salwa Judum meetings at Basaguda camp. That whenever the police came to their village, they used to run to the forest. That on one occasion Salwa Judum activists and Police took some youths of the village to the Basaguda Police Station. Later 30 women went to the police station to get them released where they were beaten by the police. That during December 2006, Salwa Judum activists, SPOs and Police went to Boruguda and Kottur and burnt houses in the village. Later they came to Lingagiri

> village and burnt all the 150 houses in the village and killed Pujari Ramaiaha, Pujari Motiram, Soyam Ramulu and Gantal Kanaiaha. That they also raped and killed Gantal Sridevi. (6.6.2)
>
> The enquiry team visited Lingagiri village and on the way saw Basaguda village, Kummarguda village and Dharmapuram village. Some of the houses were damaged, while others were found abandoned. Lingagiri is a big and a rich village. There are about 12 bore wells in the village. However, the team found all the houses either burnt or damaged. Nobody was found to be staying in the village. In some houses the team found school books scattered. The team also found some houses to have been ransacked. (6.62.2)
>
> The influence of the Naxalites is quite evident in this village. The team found slogans of 'Naxal Zindabad', 'Salwa Judum Murdabad', and 'Lal Salaam' to those who died in the village on the walls of classrooms. (6.62.3)
>
> Thus, the houses in this village were found to have been burnt and ransacked, but it could not be verified as to who was responsible for the same. The alleged killings of the persons also could not be verified since no one was available in the village. However, it was verified and found to be true that Ramaiaha, Motiram, Ramulu and Kanaiaha are from village Lingagiri because their names figure in the voters list collected by the team. (6.62.4)

Here we have a case where the NHRC found that all houses in Lingagiri were burnt and the village abandoned. The relatives of people killed submitted testimonies to the NHRC team. But the NHRC 'could not verify' what happened, and left the matter at that.

Despite their best efforts to whitewash the massacres, justify the Salwa Judum as necessary self-defence and praise the SPOs, the NHRC report could not but expose some of the horror of what was happening. Every village they visited was burnt, and several revealing paragraphs managed to slip through, like this one about sangham members:

> These villagers were specifically targeted when Salwa Judum was on the rise. The enquiry team has come across instances where some of these villagers were even killed (no criminal cases were, however, either reported or registered). Though the State has taken action against SPOs in some cases for violations like murder and attempt to murder, but these cases do not pertain to the violence let loose on innocent villagers during operations against Naxalites. (5.04)

The NHRC also made some useful recommendations to the state government – that the villagers in camps and in Andhra Pradesh should be rehabilitated in their own villages, that people should be compensated for the loss of their houses and belongings, that a list of missing persons should be prepared, that the security forces should vacate schools, that FIRs should be registered on all complaints and compensation given, regardless of the perpetrator.

Our lawyers counselled making the best of the NHRC report, culling the evidence provided to frame our own arguments. Fortunately, Justice Balakrishnan himself read the report with a discerning eye, expressing shock in court at the scale of the violations. On 16 December 2008, the Chief Justice asked the Chhattisgarh government to file an 'Action Taken Report' on the NHRC recommendations by 30 January 2009.

The Rehabilitation Plan of 2010

There was no proper hearing throughout 2009. The state government filed successive reports on the action they had taken, and we filed consecutive counter-affidavits showing how vague they were and how no action was actually transpiring. For instance, of the 103 villages we said had been burnt, the NHRC visited 16 and found them all burnt. But the state government filed FIRs only in six cases.

On 18 February 2010, the counsel for Chhattisgarh blithely assured the court that the security forces had left all the schools they had occupied. Six years on, this is still untrue, with many CRPF camps abutting school or hostel premises. At this same February hearing, since it was abundantly clear that the state government would do nothing to rectify the situation, Justice Balakrishnan asked us to prepare a rehabilitation plan.

At the end of March 2010, we submitted a rehabilitation plan based on national and international principles, framed after wide consultations – with senior civil servants, members of the Child Rights Commission, and international humanitarian organizations – on best practices from other conflict situations. The plan provided both for humanitarian relief and rehabilitation, and criminal investigation and prosecution, stressing the importance of a 'high-level monitoring committee' which would ensure its implementation.

The rehabilitation plan also provided for a survey of all the people killed, raped or arrested, village by village. We had had no way, before filing the case, of investigating all the cases we listed, since movement in the area was made impossible by the Judum and the security forces. But we were frank about our fallibility to the court, and submitted revised and more accurate lists whenever we could. We also found people killed by the Maoists who had never been recorded or compensated. Had this plan been implemented, much of the subsequent history of Bastar might have been different.

As usual, fate in the form of a Maoist attack intervened. After the Tadmetla ambush of April 2010, Justice Balakrishnan said he was nervous about sending independent monitors. Nevertheless, on 6 May 2010, on a day that Justice Rajinder Sachar and I argued in court because none of our usual lawyers were available, he asked us to file letters of consent from people willing to serve on a monitoring commission in Bastar. Once again, several public-spirited former justices and senior bureaucrats readily agreed. Justice Balakrishnan retired. Thus ended the first two phases of our litigation, and we spent the summer of 2010 waiting for the next development.

17

The Legal Death and Reincarnation of the Salwa Judum

> Tax breaks for the rich, and guns for the youngsters amongst poor, so that they keep fighting amongst themselves, seems to be the new mantra from the mandarins of security and high economic policy of the State.
>
> 5 July 2011 Judgment of Justice Reddy and Justice Nijjar in WP (Civil) 250/2007

In July 2010, our matter was transferred to the court of Justice B. Sudershan Reddy and Justice S.S. Nijjar, who were already hearing another matter relating to Dantewada: the Gompad massacre in which nine people were killed.[1] After the 2011 judgment, Mahendra Karma and others put it out that they had not been well represented in court, but in fact, the state of Chhattisgarh had engaged top lawyers like Mukul Rohatgi, Harish Salve and Ranjeet Kumar, paying them enormously high fees to save themselves from compensating their starving citizens.[2]

Chhattisgarh was also rescued in court by the then Solicitor General Gopal Subramaniam, arguing for the Union, who fended off the idea of an independent monitoring committee by propping up the Centre's Integrated Action Plan as an alternative. A plan to provide welfare services, which the state was duty-bound to provide in any case, had nothing to do with prosecution for killings and rapes, or compensation for arson. As for the state government, it continued to be brazen, suggesting a monitoring committee headed by Mahendra Karma, one of the prime accused. It could not have made its contempt for the whole judicial process more evident.

During one of the hearings, Gopal Subramaniam asked us, as petitioners, to go to Dantewada and see the good work the Collectors were doing with the IAP, assuring us that he would get the government of Chhattisgarh to provide access. Taking these assurances at face value, in October 2010, the journalist Chitra Padmanabhan and I went to Dantewada. But almost as soon as we reached, we were surrounded by some 50 armed SPOs led by a Subdivisional Officer of Police. They refused to let us out of their sight for the next five days, saying they were under orders from the SSP, Kalluri. This was not the first time Kalluri had done this: in January 2010, my colleague Ujjwal Singh and I were followed everywhere we went by two unmarked jeeps of armed SPOs; the police had also instructed all the lodges not to give us rooms, and we were forced to take shelter in a college hostel, with the SPOs patrolling around us all night.

Chitra and I decided to use the opportunity provided by our police escort to visit the Salwa Judum camps. These had so far been difficult for me to access, given the hostility of Salwa Judum leaders to human rights activists. To our surprise, several of the Judum leaders approached us in camp, asking whether we could broker peace talks; they even sent letters through us to the Supreme Court, describing the poor conditions in camps and saying they had made a mistake in joining the Judum. In Jagdalpur, the SP Sunder Raj had arranged for us to meet the Bastar Chambers of Commerce, who, while aggressive about 'outsiders' stopping the Tata steel plant, also asked us to help in bringing peace.

Despite this newfound bonhomie, we were not off the hook till we actually left the state. The SP sent a constable, supposedly in disguise but easily recognisable, to follow us on the bus and get our boarding pass numbers. At the last bus stop, we waved at him cheerily and took an auto to the airport. Our dedicated tail then hailed a passing police car and got it to chase our auto, but without telling the Raipur police why. The car caught up with us just as we were about to enter the airport, a policeman leapt out and said, 'Crime Branch Raipur wants you.' Our hearts sank. Fortunately, our very own spy came and let us go. It all felt like a B-grade crime movie.

A letter from the Chief Secretary of Chhattisgarh, P. Joy Oommen, to E.A.S. Sarma, dated 6 September 10, showed that the government never had any intention of honouring its lawyers' statements in court. In response to questions regarding the status of the rehabilitation the state claimed to be carrying out, Oommen wrote:

> It is not clear to us what is the purpose of such detailed information … including 'the state government's plan for alternative land or livelihood for these people'. We do not keep a list of anyone called Salwa Judum member. I cannot help mentioning that many of the questions you have asked amount to conducting an inquisition of our officers in the field.

He concluded, with what must have seemed to him a grand poetic touch, reminiscent of the literary correspondence of colonial civil service officers:

> I do hope that your exertions would help the cause of development of Bastar and its people. And that, some day we would be able to work together to find solutions to the many problems facing our tribal areas instead of wasting our lives fighting in the dark jungles and in dreary law courts.

Till mid-March 2011, we went back and forth in court, with Ashok Desai asking for a monitoring committee, and the court instead repeatedly asking the government of Chhattisgarh to submit affidavits showing what they were doing to wind up camps and rehabilitate villagers. To me, it seemed as if the judges were trying to broker a compromise, and were avoiding giving a judgment.

In mid-March 2011, after the SPOs and police raped and killed people in Tadmetla, Timapuram and Morpalli, the Judum drove away Swami Agnivesh, and the matter was reported in the national press, the discourse shifted. Till May 2011, the attention of the court was focused on the recruitment, training etc. of the SPOs, and all talk of a monitoring committee was put aside. Orders were reserved over the summer.

The state government swore before the court that in the two months of training the SPOs received, they were taught the law in 24 periods (the Penal Code, Criminal Procedure Code and Evidence Act); human rights and other provisions of the Indian Constitution in 12 periods; the use of scientific and forensic aids in policing in six periods; and the culture and customs of Bastar in nine periods.[3] Given that many of the SPOs had not even graduated from primary school, this training programme strained everyone's credulity. Later, in scrambling to tweak the SPOs into an armed auxiliary force, many of the SPOs were given false certificates to show they had at least passed class 5.

As for the attacks on Tadmetla and Swami Agnivesh, the Chhattisgarh government said that it was Agnivesh's own fault that he was attacked in Dornapal. They claimed he raised 'Maoist slogans' at the jan adalat where he had got five Chhattisgarh policemen released after the Maoists kidnapped them.[4] [It turned out that what they were calling Maoist slogans was merely Agnivesh politely saying 'Lal Salaam' while reciprocating the Maoists' 'Lal Salaam'.] Harish Salve tried to rescue the state from its cavalier attitude by saying he would ensure that the chief minister appointed a sitting judge into the March 2011 attacks. On 12 May, he was rewarded by the appointment of Justice T.P. Sharma, former law secretary turned high court judge, to head the Commission of Enquiry into Tadmetla.

From the Heart of Darkness to Light

The judgment of 5 July 2011 came as a complete shock. My field notes read:

> I had to go to the department in the morning because I was in charge of the admissions entrance exam. Why does it always happen to me that dates clash?!! There was a huge traffic jam near Pragati Maidan. When I reached, Justice Reddy had already started reading the judgment. I was panting for the first few minutes and when he said 'the horror, the horror', wasn't sure if I was hearing right. Nearly landed on the lap of an old lawyer gent sitting behind me in shock. I was confused as to what happened after that, but I know the lawyers and I came out and hugged each other. There was a phalanx of cameras, and I said something about how the Constitution had won. Fortunately, I remembered at the end to mention that Kartam Joga was in jail. Then I came back to the department to finish conducting the exam. I tried telling someone we had just got a major judgment, but was met with a blank look.

The judgment delivered by Justices Reddy and Nijjar rested on the violation of Articles 14 and 21 of the Constitution. They held that the use of poorly trained, low-paid SPOs in counter-insurgency operations violated their right to equality (Article 14) compared to better-trained security forces which suffered less fatalities (173 out of 3000 SPOs had been killed compared to 538 out of 45,000 security forces). This not only violated their own right to life, but also endangered the lives of others (Article 21). Many of the SPOs were selected precisely because they harboured feelings of revenge against the Naxalites, which was not a sound basis for recruitment. The court directed the state to disband and disarm all SPOs, and stop using them in combat against the Maoists. Those of them who were not guilty of any criminal action could be redeployed for traffic policing or disaster management. The Union of India was ordered to stop funding SPOs in Naxalite operations.

The judgment also directed the Chhattisgarh government 'to prevent the operation of any group, including but not limited to Salwa Judum and Koya Commandos, that in any manner or form seek to take law into private hands, act unconstitutionally or otherwise violate the human rights of any person', and to investigate and prosecute all human rights violations. They ordered a CBI enquiry on the Tadmetla incidents, saying that they had little faith in the outcome of any enquiry commissioned by Chhattisgarh.[5] The principle that we started out with – that state support for vigilantism was unconstitutional – had finally been established. Far from negotiating a compromise, as I had feared, the court came out strongly in defence of the Constitution.

The judgment was greeted extremely favourably by the liberal public at large. Several activists wrote in to say that it restored their faith in the judiciary. It was described as one of the most important judgments of the year, appeared as a question in civil service exams, and has since been written about by legal scholars.[6] At least part of the excitement over the judgment was generated by its literary references to Conrad:

> As we heard the instant matters before us, we could not but help be reminded of the novella, 'Heart of Darkness' by Joseph Conrad…
>
> … modern constitutionalism posits that no wielder of power should be allowed to claim the right to perpetrate state's violence against any one, much less its own citizens, unchecked by law, and notions of innate human dignity of every individual.
>
> … Human beings are not individual blades of dry grass. As conscious beings, they exercise a free will. Armed, the very same groups can turn, and often have turned, against other citizens, and the State itself. Recent history is littered with examples of the

> dangers of armed vigilante groups that operate under the veneer of State patronage or support.
>
> Our constitution is most certainly not a 'pact for national suicide.' In the least, its vision does enable us, as constitutional adjudicators to recognize, and prevent, the emergence, and the institutionalization, of a policing paradigm, the end point of which can only mean that the entire nation, in short order, might have to gasp: 'The horror! The horror!'

Part of the enthusiasm for the judgment was also generated by its acknowledgement of the role of neo-liberal policies that were facilitating the acquisition of land and forcing people into resistance:

> The problem rests in the amoral political economy that the State endorses, and the resultant revolutionary politics that it necessarily spawns.
>
> Policies of rapid exploitation of resources by the private sector, without credible commitments to equitable distribution of benefits and costs, and environmental sustainability, are necessarily violative of principles that are 'fundamental to governance', and when such a violation occurs on a large scale, they necessarily also eviscerate the promise of equality before law, and equal protection of the laws, promised by Article 14, and the dignity of life assured by Article 21.

Security experts and right-wing commentators, however, castigated the judgment as long on ideology and ignorant of the practicalities of conducting counter-insurgency. Following the tone set by the state and the Centre, the media focused entirely on the plight of the SPOs who were to be disarmed, claiming this would make them vulnerable to the Maoists, and how this was a big setback for the anti-Naxal operations, which were taken as a given.[7]

Sadly, no one interviewed Kartam Joga's family on his false incarceration and how they felt about the order. Nobody interviewed the villagers who had suffered at the hands of the SPOs and security forces. Instead, media coverage of the verdict focused on the reactions of the accused, interviewing alleged rapists for whom there was a standing arrest warrant, like the SPO Kartam Surya. Naturally, they described the Supreme Court order as a bad thing.[8]

The judgment was also criticized for ignoring the role of the security forces.[9] Our petitions had, in fact, named both. Neither the media nor activists highlighted or mobilized around the part of the order that directed investigation and prosecution of criminal offences, which could have included in its ambit those committed by the security forces, as well as the order directing compensation to all victims. And while the judges sought to establish the constitutional principle that counter-insurgency could not be outsourced to untrained civilians from the same community and must rely on formally appointed forces, they also rebuked the state for seeing the problem in militaristic terms.

The Chhattisgarh Government Shrugs Off the Order

The Centre and Chhattisgarh immediately worked to nullify the effects of the order. Within the month, on 28 July 2011, the Chhattisgarh government passed the Chhattisgarh Auxiliary Armed Police Force Ordinance, regularizing all SPOs with effect from 5 July 2011, the date of the judgment, and increasing their pay to Rs 7000. The spin that the Raman Singh government put out was that the court had simply objected to the lack of training and pay of the SPOs, and this was supposedly addressed by the ordinance. In fact, the ordinance – and the Act it subsequently became – explicitly stated that the armed auxiliary forces would be used to combat Maoists, the very activity that had been ruled unconstitutional. The SPOs, ultimately, turned out to be the biggest beneficiaries of the judgment – with higher pay, better guns and more job security.

The Union too moved swiftly, claiming that the order hampered its anti-Naxalite operations, and filed a review petition on 12 August.[10] At issue, it said, were the rights of '28,566 SPOs who had been hired for 7 LWE [left wing extremism] States'. The Union launched into a full-fledged defence of the right of citizens to bear arms for self-defence – a right they said could not be denied to SPOs. Not surprisingly, this right is never recognized for citizens defending themselves against a predatory state or against police excesses. The Union, disingenuously, also took up for the rights of the adivasis, who they usually always castigate as backward: 'To state that villagers cannot participate in their own community policing because of low levels of literacy is an elitist view.'

By this time, since Justice Reddy had retired, Justice Nijjar was sitting with the Chief Justice, Altamas Kabir. On 18 November 2011, Ashok Desai and Rohinton Nariman, then Additional Solicitor General appearing for the Union, agreed in court that the Salwa Judum order would be restricted to Chhattisgarh. Desai's logic was that to insist that the ban on using SPOs be applicable to all states, when we had argued only in the context of Chhattisgarh, would expose us to long and complicated litigation. Inevitably, the press reported it as a major victory for the Centre and Chhattisgarh.

In February 2012, the SPOs attacked the CBI team that had gone to investigate the March 2011 attack on Tadmetla (see below). No further proof was needed of how little the state had done to rein them in. A month later, in March 2012, we filed an application for contempt of court. Between Chhattisgarh-sought adjournments and court delays, Justice Nijjar asked Chhattisgarh to file a response, but after he retired in the summer of 2014, the contempt has not even been listed. In 2016 as the situation worsened, we filed a fresh application for a monitoring committee.

The CBI's Investigation

Even though the CBI was supposed to submit a preliminary report in six weeks, they visited the villages only after six months, in January 2012. They based their investigation on the FIRs filed by the police, which blamed the Maoists for arson, and made no mention of any rapes and killing. The very fact that the SPOs and Judum leaders went to such lengths to stop anyone visiting the affected villages should have been enough to cast doubt on the FIRs. At this initial visit, the CBI was flown into Chintalnar by helicopter and stayed at the CRPF camp. When I reached a day later, accompanied by local journalists, villagers from Timapuram and Pulanpad had already come to Chintalnar to depose. The setting was a small panchayat bhawan some 500 metres from the CRPF camp. As the women testified, SPOs walked up and down, sat under a tree and stared at them. They included some of the SPOs who had been part of the attack. But the women who had come – and it was mainly women, with their children – refused to be intimidated. The CBI also visited Morpalli and Tadmetla on this visit.

The CBI team left, saying they would come back and get more testimonies from the villagers. But in February 2012, when the CBI team was at Dornapal, they were attacked by the SPOs, who were so emboldened by their newly found status as armed auxiliary forces and their guns that their own superiors meant nothing to them. The immediate provocation was the killing of their leader Kartam Surya in a Maoist blast. By local accounts, Surya and D.S. Marawi who had led the police attacks on Tadmetla were on their way to threaten villagers not to depose against them. Surya was now a police constable posted elsewhere, and along with Kiche Nanda, another SPO leader, had come to Dornapal to ensure 'his boys' were not harassed by the CBI investigation.

The CBI affidavit describes the scene graphically:

> After some time the erstwhile SPOs (now members of District Auxiliary Force as Asst. Police Constables) who were heavily armed with automatic weapons, hand grenades etc, rushed towards the CBI team. Seeing the mood of the agitating SPOs, some police officers advised the CBI team to go inside the rooms where they were staying and the team of CBI officials was holed up in one of the rooms. Later on, the SPOs surrounded the rooms and started banging the doors,

> they even tried to break open the doors which were secured by placing almirah, beds etc. against the doors, by CBI officials.

The CBI officials immediately informed their seniors and were told that SP Sukma would handle it, but he too was 'manhandled' and 'heckled' along with other police officers who tried to pacify the SPOs. When they were finally rescued by the CRPF and taken to their camp, there was firing on the camp which lasted for a couple of hours, and the CRPF had to fire three para-bombs and several rounds in retaliation.[11]

After this, the CBI decided it was unsafe for their officials to visit the area. Instead, they sent word, through the local administration, for the villagers to come to Jagdalpur. The administration made no effort to pass on the information to the villagers. The bureaucracy was rather more cooperative with the Justice T.P. Sharma Commission which, judging by its hostile questioning of the villagers, helped by media attempts to show that I was tutoring witnesses,[12] was set up to whitewash the attacks.

But on at least two occasions, when the CBI asked for our help to summon witnesses, the villagers did come, giving up their daily wage labour for a week. They were eager to tell their story and get justice – desperate enough to come standing 187 kilometres each way on the most awful rutted tracks in cattle pick-ups. The road from Dornapal to Chintalnar passes through at least eight CRPF camps. At each camp they are stopped and checked and their names written down. Women came with their small suckling babies, braving the heat, the mosquitoes and the general discomfort. The local administration was responsible for their food and transport, which meant they were either not fed or fed erratically. In one case, we drove for ten hours, waited for an hour to be cleared by a CRPF camp, rounded up a sozzled witness from a wedding, dunked him in water, sobered him up and took him to the CBI hearing, only to find that, due to some miscommunication among CBI staff, he left for home the next morning without his deposition being taken.

In November 2015, after we flatly refused to submit the villagers to any more torture by making them come all the way to Jagdalpur, the CBI – now with its third team of investigators – decided to attempt to go to Chintalnar again. This time too the Chhattisgarh police tried to intimidate them, providing them with a drunk escort, claiming the Maoists were out to ambush them, and banging on their door in the middle of the night. But given a BJP-controlled CBI at the Centre intent on protecting a BJP-ruled state, the CBI was not keen on making this an issue.

After much delay before a new Supreme Court bench (our third since we first filed), in October 2016, the CBI charged seven SPOs with burning Tadmetla and Timapuram and twenty-six Salwa Judum leaders for attacking Swami Agnivesh. Even though this indictment was so weak, ignoring the much greater crimes of rape and murder, IG Kalluri and his men went into vindictive overdrive. At a press conference, Kalluri admitted directing the operations as SSP Dantewada in 2011. He accused the CBI of lying. The police then burnt effigies of six human rights activists, including me, in a professionally organized manner, dressing the effigies in new clothes with colour photos of our faces pinned on. A successor organization of the Salwa Judum, calling itself Agni, the Hindi word for fire, attacked Manish Kunjam while he was holding a press conference on the CBI charges.

I was in New York on 8 November, when I got a call around 1 a.m. from an Indian TV channel asking for my reactions to the murder charge against me and others, including JNU historian Archana Prasad, CPI members Vineet Tiwari and Manju Kawasi and Sanjay Parate, state leader of the CPM. According to the police story, Vimla Baghel, wife of the murdered man, Shyamnath Baghel, had walked 14 km to the police station just after giving birth and given full details of how the six of us had murdered her husband. The police charged us with murder, rioting, bearing arms and also the UAPA (Unlawful Activities Prevention Act).

However, Vimla told a television journalist who trekked down to Nama to get the real story that she knew nothing about the complaint. (After this, the police decided they could not risk any more interviews and gave her a job in the force.) This, and the support of our lawyers, students, friends and colleagues, ensured we got a reprieve from the Supreme Court. The judges asked for an assurance from the Chhattisgarh government that we would not be arrested or even interrogated without being able to approach the Court for protection.

We had last visited the area six months previously to investigate the formation of a new vigilante force, the 'tangiya gang' and reported on how the villagers were being terrorized by both the Maoists and the police (see page 184–85). The charges, though clearly unsustainable, were successful from the police viewpoint, helping to spread the spectre of an urban Maoist network among the lay public. The fact that Archana Prasad worked at Jawaharlal Nehru University (JNU) capitalized on the ongoing demonization of JNU as an anti-national left-wing university. The police also put pressure on our universities to act against us but did not succeed. Eventually in 2019, the charges against us were dropped, and in 2020 the NHRC even ordered compensation of Rs 1 lakh to each of us for 'mental agony arising out of false charges'.

Kalluri was moved from his post as IG Bastar, following strictures by the NHRC after a string of attacks on civil society activists in 2016 (including a fact-finding team from Telangana which was jailed for six months before being acquitted). However, even the Congress government which came to power in 2018 took no action against him.

Former CPI activist Podiyam Panda, who brought the Tadmetla burnings to light, is a victim of 'collateral damage' from both sides. In April 2017, soon after the Maoists killed twenty-five policemen in an ambush near Chintagufa, the police managed to capture him. After days of uncertainty when his whereabouts were unknown, his wife filed a writ of habeas corpus. Under duress, and flanked by police, Panda told the Chhattisgarh High Court that he had 'voluntarily surrendered'. We later learnt he had been severely tortured. For their part, the Maoists abducted his wife and brother for twelve days and accused them of helping the police.

For two years (2016–18) the Supreme Court tried to pass the buck to the NHRC to investigate the hundreds of cases of rapes and killings in our petitions, but the NHRC did nothing. When finally pressed, they made all sorts of excuses such as that we had listed the victims by home village rather than place of encounter. They said that if villagers had a problem, they could 'google' the NHRC special rapporteur and send email complaints to NHRC. A final hearing of our matter had just resumed in October 2018 when the judges retired again, and since then there has been no hearing.

T.R. Andhyarujina, Ashok Desai and Justice Nijjar have passed away. As part of a concerted attack on lawyers, human rights activists, writers and others by the BJP government, Sudha Bhardwaj was jailed and is currently out on bail.

Reflections on the Legal Process

We got almost all the orders we wanted except for a monitoring committee, but no implementation. None of the thousands of desperately poor villagers whose homes were burnt have got compensation. Chhattisgarh claimed they had obeyed the order to compensate 'victims of violence' by giving the families of Congress politicians Mahendra Karma and V.C. Shukla Rs 5 lakh each, after Maoists killed them in 2013. Neither could be said to need the money. On paper, petitioner Dudhi Joga was given the grand sum of Rs 10,000 for his burnt house and the destruction of all his household possessions. But in fact, even this laughably measly amount has not been paid. Those who wanted to return from Andhra or the camps have done so on their own, without help from the state. Nobody has been prosecuted for the hundreds of rapes and murders committed. When contesting the elections in 2018, the Congress promised to release the hundreds of ordinary adivasis in jail. But large-scale arrests continue as do extrajudicial killings. An estimate given by villagers to the press in June 2021 claimed 187 deaths in fake encounters between 2015 and 2021. Although the Sarkgeuda and Edesmetta judicial enquiries vindicated the villagers, there has been no attempt to prosecute anyone responsible or provide compensation. The CBI case on Tadmetla is also languishing. Far from obeying the Supreme Court's 2011 directions, the CRPF has formed a Bastar battalion, drawing on local recruits – a 4.0 version of the SPOs, Armed Auxiliary Forces and the District Reserve Guard. As scholar Vani Xaxa once said to me in conversation, Bastar has become a liberated zone in more senses than one – liberated from the protection of the Constitution.

One might think that in politically contentious cases, especially those concerning 'national security', court processes would play out differently from more 'regular' matters. However, many of the problems we experienced are endemic to the judicial system as a whole: overloaded dockets, lengthy delays and a procedural bias in favour of the government.[13] In fact, no-one is more aware of the overload and the consequent pendency of cases, than the judges themselves.

From the perspective of the genesis of PILs – as a weapon of the weak – the endemic delays, however, mean that its very rationale is defeated. Far from any relaxation of procedure, as Justice Bhagwati originally envisaged for PILs, the onus has been on us to 'prove' every single charge under severely restricted conditions. If women who are gang raped by SPOs or security forces cannot name their rapists, this is used against them. Fresh rights violations keep occurring even as old ones are left unaddressed. The court could have devised stronger mechanisms than simply asking for compliance or asking the police to prosecute themselves. The oversight of an independent monitoring committee was critical.

With every request that the court made for an update, the hope of relief receded, as the state of Chhattisgarh used the occasion to delay and lie their way through the system. There is a large difference between court time and chronological time, and judicial decrees are sometimes framed as though time has stood still from when the case was first filed. By January 2011, when the court ordered the Chhattisgarh government to respond on winding up the Judum camps, most people had already returned home.

Police officers always describe the Maoist jan adalats as kangaroo courts, in which terrified villagers carry out brutal punishment at the behest of the armed squads, while the Maoists claim that the punishments are determined by popular demand. Not having seen a jan adalat, I cannot comment on this, though the truth is likely to lie somewhere in between. What I do know is that the formal legal system, with its endless adjournments and non-hearings, does not amount to due process either. Our matter was listed some hundred times between May 2007 and May 2018, and actually heard some sixty times. The government cannot, by definition, get tired – but the whole thrust of its participation in any litigation is to wear out its opponent, an objective that the court system fully facilitates.

In cases like rape, courts often reproduce the trauma they are called upon to address. Here too, the state's strategy, including the supposedly independent NHRC, was to put the petitioners – rather than those responsible for the murders and arson – on trial. More importantly, they harassed villagers who dared complain, and I constantly worried about whether their decision to testify took account of the potential costs to them. The biggest problem in Indian law, however, is that the masterminds of the Salwa Judum strategy – both at the Centre and in the state – cannot be held to account for command responsibility. It is the civil-war-cum-vigilantism imagery of 'brothers pitted against each other' and 'divided villages' that has captured the national imagination, ignoring how these divisions were consciously created as part of a planned counter-insurgency operation. While Mahendra Karma could have been arraigned, because he was seen leading specific arson attacks, the law as it stands in India has no room to indict Chief Minister Raman Singh or Prime Minister Manmohan Singh for enabling the lawlessness generated by the Salwa Judum.

In cases involving state participation in mass violence like 1984 and 2002, it is often easy for the courts or human rights commissions to order compensation, while the prosecution agenda is abandoned. While compensation is extremely important for victims, it also runs the risk of being divorced from any acknowledgement of culpability. The criticism commonly made of legal human rights discourse – that it depoliticizes issues and converts people into individual victims, rather than populations in resistance attempting to frame collective political goals – is also largely fair. Here the state refused to comply even with the direction to compensate, leave alone punish.

The law is incapable of dealing with sociological or moral culpability. Questions of culpability were constantly being debated outside the court: whether the Maoists were culpable for using adivasis as pawns in their larger struggle for control over the state or whether adivasis were willingly participating to defend their resources; whether the government's culpability for not providing basic services over the years, expropriating resources and creating the grounds for disaffection could be minimized, just because people had taken up armed struggle against it. Justices Reddy and Nijjar addressed these issues in their preamble, but could not in their orders.

In principle, the law cannot create a hierarchy of good and bad killings, but in practice, the state construes culpability depending on the status of the victim. The killing of a man like Mahendra Karma, who was responsible for thousands of homes being burnt and women raped, was followed up by an enquiry by the National Investigative Agency. However, the people who were killed and raped on his orders and under the watch of the chief minister disappeared into the abyss of impunity.

The police put the labels 'Naxalite' and 'encounter' on what they do as part of the legal justification of any killing. The struggle by human rights groups is to show that these labels do not constitute a self-evident defence. Not everyone whom the police term a Naxalite is one, and even more, the police are not entitled to kill everyone who is a Naxalite. It must be shown that they were firing in self-defence, and that arrest was not a possibility. The Maoists treat 'informer' as a similar self-evident label – as if that was enough to justify their killing. Both the state and the Maoists set up a hierarchy of good victims and bad victims, and both release lists of 'martyrs' which ignore their own killings. Neither the state nor the Maoists nor the law has a name or place for double agents, and civil wars produce plenty of those.

In *The Hollow Hope*, based on the history of US law, Rosenberg argues against what he calls the 'dynamic court view' – the idea that courts can change the social landscape on their own through landmark court decisions like *Brown* v. *Board of Education*, or *Roe* v. *Wade*. Instead, the courts operate under several constraints: having to frame remedies under existing rights/legislation; a fear of overstepping the boundaries of judicial independence and upstaging elected governments; and above all, lack of any powers to ensure implementation of their judgments. They are only able to effect social change under certain conditions, for instance, when the state has a reason of its own to push a court judgment or there is powerful mobilization in society in favour of those decisions. In fact, progressive judgments may invite so much flak that they may push the cause backward.

In this case, the courts did play an important role, producing, as Marc Galanter writes, 'not only decisions but messages'.[14] The 2011 judgment is a powerful symbolic resource against vigilantism. The signalling had begun even before the Reddy–Nijjar court, with other judges who heard the case – such as Justice Balakrishnan – also able to see through Chhattisgarh's vague responses to the compelling evidence of mass violence. The ongoing court case helped to stop further escalation of the Judum, though it was not able to prevent the conversion of the counter-insurgency into Operation Green Hunt.

Did the media campaigns play a role in this judgment? Assessing this is tough.[15] While the Binayak Sen campaign gave negative publicity to the Judum, it was heavily outweighed by pro-government reportage. Ultimately, what seems to have motivated Justice Reddy was his own strong sense of the Constitution, which was likewise reflected in the 'Black Money' order of 2011, in which he and Justice Nijjar ordered a special investigation team to monitor the repatriation of illegally stashed money. Justice Reddy's roots in Andhra had also given him a comprehensive understanding of the Maoist movement.

Postscript (2022)

Law, fortunately, is not the only source of hope. Even as more security camps have come up, taking over cultivated fields and sacred spaces, people have begun to resist in new ways. On 17 May 2021, thousands of unarmed villagers gathered to peacefully protest against a camp in Silger village. The CRPF opened fire, killing three persons and injuring several others. Since then, Silger has become a symbol of non-violent resistance, sparking many similar struggles across the region. People are demanding justice in all its forms – an end to CRPF camps, prosecution of those responsible for killing civilians and appropriate compensation. They are also demanding schools and health centres. The administration is finally reopening about half the schools that were shut down in the Judum.

The most remarkable aspect is that these movements are mainly led by youth, both men and women. Most of them are barely out of school. They remember the Salwa Judum as a time of great privation and distress but are determined that come what may, unlike their parents, they will not flee their villages but will fight for their rights. Despite the administration's attempts to arrest them and intimidate them in all sorts of ways and to stop people coming to their rallies, they have sustained their protest for over a year now. When not studying, protesting, helping out in their family farms or doing coolie labour, they compose songs, play volleyball, dance the nights away and pose for selfies like youth everywhere. They have truth on their side.

Epilogue: A New Compact

In the novel *Atonement*, the protagonist cannot endure the unbearable sadness of what actually happened. So she decides to write an alternative happy ending.

Like her, in my other story, I see the forested hills of Bastar around me, with no sign of a paramilitary camp. The jungle has grown over to cover the scars.

Following a change of government, there was an accord, and all those responsible for mass crimes were put in jail. A new Constitution gave all people the right to decide how they wanted their resources to be used. Eminent domain, under which the government claimed ownership of all land, was banished forever. All the royalties from the existing Bailadilla mines, and the profits from the steel plant in Nagarnar went to an elected council managed, among others, by village elders and former adivasi guerrillas. They used it to level fields, and built ponds, schools, hospitals, etc. Everything else, the villagers decided, would be left as forest. The people set up small cottage industries to add value to the minor forest produce they were collecting. In any case, they got a fair price for all their labour, and the traders no longer made huge profits by cheating them. New methods made agriculture sustainable and also ensured the villagers got healthy organic grain to eat. Primary health care centres started working in every panchayat, and children were no longer pot-bellied with hunger. No one was landless, no one migrated for labour.

In my narrative, I walk through dense and fragrant forests, and I can hear the koel calling. Schools teach in Gondi, Dhurwa, Hindi and English – with options to learn Spanish, Arabic or Chinese. They have well-equipped chemistry labs and large playing fields. School projects include making and editing Gondi films, recording traditional songs and cataloguing the plants that grow in their forest. Immigrant children also learn the local languages in school, and take pride in adivasi culture instead of looking down on it. Once they grow up, some of them, like Hidme and Hadma, Masa and Deve, become novelists, lawyers, politicians and scientists, using their knowledge of the forest to create life-saving drugs. But they always come home for the village *mandai*, to worship their hill gods. My story dances with abandon to the sound of the Madia dhol under a full moon night, where my friends and I raise a toast of mahua to hope and the future.

Notes

1. Burnt Rice

1. The former princely states of Bastar and Kanker were combined to form Bastar district after Independence. In 1998–99, Bastar district was trifurcated into North Bastar–Kanker, Bastar and South Bastar–Dantewada districts, and subsequently into seven smaller fragments: Bastar, Kondagaon, Kanker, Narayanpur, Dantewada, Bijapur and Sukma. The latter two were carved out of Dantewada district in 2007 and 2012 respectively. The state of Chhattisgarh was separated from Madhya Pradesh in 2000.
2. David French, *The British Way in Counter-Insurgency, 1945–1967* (New York: Oxford University Press, 2011); Daniel Marston and Carter Malkasian, eds, *Counterinsurgency in Modern Warfare* (Oxford: Osprey, 2008).
3. Ranajit Guha, *Elementary Aspects of Peasant Insurgency in Colonial India* (Delhi: Oxford University Press, 1983).
4. Aman Sharma, 'Govt to recruit 7350 men for paramilitary forces from Naxal affected districts', *Economic Times*, 12 April 2013; Rashmi Drolia, 'Chhattisgarh budget: Raman announces 4 new battalions in Bastar to fight rebels', *Times of India*, 9 March 2016; Diptiman Tiwary, 'Bastar: CRPF tribal battalion to counter Maoists threat in Bastar', *Indian Express*, 12 July 2016.
5. During the Second Boer War (1899–1902), more Boer women, children and blacks died than male Boer combatants after being regrouped in

British 'concentration camps'; in Vietnam, over 8.5 million people had been settled in 7205 strategic hamlets by 1963; in Algeria during 1954–61, 1.9 to 2.3 million civilians were grouped by the French; and in Kenya over a million people were resettled in 854 villages to crush the Mau Mau revolt. Nandini Sundar, 'Interning insurgent populations', *Economic and Political Weekly* 46, No. 6 (2011), pp. 47–57.

6. P. Sundarayya, *Telangana People's Struggle and Its Lessons* (New Delhi: Foundation Books, 1972); on the grouping of Koya villages, see pp. 187–9.
7. An army officer's reminiscences reproduced in Lalkhama, *A Mizo Civil Servant's Random Reflections* (Ghaziabad: Express Print House, 2006).
8. Art. 14 of the Additional Protocol (II) to the Geneva Convention, relating to the protection of victims of non-international armed conflict, 8 June 1977, https://treaties.un.org/doc/Publication/UNTS/Volume%201125/volume-1125-I-17513-English.pdf
9. Through most of the book, I refer to the region as Andhra Pradesh rather than Telangana, because that is more accurate for most of the period described here. Moreover, while Khammam has been transferred to Telangana, seven mandals which will be affected by the proposed Polavaram project have been retained with Andhra Pradesh. These are primarily the areas to which the Chhattisgarh villagers fled. See the Andhra Pradesh Reorganisation Act, No. 6 of 2014. In the maps, Andhra Pradesh has been used when the maps show events before 2014, and Telangana when showing the boundaries as of 2016.
10. Arshad Bhat, 'The case against village defence committees', *Greater Kashmir*, 16 August 2013; Anis Zargar, 'Should village defence committees in Kashmir be disbanded', *DNA*, 22 December 2015.
11. Victoria Sanford, *Buried Secrets: Truth and Human Rights in Guatemala* (New York: Palgrave Macmillan, 2003). Sanford writes of army units encircling villages at dawn; of minors conscripted by the army into joining 'civil patrols' who were sent to hunt survivors from their own villages in the mountains, burn food and steal livestock; of 'communities of resistance' protected by armed guerrillas who themselves had no food; and 'community surrenders' to come and live in army-controlled 'work

resettlement camps' which they could not leave without permission.

12. Ram Narayan Kumar and Amrik Singh, *Reduced to Ashes: The Insurgency and Human Rights in Punjab* (Kathmandu: South Asia Forum for Human Rights, 2003); Nanda Talukdar Foundation (NTF) and Human Rights Law Network (HRLN), *Secret Killings of Assam* (Guwahati and New Delhi: NTF & HRLN, 2009).
13. Sheikh Mushtaq, 'Much ado in Kashmir over Padma Shri for Mir', Reuters, 3 February 2010.
14. Rashmi Drolia, 'Mission 2016: DRG force pressed into anti-Naxalite ops in Chhattisgarh', *Times of India*, 5 February 2016.
15. Amrita Rangasamy, 'And then there were none: A report from Srikakulam', *Economic and Political Weekly* 8, No. 46 (17 November 1973), pp. 2041–2.
16. National Crime Records Bureau, 2013, http://ncrb.nic.in/PSI-2013/CHAPTER-2.pdf.
17. Rashmi Drolia, 'Chhattisgarh budget: Raman announces 4 new battalions in Bastar to fight rebels'.
18. See, for instance, Judith Butler, *Frames of War: When Is Life Grievable?* (London: Verso, 2009).
19. *Indian Express* editorial, 7 January 1967.

2. Iron in the Soul

1. Letter to NHRC, 'Police atrocities on Madia (Gondi) adivasi women in Lohandiguda, Bastar', 28 March 2007, signed by Ramuram Maurya of the Prastavit Tata Steel Jan Adhikar Samiti and Bela Bhatia.
2. http://www.narendramodi.in/mous-signed-at-dantewada-in-the-presence-of-prime-minister-shri-narendra-modi-9785.
3. Bilge Erten and José Antonio Ocampo, 'Super-cycles of Commodity Prices since the Mid-nineteenth Century', United Nations Department of Economic and Social Affairs, DESA working paper No. 110, February 2012. I am grateful to Gavin Capps for the reference.
4. Government of India, *Report of the High Level Committee on Socio-economic, Health and Educational Status of Tribal Communities of India*

(henceforth Xaxa Committee Report) (New Delhi: Ministry of Tribal Affairs, 2014), Table 8.12, p. 272.

5. Minerals contributed 19.23 and 64.41 per cent of the total revenue and non-tax revenue, respectively, of the state in 2010–11. Performance Audit on 'Assessment, Levy and Collection of Major and Minor Mineral Receipts' of the Government of Chhattisgarh, conducted by the Comptroller and Auditor General, http://www.indiaenvironmentportal.org.in/files/file/chhattisgarh%20performance%20audit%20on%20mining.pdf.
6. Supriya Sharma, 'Iron ore mines going for Rs 1 lakh in Chhattisgarh?' *Times of India*, 2 August 2010. In 2013, 18 mining leases were sanctioned in Chhattisgarh of which 12 were located in Bastar alone; and of the 21 prospecting licences given in the state, over 95 per cent were to private companies. Letter dated 7 November 2013 from the Chhattisgarh Bachao Andolan, a consortium of groups in the state struggling over rights to natural resources, to the Ministry of Tribal Affairs protesting termination of the M.B. Shah Commission of Enquiry.
7. Federation of Indian Chambers of Commerce and Industry, *Task Force Report on National Security and Terrorism* (New Delhi: FICCI, 2009), http://www.ficci.com/SPdocument/20032/terrorism-report.pdf.
8. *Daily Chhattisgarh*, 13 September 2006, translated from Hindi by the moderators of CGNet.
9. National Environmental Engineering Research Institute, *Rapid Environmental Impact Assessment for Mining and Infrastructural Facilities at Raoghat, District Bastar, Chhattisgarh, 2006*.
10. For instance, in police firings at Maikanch village in Rayagada district, Odisha, three people were killed protesting against land acquisition for bauxite mining (2001); at Tapkara in Ranchi district, Jharkhand, nine were killed protesting against the Koel Karo dam (2001); at the Khuga dam site in Churachandpur district, Manipur, three were killed (2005); at Kalinganagar in Odisha, 12 were killed protesting against a Tata Steel plant (2006); at Nandigram in West Bengal in 2007, 15 were killed protesting against land acquisition for a special economic zone.

11. Rambhau Mhalgi Prabodhini (RMP), *Development and Internal Security in Chhattisgarh: Impact of Naxalite Movement: A Report* (Mumbai, 2005–6), p. 47. I also conducted interviews with people from Satwas and neighbouring villages. The ashram at Gumargunda is actually Divya Jivan Sangh.
12. 'Final Report of the Lokayukt Committee on the Felling of Trees on Malik Makbuja and Other Government Land in Bastar District (M.P.)', (MP Lokayukta, March 1998), pp. 22, 31.
13. In 2009, the police–population ratio was 194.4 (sanctioned) and 138.16 (actual) policemen per 1,00,000 persons, going up to 268.92 (sanctioned) and 184.5 (actual) in 2013. The All-India average in 2013 was 181.47 (sanctioned) and 136.42 (actual). Answer to Rajya Sabha Starred Question No. 405 for 06 August 2014.
14. For police figures, see: https://data.gov.in/catalog/all-india-and-state-wise-actual-police-strength (accessed 21 June 2015); http://ncrb.gov.in/CD-CII2012/cii-2012/Chapter%2017.pdf (accessed 21 June 2015).
15. MHA Annual Reports, 2014–15, 2015–16.
16. Aman Sharma, 'Bastar set to become the most militarized zone', *Economic Times*, 10 June 2014.
17. W.V. Grigson, *The Maria Gonds of Bastar* (Delhi: Oxford University Press/Vanya Prakashan, 1938/1991), pp. 13–14.
18. Special correspondent, 'Rs. 50 crore a year to develop Naxal-hit and backward areas', *The Hindu*, 8 August 2010.
19. I am grateful to Farah Naqvi for relaying this conversation.
20. Ejaz Kaiser, '75,000 applications for 30 peon posts, officials cancel Exam', *Hindustan Times*, 24 August 2015.
21. Earlier on http://bastar.nic.in.
22. Abhishek Bhalla, 'Meet the dogs that have instilled fear among Maoists in the red zone', *Mail Today*, 15 April 2016
23. Shale Horowitz and Deepti Sharma, 'Democracies fighting ethnic insurgencies: Evidence from India', *Studies in Conflict & Terrorism* 31 (2008), pp. 749–73; Anna Getmansky, 'You can't win if you don't fight: The role of regime type in counterinsurgency outbreaks and outcomes', *Journal of Conflict Resolution* 57 (2013), pp. 709–34; Jason Lyall, 'Do

democracies make inferior counterinsurgents? Reassessing democracy's outcome on war outcomes and duration', *International Organization* 64 (Winter 2010), pp. 167–92.

24. 'Kishenji's dead, not the Maoist threat', *Hindustan Times*, 27 November 2011.

3. 'Because I Want Peace'

1. While both the Maoists and other commentators treat Naxalbari 1967 as the spark for the Maoist movement in India, the Telangana armed struggle, and the Tebhaga and Warli peasant movements are important precursors. The 'right wing' of the party advocated stopping the Telangana movement on the grounds that the armed squads were not equipped to confront the Indian army and that they would lose the support of the rich peasantry if they fought against India. While initially the party resolved to cease armed struggle only if the peasants could keep the land they had occupied, if cases against all prisoners connected with the struggle were closed and the ban on the party lifted, eventually, in the face of Congress intransigence, pressures to fight elections and internal differences, the resistance was withdrawn unconditionally in 1951. The people surrendered their arms.

   In 1964, the CPI split on Sino-Soviet lines into the CPI and CPI(M). Broadly speaking, those who had advocated continuing the Telangana armed struggle went over to the CPI(M), and later, in 1968, the Maoists in the CPI(M) split to form the Andhra Pradesh Co-ordination Committee for Communist Revolutionaries, taking a substantial number of the cadre with them. Within the Andhra Maoists, some of them supported the Charu Majumdar group of Bengal Maoists, and the All India Co-ordination Committee of Communist Revolutionaries which had been formed after the Naxalbari uprising in 1967 and which subsequently became the Communist Party of India (Marxist–Leninist), CPI(ML), in 1969. In particular, the group which led the Srikakulam struggle sided with Charu Majumdar, while Chandra Pulla Reddy, T. Nagi Reddy and D. Venkateswara Rao advocated a more protracted struggle, believing that the situation was not yet ripe for armed revolution everywhere and mass struggles were needed to address people's immediate needs. This group was active in Khammam and Warangal districts.

In the meantime, of course, the CPI(ML) had been working in other states, following a programme of annihilations of individual landlords, attacks on police, as well as mobilization of urban youth. After Charu Majumdar's death in 1972, the movement splintered, but parts of it came together again as the CPI (ML) Central Organising Committee in 1974. There were other groups like the Dakshin Desh which had never been part of the CPI (ML), but which later became the Maoist Communist Centre, working in Bihar and various other permutations and combinations of ideological groupings, which worked in different states. For readings, see Sumanta Banerjee, *In the Wake of Naxalbari* (Calcutta: Subarnarekha, 1980); CPI (Maoist), *30 Years of Naxalbari* (2000); Shanta Sinha, *Maoists in Andhra Pradesh* (New Delhi: Gyan Publishing House, 1989); P. Sundarayya, *Telangana People's Struggle*; N. Venugopal, *Understanding Maoists* (Kolkata: Setu Prakashani, 2013).

2. Christoph Von Fürer-Haimendorf, *Tribes of India: The Struggle for Survival*, Postscript, May 1981 (Delhi: Oxford University Press, 1991, 2nd impression), pp. 323–6.
3. Sundarayya, *Telangana People's Struggle*, pp. 198, 278–9, 372; V.P. Patel, 'Tribal Unrest and Adventures of Naxalites', in V.P. Patel, *Studies in Development Anthropology* (Madhusudan Nagar, Society for Anthropological and Archaeological Studies, 1986), pp. 30–1.
4. Patel, 'Tribal Unrest and Adventures of Naxalites', pp. 30–3.
5. The police list eight squads in Bastar: Konta Sukma and Bailadilla dalams (1984), Maded and National Park dalams (1983), Abujhmarh dalam (1988), Bhamragarh dalam, Keskhal dalam and Etapalli dalam. Of the 15–30 men in each squad, the leaders and half the members were from Andhra. A.N. Singh, 'Naxalpanthi Gathividhiyan Sambandhi Teep', cyclostyled document prepared by I.G. Singh, Bhilai Zone, Bhilai, 1992; see also 1990 police note on the Jan Jagran Abhiyan.
6. Patel, 'Tribal Unrest and Adventures of Naxalites'. pp. 18–23, 34–5.

7. Grigson, *Maria Gonds of Bastar*, p. 32.
8. Nandini Sundar, *Subalterns and Sovereigns: An Anthropological History of Bastar*, 2nd edn. (Delhi: Oxford University Press, 2007), pp. 167–8.
9. Peddi Shankar was shot in the back by the police in 1980, becoming the 'first martyr' of the People's War in Dandakaranya.
10. P. Shankar, *Yeh Jungle Hamara Hai* (Delhi: New Vistas Publications, 2006), p. 16.
11. Cable from Mumbai to Washington, 11 January 2010, https://wikileaks.org/plusd/cables/10MUMBAI12_a.html.
12. 'Should India ban iron ore export?' Zeebiz.com, 30 July 2010.
13. Additional affidavit dated May 2015 of Centre for Public Interest Litigation in WP (Civil) 128 of 2015 (*CPIL* v. *Union of India and Ors.*).
14. 'I funded these leaders' campaigns, introduced those firms to Maoists', *Indian Express*, 24 January 2014.

4. The Maoist State

1. MHA Annual Report, 2004–5, p. 44.
2. Rahul Bedi, 'Maoist insurgency spreads in India', *Jane's Intelligence Review*, 18 (7): 21–5.
3. Whatsapp release by Bastar police, 22 November 2015.
4. Amitav Ghosh, *Flood of Fire* (Gurgaon: Hamish Hamilton, 2015), p. 472.
5. CPI (Maoist), *New People's Power in Dandakaranya* (Calcutta: Biplabi Yug Publications, 2000), p. 7; Shankar, *Yeh Jungle Hamara Hai*, p. 9.
6. Madhu Ramnath, 'Tropical deciduous forests and the Adivasi: Indigenous traditions as response to leaf fall in Bastar, India', *Natural Resources Forum* 27 (2003), pp. 304–9.
7. CPI (Maoist), *New People's Power in Dandakaranya*, pp. 19–58.

5. A 'Peaceful People's Movement'

1. 'Shun bullets, join ballots', Raman Singh tells Maoists, webIndia 123, 15 August 2007; *Times of India*, 2 May 2010.

2. NHRC annexures, G1–G8: Document titled 'Naxal incidents since Salwa Judum was started', 26 May 2005–25 June 2005; G1, Monthly returns from DC, Dantewada, 26 December 2002–25 December 2007. Unless specifically mentioned otherwise, all references to police and official correspondence and reports should be assumed to be taken from these annexures, which are not available with the main report but are kept in the Supreme Court record room. The main report is available on the NHRC website as NHRC (Investigation Division): *Chhattisgarh Enquiry Report* (On the remit from the Hon'ble Supreme Court of India in Writ Petition (Civil) No. 250/07 *Nandini Sundar and Ors* v. *State of Chhattisgarh* and Writ Petition (Criminal) No. 119/07 (*Kartam Joga and Ors* v. *State of Chhattisgarh*).
3. These are armed police forces which belong to particular states rather than the Centre, but which can be deployed anywhere in India.
4. MHA Annual Report 2003–4, p. 44.
5. Police Note, 1991: Details of Jan Jagran Abhiyan 1990. NHRC annexures, D2.
6. Translated from '*Har Sham ke bad, Naxsaliyo ka raj*' (Naxals rule when the sun sets), *Navbharat*, 8 December 1991.
7. On Baba Bihari Das, see Nandini Sundar, *Subalterns and Sovereigns*, pp. 234–43.
8. My interviews with villagers, 2005, 2009.
9. 'Salva Judum, Rising against Naxalism'. No official credit is provided for this film.
10. G. Manju Sainath, 'People's battle against People's War', *The Hindu*, 29 June 2005.
11. Shivanand Shukla, 'Maoists have made us refugees in our own land', *Pioneer*, 26 October 05.
12. Shivanand Shukla, 'Tribal uprising against Maoists in Chhattisgarh', *Pioneer*, 29 June 2005.
13. 'Raipur mulls arming tribals against Naxals', *Asian Age*, 22 July 2005.
14. It is unlikely, however, that the plan originated with the Collector, since it allots duties to different departments, including his superiors at the state level.

15. Brief memorandum on Jan Jagran Abhiyan (Salwa Judum), District South Bastar (Dantewada), January 2007.
16. Minutes of the 20th Coordination Centre meeting held on 31 March 2006, Vigyan Bhawan, New Delhi.
17. See Amit Jogi's record of the conversation with Bhopalpatnam villagers at http://naxalrevolution.blogspot.in/2013/05/mahendra-karmas-annihilation-cpi-maoist.html.

6. Between Fear and Courage

1. These testimonies were translated by Omprakash, Charu and me as part of the submissions in WP (Criminal) 119 of 2007.
2. *'Being Neutral Is Our Biggest Crime': Government, Vigilante, and Naxalite Abuses in India's Chhattisgarh State* (New York: Human Rights Watch, 2008), p. 63.
3. NHRC annexures, D1.
4. 'Preliminary observations and findings of the IAPL team on the human rights situation in Chhattisgarh, India, particularly of the adivasis in the Bastar region' (IAPL, 2007).

7. The Sorrow of the Sabari

1. 'Multisector assesment of IDP camps in Dantewada district of Chhattisgarh state', 19–24 June 2006 (UNICEF, 2006).
2. On numbers in camps see Chhattisgarh affidavit, 12 February 2011, para 6; for money spent, see Chhattisgarh affidavit, 30 May 2010, in WP 250/2007 (total summing up mine).
3. NHRC Annexure C, Documents related to visits to temporary relief camps in District Bijapur and Dantewada (CG). Calculations drawn from our Written Submissions for August 2010, in WP 250/2007.
4. S. Karimuddin, 'Birth rate plunges in Salwa Judum-hit South Bastar', *Hindustan Times*, 8 December 2006.
5. Nitin Mahajan, 'Cops ran away, let Naxals mow down 55: Official probe', *Indian Express*, 1 September 2007.

6. CPI (Maoist), *Women Martyrs of the Indian Revolution* (nd, online pdf version).

8. Border Crossings

1. For the use of Andhra Pradesh rather than Telangana, see Chapter 1, endnote 9.
2. Representation to the Director, Women Development and Child Welfare Department, Government of Andhra Pradesh, 2009.
3. The police 'daily diary' of Dornapal thana for 15 April 2006 records that the police provided protection to Mahendra Karma's rally in Cherapalli village, NHRC Annexure G1.
4. Pavan Dehat, 'Sukma encounter fake: Victim's kin', *The Hindu*, 5 November 2015.

9. Notes on an 'Operation'

1. Interviews, 22 October 2009, 4 March 2010, 6 March 2010, 27 May 2010, 4 March 2011.
2. Communist Party of India (Maoist), Press statement on the Dantewada guerrilla attack, dated 8 April 2010, *People's March* 11, No. 3 (March–April 2010), p. 42.
3. Dilip Kumar Mekala, 'Revisiting the horrors of Chintalnar massacre', *Force India*, 2012.
4. 'Dantewada's torture tapes', 2 April 2013, http://www.thefreelibrary.com/DANTEWADA'S+TORTURE+TAPES.-a0324484072; 'Mahendra Karma's annihilation' – CPI (Maoist) statement, 29 May 2013, http://naxalrevolution.blogspot.in/2013/05/mahendra-karmas-annihilation-cpi-maoist.html.
5. Aman Sethi, 'Chhattisgarh villages torched in police rampage', *The Hindu,* 23 March 2011; Anil Mishra, '300 homes burnt in Bastar', *Rajasthan Patrika*, Raipur edition, 23 March 2011.
6. Supriya Sharma, 'In Dantewada, Collector & SP not on same page', *Times of India*, 24 March 2011.

7. Aman Sethi, 'Burning of villages: Chhattisgarh government blames it on Maoists', *The Hindu,* 29 March 2011; 'Tadmetla Kand done by Naxals: Gurudas Kamath' (Minister of State for Home), *Deshbandhu*, 13 April 2011.
8. Ejaz Kaiser, 'Absconding, but on duty', *Hindustan Times*, 29 March 2011.
9. Aman Sethi, 'Chhattisgarh Congress MLAs on way to arson site held, released', *The Hindu,* 30 March 2011.
10. Notarized affidavit by Swami Agnivesh, 1 April 2011, in WP 250/2007; see also Joseph John, 'Agitated crowd attack Swami Agnivesh in Chhattisgarh', *Indian Express*, 26 March 2011.
11. English translation of FIR No. 0/2011, 27 March 2011, P.S. Sukma. Marawi was also the man who led the attacks on Tadmetla and other villages, and who filed the FIRs, claiming the Maoists did it. Clearly, Marawi had no option but to file a truthful FIR in this case, since there were too many witnesses.
12. Ashutosh Bhardwaj, '70% of Naxal surrenders are neither Naxals nor surrenders', *Indian Express*, 8 December 2014; Dipankar Ghose, 'Outsiders versus patriotic voices: The new lines in Bastar', *Indian Express*, 6 March 2016.
13. Fact-finding reports by WSS, 'Rampant Looting and Sexual Violence by Security Forces in Villages in Bijapur, South Chhattisgarh, October 19/20–24, 2015'; 'The Violent Truth of Anti-Naxal Operations in South Chhattisgarh Border Villages of Sukma and Dantewada', January 2016.

10. The Renegade and the Rifleman

1. Cited in Neville Maxwell, *India's China War* (Harmondsworth: Penguin Books Ltd, 1970), p. 14.
2. Joseph John, 'Tribals see conspiracy in notice to Salwa Judum leader before election', *Indian Express*, 16 October 2008.
3. Chhattisgarh affidavit, 3 May 2011, para 10, in WP 250/2007.
4. In the country as a whole, according to home ministry figures, there

were 70,046 SPOs, of which the bulk worked in Jammu and Kashmir (30,474). Union of India affidavit, 2 May 2011, in WP 250/2007.

5. Ashutosh Bhardwaj, 'The Hunted: Maoists who surrender want a family life, but nothing really changes for them', *Indian Express*, 5 January 2015.
6. NHRC annexure E-2.6, where the Chhattisgarh government has replied to a query from DIG NHRC.
7. Chattisgarh affidavit, 21 July 2012, in WP (Civil) 250/2007.
8. Malini Subramaniam, 'The ghosts of Salwa Judum refuse to leave Chhattisgarh', Scroll.in, 8.8.2015.
9. Dipankar Ghose, 'Outsiders versus patriotic voices: The new lines in Bastar'; 'Learn who the Naxals really fear', *Dainik Rashtriya Ujala*, 5 February 2016.
10. PTI, 'District Reserve Group adds impetus to anti-Naxal operations in Chhattisgarh', *Economic Times*, 5 February 2016.
11. Pavan Dahat, 'Plans on for major anti-Maoist offensive in Bastar', *The Hindu*, 28 November 2015.
12. This is, no doubt, what explains an internal Chhattisgarh police report that lists 325 encounters in 2006, 250 Naxalites killed but only 69 bodies recovered.
13. 'Mizo jawans abuse women', *Hindustan Times*, 24 November 2007.
14. Deeptiman Tiwary, 'Some states want Maoism to continue: CRPF chief', *Times of India*, 28 November 2014.
15. http://mha1.nic.in/par2013/par2014-pdfs/rs-190214/2694.pdf
16. Nandini Sundar, 'The trophies of Operation Green Hunt', *Outlook*, 5 July 2010; 'Slain Maoists bodies shifted to Chhattisgarh amidst protests', *The Hindu*, 18 April 2013; 'Commando's body lay in open for three days till journo fetched it', *Indian Express*, 26 April 2013; 'The Maoist who planted the bomb in the jawan's corpse was subsequently killed along with four children, in what locals alleged was a fake encounter.' Santosh Singh, 'Four children among 12 "Maoists" killed by CRPF, Jharkhand police', *Indian Express*, 10 June 2015; IANS, 'Bodies of martyred Chattisgarh cops ferried in garbage truck', *Hindustan Times*, 28 June 2011.

11. Security or Development?

1. Xaxa Committee Report, Table 5.40, p. 148, on poverty; Table 7.9, p. 211, on BMI.
2. Rs 542.16 crore was released for police station fortification in 2010–14.
3. SRE includes compensation to those killed on duty, rehabilitation of surrendered Naxalites, community policing, village defence committees and publicity material.
4. The special infrastructure scheme includes creating helipads, building roads in accessible areas, creating camping grounds, etc.
5. In January 2015, the central government allotted a further Rs 4000 crore for 1000 kilometres of roads in the Naxalite-affected regions of Chhattisgarh. 'Nitin Gadkari announces Rs 20,500 cr package for roads in Chhattisgarh', niticentral.com, 30 January 2015.
6. Rs 9059 crore was released till 2015.
7. Kaveri Gill, Rajesh Bhattacharya and Snehashish Bhattacharya, *The Political Economy of Capitalism, 'Development' and Resistance: The State and Adivasis of Mainland India* (Oxfam, 2013).
8. Union of India affidavit, 26 October 2010, in WP 250/2007, Annexure R1.
9. Aman Sharma, 'Fighting Maoists a national issue, but NDA asks state to meet the expenses', *Economics Times*, 27 November 2014.
10. Gautam Navlakha, 'Armed forces and livelihood and state power', kafila.org, 2 December 2015.
11. Figures taken from Table T01-2217, 2011 census for Dantewada, T01-T03-2218. 2011 census. In Bastar division, the blocks and tehsils coincide.
12. Administrative districts in India started out as revenue collection units, hence the term Collector for the head of the district.
13. 'Naxals torch passenger bus in Chhattisgarh, none hurt', NDTV.com, 24 November 2015.
14. Konta block had 194 primary schools for 241 villages; Bhairamgarh block had 127 primary schools for 218 villages; and Bijapur block had 45 primary schools for 95 villages. 2011 census.

15. In Usoor and Bhairamgarh blocks of Bijapur district, the literacy rates were as low as 30.73 per cent and 32.46 per cent respectively; while in Konta block, the literacy rate was 27.64 per cent. 2011 census.
16. Pratiyogita Darpan, November 2007, 2 (17): 770.
17. Ejaz Kaiser, 'Now Maoists writing kids textbooks', *Hindustan Times*, 22 October 2012.
18. 'Statistical Profile of Scheduled Tribes in India 2013' (Government of India, Ministry of Tribal Affairs, 2013), Tables 4.10–4.19, pp. 240–9.
19. Javed Iqbal, 'Cholera outbreak kills over 60 in Bastar', *New Indian Express*, 9 July 2010; Aman Sethi, 'Death stalks Dantewada', *The Hindu*, 9 October 2010.
20. Siddharth Ranjan Das, 'In this part of Chhattisgarh, medical help means a 10 km walk', NDTV.com, 19 September 2015.
21. Sanjib Kr. Baruah and Rajesh Ahuja, 'Narendra Modi govt cracks down on NGOs, prepares hitlist', *Hindustan Times*, 24 January 2015.
22. Suvojit Bagchi, 'Red Cross asked to stop work in Naxal-affected Bijapur', *The Hindu*, 14 June 2013.
23. MHA Annual Report 2014–15, p. 25.

12. The Amnesias of Democracy

1. Girija Shivakumar, 'Attack shows Maoists don't have faith in democracy', *The Hindu*, 26 May 2013; 'Jairam Ramesh describes Maoist attack as holocaust', IANS, 26 May 2013.
2. Statement of the Dandakaranya Special Zonal Committee, 26 May 2013, http://naxalrevolution.blogspot.in/2013/05/mahendra-karmas-annihilation-cpi-maoist.html.
3. V.I. Lenin, *'Left-Wing' Communism: An Infantile Disorder* (New York: International Publishers, 1940), pp. 41–2.
4. CPI (Maoist) spokesperson Comrade Abhay's interview on the 2014 Lok Sabha election, BannedThought.net, 24 March 2014.
5. Abhay, BannedThought.net.
6. Ashutosh Bhardwaj, 'Chhattisgarh Assembly polls: Democracy comes to Maoist heartland', *Indian Express*, 3 November 2013.

7. S.Y. Qureshi, *An Undocumented Wonder: The Making of the Great Indian Election* (New Delhi: Rupa, 2014), p. 3.
8. Suvojit Bagchi, 'Chhattisgarh seeks record number of central forces for polls', *The Hindu*, 3 October 2013.
9. Bhardwaj, 'Chhattisgarh assembly polls'.
10. PTI, 'Naxals worried over impressive voter turnout in Chhattisgarh', *Indian Express*, 2 May 2014.
11. '80 booths in Chhattisgarh's Bastar LS seat categorized as critical', *Times of India*, 8 April 2014.
12. Ejaz Kaiser and Rajesh Ahuja, 'Maoists kill 14 in two attacks in Chhattisgarh', *Hindustan Times*, 13 April 2014.
13. Azad, 'On the election boycott tactic of the Maoists', in *Maoists in India: Writings & Interviews by Azad* (Friends of Azad, 2009), p. 40.
14. 'Mining leases being doled out in the state ahead of elections: Congress', ibnlive.in.com, 7 August 2013.
15. Ashutosh Bhardwaj, 'Chhattisgarh govt pays for all TV news that is fit to buy', *Indian Express*, 7 December 2012.
16. Ashutosh Bhardwaj, 'Chattisgarh tapes: "We have to go up to 7 at least, he is expecting 10. We will bring him down"', *Indian Express*, 6 January 2016.
17. Tariq Thachil, *Elite Parties, Poor Voters: How Social Services Win Votes in India* (Cambridge: Cambridge University Press, 2014).
18. 'After Phase-1 we resorted to "cluster bombing", says Raman Singh', *The Hindu*, 22 December 2013.
19. Ajit Jogi, 'Time to call off the Salwa Judum', *Indian Express*, 30 June 2006.
20. Impressions based on an email from Sonia Gandhi to one of her ministers who had forwarded the ICI photos to her; interview with Rahul Gandhi at his behest; meetings with K.C. Deo, Mani Shankar Iyar, Jairam Ramesh, P. Chidambaram, Sriprakash Jaiswal and Shivraj Patil; newspaper statements by P.C. Kyndiah.
21. Ejaz Kaiser, 'Salwa Judum divides Congress in Chhattisgarh', *Hindustan Times*, 28 December 2006.

13. The Rights and Wrongs of Human Rights

1. 'Chidambaram slams Maoist sympathizers', Times Now, 26 October 2009.
2. 'Chidambaram seeks bigger mandate, singles out activists for blame', *Times of India*, 18 May 2010.
3. On the history of the civil liberties movement in India, see Amit Upadhyay, 'From "Civil Liberties" to "Human Rights"? The Shifting Grounds of Civil Liberties Activism in India', thesis submitted to the University of Hyderabad, 2014; Ujjwal Kumar Singh, ed., *Human Rights and Peace: Ideas, Laws, Institutions and Movements* (New Delhi: Sage, 2009); essays by Balagopal, many available on balagopal.org. I am grateful to the HRF for sending me Balagopal's unpublished essays.
4. Open Letter from the CPI to the President, 16 November 2005.
5. HRF press releases, August 2005 and May 2006.
6. The detailed report came out five months later. PUCL, Chhattisgarh and PUCL, Jharkhand, PUDR, Delhi, APDR, West Bengal, and IAPL, *When the State Makes War on Its Own People* (April 2006).
7. Independent Citizens Initiative, *War in the Heart of India* (July 2006).
8. Asian Centre for Human Rights, *The Adivasis of Chhattisgarh: Victims of the Naxalite Movement and Salwa Judum Campaign* (February 2006); CAVOW, *Salwa Judum and Violence on Women in Dantewara* (December 2006); Human Rights Forum, *Death, Displacement and Deprivation in Dantewara* (December 2006); *'Being Neutral Is Our Biggest Crime'*.
9. Rambhau Mhalgi Prabodhini (RMP), *Development and Internal Security in Chhattisgarh: Impact of Naxalite Movement, A Report* (Mumbai, 2005–6).
10. The parallels with the military's human rights discourse in Colombia are striking, suggesting this is a global phenomenon. See Winnifred Tate, *Counting the Dead: The Culture and Politics of Human Rights Activism in Colombia* (Berkeley: University of California Press, 2007).
11. Himanshu Kumar, 'Two roads parted in the woods', *Tehelka*, 26 October 2013.

12. Ashutosh Bhardwaj, 'The Gandhian as a Maoist: Journalist Prafulla Jha fights back his sedition charges', *Indian Express*, 27 October 2013.
13. Minnie Vaid, *A Doctor to Defend* (Delhi: Rajpal & Sons, 2011); see also Dilip D'Souza, *The Curious Case of Dr. Binayak Sen* (New Delhi: HarperCollins, 2012).
14. Joseph John, 'Bastar attack kingpin studying in Delhi, knows Roy, Patkar: Cops', *Indian Express*, 12 July 2010.
15. Shoma Chaudhury, 'The inconvenient truth of Soni Sori', *Tehelka*, 15 October 2011.
16. Rashmi Drolia, 'Women in politics: One front runner, another voice of tribal people in Bastar', *Times of India*, 25 April 2015.
17. Clifford Bob, *The Marketing of Rebellion, Insurgents, Media and International Activism* (Cambridge: Cambridge University Press, 2005), p. 64.
18. 'Ganti Prasadam gets bail, refuses to leave jail', PTI, 23 February 2011.
19. Nitin Mahajan, 'End Salwa Judum, kids to tell Kalam on state anniversary', *Indian Express*, 6 November 2006.
20. Gautam Navlakha and Ashish Gupta, 'The real divide in Bastar', *Economic and Political Weekly* 44, No. 33 (2009), pp. 20–3.

14. To Talk or Not to Talk?

1. Manan Kumar, 'Centre spares Naxalite "friends"', *Telegraph*, 11 April 2007.
2. B. Vijay Murty, 'Tribal, dalit officers are soft targets for Maoists', *Hindustan Times*, 2 July 2013.
3. Arun Janardhanan, 'With Che as hero, Alex Paul Menon roamed the badlands', *Times of India*, 24 April 2012.
4. G. Haragopal, 'Abduction of the District Collector of Sukma, Chhattisgarh', *Economic and Political Weekly* 47, No. 43 (2012), pp. 34–39; G. Haragopal, 'Malkangiri kidnap in Orissa: Negotiating peace', *Economic and Political Weekly* 46, No. 26 & 27 (2011), pp. 23–27; G. Haragopal, 'The Koyyur kidnap: Question of human rights', *Economic and Political Weekly* 4 December 1993, pp. 2650–2.

5. Sarva Dharma Sansad, PUCL, PUDR, *Of Human Bondage: An Account of Hostage Taking in Bastar: Report of the Team of Human Rights Activists who Secured the Release of Five Policemen-hostages in Chhattisgarh* (January–February 2011).
6. G. Haragopal, 'Malkangiri kidnap', p. 24.
7. Suvojit Bagchi, 'Justice deliverance slowing down in Chhattisgarh district, RTI reveals', *The Hindu*, 29 October 2013.
8. See *Of Human Bondage*, on the Narayanpur kidnappings of policemen.
9. K. Balagopal, 'Beyond violence and non-violence', kafila.org, 23 January 2009.
10. Ganapathi, General Secretary CPI (Maoist), 'Open reply to Independent Citizens Initiative on Dantewada', *Economic and Political Weekly* 6 January 2007, pp. 67–71.
11. See Balagopal, 'Beyond violence'.
12. Balagopal, 'Civil Liberties Movement and Revolutionary Violence', HRF compilation.
13. Suhas Palshikar and Yogendra Yadav, 'The Week-CNN-IBN-CSDS poll inside India's war zone', *The Week*, 20 August 2010; Rupashree Nanda, 'State of the nation: Government preferred over Naxals', IBN Live, 9 August 2010; Times Insight Group, 'State worse for us than Naxals, say 58% in poll', *Times of India*, 28 September 2010.

15. The Propaganda Wars

1. Herbert Gans, *Deciding What's News*, new ed. (Evanston: Northwestern University Press, 2004).
2. Shubhranshu Choudhary, 'The art of not writing', Inforchangeindia.org, 2009; Ashutosh Bhardwaj, 'Chhattisgarh govt pays for all TV news that is fit to buy'; Suvojit Bagchi, 'Whose journalism is it anyway', *The Hindu*, 28 January 2014; Sandeep Pai and Ejaz Kaiser, 'Auditor raps Chhattisgarh for paying for coverage', *Hindustan Times*, 30 January 2014.
3. It was later renamed CGNet Swara, training local reporters and ordinary villagers to relay news using mobile phones.

4. Sujeet Kumar, 'Pizza and Pepsi threaten Maoist fiefdom', IANS, 7 August 2005.
5. '"Scribes should be jailed for glorifing Maoists": BJP MP', IANS, 1 September 2005.
6. Rajendra Mohanty, 'Naxals versus the people', *Tehelka*, 24 September 2005.
7. This is based on a close study of articles that appeared on CGNet, and corroborated by compilations made between 2005 and 2007 from the English press by the Commonwealth Human Rights Initiative.
8. Somini Sengupta, 'India's unrelenting "People's War"', *New York Times*, 12 April 2006; Randeep Ramesh, 'Inside India's hidden war', *Guardian*, 9 May 2006; John Lancaster, 'India's ragtag band of Maoists takes root among rural poor', *Washington Post*, 13 May 2006; Jill McGivering, 'Displaced by India's red threat', BBC.co.uk, 30 June 2006; 'A spectre haunting India, *The Economist*, 17 August 2006.
9. Stuart Hall, et al., *Policing the Crises: Mugging, the State and Law and Order* (New York: Holmes & Meier Publishers, 1978).
10. For a range of ways in which the media distorts facts – using selective or even fictional reporting, dumbing down issues, etc. – see Malcolm Dean, *Democracy under Attack: How the Media Distort Policy and Politics* (Bristol: Policy Press, 2012).
11. Ashutosh Bhardwaj, 'Chhattisgarh govt pays for all TV news that is fit to buy'.
12. See Robin Jeffrey, *India's Newspaper Revolution: Capitalism, Politics and the Indian Language* (New York: St. Martin's Press, 2000); Sevanti Ninan, *Headlines from the Heartland: Reinventing the Hindi Public Sphere* (New Delhi: Sage, 2007).
13. CPI (Maoist) spokesperson Comrade Abhay's interview on general elections, 2014. The interview was released to the media on 24 March 2014.
14. Chitrangada Choudhury, 'Arrested, tortured, jailed in South Bastar', *The Hoot*, 8 October 2015.
15. '"Not a single journalist working without fear or pressure": Editors Guild on Bastar', Scroll.in, 29 March 2016; see also Furquan Amin

Siddiqui, 'Pen or gun: Journòs in Chhattisgarh stuck between cops and Maoists', *Hindustan Times*, 16 December 2015.

16. Smita Gupta, 'The shy peace hunter', *Outlook*, 15 May 2006; Maureen Mitra, 'Chhattisgarh tangle', *Down to Earth*, 31 October 06.
17. Michael Schudson, *The Sociology of News* (New York: W.W. Norton, 2003).
18. Devi Leena Bose, '"Reporting Dantewada": Televisual construction of Maoism', indianmedialogue.com, 27 December 2007 (reporting on the April 2010 attacks in which 76 CRPF and 8 Naxals were killed); Aritra Bhattacharya, 'Media does not hide its colour', *The Hoot*, 5 June 2013 (on the media coverage of the killing of Mahendra Karma).
19. Naveen Mishra, 'Power to define: Framing of Naxalites in the Indian media', *Global Media Journal* 6, No. 2, Mediterranean Edition (Fall 2011), pp. 23-35; Pradip Ninan Thomas, 'The "Red Surge": Media framing of Maoist struggles in India', *International Communication Gazette* 76, No. 6 (2014), pp. 485–504.
20. Arundhati Roy, 'Walking with the comrades', *Outlook*, 29 March 2010.
21. Robert M. Entman, Steven Livingston and Jennie Kim, 'Doomed to repeat: Iraq News, 2002–2007', *American Behavioral Scientist* 52, No. 5 (2009), pp. 689–708.
22. 'Country will meet Maoist challenge by 2–3 years, says Chidambaram', rediff.com, 31 March 2010. 'Maoists looking at armed overthrow of state by 2050', *Times of India*, 6 March 2010
23. E.S. Herman and N. Chomsky, *Manufacturing Consent: The Political Economy of Mass Media*, new edn. (New York: Pantheon Books, 2002), pp. 37–86.
24. MHA Annual Report, 2014–15, p. 25; see also MHA Annual Report 2006, pp. 6–10, for expenditure on propaganda.

16. Praying for Justice

1. Gerald N. Rosenberg, *The Hollow Hope: Can Courts Bring about Social Change?* (University of Chicago Press, 2008).
2. Nick Robinson, 'A court adrift', *Frontline*, 3 May 2013.

3. This is supported by an analysis of the media coverage of the Salwa Judum on google trends, an admittedly imperfect measure.
4. History of the Supreme Court, supremecourt.nic.in.
5. Status Paper on the Naxal Problem, Internal Security Division, MHA, 18 May 2006; Minutes of the 20th Coordination Centre meeting held on 31 March 2006 at Vigyan Bhawan, New Delhi.
6. Letter from Raghu, Program Officer in ActionAid, to the NHRC, 18 June 2008.
7. Shubhranshu Choudhary, 'A rustic version of police-Naxal encounter', *Daily Chhattisgarh*, 13 April 2007.
8. Nitin Mahajan, 'Autopsy confirms foul play, cops file FIR', *Indian Express*, 10 May 2007.

17. The Legal Death and Reincarnation of the Salwa Judum

1. This petition had been filed by Himanshu Kumar of the VCA, along with some of the Gompad villagers. The Chhattisgarh police abducted the Gompad petitioners before they reached court, and after they had been in custody for a while, they testified that their relatives had been killed, but 'could not say by whom'. The Gompad matter then went into limbo, and after a long gap, it is being heard again in 2016.
2. Paramita Chatterjee and Reshmi R. Dasgupta, 'Star lawyers get Rs. 5 lakh for 5 minute job', *Economic Times*, 31 October 2009.
3. Chhattisgarh affidavit, 25 April 2011.
4. Reply affidavit by Chhattisgarh in response to Swami Agnivesh's affidavit, 13 April 2011, in WP 250/2007.
5. For many decades, a 'CBI investigation' has been shorthand for an impartial and professional investigation; evidence of the distrust in which the regular police are held across the country. Unfortunately, as the CBI's behavior in this, and other cases shows, institutional overload and politicization means that this bastion too is crumbling.
6. See, for instance, Judith Resnik, 'Globalization(s), Privatization(s), Constitutionalization, and Statization: Icons and Experiences of Sovereignty in the 21st Century', *I•CON*, 11 No. 1 (2013), pp. 162–99.

7. Dhananjay Mahapatra, 'SC defangs SJ, anti-Naxal ops may be hit', *Times of India*, 6 July 11; Ejaz Kaiser, 'Post-SC order, Maoist threat looms over SPOs', *Hindustan Times*, 7 July 11; Supriya Sharma, 'SC ruling hit us like a storm, death threats to disarmed tribals', *Times of India*, 9 July 11.
8. Ejaz Kaiser, 'Chhattisgarh to seek review of Supreme Court's Salwa Judum order', *Hindustan Times*, 5 July 2011.
9. Bela Bhatia, 'Judging the judgement', *Economic and Political Weekly* 46, No. 30 (23 July 2011), pp. 14–16.
10. WP (Cr) 119/2007), *Union of India* v. *Kartam Joga & Ors.*, Application for modification/recall of the 5 July 2011 order.
11. CBI application for directions, 12 March 2012, in WP 250/2007.
12. '*Gawahon ne sweekara, Professor Nandini ne jaisa bolne kaha, vaise hi diya bayaan*', *Jagdalpur Patrika*, 15 June 2014; '*Nandini Sundar Maowadiyaon ke seedhe sampark mein, videsh se funding bhi*', *Jagdalpur Patrika*, 11 July 2014.
13. See Upendra Baxi, *The Crises of the Indian Legal System* (Delhi: Vikas, 1982).
14. Mark Galanter, 'Justice in many rooms: Courts, private ordering and indigenous law', *Journal of Legal Pluralism* 19 (1981), pp. 1–47.
15. Sir Mark Potter, *Do the Media Influence the Judiciary?* (Oxford: The Foundation for Law, Justice and Society, 2011).

Appendices

Appendix 1
Official Data on Deaths in the State–Maoist Conflict in Chhattisgarh, 2005–16

Year	No. of civilians killed (a)	No. of security personnel killed (a)	No. of Maoists killed (a)	Total casualties, MHA data on SATP (a)	Total casualties, MHA annual reports (b)	Total casualties, SATP data (c)
2005	121	47	32	200	168	126
2006	304	84	74	462	388	361
2007	171	198	66	435	369	350
2008	157	85	76	318	242	168
2009	163	127	142	432	290	345
2010	171	172	83	426	343	327
2011	124	80	34	238	204	176
2012	63	46	38	147	109	108
2013	67	44	38	149	111	128
2014	52	59	35	146	112	113
2015	NA	NA	NA	97	97	120
2016	20	15	47	35*	35*	97**
Total	NA	NA	NA	3085	2468	2419

* updated till 31 March 2016

** updated till 22 May 2016

(a) My compilation of Chhattisgarh data year-wise based on Ministry of Home Affairs (MHA) data, at the South Asia Terrorism Portal (SATP) satp.org, http://www.satp.org/satporgtp/countries/india/maoist/data_sheets/fatalitiesnaxalmha.htm.
(b) My compilation of Chhattisgarh data from MHA annual reports, 2005–16, at mha.nic.in
(c) SATP table compiled from news reports, http://www.satp.org/satporgtp/countries/india/maoist/data_sheets/fatalitiesnaxal05-11.htm. According to SATP data, 721 civilians, 891 police personnel and 807 Maoists were killed between 2005 and 2016 in Chhattisgarh.

SATP data also shows that Chhattisgarh is the clear leader in conflict-related deaths, followed by Jharkhand with a total of 1411 deaths, Andhra Pradesh with 729, West Bengal with 699, Odisha with 671, Bihar with 629 and Maharashtra with 452, during this period. Across India, 7072 people died in the state–Maoist conflict between 2005 and 2016.

Seventy people were killed in 'Naxalite-related incidents' between 1968 and 1998.[1] In the years prior to the Salwa Judum, i.e. 2003 and 2004, the total number of deaths in Chhattisgarh due to the state–Naxalite conflict were 74 and 83 respectively,[2] showing the overall casualties went up drastically after the Salwa Judum began.

---

[1] Figures provided by the Office of the Inspector General of Police in Jagdalpur, 1998.
[2] MHA annual reports, 2003, 2004.

Appendix 2

Timeline

1980–95	Communist Party of India (Marxist-Leninist) People's War establishes roots in South and West Bastar and Abujhmarh
1990	First Jan Jagran Abhiyan in Bijapur block; police-sponsored rallies against Maoists led by Congress leader Mahendra Karma
1998	Second Jan Jagran Abhiyan in Bhairamgarh block (short-lived)
2000	Formation of the state of Chhattisgarh (carved out of Madhya Pradesh)
2003	Raman Singh/BJP wins assembly elections replacing Ajit Jogi/Congress Liberalization of the national mining policy
2004	Formation of CPI (Maoist) out of merger of People's War and Maoist Communist Centre CGNet set up by Shubhranshu and Smita Choudhary
2005	Third Jan Jagran Abhiyan started around Kutru in Bhairamgarh block; renamed Salwa Judum around August

	MOUs announced with Tata and Essar to build steel plants in Lohandiguda and Dhurli/Bhansi respectively; Special Economic Zone Act passed CPI (Maoist) banned and Chhattisgarh Special Public Security Act enacted
June 2005–February 2006	Villages burnt, inhabitants forcibly evacuated into Salwa Judum camps in Bhairamgarh and Bijapur blocks
February 2006	The Salwa Judum comes to Usoor and Konta blocks; hundreds of villages are attacked, and camps come up along the Sukma–Konta highway
February 2006–March 2007	Sustained Salwa Judum and security force attacks in and around Bhairamgarh, Bijapur, Usoor and Konta blocks; in March 2007, attacks on villages on the border with Andhra Pradesh
April, July 2006	Two major fact-finding reports – by All India Fact-Finding and Independent Citizens Initiative – released
December 2006	Scheduled Tribes and Other Traditional Forest Dwellers (Recognition of Forest Rights) Act, 2006 passed
31 March 2007	Santoshpur fake encounters reported in real time
May 2007	Nandini Sundar and others heard in the Supreme Court (SC) Binayak Sen, PUCL Secretary, arrested
October 2007	'Kartam Joga and ors' writ petition heard in the SC
November 2007	Massive Adivasi Mahasabha/CPI rally in Jagdalpur, after which people start returning home from Salwa Judum camps and Andhra Pradesh

March–April 2008	Chief Justice C.J. Balakrishnan says arming citizens is abetting crime and asks NHRC to investigate
June 2008	NHRC investigation
August 2008	NHRC submits its report; the media reports 'clean chit' to the Salwa Judum even before the SC sees the NHRC report
October 2009	Operation Green Hunt, the name for concerted police operations against Maoists, begins across India Citizens Initiative for Peace formed to campaign for peace talks
2009–10	Combing operations begin in Darbha block of Bastar; attacks on Gompad and other villages – large numbers killed
April 2010	76 CRPF men killed in Maoist ambush, Tadmetla
August 2010	Kartam Joga and other CPI activists arrested; released only two years later
March 2011	Tadmetla, Morpalli and Timapuram burnt for the second time, villagers killed and raped; Salwa Judum leaders attack Swami Agnivesh
July 2011	SC order declaring the Salwa Judum unconstitutional, asking state to disband SPOs Chhattisgarh renames SPOs armed auxiliary forces; starts increasing number of CRPF camps
September 2011	Soni Sori campaign starts
March 2012	Nandini Sundar and others file contempt case in SC – still not heard (till 2016)
April 2012	Alex Paul Menon, Collector of Sukma, kidnapped; released after 12 days

June 2012	17 villagers killed by security forces in Sarkeguda, Bijapur district
May 2013	8 villagers killed by security forces in Edesmetta, Bijapur district Mahendra Karma and other Congress leaders killed in Maoist ambush at Jeeram Ghati; the war intensifies around the Kanger forest, Darbha block
November 2013	Raman Singh/BJP wins third term in assembly elections
May–June 2014	Narendra Modi and NDA win national elections S.R.P. Kalluri posted back as IG Bastar
May 2015	Modi announces plans for a mega steel plant at Dilmilli in Bastar district Chavindra Karma announces plans for Salwa Judum II
September 2015–ongoing	Jan Jagran Abhiyan restarted; sharp rise in fake encounters and fake surrenders; mass gang rapes of women in Bijapur and Sukma
February–May 2016	Police-sponsored vigilante groups, Samajik Ekta Manch and others, intimidate and drive out journalists, researchers, lawyers and activists
October 2016	CBI charged SPOs with arson in Tadmetla and Salwa Judum activists with attacking Swami Agnivesh
November 2016	Nandini Sundar and ors charged with murder; charges dropped in February 2018
December 2018	Congress Government replaces BJP in Chhattisgarh
May 2021	Silger protest begins
2019–22	Sarkeguda and Edesmetta Enquiry Reports show CRPF killed innocent villagers

Acronyms and Abbreviations

AFSPA	Armed Forces Special Powers Act
AID	Association for India's Development
AP	Andhra Pradesh
APCLC	Andhra Pradesh Civil Liberties Committee
APDR	Association for the Protection of Democratic Rights
ASDS	Vyavasayaka Mariyu Sanghika Abhivrudhi Samstha
BJP	Bharatiya Janata Party
BSF	Border Security Force
BRICS	Brazil, Russia, India, China and South Africa
BRO	Border Roads Organisation
CAF	Chhattisgarh Armed Forces
CAPF	Central Armed Police Forces
CG	Chhattisgarh
CIP	Citizens Initiative for Peace
CISF	Central Industrial Security Force
COBRA	Commando Battalion for Resolution Action
CNM	Chetna Natya Manch (locally called 'Cinem batch')
CPI	Communist Party of India

CPI(M)	Communist Party of India (Marxist)
CPI (ML) PW	Communist Party of India (Marxist-Leninist) People's War
CPI (Maoist)	Communist Party of India (Maoist)
CPJC	Campaign for Peace and Justice in Chhattisgarh
CRPF	Central Reserve Police Force
CrPC	Criminal Procedure Code
CSPSA	Chhattisgarh Special Public Security Act
DAKMS	Dandakaranya Adivasi Kisan Mazdoor Sangathan
DIG	Deputy Inspector General
DK	Dandakaranya
DKSZC	Dandakaranya Special Zonal Committee
DRG	District Reserve Guard
DSS	Dantewada Samanvay Samiti
FFDA	Forum for Fact-finding, Documentation and Advocacy
FICCI	Federation of Indian Chambers of Commerce and Industry
FINS	Forum for Integrated National Security
FIR	first information report
FRA	Forest Rights Act (The Scheduled Tribes and Other Traditional Forest Dwellers [Recognition of Forest Rights] Act)
HRF	Human Rights Forum
IAP	Integrated Action Plan
IAPL	International Association of People's Lawyers
ICI	Independent Citizens Initiative
ICRC	International Committee of the Red Cross
IDP	internally displaced person
IED	improvised explosive device
IG	Inspector General of Police
INSAS	Indian Small Arms System
IPC	Indian Penal Code

IRB	India Reserve Battalion
ITBP	Indo-Tibetan Border Police
ITDA	Integrated Tribal Development Agency
JAGLAG	Jagdalpur Legal Aid Group
JJA	Jan Jagran Abhiyan
KAMS	Krantikari Adivasi Mahila Sangathan
LGS	Local Guerrilla Squad
LOS	Local Organization Squad
LWE	left-wing extremism
MCC	Maoist Communist Centre of India
MHA	Ministry of Home Affairs
ML	Marxist Leninist
MLA	Member of the Legislative Assembly
MP	Member of Parliament
MSF	Médecins Sans Frontières
NAPM	National Alliance of People's Movements
NCST	National Commission for Scheduled Tribes
NCPCR	National Commission for Protection of Child Rights
NCW	National Commission for Women
NDA	National Democratic Alliance (BJP led)
NHRC	National Human Rights Commission
NMDC	National Minerals Development Corporation
NREGA	National Rural Employment Guarantee Act
NTFP	non-timber forest produts
NSS	Nagrik Suraksha Samiti
PCPA	People's Committee against Police Atrocities
People's War	Communist Party of India (Marxist-Leninist) People's War
PESA	Panchayats (Extension to Scheduled Areas) Act
PIL	public interest litigation
PLGA	People's Liberation Guerrilla Army
POR	preliminary offence report
PUCL	People's Union for Civil Liberties

PUDR	People's Union for Democratic Rights
RMP	Rambhau Mhalgi Prabodhini
RPC	Revolutionary People's Committee
RSS	Rashtriya Swayamsevak Sangh
UNICEF	United Nations Children's Emergency Fund
UPA	United Progressive Alliance (Congress led)
SC	Scheduled Caste
SDM	Sub-Divisional Magistrate
SHRC	State Human Rights Commission
SLR	self-loading rifle
SP	Superintendent of Police
SPO	Special Police Officer
SRE	security related expenditure
SSP	Senior Superintendent of Police
ST	Scheduled Tribe
ULFA	United Liberation Front of Asom
VCA	Vanvasi Chetna Ashram
VDC	Village Defence Committee
WSS	Women against Sexual Violence and State Repression

Glossary

aonla	*Phyllanthus emblica*
adivasi	Scheduled Tribe
anganwadi	pre-primary childcare centre
anudeshika	teaching assistant
baap	father
baheda	*Terminalia bellirica*
bandh	strike
beedi	local cigarette (tobacco wrapped in tendu leaf)
beeja pandum	seed-sowing festival
benami	usually refers to illegal transactions or property held in another's name
bhajans	Hindu devotional songs
bhawan	building
bhum	earth
bhumkal	war to defend the earth; 1910 rebellion
bhum pandum	seed-sowing festival
bhoj	feast/food
biere metta	big mountain
bija	*Pterocarpus marsupium*
chakka jam	road blockade

char	*Buchanania lanzan*
chhind	*Phoenix sylvestris* (date palm)
chhindras	fermented sap of date palm
chowk	crossroad/market centre
dada log	elder brothers (colloquial term for Maoists)
dalal	middleman
dalam	armed squad
devi gudi	mother goddess shrine
desi	native/local
dhaora	*Anogeissus latifolia*
dhol	double-headed drum
gaita	priest
garh	fort (headquarters of small chieftainships)
gaddi pandum	ancestor spirit festival
ghotul	youth dormitory
gopniya	secret
haat	weekly market
inami	rewarded
inda	wide waters (river/sea)
Ikhwani	Kashmiri pro-government militia, consisting of surrendered militants
jaga	earth deity
jan adalat	people's court
Jan Jagran Abhiyan	Public Awakening Campaign
jan militia	people's militia
jan sunwai	people's hearing
janathana sarkar	people's government
jatra	sacrifices/festivals
jawans	soldiers (paramilitary men)
jhola	cloth bag
Judum	long collective hunt (traditionally), counter-insurgency operation (since 2005)
karum/kurmi pandum	new millets festival

khapra	baked-brick roof tiles
khas aadmi	close followers/friends
khichdi	rice and lentils cooked together
koi/koitor/koya	human/person (Gondi)
korta pandum	new rice festival
kothar	field shelter to guard crops
ladi	open shelter with thatched roof in fields or threshing grounds
Lal Salaam	red salute
landa	rice beer
lathi	stick
lungi	cotton wrap-around worn by men
mai-baap	mother–father
majhi	headman of pargana (cluster of villages)
malik makbuja	owner's right to cut trees on his/her own land
mahua	*Madhuca indica*
mandai	pargana festival
mantri mahoday	honourable minister
marh	hill range
marka pandum	new mango festival
mata	mother goddess
mati	earth (deity)
mitanin	village-level health worker
moong	green gram
murdabad	death to
nala	rivulet
panchayat	village self-governance unit
pandum	festival
para	hamlet
pargana	cluster of several villages (traditional administrative division)
patel	village headman

patta	land title document
patwari	revenue officer in charge of land records
peedith	victims
perma	earth priest
pucca	permanent
pujari	priest
prabhari mantri	minister in charge of an area
razakar	private militia under the Nizam of Hyderabad
saga	affinal relatives
sainik	soldier
sal	*Shorea robusta*
salwa	pacification/purification
Salwa Judum	purification hunt (counter-insurgency operation since 2005)
samiti	committee
samosa	fried snack
sangham	village-level organization set up by Maoists
sangharsh	struggle
sarkar	government
sarpanch	elected head of a village panchayat
sarv samaj	all-community platform
shikshakarmi	contract schoolteacher
shivir	refugee camp
siraha	shaman
sulphi	*Caryota urens* (fishtail palm)
tehsil	revenue administrative unit
tendu	*Diospyros melanoxylon*, leaf used for local cigarettes
tilli	sesame
thana	police station
thanedar	person in charge of a police station

tora	fruit of *Madhuca indica*
wadde	herbal healer
vikas	development
vetta	short hunts around seed-sowing time
zindabad	long live

Acknowledgements

Of all the books I have written or edited, this has been the hardest one to do, in part because I have so much invested in the situation. Acknowledging people is even harder because there is no way to measure comradeship, concern, affection, selflessness and the inspiration provided by those around me.

I am deeply grateful to Manish Kunjam, Podiyam Panda, Rama Sodi, Kartam Joga, and others in the Communist Party of India, all of whom I cannot name, with whom I have had many long discussions. In particular, I admire Manish Kunjam for his insights, his ability to laugh even in the midst of conflict, and his courage. I thank Podiyam Panda for those winter dawn conversations, for never losing heart despite his own dire situation, and instead advising me to take things 'one step at a time'.

In Bastar, many people have helped in a variety of ways; I cannot name them for their own safety. My old friends from the 1990s, when I first lived in the region as a researcher, have always been there for me.

The Maoists have never taken me on a guided tour of 'their' areas, as they have done with other journalists and writers. I was told it was because I asked too many difficult questions. However, I am grateful to village friends of long standing for sharing their experience of the Maoists with me, and to former Maoists who very kindly recounted their histories. I would especially like to thank Lanka Papi Reddy for his account of the early years.

One enjoyable aspect of the past 10 years has been learning how a different profession operates. Ashok Desai is a master of knowing when and how to respond, how to be courteous to one's opponents and yet make one's point. Nitya Ramakrishnan has been the backbone of our litigation. I am grateful to T.R. Andhyarujina for taking on the Salwa Judum matter in 2007. Sumita Hazarika and her office have borne with us for almost a decade now, with rare cheerfulness.

Rahul Kripalani has been a constant source of support and work on this case, and I am deeply grateful to him. Ashish Chugh and Pragya Singh provided my first insight into how hard and skilfully junior lawyers worked, an appreciation which was reinforced after meeting Suhasini Sen. I thank Menaka Guruswamy for all her work and support on this matter. I am also grateful to Rajinder Sachar, Kanak Tiwari, Tridip Pais, R. Nitin, Sarim Naved, Rhea Sawhney, Anu Bindra, Bipin Aspatwar, Sharma ji, Shatru and Pooran. Ujjwal Singh's backing and help in this litigation has been indispensable. And of course, I am deeply grateful to all my co-litigants.

Himanshu and Veena Kumar were generous with their hospitality. I also thank the Vanvasi Chetna Ashram staff for their help. I am deeply indebted to Gandhi Babu and Venkatesh of ASDS along with all their staff, Raghu and G. Rajshekhar of Action Aid Hyderabad, Sharanya Nayak and C. Sudhakar.

Omprakash's help in translating the testimonies in the Kartam Joga matter was invaluable. I truly appreciate the help provided by Aditya Swaroop, Sanchita Bakshi, Sridevi Pannikar, Kamal Choubey, Preeti Chouhan, Vikas, and Pratyush Chandra during the NHRC visit to Bastar in 2008. Sushant Panigrahi provided able research assistance in interviewing SPOs.

I am grateful to the other members of the All India Fact-Finding team of 2005, and to the late B.G. Verghese, E.A.S. Sarma, Ramachandra Guha, Harivansh and Farah Naqvi of the Independent

Citizens Initiative. J.P. Rao, Ajay Dandekar, Kopa Kunjam, Ujjwal Singh, Chitra Padmanabhan, Suresh Kumar, Prabhat Pattavi, Rahul Kripalani, Archana Prasad, Aradhna Markam, Manju Kawasi and Vineet Tiwari have accompanied me on some of the other trips that I describe in this book. I am deeply grateful to all of them, including for putting up with the harassment of the Chhattisgarh police. I would like to especially acknowledge J.P. Rao for insisting over the years that something must be done about the crisis in Bastar, whether it was relief to internally displaced persons, setting up the Campaign for Peace and Justice in Chhattisgarh, contacting the National Commission for the Protection of Child Rights or envisioning legal aid in Bastar. His quiet, facilitative role has been critical, but largely unrecognized even by people following the region.

Shubhranshu and Smita Choudhary played a critical role through CGNet, especially in the early years of the Judum. I am grateful to them as well as Vijayan, Vani, Rohit, Praveen and others in CPJC and to all those who came together to carry forward the Citizens Initiative for Peace. I am obliged to the late S.R. Sankaran, the late Nirmala Deshpande, K.B. Saxena, D. Bandopadhyay, Swami Agnivesh, V.S.K. Krishna and other members of the Human Rights Forum, Sudha Bhardwaj, Rajendra Sail and others in Chhattisgarh PUCL, Kavita Srivastav, Malini Subramaniam, Shalini Gera, Isha Khandelwal, Usha Ramanathan, Radha Kumar, Ravi Nair, Harsh Mander, Maja Daruwala and others from the Commonwealth Human Rights Initiative, as well as the ICRC and MSF for different kinds of help. Were I to name all those who have encouraged and assisted me at various points along the last 10 years, my task would never end.

I have met several members of different political parties in connection with the conflict; in particular, I would like to thank D. Raja and Jairam Ramesh for their concern on this issue. I thank the senior officials in the security establishment who agreed to be interviewed including former DGPs Viswaranjan and Ramnivas, A.N. Upadhya, Brigadier B.K. Ponwar, M.K. Narayanan and D.M. Mitra.

I am grateful to my colleagues and students at the Department of Sociology, Delhi University for creating a space where Bastar's problems did not matter. Keeping the two parts of my life – teaching and litigation – separate has been difficult but also important to me. I also thank all the people who invited me to share my ideas on civil war, and who coped with my last-minute cancellations or my failure to submit articles on time, because of the exigencies of the litigation.

I am grateful to all the people who read this book either in whole or in part and gave me useful suggestions – Aparna Sundar, André Béteille, Anuradha Roy, Anushrut Ramakrishnan Aggrawal, Karthika V.K., Kiran Bhatty, V.S.K. Krishna, Nitya Ramakrishnan, G.V.K. Prasad, G. Rajshekhar, Rahul Kripalani, S. Sundar, Ujjwal Singh, N. Venugopal, Vikram Seth and Vineet Tiwari. Ramachandra Guha, Javed Iqbal, Gita Gopalkrishnan, Kaveri Gill and Siddharth Varadarajan heroically read the whole.

I am extremely grateful to Nandini Mehta for her editorial eye, and for insisting over several iterations that the manuscript be shortened and made more accessible, to Chiki Sarkar for taking it on and to the entire Juggernaut team who have worked on this book, especially Jaishree Ram Mohan and Gavin Morris. I thank Dipankar Deepak for drawing the maps.

I have been very fortunate in my friends, who have provided support in many different ways. In particular, I would like to thank Ajay Dandekar, Alessandro Monsutti, Ali Ahmad, Amita Baviskar, Carol Upadhya, Chitaroopa Palit, Daniela Berti, Dilip Simeon, Farah Naqvi, Gilles Tarabout, Jitendra Kumar, Jyotirmaya Sharma, Karen Hebert, Kaveri Gill, Khurram Hussain, Laura Sayre, Kiran Bhatty, Madhu Sarin, Mahesh Rangarajan, Michael Burawoy, Nicolas Jaoul, Nitya Ramakrishnan, Rita Brara, Sanghamitra Misra, G. Rajshekhar, Ujjwal Singh, Radhika Singha, Shashi Bhushan Pathak, Susan Visvanathan and Ravi Vasudevan. There are few scholars as generous as Ramachandra Guha, both personally and intellectually. It is hard to describe how much I owe him.

The bulk of the writing was done in three-week spells over three summer and winter vacations from June 2014 to July 2015, though I had drafts of several unpublished conference papers and presentations starting from 2006, and this book has been in the planning since 2008, when thanks to James Scott and K. Sivaramakrishnan, I got some thinking space. It would never have been possible without the generosity of my mother-in law, Usha Varadarajan, who provided two lovely homes away from Delhi. I wish this book had come before my father-in-law, M. Varadarajan, passed away. He was the most undemanding father-in-law one might have asked for, unstinting with his help and affection.

I am very grateful to my parents, Pushpa and Sundar, for their love and support in everything I do, and to my mother, in particular, for keeping in check my father's anxieties whenever I travel to Bastar. Among the many things I have to thank Aparna Sundar and Terrence Maccagno for, producing Rosa and Ilan is by far the most important. They are the best things to have happened to the entire Sundar family.

And as always, Siddharth, my companion and closest friend for the last 27 years, has borne the brunt of my obsessions and anxieties. Despite his workaholism tempered only by his love for Ambassador cars, old maps and cigars, none of which I share, we have fun together. I will never have a way of thanking him enough.

NOTE

Over the years I have lectured and written extensively on this issue. Despite my best attempts to avoid this, there may be some degree of self-repetition in what I have written here. I have directly taken the following passages from my earlier articles: portions of the preface, the last paragraph of chapter 2 and a couple of paragraphs on SPOs have been taken from 'Mimetic Sovereignties, Precarious Citizenship: State Effects in a Looking Glass World', *Journal of Peasant Studies* 41, No. 4 (July 2014), pp. 469–90. The description of the 2010 Tadmetla encounter in chapter 9 has been taken from 'Winning Hearts and Minds: Emotional Wars and the Construction of Difference', *Third World Quarterly* 33, No. 4 (2012), pp. 1–17. The discussion on malik makbuja in chapter 2 has been expanded from 'Is Devolution Democratisation', *World Development* 29, No. 12 (2001), pp. 2007–24. Some sections on the Maoists have earlier been written up as 'Insurgency, Counter-insurgency and Democracy in Central India', in Robin Jeffery et al., eds., *More than Maoism*, pp. 149–68, New Delhi: Manohar, 2012. General references to Bastar's history are taken from my book *Subalterns and Sovereigns: An Anthropological History of Bastar (1854–2006)*, 2nd edn., New Delhi: Oxford University Press, 2007.

Many names, especially of villages and rape survivors, have been changed. I have left in only the names of people who are already well-known actors in this conflict and those of villages where much has already been reported on them (for example, in chapter 9). In these cases, while I have retained the names of the dead, I have changed the names of anyone still alive. I have also left in the Salwa Judum leaders who are well known, but changed the names of most of the SPOs.

Index

1861 Police Act, 193

Aam Aadmi Party (AAP), 272
Action Aid, 154–5, 266
activists, 256, 279, 290
  against the Judum, 257–61, 263–6, 277–8; *see also* human rights
  against the Maoists, 261–3, *see also* Salwa Judum, vigilantism
  against Operation Green Hunt, 270–3
  cause célèbre, 267–76
  cyber-activism of, 46, 275–6, 307
  attacks on, 17, 113, 179–81, 241, 264–5, 273, 277, 281–3, 307, 333
  local Bastar, 277–8
Additional Central Assistance Plan, 233
  See also Integrated Action Plan (IAP)
adivasis, 8, 11
  and forests, 8–9, 59
  and health care, 11, 13, 29, 34, 53, 69, 76, 79, 145, 147, 221–3, 230–3, 245, 263, 266, 267, 351
  and land, 9, 11, 13, 14, 25, 41, 53–8, 59, 61; acquisition of, 27–9, 31–4; alienation of, 35–7, 39–40
  and mass arrests, 12, 39, 147, 158, 183–5, 251, 346
  and mining, 9–10, 27, 29–33, 38, 40–1, 43–4, 65, 67, 86, 220
  Bhatras, 9
  children and education, 227–8
  'civilization' of, 38–9, 43, 229
  dehumanization of, 41, 188, 198
  Dhurwas, 9–11, 56, 81, 131, 165–6, 184
  Dorlas, 9, 55–6, 81, 110, 131, 148
  employment, lack of, 41, 43, 85–6, 130, 134, 152, 189, 195, 235
  escaping from Judum, 146
  exploitation of, 38–40

extortion by lawyers, 126–7
grouping, 15, 17–9, 33
Halbas, 9
houses, 131
hunting, 107
Koyas, Gotti, 149, 151, 153
ill-treatment of, 11–2, 28
life in villages, 11–2, 151–3
laws for the protection of, 220
literacy, 41
Madia, 9, *see also* Koya
malnutrition, 154
media reporting, 24, 105, 283, 292–5
Muria, 9, 109–10
poverty, 220, 234
rebellion against the Raj, 13
securing rights, 287
way of life, 19, 89–90
welfare budget, 222
Afzal, Mohammad, 298
Agarwal, Pratap, 277
Aiyar, Mani Shankar, 248
Ajay, T.G., 241, 268
Adivasi Mahasabha, 32, 116, 249–50, 313, 380
All India Fact-finding Team, 12, 99, 103, 113, 210, 295, 298
Ambeli, 95–6
Amnesty International, 271
Andhra Pradesh, 14, 20, 31, 46, 105, 114
forest department, 151
mass migration to, 85, 149, 150–1
Andhra Pradesh Civil Liberties Committee (APCLC), 266, 288
Andhyarujina, T.R., 312
Apte, Bal, 261
Armed Auxilliary Forces, 200, *see also* SPOs
Armed Forces Special Powers Act (AFSPA), 239
arrests, *see* adivasis, jail, prison, prisoners
Art of Living, 179–80
Association for India's Development (AID), 266
Association for the Protection of Democratic Rights (APDR), 268
ASDS (Vyavasayaka Mariyu Sanghika Abhivrudhi Samstha/ Agriculture and Social Development Society), 154, 266
Atami, Chaitram, 93, 132
Athalye, Dr Anil, 261
Azad (Cherukuri Rajkumar), 83, 244, 270, 283, 289
Azadi Bachao Andolan, 282

Babu, Gandhi, 266
Babu, Justice Rajendra, 323
Bailadilla, 28, 65
hills, 8, 27, 32
mines, 10, 41, 220, 351
Balagopal, K., 255, 279, 287–8, 310
Balakrishnan, Chief Justice, 322, 330–1, 349
Bandyopadhyay, D., 255
Banerjee, Mamata, 14, 242
Bardhan, Comrade A., 313
Bastar, 4, 9–10, 12–5, 21, 23, 27, 37–8, 51–2, 61, 68, 84, 86, 130, 163, 207, 220, 243, 294, 297, 351
autonomy, 188
Darbha block, 163–6
division into smaller districts, 223

elections, 243–4, 246–7
immigrants into, 39–40, 59, 110
Gonds, 40, 56, 81, 109–10, 131, 165–6, 184
mineral wealth, 29, 33
police, 202, 207–08
tourism website, 42
Bastar Bandhu, 94, 263
Bastar Division Journalists' Association, 301
Bastar Parivahan Sangh, 59
Bastar Sambhag Kisan Sangharsh Samiti, 277
Bastar Sangharsh Samiti, 16
beeja pandum, *see* seed-sowing festival
burning of villages 2–3, 15, 17–20, 34, 73, 93, 97, 102, 106–8, 110, 114–20, 136–7, 143–4, 146–50, 152, 156–9, 167, 171, 174–8, 181–3, 189, 191, 197, 205, 209–10, 214, 225, 227, 239, 254, 298, 309, 313, 319, 328–30, 343, 345
Bhairamgarh, 58, 61, 76, 92–4, 100, 105, 107, 109, 113, 130, 191, 198, 222, 226, 234
Bharadwaj, Sudha, 199
Bharatiya Janata Party (BJP), 15–6, 35, 42, 64, 67, 89, 169, 188–90, 241–3, 245–7, 254, 261–2, 264, 269, 282, 296, 305, 307, 321, 343
Bhardwaj, Ashutosh, 244, 268
Bhardwaj, Parijat, 272–3
Bhatia, Bela, 255, 272
Bhattacharya, Buddhadeb, 162
Bhopalpatnam, 52, 111, 130, 277, 298
Bhumkal, 13, 165, 187–8, 300
Bhumkal (magazine), 308
Bhushan, Prashant, 281
Bijapur, 7, 11, 25, 38, 58, 61, 67, 90, 92, 95, 100, 105, 107, 111, 135, 145, 147, 167, 181, 223, 226, 234
mass rapes, 248
Bodhghat hydroelectric project, 188
Border Roads Organisation (BRO), 125, 224
Border Security Force (BSF), 16, 170, 211
Buch, Nirmala, 285

CGNet, 236, 270, 293, 295, 298
Campaign for Peace and Justice in Chhattisgarh (CPJC), 279–81
Campaign for Survival and Dignity, 47
Central Armed Police Forces (CAPF), 16, 37, 235
Central Bureau of Investigation (CBI), 34, 180, 213, 340–3
Central Industrial Security Force (CISF), 257
Central Paramilitary Forces (CMPF), 207
Central Reserve Police Force (CRPF), 16, 22, 24, 37, 55, 72, 85, 94, 113, 119, 125, 131, 138, 142, 144, 155, 161–4, 166–9, 170–1, 184, 176–8, 181, 196, 209–14, 222, 224, 227–8, 230, 232–3, 236–7, 243–4, 251–2, 265, 274, 288, 304–5, 309, 341–2
and Morpalli, 174–5, 178
and Tadmetla, 171–3, 176–8
arson, 181–2

camps, 151, 202–3
raping, 174, 177, 185, 237
Chasi Mulia Adivasi Sangh, 236, 286
Chaudhuri, Mohuya, 295
Chauhan, Vijay, 180
Cherapalli, 155–6, 158, 161
burning down of, 157
Chetna Natya Manch (CNM or Cinem batch), 69, 170
Chhattisgarh, 7–8, 14, 29, 37, 85, 91, 296
Armed Forces (CAF), 196–7
Auxiliary Armed Police Force, 21, 200, 335, 339, 341
Chhattisgarh Scheduled Tribe Commission, 100
defence expenditure, 222
Directorate of Economics and Statistics, 41
High Court, 268, 277, 312
migrant labourers, 152–53
police, 16, 94, 173, 271
Special Task Force, 161
Police Act of 2007, 193
prison statistics, 23
Shramjivi Patrakar Sangh (Working Journalists' Union), 298
Special Public Security Act (CSPSA), 22, 263, 267–8, 294, 298–9
Chhattisgarh Bachao Andolan, 272–3
Chidambaram, P., 39, 236, 248, 258, 265, 283, 306
Chinnalu, Jannu, 50
Choudhary, Shubhranshu, 270, 293
Citizens Initiative for Peace (CIP), 281
civilian deaths, 138, 141, 166–7, 182, 209, 224, 233, 239, 258
Code of Criminal Procedure (CrPC), 22
Commonwealth Human Rights Initiative, 323
Communist Party of India (CPI), and Mahendra Karma, 188
Cherla rally, 114, 149, 153, 250, 255, 313, 320, 325, 328
early history, 18, 52, 356
electoral politics, 245, 247, 272, 276
image problem, 275–6, 348
litigation in Court, 313–4, 325
mobilization for adivasi rights, 10, 36, 56
mobilization against land acquisition, 28, 40, 245
police attacks on, 202, 276 (*see also* CPI prisoners)
prisoners, 125–8, 251, 267, 272–6
relations with CPI (Maoist), 92, 157, 164, 241–2, 276
stand against Judum, 111, 114, 123, 126, 140, 156, 164, 167, 177, 199, 249–52, 260, 269, 298
see also Adivasi Mahasabha, Manish Kunjam, Rama Sodi
CPI Maoist, *see under* Maoists
CPI Marxist-Leninist (ML),
People's War, 13, 49–86, 91, 356; early history 49–59, 356; *see also* Maoists
New Democracy, 148

Congress Party, 15–6, 35, 40, 179,180, 188–9, 238, 241–3, 246, 296
opinion on Judum, 248–9
Constitution of India, 45, 47, 187–8, 335, 346, 350–1
conversion, religious
in camps, 135
in Andhra Pradesh, 25, 156
in Bastar villages, 26, 93
counter-insurgency, 12, 14–6, 19, 21, 23–4, 43, 68, 189, 200, 212, 235
and democracy, 45, 239
and the law, 22, 263, 298

dalam (People's War squads), 52–5, 60, 74, 76–9, 107, 110, 123, 127, 157, 161, 241, 247, 300
development work, 234
killings, 238, 300
local guerrilla squads (LGS), 69, 71
local organization squad (LOS), 69, 71
Dandakaranya, 8, 51–52, 55, 76
Dandakaranya Adivasi Kisan Mazdoor Sangathan (DAKMS), 69
Dandakaranya Special Zonal Committee (DKSZC), 69
Dandekar, Ajay, 167
Dantewada, 7, 12, 23, 25, 28–9, 31, 44, 58, 62, 72, 84, 103, 108–9, 144, 151, 163, 170, 190, 199, 232, 234, 247, 259, 280
jailbreak, 127
Dantewada Samanvay Samiti (DSS), 93–4
Das, Baba Bihari, 93
Delhi 1984 massacres, 16
Deo, K.C., 248
democracy, 13, 14, 43, 45–7, 238–56
and elections, 240–7
and political parties, 247–52
and statutory institutions, 253–6
Desai, Ashok, 314, 320, 334, 340
Deva, Kalma, 55
Devi, Mahasweta, 281
'District Reserve Guard' (DRG), 21, 161, 186, 201, *see also* SPOs
displacement
as a weapon of war, 15, 19–20, 129–61, 247–8, 280
of adivasis by large projects, 41, 43, 45, 55, 249, 262, 272
Divya Seva Sangh, 34
Dornapal, 4, 134–6, 140, 179–80, 191, 197, 200, 211, 222, 224, 250, 335
Doval, Ajit, 183, 255
Dutt, Shekhar, 181, 262

Edesmetta, 163, 346
Editors Guild, 301
education, *see* schools
Ekal Vidyalaya, 245
Ekta Parishad, 36
elections, *see under* democracy
Election Commission, 244
extrajudicial killings, 45, 167, 224, 254, 283, 307, 328
encounters, fake *see* extrajudicial killings
Errabor, 106, 130, 135, 192, 232
camp, 110, 114, 132, 140–1, 277, 323

Essar Steel, 32, 63, 65–6, 78, 188, 245, 250, 263, 271, 279–80

Federation of Indian Chambers of Commerce and Industry (FICCI), 32
Fifth Schedule, 220, 322
Forest Rights Act (FRA), 39, 47, 220, 313
Forum for Fact-finding, Documentation and Advocacy (FFDA), 254, 327
Forum for Integrated National Security (FINS), 261–2, 269

Gandhi, Rahul, 249
Gandhi, Rajiv, 246
Gandhi, Sonia, 249
Garg, Ankit, 271
Garg, Ruchir, 294
Gautam, Avdhesh, 251, 270–1
Gayatri Parivar, 34, 135
Gera, Shalini, 272–3
Godavari Ispat, 67
Gompad, 72, 169
  massacre, 264, 332
  victims, 281
Grigson, Wilfred, 38–9, 57
Grouping 15, 17–9, 112–3, 130–42; *see also* Salwa Judum camps
Guha, Piyush, 267
Guha, Ramachandra, 12, 113, 207, 260, 311–2
Guha, Ranajit, 14
Gujarat 2002 massacres, 16, 296
Gupta, Smita, 302

Haimendorf, Christoph von Fürer, 51
Haragopal, G., 284
health, *see under* adivasis
hostages, 283–6
Human Rights
  activists 32, 44–5, 190–1, 256–78, and peace talks 279–90
  violations of, *see under* burning of villages, displacement, Maoist killings, rapes, Salwa Judum, starvation
Human Rights Forum (HRF), 152, 260, 266, 279, 288
Human Rights Watch (HRW), 119, 268, 271
hunger, 133, 351 *see also* starvation
Hydroelectric projects, 29
  Bodhghat, 188
  Polavaram, 28, 285

Ikhwanis, 21, *see also* renegades
Independent Citizens' Initiative (ICI), 12, 37, 113, 120, 141–2, 187–8, 254, 260, 287, 302, 305, 311–2, 322
India Reserve Battalion (IRB), 210
  Mizo jawans, 211
  Mizo Reserve Battalion, 200, 211
  Naga forces, 147, 197 210–11, 294–5
India Today, 212
Indian Army, 18
Indian Express, 24, 190,195, 268, 244–5, 296
Indian government,
  and land acquisition, 27–9, 31–5, 39
  and media representation, 296, 307

and road construction, 223–4
and tendu leaves, 60–1, 64, 86
crackdown on Maoists, 32–4, 38, 44, 89–90, 95–6, 100–04, 115–21, 163, 169, 173, 184, 251
discomfort with activists, 271–5
relief to villages, 178–9, 263
repatriation of villagers, 140–1, 155, 331
standpoint on Judum, 302
welfare of STs, 220–3
education, 225–30
health care, 230–3
Indian Penal Code,
Section 124, 267
Section 144, 33
Indo-Tibetan Border Police (ITBP), 16, 212, 222
Indrawati, 7–8
Indrawati National Park, 11, 55
Induwar, Francis, 283
Integrated Action Plan (IAP), 221–2, 333
and development, 233–4
misuse of funds, 221–2
See also Additional Central Assistance Plan (ACA)
Integrated Tribal Development Agency (ITDA), 265–6
Intelligence Bureau (IB), 183, 232
Internally Displaced Persons (IDPs), 150, 154, 169, 173, 251, 254–5, 266, 269, 327
International Association of People's Lawyers (IAPL), 125–6
International Committee of the Red Cross (ICRC), 232, 263, 272, 331
Iqbal, Javed, 270
Jagdalpur, 7, 23, 27–8, 33, 38, 95, 125, 140, 163, 342–3
Jagdalpur Legal Aid Group (JAGLAG), 125, 272–3
Jai Johar Seva Sansthan, 263
jailbreak 72, 127; *see also* prison
Jain, Nemichand, 300
Jaiswal, Deepak, 301
Jaiswal, Sriprakash, 248
Jan Jagran Abhiyan (JJA), 16, 96, 99–100, 103, 249, 294
of 1990, 62, 92–3, 187, 294
of 1998, 92
of 2005, 94
of 2014–16, 187
See also Mission 2016
Jan Natya Mandali, 50
Jan Swasthya Abhiyan, 323
Janathana Sarkar, 24, 61–2, 76, 78, 82, 235
policy programme, 82–4
Jayaswal Neco, 67
Jha, Praful, 268
Jha, Prateik, 268
Jhabua, 44
Jharkhand, 29, 42, 86, 91–2, 99, 201, 215, 283, 286, 296
Joga, Dudhi, 311, 313, 326, 345
Joga, Kartam, 250–2, 270, 311, 313–4, 319, 326, 336, 338
Jogi, Ajit, 138, 189, 246, 248
Jogi, Amit, 245
Jungle Warfare College, 29, 40, 91, 122

Justice T.P. Sharma Commission, 342–3

Kabir, Chief Justice Altamas, 340
Kalam, President APJ Abdul, 277
Kalluri, S.R.P., 161, 173, 179, 183, 191, 200–01, 207–8, 251–2, 270, 273, 301, 308, 333
Kanker, 23, 91, 294
Kannabiran, Kalpana, 254
Kannayya, Dubba, 62
Karkeli, 11, 94–6
Karma, Chhavindra, 248
Karma, Deepak, 239
Karma, Devati, 238
Karma, Mahendra, 16, 32, 34–6, 66, 78, 92, 94, 97, 101, 103, 105–6, 119, 157, 160, 187–9, 191–2, 238–9, 241, 245, 248, 254, 263–4, 294, 305, 313, 326, 333, 345–8
  National Investigative Agency, 348
Kashmir, 20, 24
Kashyap, Baliram, 294
Kashyap, Dinesh, 243
Kashyap, Kedar, 100
Kejriwal, Arvind, 323
Khammam, 148, 151, 154, 265
Khandelwal, Isha, 272–3
Kistaram forest, 57, 107, 266
Kocherry, Thomas, 282
Kodopi, Lingaram, 66, 270–1, 275
Konta, 56, 58, 76, 80, 84, 90–2, 105–6, 110, 117, 126, 130, 134–5, 138–40, 148, 151–2, 157, 183, 190, 192, 197, 199, 211, 224, 226, 232, 234, 242, 251, 265
  killings, 169
Koraput, 10, 285
Kotrapal, 96–7, 99
Koya Commandos, 173, 176–8, 181, 200, 337
Koya Samaj, 26
Krantikari Adivasi Mahila Sangathan (KAMS), 69, 73, 79
Krishna, Vineel, 276, 283, 304
Kumar, Himanshu, 113, 154, 263–5, 270–1, *see also* VCA
Kumar, Indresh, 262
Kumar, Ranjeet, 332
Kunjam, Kopa, 128, 167, 181, 251, 264
Kunjam, Manish, 35, 111, 116, 126, 241, 245, 249–50, 253, 275–6, 284, 311, 313, 323
Kunjam, Sudruram, 251
Kuswaha, Ram Bhuwan, 119, 157, 191, 324
Kutru, 11, 61, 99, 113, 189–91, 233, 249
Kyndiah, P.R., 248

Lachanna, 50, 53, 55–6, 61–2, 81, 92–3, 308
Lala, B.K., 66
Lalgarh movement, 13, 304
Land Acquisition Act, 47
Lingagiri, 157, 328–9
Lokayukt, 36, 188

Ma Danteshwari Swabhimaan Manch, 190
Madhukar, 94, 189–91, 261
Mahato, Chatradhar, 162
Mahila Ekta Manch, 273
Majumdar, Charu, 50, 82

Malaya, 17, 19–20
  Communist Party of, 17
malik makbuja, 35–6, 188, 275
Mandavi, Bhima, 243, 245
Mandavi, Vikram, 138, 198
Mander, Harsh, 181, 323
Maoists, 2, 4, 12–7, 21–2, 31, 51–3, 76, 91–2, 108, 114, 148, 155, 157, 170, 207, 242, 257, 293–4
  against mining, 285
  ambush, 169, 200, 238
  and Comprador Big Bourgeoisie (CBB), 65
  and contractors, 63–6, 166
  and corpses, 214–5
  and Judum, 17, 20–21, 41, 106–11, 129, 132–6, 141–6, 195, 234
  and medical relief, 233
  and PDS, 234–5
  and traders, 54, 63–7, 80, 133, 143, 145–6, 192, 235, 270
  and villagers, 43–4, 54, 57, 62–3, 78–81, 85–6, 95–6, 109, 142–3, 146, 164–5, 234–5
  empowerment, 287
  women, 79–80
  architecture/memorials, 83, 170, 174, 192
  attacks by, 23, 66, 72, 91, 94, 96, 108–11, 141–2, 162–3, 166, 170, 184, 303
  Central Committee, 65–7, 235
  Dalits, 248, 284
  Darbhaguda blast, 253
  destroying schools, 226, 230
  electoral boycotts, 241–4, 247, 250
  ideology, 44, 49–50, 82–4, 239–40, 288–9
  insurgency, 20, 24, 32, 42–4, 49–50, 68
  kidnappings, 283–6
  killings/encounters, 24–6, 78 120–1, 214
  guerrilla squads, 18
  Martyrs' Week, 82, 223
  martyrs, 142–3, 169
  nexuses, 67, 212
  organizing village labour, 58–9, 77, 165
  party schools, 73, 230
  peace talks, 279–83
  People's Democratic Government, 82
  perception of, 42, 49, 54, 224, 287
  poster campaign, 308
  propaganda against, 102
  public sympathy, 54–5, 75, 110, 137, 195, 262
  recruitment, 75, 165
  red corridor, 42
  repatriating villages, 160
  resistance to JJA, 93
  revolutionary people's committees (RPCs), 76
  sangham, 62, 77–8, 81–2, 92, 95–6, 100, 105, 108, 117, 120, 125, 149, 157, 165, 195, 198, 234, 300
  state committees, 69
  training, 75, 165
  public perspectives on, 44, 46–7, 164, 290, 292
  women cadres, 72–5,196, 320
  Women's Day, 82

Maoist Communist Centre of India, 91
Marawi, SP D.S., 179–80, 341
marh, 8, 43, 53, 61, 73, 130, 304
media,
  anti-activist, 258, 275, 280
  arrest of journalists, 306
  complicity in reductionism, 259, 283–4, 292–3, 297–8, 339
  corporate takeovers, 305
  cyber representations, 309
  ignoring the conflict, 163–4, 293–8, 302
  investigation into Judum activities, 260
  'Naxalite incidents', 10, 53, 93, 102, 164,166, 258, 284, 302
  reporting of encounters, 37, 283
  partisan views, 302–4
  tendencies, 23–4
Médicins Sans Frontières (MSF), 118, 232, 263, 280, 298
Menon, Alex Paul, 275, 283–5, 304
mining, 34, 38, 44, 244–5, 281, 289–90, 296
  activism against, 275
  and industrialization, 40–1, 43
  corruption, 262
  devastation, 86
  displacement, 272
  Raoghat, 8, 28, 33, 38
  companies, 32, 46, 65, 285
  formal and informal, 31
  private partnerships in, 29
  Bailadilla, 10, 41, 220, 351
  mining policy, 31, 91
  steel companies, 65, 67, 277
  waste dumps, 33
Ministry of Home Affairs, 71, 189, 193, 322
  and Naxalite Cell, 205
  and report on left wing extremism, 221
Ministry of Tribal Affairs, 220, 248
Mishra, Amaresh, 168
Mishra, Anil, 178
Mission 2016, 24
  See also Jan Jagran Abhiyan (JJA)
Mizoram, 16, 18, 20, 24, 115
Modi, Narendra, 16, 28, 39, 246, 287
  government, 47, 290
Mohapatra, Subhash, 254, 327
Mooka, Soyam, 190, 199, 325
Morna, 146–7
Morpalli, 173–5, 177–8, 213, 335, 341
  attacks, 341
  starvation deaths, 181

NGOs/activists (local), 154, 190–1, 193, 256, 262–3, 273
  Goonj, 266
  Rupantar, 267
  see also ASDS, RMP, VCA, Vivekanand Foundation
Nag, Sukal Prasad, 114, 127–8
Nagaland, 20, 91, 210–11
  armed struggle for independence, 19
  human rights groups, 210
  see also IRB
Nagarnar, 27–8
Nagrik Suraksha Samiti, 91–2
Naidu, Vijay, 180
Nanda, Kiche, 140, 200, 341

Naqvi, Farah, 113, 260
Nariman, Rohinton, 340
Nath, Ratneswar, 36
National Alliance of People's Movements (NAPM), 47, 281–2
National Commission for Protection of Child Rights (NCPCR), 251, 254–5, 331
National Commission for Scheduled Tribes (NCST), 220, 253
National Commission of Women (NCW), 191, 253–4, 280
National Democratic Alliance (NDA), 183
National Human Rights Commission (NHRC), 45–6, 90, 119, 121–3, 154, 180, 236, 251, 254, 260–1, 297, 318, 322–6, 345
  hierarchy of truths, 327
  investigation, 325–30
  report on Salwa Judum, 326, 329–30
National Minerals Development Corporation (NMDC), 27–8, 31, 72
National Rural Employment Guarantee Act (NREGA), 134, 149
National Rural Health Mission, 222
National Remote Sensing Agency, 91
National Security Adviser, 183
Navlakha, Gautam, 222, 255
Naxal Peedith Sangharsh Samiti, 16
Naxalites, 15, 22–3, 32, 37, 42, 49, 71, 91, 94, 104, 122, 171, 209
  abused by the legal system, 127
  anti-Naxal movement, 100, 248
  media representations, 292
  'Naxali offence', 125
  Naxology, 43
  sympathizers, 199, 204, 259
  see also Maoists
Nayar, Kuldeep, 281
Nelson Mandela Centre for Peace and Conflict Resolution, 279, 282
Nijjar, Justice S.S., 318, 332, 336, 340, 348–50
Niyogi, Shankar Guha, 52, 267
Non-timber forest products (NTFPs) 59, *see also* tendu

Odisha, 7, 14, 29, 31, 130
Operation Green Hunt 16, 24, 81, 120, 162–85, 189, 249, 251, 259, 270, 275, 276, 281, 283, 285, 289, 295, 304, 322, 349
Oommen, P. Joy, 334
other backward classes (OBCs), 41, 184
  Dhakads, 9
  Gadhwas, 9
  Kallars, 9, 109
  Kumhars, 9
  Marars, 9
  Rauts, 9
  Sundis, 9

Padmanabhan, Chitra, 333
Paikra, Kamlesh, 298
Pal, Yash, 282
Pambhoi, Rajendra, 97, 189–90
Panchayats (Extension to Scheduled Areas) Act (PESA), 31–2, 39, 220, 253

Panda, Muye, 252
Panda, Podiyam, 47, 123, 178, 199, 252, 275
Pandey, Hem Chandra, 283
Pandey, Sandeep, 190
Panigrahi, Sushant, 194–6, 198
Panikkar, Sreedevi, 124
pargana majhis, 61
Patel, V.P., 53
Patel, Bandi, 62, 92
Patel, Nand Kumar, 239
Patil, Shivraj, 37, 248, 322
Patkar, Medha, 190, 270
Pawar, Manturam, 245
peace talks, 279–83, 333
People's Committee against Police Atrocities (PCPA), 162, 242, 286
People's Liberation Guerrilla Army (PLGA), 69, 75, 142, 170, 299, *see also* dalam
People's Liberation Front of India, 13
People's March, 120, 142
People's Union for Civil Liberties (PUCL), 180, 199, 241, 260, 267–9, 280, 312, 331
People's Union for Democratic Rights (PUDR), 268, 312
People's Watch, 323
Pillai, G.K., 306
Pillai, N.R.K., 299
Pisda, K.R., 99, 103, 106, 226
Pituri, 308
Planning Commission, 43, 233, 255, 260, 280, 324
police, 257
  arbitrary arrests by, 125–6, 267–8
  atrocities on villagers, 51, 107
  coerced surrenders of Maoists, 184, 305, *see also under* surrenders
  'Jan Jagran' meetings, 183, *see under* Jan Jagran
  justification for violence, 102–4
  manipulating regional differences, 308
  manipulation of facts/figures, 305, 327–8
  propaganda, 308
  staged arrests, 184
  violence, 71
  war on Maoists, 100
political positions on Maoists, 44–5
Ponwar, Brigadier B.K., 40–1, 122
Pordu, 308
Poyam, Lachman, 95
Prabhat, 170, 308
Prabhat, Nalin, 170
Prabhat Khabar, 260
Prasad, Ganti, 276
Prasanna, R., 155, 178
prison 219, 271–2,
  conditions, 22–3, 125–8, 251
  camps as, 113, 137
  and civil liberties, 267, 269
  and legal aid, 272–3
prisoners
  activists as, 251, 264, 267, 271–2, 276, 336
  '___of conscience', 271, 278
  demand for release of, 285, 308, 356
  journalists as, 299–301
  Maoist, 50
  women, 122, 125, 253–4

Purushottam of Gudma, 95, 101
Putul, Alok, 294

Qureshi, S.Y., 243

Radical Students Union, 50
Radical Youth League, 50
Raipur Satyagraha, 268
Raj, SP Sunder, 333
Ramakrishnan, Nitya, 314
Ramanna, 55
Rambhau Mhalgi Prabodhini (RMP), 261
Ramesh, Jairam, 236, 248
Rammohan, E.N., 170
Ramnad, Madhu, 80
Rangasamy, Amrita, 22
Rani Bodli,
  attack on SPO camp, 96, 141, 198, 205
  police memorial, 320
Rao, J.P., 114, 167–8, 266
Rao, Mallojula Koteswara (aka Kishenji), 46, 290, 304
Raoghat, 8, 28, 33, 38
rape,
  as a weapon of war, 15, 17, 21, 47, 72, 119, 161, 190, 198, 200, 239, 252, 273, 288, 305–6, 331, 344–6
  specific incidents of, 28, 74, 92, 114, 116, 122–5, 146, 159–60, 169, 173–4, 177, 179, 185, 191, 199, 201, 248, 254, 304, 319, 323, 326, 329, 335, 341, 343
  see also violence on women
Rapid Environmental Impact Assessment report, 33
Rashtriya Swayamsevak Sangh (RSS), 33–4, 81, 132, 135, 228, 245, 261–2, 307
  indoctrination, 228, 245
  Sangh Parivar, 34
  schools, 229, 245
Rathore, O.P., 103, 207
Ray, Rabi, 281
'red corridor', 303
Reddy, Justice B. Sudershan, 318, 332, 336, 340, 348–50
Reddy, Patel Sudhakar, 83
Reddy, Sai, 299
refugees, 3–4
  East Pakistan Displaced Persons, 10
  from Judum attacks, 107, 130, 146–7, 151–2, 155, 164, 222
renegades 20–2, 122, 195–8, 201–3
Revolutionary Writers' Association (Virasam), 50
Right to Education Act (RTE), 228
roads
  government focus on, 20, 25, 27–9, 38, 69, 134, 203, 221–4, 305–7
  Maoist opposition to, 20, 85, 144, 166, 223–4, 305, 307
  settlement along, 17, 39, 102, 105, 241–4, 294
Rohatgi, Mukul, 320, 332
Rosenberg, Gerald, 310, 349
Roy, Arundhati, 270, 304
Ryotu Coolie Sangham, 51

Sabari river, 7, 138–9
  pollution by corpses, 138
Sachar, Justice Rajinder, 281, 331

Saini, Dharampal, 229
Salve, Harish, 332, 335

Salwa Judum, 1, 12, 16, 21–6, 32–4, 40, 46, 64, 73, 75, 78, 81, 93–5, 105, 111–2, 129, 143, 162–3, 183, 186–92, 198–206, 269, 275, 294, 297, 304, 309
- and CPI, 249–50, 260
- and schools, 225–7
- and villagers, 102, 134–6, 139, 143–4, 154, 185
  - alerting system, 144
  - discrimination, 145
- arbitrary killings, 138, 155–6, 158–9, 167, 176
- atrocities on villagers, 19, 31, 41, 105–8, 114–22, 130, 144, 146, 148, 162, 169, 279, 313, 324
  - Cherapalli, 156–8
  - memorial stones, 120
  - Morpalli, 174–5
  - Pulanpad, 175–7
  - Rigarnad, 118–9
  - Surpangada, 119
  - Vengaipadu, 168
- atrocities on women, 122–5, 159–60
- attacks on Maoists, 107–9
- beginnings, 15, 37, 41, 96, 100–1
- breach of promise, 180
- causing demographic shifts, 222–3
- civilian victims, 108, 137, 146, 163
- cross-border, 151
- defection, 193, 198, 333
- forced conscription, 105–7, 195
- human shields, 139
- investigation into, 260–1, 279
- leaders 93, 95, 132, 180, 191, 239, 248, *see also* Karma, Kuswaha, Madhukar, Vikram Mandavi, Mooka, Naidu, Purushottam, Surya, Vijay
- media representations of, 293–5, 305
- public demonstration against, 114, 140, 180, 242, 277, 303
- rallies, 277
- recruitment, 193–5, 335
- relief camp, 4, 17, 19–20, 25, 77, 113, 130–1, 137, 333
  - deaths, 137
  - exodus from, 140
  - held hostage, 137–9
  - liquor, 134
  - Maoist attacks, 141
  - mass weddings, 135
  - rations, 133
  - religious conversions, 135
  - sanitation, 132
- teachers in the campaign, 189–90
- victims, 246, 348
- written complaints against, 116–7, 179, 180

Special Police Officers (SPOs), 21, 40–1, 91, 95–6, 103–4, 107, 112, 115, 118, 125, 129, 133, 135, 138, 144–5, 151, 158–9, 167–9, 176, 178, 186, 189, 206, 247, 265, 299, 327
- and Judum, 193–8
- compensation for death, 198
- contempt of SC order, 341
- District Auxiliary Force, 341

erstwhile Maoists, 195–8
female SPOs, 196–7
killed by Maoists, 201
killing civilians, 138, 141, 168, 197
moral dilemma, 197
posing as Maoists, 201–2
raping by, 159–60, 167, 171–2, 185, 197, 199, 335
recruitment/attrition, 193–8
regularization of, 339–40
resisting investigation, 178
state support of, 254, 261–2, 319, 327–30, 346
Supreme Court judgment on, 336–8
threatening rape victims, 305
Samaj Parivartana Samudaya, 36
Samajik Ekta Manch, 16, 191–3, 273, 277
Sangharsh Samiti Dhurli, 32
Sankaran, S.R., 248, 279, 280, 288, 313, 331
-led Committee, 279
Santoshpur, 254, 327
Sanyal, Narayan, 267, 268
Sarkeguda, 25, 155, 163, 181–2, 248
Sarma, E.A.S., 12, 260, 266, 311–2, 334
Sarv Adivasi Samaj, 277
Sarv Mool Samaj, 277
Sarva Samaj, 167
Scheduled Castes (SCs), 41
Maharas, 9, 109–10
Mrigans, 9
of Bihar, 13
Pankas, 9
Scheduled Caste/Scheduled Tribes Prevention of Atrocities Act, 220
Scheduled Tribes (STs), 41, 220, *see also* adivasis
schools, 225–7, 236–7
military occupation of, 228, 252
Portacabins, 228–9
shikshakarmi, 208, 227
seed-sowing festival 56, 80–1, 89, 95, 156, 182, 326
Sehrawat, Tarun, 304
Sen, Binayak, 241, 267–70, 274–6, 304, 348
Sen, Ilina, 267–8
Sethi, Aman, 178
Sharma, B.D., 253, 284
Sharma, Bhanwari Lal, 282
Sharma, Justice T.P., 335
Sharma, Rahul, 320
Shukla, V.C., 345
Singh, Mamta, 323–4
Singh, Manmohan, 13, 248, 347
Singh, Prabhat, 301
Singh, Pragya, 312–3
Singh, Prakash, 203, 255
Singh, Rajnath, 306
Singh, Raman, 89, 100, 167, 179, 181, 188, 190, 245–6, 262, 269, 282, 284, 324, 339, 347
Singh, Ujjwal, 333
Sinha, Shanta, 254–5
Sitaramaiah, Kondapalli, 49–50
Sixth Schedule, 188, 220, 250, 252
Sivananda Ashram, 93
Sodi, Rama, 313
Sori, Soni, 66, 73, 270–6
Special Police Force, 2
Cobras in Chhattisgarh, 42, 176, 178

Greyhounds in Andhra Pradesh, 42, 72, 107, 163, 247
Jaguars in Jharkhand, 42
Srikakulam Naxalite uprising, 18, 22
starvation, 15, 19–20, 116–7, 133–4, 142–7, 153–4, 175, *see also* hunger
State Human Rights Commission (SHRC), 254, 327
steel plants,
Nagarnar, 27–8, 351
Dilmilli, 28, 252
Tata in Lohandiguda, 28, 32, 40, 253
Essar in Bhansi/Dhurli, 32, 253
strategic hamletting, *see* grouping
Subramaniam, Gopal, 321, 332
Subramaniam, Malini, 273, 301
Sukma, 38, 55–6, 58, 64, 72, 111, 135, 149, 166, 192, 208, 223, 226, 250, 283, 325
surrenders, by Maoists/sangham members, 21, 57, 65–6, 85–6, 92, 96–7, 99, 105, 108, 117, 183–5, 192, 195, 197–8, 201, 203, 212–3, 224, 235, 243, 294, 305, 307–8
Sundarayya, P., 51
Supreme Court of India, 12, 21, 36, 90, 99, 132, 137, 140–1, 154, 193, 199–200, 213, 228, 247, 249–50, 252, 267, 269, 285, 302, 314–5, 333
bail to Binayak Sen, 267
orders on compensation to victims, 247, 297, 328, 330, 339, 344, 346
contempt of order, 340–1, 343–8
judgment on Salwa Judum, 21, 200, 336–9
Gompad massacre case, 332
malik makbuja case, 36
media reporting on, 302, 313, 317, 338–9, 349
order on schools, 228, 237, 285
PILs, 310–4, 331, 346
Right to Food case, 181
testimonies submitted by victims to, 114–9, 123, 160, 178, 254–5, 313, 319–20
working procedure, 315–7
Writ Petitions against Salwa Judum, 310–48
and NHRC, 46, 90, 119–22, 138, 154, 251, 261, 297, 318, 322–30, 345
Surrendered United Liberation Front of Asom (SULFA), 21
Surya, Kartam, 21, 178, 200, 339, 341
Surya Foundation, 42, 261–2
Swami Agnivesh, 178–80, 190, 282–3, 285, 335

Tadmendri, 96
Tadmetla, 24, 170–1, 176, 213, 248, 251, 335
ambush, 304, 331
burning of, 178, 181–2, 247
CBI enquiry, 337, 340–3
Commission of Enquiry on, 335
Tata Group, 28, 32, 63, 78, 188, 250, 287, 294, 333
Tata Institute of Social Sciences, 325

Tehelka, 271, 295, 304
Telangana, 7–8, 13, 16–7, 19, 25, 266
  armed struggle, 49, 52
  see also Andhra Pradesh
Telugu Desam Party, 149, 243
tendu leaves, 60–1, 64, 86, 89–90
Todem, Rajaram, 35–6, 100
Trinamool Congress (TMC), 14, 242

UNICEF, 131–2, 232, 280
United Progressive Alliance (UPA), 40, 47, 261, 321
United States of America (USA), 306
Unlawful Activities (Prevention) Act, 298
Usendi, Gudsa, 141, 309
Usendi, Vikram, 246
Usoor, 92, 105, 129

Vanvasi Chetna Ashram (VCA), 138, 154–5,167, 199, 263–5, 325
Vanvasi Kalyan Ashram, 34, 228, 245
Verghese, B.G., 160
Vidya Bharati, 34
Vietnam, 17
vigilantism, 16, 23, 255, 260, 273, 337, 347, 349, *see also* Salwa Judum, Samajik Ekta Manch
Joint Action Committees (JACs), 259
Vijay, P., 190, 192, 325
violence,
  by the state, 287
  debates on, 213–4, 257–9, 286–8
  on Judum members, 110–11, 141
  on minorities, 16
  on villages, 2–4, 15, 17, 25, 71
  on women, 2, 17, 53, 72–4, 114, 122–5, 159–60, 167, 169, 174, 185, 201, 237
  protest against, 276–7, 282
Vishwa Hindu Parishad (VHP), 26
Vishwaranjan, DGP, 181, 206–7, 299, 320, 322
Vivekanand Foundation, 261

Yadav, Santosh, 301
Yugandhar, B.N., 280

Wikileaks, on Essar 65
Winning Hearts and Minds 19, 234
Women against Sexual Violence and State Repression (WSS), 185
Women Martyrs of the Indian Revolution, 72, 74

A Note on the Author

Nandini Sundar, professor of sociology, Delhi University, and winner of the Infosys Prize for Social Sciences in 2010, has been writing about Bastar and its people for twenty-six years.

Her first book, *Subaltern and Sovereigns: An Anthropological History of Bastar (1854–1996)*, is an authoritative account of Bastar's colonial and post-colonial past.